DRAGON IN A THREE-PIECE SUIT

DRAGON IN A
THREE-PIECE SUIT

THE EMERGENCE
OF CAPITALISM IN CHINA

Doug Guthrie

PRINCETON UNIVERSITY PRESS   PRINCETON, NEW JERSEY

Copyright © 1999 by Princeton University Press
Published by Princeton University Press, 41 William Street,
Princeton, New Jersey 08540
In the United Kingdom: Princeton University Press,
Chichester, West Sussex
All Rights Reserved

Library of Congress Cataloging-in-Publication Data

Guthrie, Doug, 1969–
Dragon in a three-piece suit : the emergence of capitalism
in China / Doug Guthrie
   p. cm.
Includes bibliographical references and index.
ISBN 0-691-00492-7 (alk. paper)
1.Organizational change—China. 2. Industrial
organizations—China. 3. Industrial management—China.
4. Capitalism—China. 5. China—Economic policy—1976–
I. Title. II. Title: Emergence of capitalism in China.
HD58.8.G87   1999
338.951—dc21   98-53890   CIP

This book has been composed in Times Roman

The paper used in this publication meets the minimum requirements
of ANSI/NISO Z39.48-1992 (R1997) (*Permanence of Paper*)

http://pup.princeton.edu

Printed in the United States of America

10 9 8 7 6 5 4 3 2 1

Contents

Figures

Tables

Preface and Acknowledgments _____

In 1995 I SPENT the year talking to Chinese managers about the economic strategies they are adopting in the reform era and about the ways they are changing their organizations more generally. These firm-level changes are pieces in the puzzle of China's transition to a market economy, and as I put these pieces together, this is what I see: a glaring clash of cultures; superficial systems imposed on the foundations of Chinese-style socialist enterprises; a giant, proud, imperious serpent squeezing into Western garb; a dragon in a three-piece suit. More than anything, the practices Chinese firms are adopting in the reform era reflect the search for the strategies and structures that say to the world: We have arrived; we understand the meaning of doing business in the modern world.

The increasingly popularized notion of "The Modern Enterprise System" [*xiandai qiye zhidu*] is very much about giving a face-lift to the state-run organizations that are the legacy of industrial policy in Mao's China. It is about encouraging Chinese organizations to look to the rest of the world for examples of "efficient" market practices. It is about encouraging Chinese organizations to structure themselves so they can "get on track with the international community" [*gen guoji jiegui*] (another very popular idea among managers and officials in reform-era China). It is about Chinese managers hanging up their traditional Communist Party uniforms and donning a sleek set of threads that would place any Western boardroom at ease. It is about those same managers changing the structure and operations of the organizations they run to assure those same Western boardrooms that we are all on the same page about organizational structure and management. A question that naturally arises is how deep do these changes run? What do they actually mean? Organizations can institutionalize new structures—just as managers can throw on a three-piece suit—but what do these cosmetic changes mean for how organizations actually operate in reform-era China? Further, what does it mean for theories of economic action and efficiency that Chinese managers are adopting practices which only appear to be efficient or legitimate?

The realities of organizational practices in China's reforms give rise to an interesting set of theoretical questions that have to do with the structure of markets, market practices, and more general economic principles. I argue that economic strategies and firm structures in China are adopted for cosmetic reasons in the reform era, essentially because Chinese organizations mimic the practices and structures of organizations most admired in the marketplace (i.e., Western organizations). If this is the case, what does this process tell us about the structure of markets in transitional economies? What does it tell us about the notion of transcendental market principles? Although many economists would argue that it is the market push toward efficiency that has led Chinese organizations to set up rational bureaucratic structures, little about transcendental market principles or market practices is reflected in the decisions and practices of organizational actors in China. The Chinese case seems to affirm more than ever the notion that markets are socially constructed arenas in which economic actors make decisions and adopt practices for a variety of reasons, which include uncertainty in the marketplace, the impulse to mimic others in the market, and political pressure from new laws and government agencies. The notions that economists hold so dear of rational profit maximization and that magical push of the market toward efficiency are only two of many possible reasons behind why economic actors do what they do in the turbulent markets of China's transitional economy.

The punch line here, however, is that, although these changing firm structures are often adopted by Chinese organizations to help them *appear* legitimate and market-savvy in the eyes of foreign investors, these new practices do have substantive consequences. For example, when Chinese firms institutionalize mediation committees [*tiaojie hui*] in their organizations, individuals are significantly less likely to file complaints with the local labor bureau; when organizations institutionalize formal hiring procedures, managers are significantly less likely to report using connections in hiring decisions. Thus, while these firms may adopt strategies and practices for reasons of legitimacy, these new organizational structures have real implications for the environments they create in the firm. They have real consequences for the structure of authority relations in the Chinese workplace, the reliance on informal networks and social ties in economic decision making, and the overall rationalization of Chinese business relationships. In China's economic transition, important structural changes are occurring at the state and firm levels, and these changes have radical implications for the structure of economic and social life in China.

Without the financial, administrative, intellectual, and emotional support that many institutions and individuals provided me over the course of this research and writing, this project would not have been possible. It is difficult in a few short sentences to do justice to all those who contributed in significant ways to the project. First and foremost, I would like to thank the Chinese managers and officials who generously gave many hours of their time to this project. The ideas presented in this study are theirs as much as they are mine.

The bulk of the research was funded by the Social Science Research Council and the American Council for Learned Societies with Funds Provided by the Ford Foundation. The University of California, Berkeley, also funded research trips that were crucial to the project. In addition, Berkeley provided funding for a year of writing. While conducting the field research, I was affiliated with the Shanghai Academy of Social Sciences (SASS), an educational institution located in the heart of Shanghai. The Foreign Affairs Office and the Department of Sociology of SASS provided administrative support for the project. In particular, I would like to thank Li Yihai, Lu Hanlong, Zhao Nianguo, and Lu Xiaowen. Among my many China contacts and informants, I would also like to thank Diane Long and Dashiell Chien, who proved to be invaluable advisors for my research.

While all the analyses presented here are original, parts of some chapters were adapted from journal articles. Part of chapter 4 originally appeared in "Organizational Uncertainty and Labor Contracts in China's Economic Transition," *Sociological Forum* 13:457–94 (© 1998 Plenum Publishing Corporation; all rights reserved). Part of chapter 6 originally appeared in "Between Markets and Politics: Organizational Responses to Reform in China," *American Journal of Sociology* 102:1258–1303 (© 1997 University of Chicago Press; all rights reserved). Chapter 8 was adapted from "The Declining Significance of *Guanxi* in China's Economic Transition," *China Quarterly* 154:31–62 (© 1998 School of Oriental and African Studies; all rights reserved).

Many friends and colleagues were sources of support, intellectual guidance, and inspiration. I have particularly benefited from conversations with Richard Arum, Judith Robinson, Josh Gamson, Leo Hsu, and Elissa Wald. Lynne Haney and Jim Ron read parts of the manuscript and provided candid advice when I needed it most. Bruce Carruthers and Frank Dobbin gave the manuscript a very thorough read and offered comments that helped shape the final product in significant ways, as did several other reviewers who remained anonymous.

I would like to especially thank my committee members. Many of their ideas guided this research in more ways than I can rightfully acknowledge. Ann Swidler and Mike Hout both provided timely and penetrating insights and analytical rigor at several points over the course of the research and writing. As my mentor in the China field, Tom Gold was an invaluable part of my graduate career. From my first semester in graduate school on, Tom supported my graduate work in a number of ways—from summer research jobs, through which I learned much about academic research, to general support, feedback, and guidance in the various theoretical and substantive directions my interests took me. Throughout my dissertation research, Tom provided much needed advice about life and research in China, and he provided many contacts that were forged through his own research in China. I could not have done my research in China without Tom's help. Tom also gave the manuscript a thorough reading and provided crucial insights.

One need not be deeply familiar with Neil Fligstein's work to recognize the intellectual influence he has had over me. It is Neil's creative ways of thinking about markets, institutions, and data collection that inspired many of the theoretical and methodological decisions that went into the formulation of this project. At the very heart of this manuscript lie insights drawn from Neil's work on the organizational and institutional structure of American capitalism, his more recent work on the European Union (EU), and his theory of "markets as politics." In addition, Neil has always been extremely generous with his time. Beyond reading the manuscript in its entirety, Neil read some of the chapters and articles more times than I can count. Throughout the project, Neil's ability to provide astute insights that have application for social processes occurring in economic transitions in China and across the world never ceased to amaze me.

Family members have also been important in the completion of this project. My grandparents, Marge and Mack Ralston, helped me very early on by financing my first trip to Asia to do language work, those many years ago. Without the advantages that trip provided me, my graduate and dissertation work would have been considerably slower, considerably more difficult, and perhaps would not have been. My parents, Joe Guthrie and Kathy Guthrie, and their spouses, Wanda Guthrie and Tim Barner, were supportive of the significant amount of time I spent on the other side of the globe; they have always been supportive of my interests and pursuits, and I feel thankful for that.

Finally, I would like to thank Sivan, without whom this research would not have been possible. Sivan accompanied me to China on the main data-gathering trip. Her zest for experiences in the Far East was infectious. Field research is difficult, wearing, and often depressing. Without Sivan there to keep my spirits up, I would have gotten less work done, and I would have felt worse about it. She also has been a wonderful intellectual partner over the past five years. Many of the ideas presented in this manuscript were first put through a filter of conversations with Sivan before they ever reached paper. She has offered interesting ideas and interpretations, and has been kind enough not to find the subject matter boring, despite having no prior connection to sociology or to China. Sivan has been with me through all the difficulties, trials, and rewards that accompany a project such as this. This book is dedicated to her.

June 1998
New York City

DRAGON IN A THREE-PIECE SUIT

One

Firm Practices in China's Transforming Economy: Efficiency or Mimicry?

> Market actors live in murky worlds where it is never clear
> which actions will have which consequences. Yet, actors
> must construct an account of the world that interprets the
> murkiness, motivates and determines courses of action, and
> justifies the action decided upon. In markets, the goal of
> action is to ensure the survival of the firm. No actor can
> determine which behaviors will maximize profits (either a
> priori or post hoc), and action is therefore directed toward
> the creation of stable worlds.
>   *(Neil Fligstein 1996a)*

> Structural change in organizations seems less and less
> driven by competition or by the need for efficiency. Instead
> . . . bureaucratization and other forms of organizational
> change occur as the result of processes that make
> organizations more similar without necessarily making
> them more efficient.
>   *(Paul DiMaggio and Walter Powell 1983)*

Prologue

This study begins with a simple observation and question. Since the late 1980s Chinese firms have been adopting a number of economic strategies and practices that resemble the rational bureaucratic systems found in firms from many advanced market societies. What are the forces and processes driving this trend? The collection of findings I present throughout these chapters provides an answer to this question. I argue that it is not the drive toward efficiency that guides organizational decisions in China's transforming economy. Rather, the decisions and practices of Chinese firms are shaped by a combination of the social networks and political institutions in which they are embedded and the economic uncertainty they experience. As they struggle to survive in the increasingly uncertain and turbulent markets of China's transition economy, Chinese firms mimic the examples of market actors that they view as being the most market-savvy, namely, foreign investors.

Groping

On the eve of the economic reforms in 1978–79, the People's Republic of China (PRC), one of the most complete totalitarian systems of the twentieth century, stood at a crossroads. The debacle of the Cultural Revolution was past, but several social problems now stood in its wake. What was to be done with all the urban residents that had just returned from a decade in the country-side? How would the current economic system absorb them? The Ten Year Plan, drawn up in 1975, was faltering, and the beginnings of unrest were start-ing to show through the cracks in the Beijing Spring movement of 1978–79. As an answer to these problems, Deng Xiaoping was positioning himself to lead the nation down a path of economic reform that would introduce a set of controlled modifications into the structure of the socialist system. However, without a defined endpoint in sight, this reform process, which the Chinese affectionately refer to as "groping for stones to cross the river" [*moshi guohe*], would unfold in unanticipated directions. In many ways, the economic reforms in China set in motion a process of radical social change that would extend far beyond the economic sphere where they began.[1]

As with the experiences in Eastern Europe, the economic reforms in China present a remarkable opportunity to observe firsthand the process of transition from a socialist to a market economic system. As the state constructs markets and the new social and economic institutions that define them, a type of natural experiment on the social, economic, and political dynamics of market transi-tion is occurring before our eyes. Yet, just as China is groping for stones to cross the river of economic reform, scholars of China's economic transition have also, to some extent, been groping. Research on economic transitions has often focused on shadows and footprints of the reforms, rather than on direct observations of economic decisions in the face of institutional change. Ex-plaining the mechanisms and processes behind institutional change is central to the story that many scholars of transition want to tell, but the data on which claims are based often fall short of the task. In economics, many studies have focused on aggregate measures of productivity across sectors and regions of the economy, attempting to infer what changes in productivity must imply about changing institutions and economic practices. In sociology, the data of choice have most often been individual or household income, as scholars guess what gains in income, returns to education, entrepreneurship, or political power must mean about labor markets and market mechanisms.

In the study of transforming economies, there are at least two situations where focus on income and productivity becomes problematic. First, because changes in income and productivity can arise from many different institutional configurations or systemic changes, observing shifts in economic indicators and inferring backward from these changes to evaluate specific institutional reforms presents a problem for transitional studies.[2] For example, poor returns to education do not necessarily indicate the absence of labor markets as some scholars have concluded; and weak returns to political capital do not necessarily mean that officials are not accruing significant advantages in the reform era.[3] Second, a lack of change in economic indicators does not necessarily imply a lack of institutional change, as some scholars have assumed.[4] It is plausible—even likely—that many economic actors in transforming economies are not experiencing growth in income or productivity *despite* changes in economic and institutional arrangements. In this scenario, a lack of change in economic indicators does not imply the absence of institutional change. Rather, it implies that economic actors are struggling to adapt and survive in the face of these radical changes. In either case, an exclusive focus on changes in standard economic indicators fails to grasp what is occurring in transforming economies.

In contrast to approaches that focus on individual-level income or aggregate measures of productivity, I explore China's transition economy by studying the specific ways that economic actors are experiencing reforms. Instead of focusing on how much money economic actors are making, I examine *what economic actors do* to make these changes in income and productivity possible. I study the *decisions and practices* adopted by firms in four sectors of industrial Shanghai. The contributions of this study are both methodological and substantive. Methodologically, I show that an empirical focus on the decisions and practices of economic actors in the marketplace sheds light on processes of transition in China that have not been adequately illuminated. If we want to understand the timing and trajectory of China's economic transition, as well as the actual impact of policy changes, we must examine specific cases of decisions, practices, strategies, and structures of organizations in the transforming economy. Firms are not passive recipients of top-down policy—rather, they interpret, adapt, modify, and even subvert the formal measures that come from on high. In the context of this contested terrain, I step beyond the focus on market competition and productivity, examining instead the adaptation of Chinese enterprises to a transforming legal/institutional environment, a changing administrative system, and the changing networks in which Chinese firms are situated.

Substantively, the results of this study add up to two basic findings. First, a process of rationalization is occurring at the firm level in China. This is a crucial process that studies focusing on income and productivity ignore. Yet, rationalist and efficiency theories of organizations do not explain why Chinese firms adopt Western-style market strategies and management practices, while institutional theories take us much further in understanding this process. Contact with foreign firms, via joint ventures, and the feeling of being set adrift by the central government—and thus the need to mimic firms from developed market economies—predict which firms will adopt Western practices. I argue that the idealized Western market practices that rationalist and neoclassical theorists believe to be responses to transcendental economic laws in fact spread across organizations not for reasons of efficiency but for reasons of legitimacy. They spread to Chinese firms that have direct contact with foreign investors and to those that are driven to copy Western practices by the belief that the supports available to them in the command economy are being removed.

Second, I deliver a nuanced message on the question of whether China's economy will eventually converge with Western advanced market economies. I show that the particular nature of China's institutional history defines its path through the reforms in profound ways, and, as a result, it makes little sense to imagine that China's economic structure can or will converge with other Western capitalist forms.[5] At the firm level, the institutional structure of state administration and, specifically, a firm's position in the industrial hierarchy of the former command economy have profound effects on how that firm will experience the reforms. In addition, building a market economy on the ruins of a socialist system has profound implications for how economic actors think about reforms. The decisions and practices that managers of firms have adopted over the course of the reforms show that neither the firms nor the managers who run them can be viewed simply as rational profit-maximizing economic actors who will pursue power and plenty given the right structural circumstances. I reject the notion that China's transition economy will eventually converge with Western-style markets, *despite* the fact that firms are adopting Western-style economic practices. While Chinese firms are adopting Western-style management practices, these activities are occurring on the foundation of an institutional system that has powerful influence over the experiences and success of organizations in reform-era China. Changes in Chinese organizations are part of a unique Chinese transitional path that will lead to an organizational configuration and market economic system at the end of transition that is distinctively Chinese.

Economic Transition and Chinese Firms

China's economic reforms comprise a fascinating case of market construction and institutional change. Where once an entire government structure rested on the administrative decisions and fiat of officials and "revolutionary" leaders, broad-based institutional changes have been introduced that shape the system in entirely new ways. "Revolutionary committees" were transformed back into "people's governments"; Chinese-foreign joint ventures were allowed to enter the economy; the provincial governments of Guangdong and Fujian were given enough autonomy from the center to formulate "separate economic regulations" for "Special Economic Zones."[6] These are but a few of the wrenching institutional changes that were enacted at the state level at the dawn of the reforms. With these changes, the Chinese government altered "the rules of the game," changing the institutional structure of society and therefore the structures that shape social and economic action.[7] This project of institution building and market construction is a fascinating instance of economic reform because it is a case where we can observe the construction of market institutions almost from scratch.

Scholars who write about Western market societies tend to take for granted an institutional environment that penetrates the firm, and they take for granted a rationalized bureaucratic system that is integral to firm structure. Yet, if we have learned anything about Chinese firms under the command economy, it is that the institutional systems around which they were structured were very different from the rationalized bureaucratic systems found in many advanced capitalist societies.[8] Currently in China, it is precisely the institutional environments that define markets and the rational bureaucratic systems within firms that are being invented and implemented. In the case of China, we have the unique opportunity to observe the construction of new institutions and markets and the adoption of many new practices within firms, an interesting window onto what one scholar has referred to as the "state-building" project of market construction and transformation.[9]

There have been a number of important studies that have systematically examined the major policy changes that have defined the economic transition in China.[10] While scholarship has focused on the effect of broad-based institutional changes on the overall economic structure, on the performance of firms, on aggregate measures of productivity across sectors, and on individual income, less attention has been given to how institutional changes translate into specific *practices* of economic actors.[11] Besides economic performance and productivity, we can observe many other organization-level manifestations of institutional change which are hidden from studies that focus on income and productivity. Organizations are structured internally by institutions and practices (e.g., grievance-filing procedures, job descriptions, etc.) that are reflections of the social and political pressures of the environments in which they are situated. They engage in economic practices (e.g., diversification), which have little to do with economic performance and much more to do with survival and stability in uncertain institutional environments. And they often adopt strategies and practices that reflect social conventions and cultural norms.[12] In the study of markets and market institutions, we need an empirical focus not only on economic performance and productivity but also on the organization-level structures and practices that are reactions to broad institutional changes defined at the state level.

In many ways, state-level institutional and policy changes are only meaningful to the extent that they have tangible consequences for actors in the changing social and economic systems. The study I have undertaken looks at the actual implementation and meaning of the reforms as viewed from the firm level. I examine the ways that these institutional changes are interpreted, incorporated, employed, and ignored by actors in the changing economy. As the state yields autonomy to economic organizations, are the internal structures of firms also moving away from the vertical ties that organized them under the totalitarian system? As a rational-legal institutional system is set in place at the state level for the economic reforms, how are the practices and the internal environments of firms changed in the process? What are the causal processes at work in institutional and structural change at the firm level? Once the policies and laws that are constructed by the state exist on paper, what factors are associated with their adoption by economic actors, and how do the meanings of these new institutions vary with organizational characteristics?

To address these questions I examine the ways that eighty-one firms, randomly sampled from four industrial sectors in Shanghai, are dealing with the reforms. I study the meaning that state-level changes have for the decisions these firms are making in the reforms, focusing on how the state-level changes, political institutions, economic uncertainty, and networks influence the practices they adopt. I present evidence on how economic actors make decisions in the transforming world of China's reforms; these decisions include inter-organizational negotiations, market strategies, and internal organizational structures. I take seriously the perspectives that managers bring to the project of economic transition and participation in new markets, and I view the organizational strategies and internal structures managers choose to adopt as the decisions of economic actors in emerging and transforming marketplaces.

Rationalist and Institutional Accounts of Organizational Action

Efficiency and rationalist theories of organizational action view organizations as profit-maximizing entities that adopt strategies and structures in the headlong pursuit of market efficiency. From this perspective, organizational decisions are based on a rational calculus where managers institutionalize internal structures and adopt market strategies that allow the organization to maximize potential. Whether the specific rationale has to do with reducing transaction costs, creating incentives for workers, or maximizing worker output, the underlying model of action rests on the assumption of profit-maximizing agents within organizations making rational decisions.[13]

Institutional theory offers a counterperspective to the rationalist and efficiency view of economic decision making.[14] Scholars in this area of research have argued that the desire to appear legitimate and market savvy in the face of political or social pressure, or simply uncertainty, in the marketplace is the primary rationale behind organizational decision making. Organizations are as likely to act according to social norms and mandates of the institutional and cultural environments in which they are embedded as they are to act according to the nebulous push of the market's invisible hand. The argument here is that "organizational structure [and action] is, in varying degrees, a symbolic phenomenon, designed to *demonstrate* appropriateness and rationality rather than to achieve efficiency."[15] From this perspective, the practices that organizations adopt are often as much symbolic as they are a rationally defined position staked out by profit-maximizing economic actors. Embedded in social and political environments, organizations adopt decisions and practices that are often reflections of the normative, legislative, and cultural pressures they face. Market pressures and fiscal constraints surely also play a role in organizational decision making, but economic pressures comprise only one of many areas of constraint that organizations and their managers face. In the institutional perspective the assumption of rational action is set aside, as patterns of decision making and individual (or organizational) choice are empirical questions, not to be simplified as assumptions for the convenience of economic modeling.

Research on China's economic transition has been heavily weighted toward rationalist and efficiency theories of economic action. On the extreme end of the spectrum sit scholars such as Jeffrey Sachs, who believe that cultural and historical particularities are irrelevant, because economic actors the world over will respond in similar ways to the efficient institutions of market economies. As an advocate of the "shock therapy" approach, Sachs argues that little attention to cultural details or experimentation is necessary: "The long-run goals of institutional change are clear, and are found in the economic models of existing market-based economies."[16] Embedded in this view is the notion that certain assumptions about economic actors are universal—actors are rational and will pursue profits given the right structural circumstances—and therefore that economic actors will respond in similar ways to certain institutional arrangements. Similarly, though focused on economic decisions at the individual level, Victor Nee's research on market transition in China is built around the assumption that given the right structural circumstances, decision making will always tend toward rational profit and utility maximization. Indeed, Nee seems to view "the pursuit of power and plenty by economic actors in society" as the linchpin of economic transitions.[17] And while Andrew Walder's work has been exemplary in identifying institutions and structural processes at work in China's transition to a market economy, there are echoes of a rationalist framework, as the perspective emphasizes incentives for officials, which are surely important, but also only part of the story.[18]

When perspectives that counter the rationalist framework are presented, the arguments rely heavily on the particularistic nature of Chinese culture. The view here is that Chinese people are embedded in a "web of social relationships," and these social ties shape economic action in the reform era.[19] Important examples of this research approach are Mayfair Yang's cultural study of connections and Yanjie Bian's research on job placement in China, both of which emphasize the cultural importance of connections in Chinese society.[20] In addition, a number of recent studies in business literatures have also focused on the cultural importance of connections in China.[21]

My analysis of China's economic transition draws primarily on the insights of institutional theory. I make no assumptions about the decision-making processes behind individual and organizational behavior, and I make no assumptions about the connection between economic efficiency and institutional change. Nor do I assume that the particularistic or network aspects of Chinese culture drive economic decision making. Instead, I focus empirically on the decisions and practices organizational actors adopt in reform-era China, attempting to make sense of these actions in the contexts of the broader institutional environments, the social networks, and the economic constraints these actors face. I argue that a process of rationalization is occurring in Chinese organizations, and this process is driven primarily by the desire to attract foreign investors and by uncertainty in the face of declining support from the state.

A caveat here: Although I present a picture in which Chinese organizations are becoming increasingly rationalized in terms of bureaucratic structures and authority relations, this does not imply that I view economic actors as reducible to a rational-actor framework. Rationalization and rational action are separate matters. The process of rationalization is about whether Chinese organizations are adopting rational bureaucratic structures, changing authority relations within the firm, adhering to contracts, and the like. A rational-actor framework would maintain that they are making these changes as part of a rational calculus about efficiency and profit maximization. While I am agnostic on the question of rational action, I believe that the *assumption* of rational action and the *assumption* that organizations only make decisions to increase efficiency cloud the waters of empirical analysis. In the end, we must get down to empirical cases, and we must rely on the information that is observable. This is exactly what I attempt to do in the analysis that follows.

Throughout much of the research on transforming economies, the central questions focus on the shape and structure of the market institutions that are emerging and the overall path of China's reform process. However, neither research focusing on individual and household data nor that focusing on aggregate measures of productivity has adequately addressed the institutional structures and practices that define market action in China today. If we want to understand what type of institutional system is emerging, we need to focus more directly on the decisions and practices of economic actors in the economy. We need to focus attention not on how much individuals (or entire sectors of the economy) have gained in income (or productivity) but rather on the institutional circumstances that have allowed these gains to take place. As

Andrew Walder aptly puts it, what is required is a "more careful conceptual-ization and measurement of the institutional conditions that affect the work-ings and impact of markets. The question is not to what *degree* markets have emerged, but what *kind* of market economy is emerging."[22] To unravel the question of what kind of market economy is emerging, we need to begin with direct observations on how economic actors are dealing with the institutional reforms that are occurring at the state level. We need to observe whether price reforms have afforded firms the ability to set prices, whether rationalized tax systems have had implications for the constraints experienced by firms and government offices, whether the Labor Law has changed the ways that firms conceive of labor relations. We need to focus specifically on what organiza-tional responses to reforms are and what these responses might indicate about state-firm relations and the course of China's economic transition. These types of observations are wholly absent from studies that draw on individual-level data of changing mechanisms of stratification or on aggregate measures of productivity. To bridge this gap, the study I report on in these pages works from the organizational level, focusing on the strategies and structures organi-zations adopt in the emerging markets of China's transition economy.

A Study of Organizations in Industrial Shanghai

In 1995 I conducted an empirical study on the ways that firms in industrial Shanghai are experiencing China's economic transition. Inasmuch as this study was carried out in one city, a few explanations and qualifications are appropriate. First, why study China's urban industrial economy? There are several reasons why such a study is important right now. In the case of China, understanding the corporate forms by which people's lives are organized is central to an understanding of social structure and social processes in Chinese society more generally. Several studies have emphasized the importance of organizational structures in contemporary Chinese society.[23] As the Party-state methodically penetrated and controlled virtually all sectors of Chinese society after 1949, few aspects of social life were left untouched by organizational structures. Organizational forms are changing rapidly in the reform era, and systematic study of how and why these organizations are changing is neces-sary for a full understanding of China's transition to a market economy. Focus on the industrial work unit allows us to explore the changing structure of the work unit and the meaning of these changes for people's lives. Andrew Walder's (1986a) work was a benchmark for understanding the structure of the work unit for life in prereform China. We now need to understand further how the changes of the economic reform have altered the structure that Walder illuminated.

Second, the industrial work unit is an important empirical site to observe the convergence of macrolevel institutional decisions and microlevel institutional practices: As institutional reforms are enacted at the state level (e.g., laws and policies), individual firms respond to these changes to different degrees and in various ways. The interesting questions for economic transition are how state-level reforms are implemented (or ignored) at the firm level, and what the reasons are behind variation in this process. This approach more directly observes the effects of institutional change in China's economic transition than does research that makes inferences about markets and institutions from observations of shifting patterns of stratification or gains in productivity.[24] Despite extensive research on organizational structure in China, particularly in the pre-reform era, we have relatively few systematic observations of the decisions and practices of urban industrial organizations during the economic transition.

An additional reason to study the urban industrial economy is that some scholars have argued that reforms have not been aggressively implemented in the upper levels of China's former command economy.[25] Since the upper levels of the administrative hierarchy are located in urban areas, it is important to study institutional and organizational changes in urban areas to gain a deeper understanding of these issues. Despite the importance of urban areas for the industrial economy (74 percent of the industrial economy is located in urban areas [State Statistical Bureau 1994], pp. 23, 296–97), many of the studies of the economic transition have focused on the meaning of the reforms for rural areas. This is because most studies of economic transition have been growth-driven—that is, scholars have assumed that growth indicates that reforms are taking hold; conversely, a lack of growth indicates that reforms are occurring at a slower rate. Since the rural economy has grown at a much faster rate than the urban economy, it has been argued that the rural economy has undergone extreme reforms while the urban economy has not experienced reforms to the same extent. However, it is a mistake to view growth as the primary indicator of reform because a lack of growth does not necessarily mean that reforms are not being enacted. Growth is but one possible outcome of introducing market constraints, as organizations could also be adopting survival and stability strategies that are indicators of the reforms but not necessarily related to growth. Systematic study of urban industrial areas, which are not experiencing the same rapid growth as rural areas, is necessary for a full picture of the changes occurring as a result of China's reforms.

The Head of the Dragon

Finally, a question of geographic location may be raised: How representative of China's economic transition is the city of Shanghai? Table 1.1 compares Shanghai to several other major cities in China. The cities compared here are

TABLE 1.1

Comparative Data on Major Industrial Cities in China in the Reform Era

	Shanghai	Beijing	Tianjin	Guangzhou	Wuhan	Shenyang	Chongqing
Population (city) (mil.)[a]	9.48	7.15	5.89	3.72	4.38	5.65	3.06
Metro area pop. (mil.)[a]	12.94	10.51	8.87	6.24	6.92	6.58	15.04
Pop. density (1,000/km^2)[a]	4.61	5.22	1.38	1.99	1.61	1.33	2.00
Density (metro area)[a]	2.04	.63	.79	.65	.82	.51	.65
Indust. lab. (city) (mil.)[b]	2.61	1.97	1.61	.89	1.19	6.10	.98
Indust. lab. (metro area)[b]	4.52	2.66	2.35	1.20	1.48	7.69	1.98
Priv. lab. (city) (10,000)[b]	5.11	5.64	5.09	6.31	4.42	6.20	3.27
Priv. lab. (metro area)[b]	5.73	5.64	5.17	9.03	5.86	6.65	7.12
No. of signed for. contracts[a]	3,864	3,765	3,544	2,620	1,081	1,129	737
For. capital inv. (bil. USD)[a]	3.18	.98	.94	1.46	.46	.56	.35
GDP (bil.)[a]	6.97	4.56	2.83	2.88	1.69	1.91	1.97

[a] 1993 data; source: *Statistical Yearbook of Chinese Cities*, 1994.

[b] 1989 data; source: *Statistical Yearbook of Chinese Cities*, 1990.

all among China's ten most populated cities. Four of the cities—Shanghai, Beijing, Tianjin, and Chongqing—are counted as official municipalities and have basically the same administrative power as provinces.[26]

Table 1.1 shows that Shanghai is exceptional in a number of ways. In 1993 only Chongqing (pop. 15.04 million) was larger than Shanghai (pop. 12.94 million) in terms of overall population; however, if we look at urban districts, Shanghai's urban population (9.48 million) was significantly larger than other major cities. In terms of population density, Shanghai is the most densely populated city overall, and only Beijing is more densely populated in urban districts. Although five of the seven cities are similar in terms of the size of their industrial labor forces, it is interesting to note that only Shenyang has a larger industrial labor force than Shanghai. Shanghai's private labor force is comparable in size to that of the other major cities, and its private labor force is similar to that of other cities in that the majority of the laborers working for private enterprises [*siying qiye*] and individual employers [*getihu*] are located in urban districts. Foreign investment has risen radically since the 1980s, and

Shanghai has landed more foreign contracts and has had more foreign capital actually invested than any of the other major cities. At the end of the 1980s, Shanghai's GDP was significantly higher than that of the other major cities. Shanghai also had the highest rate of consumption and the highest average annual salaries.

Shanghai may also be somewhat anomalous in terms of legal and institutional development, and some informants voiced this concern. One manager in the chemicals sector said:

> Shanghai is a special place in terms of the way people follow laws. The legal system is probably more developed here than it is anywhere else in China. (Interview 93*,[27] 1995)

An official in the Labor Bureau spoke more directly to Shanghai's representativeness:

> Shanghai is not representative of China. If you want to understand China, this is not the place. Shanghai is developing faster, and the people are more educated than anywhere else. It's just not like the rest of China. (Interview 40, 1995)

An official in the pharmaceuticals sector related Shanghai's atypical nature to the development of business interests there:

> All the foreign companies I work with are very happy with the situation of intellectual property rights in Shanghai. Shanghai is much better than other places in this area. Shanghai is the best place for cultured and educated people, for economic development. Shanghai may not be a good place for sight-seeing, but it's an excellent place for doing business. (Interview 65, 1995)

These statements would seem to indicate that a study of institutional change in Shanghai would tell us little that is generalizable about institutional change in China. Further, it could be argued that the selection of Shanghai as a case study amounts to selection on the dependent variable: Inasmuch as I am interested in processes of institutionalization, is it problematic that we are studying one of the most legalistic and institutionalized areas in China?

There are two answers to these issues. First, all areas of China are currently engaged in institution-building projects. Although there is certainly variation in the structure of institutional environments in different areas (e.g., Shanghai and Guangzhou), I am interested in exploring the factors and processes associated with the adoption of institutions across organizational units. In this sense, the comparative framework *within* Shanghai (across sectors, types of organizations, and levels of government administration) is much more important than the geographical location of the case study itself. Second, I view institutional and organizational change in China as a *process* of change[28]: Although Shanghai may be qualitatively different from several other areas in terms of institutional structure and change, this difference is primarily a function of degree rather than kind. Shanghai is simply further along in the process of change. As a manager in the foods sector put it:

> Many fads and trends begin in Shanghai; what Shanghai does, the rest of China will soon do. Shanghai is the head of the dragon. (Interview 74*, 1995)

This informant was speaking specifically about market trends, but I believe that the sentiment also extends to other realms in China's economic transition. I study Shanghai as a case of institutional and organizational change in China's economic transition, but the study relies on systematic comparisons across industrial sectors and organizational units to illuminate the structural factors that give rise to the process of institutional change throughout China.

Gathering Data

In 1995 I conducted a study of the decisions and practices of economic organizations in four industrial sectors of Shanghai's transforming economy. The core of the study is based on in-depth interviews with factory managers in eighty-one organizations selected in a stratified random sample of the four industrial sectors.[29] The interviews were conducted with the general or vice general manager or both at each of the eighty-one firms in the study; the interviews were unaccompanied and were conducted in Chinese.[30] Quantitative and qualitative data were gathered from the interviews with the managers. The qualitative data were as critical to the study as the quantitative data, as the perspectives articulated in these interviews guided my interpretation of the quantitative analyses. The sectors included in the study were chemicals, electronics, foods, and garments. In-depth discussions of the selection of the sectors and organizational units can be found in Appendix 1. In addition to the eighty-one interviews, I conducted seventy-four interviews with government officials, legal scholars, and managers of organizations that were not part of the random sample.

The interviews with the general managers were based on a standardized, pretested questionnaire for which all the questions were open-ended (see Appendix 3). Naturally there was variation on the open-ended nature of the questions according to the type of question being asked—some requiring more clarification and discussion than others.[31] The questions that were set up for comparisons across all eighty-one units can be broken into three main categories. The first category was made up of basic organization-level variables that had to do with the structure and economics of the organization. Among these variables were organizational size, number of retired employees, the value of the fixed assets, gross revenues (1994 and 1990), profits (1994 and 1990), percentage of production designated for the export market, and so on. The second category of variables focused on market practices (strategies) such as contractual relations with foreign firms, the decision of whether to adopt a diversification strategy, and price-setting procedures. The third category focused on the internal practices (structure) of organizations such as nonwage benefits, labor contracts, and personnel procedures (job descriptions, promotion tests, grievance filing procedures, etc.). Data were gathered on all these topics for comparisons across the eighty-one firms in the analysis. Discussions with officials and managers over these organizational variables and practices also helped contextualize the organizational practices included in the study. A set of more general rotating questions was directed toward deeper discussions of different aspects of the emerging industrial markets' organization. These questions ranged from issues such as *guanxi* (networks/connections), state control over different markets, and the fiscal systems of the reform period to the more specific questions of pricing and the effects of legalization.

Variables for Analyzing Organizational Structure and Change

The resulting data set was one of several different organizational indicators and outcome variables. Throughout the study I generally present results from one statistical model of a given organizational outcome, unless additional models reveal information essential to the discussion. A good deal of background analysis that is not presented here went into the quantitative analysis, and if a model other than the full model is presented, the reader should assume that the model presented fits the data significantly better than the full model.[32] I defer most methodological discussions of variables and coding to the appendixes. However, a few variables are critical for the analysis, and these I would like to introduce here.

INDICATORS OF AN ORGANIZATION'S ECONOMIC "HEALTH"

I focus primarily on four variables that, in diverse ways, approximate an organization's economic health. "Employee ratio" refers to the proportion of active to retired workers in the organization [active / (active + retired)]; in other words, it is a measure of the relationship between the number of productive workers an organization employs relative to the total number of workers the organization must support. Organizations with a large number of retired workers are among those that are struggling the most in China's transition, and this variable approximates that situation. As the number of retired workers appears in the denominator, larger values for this variable indicate a more positive situation for organizations in the transition. "Losses" indicate that an organization lost money in 1990.[33] "Average profit margins" are an indication of an organization's performance in the economic transition. This variable is based on profits and gross revenue. Finally, overall "organizational health" is an indicator of an organization's situation with respect to labor and input costs. The construction of this variable was somewhat more complex than that of the others, and I direct interested readers to Appendix 4 for discussion of this variable. Briefly, the variable is based on revenues, labor costs, and the money each organization must pay into the newly established pension fund [*yanglao jin*], which amounts to 25.5 percent of the organization's labor costs. Because input costs vary significantly by sector, the variable was then standardized to the average for a given organization's sector.

FORMAL RELATIONS WITH FOREIGN FIRMS:
THE JOINT-VENTURE EFFECT

Foreign investment has many effects on the economic climate in China. Although many politicians and pundits have strong opinions on the meaning of foreign investment for social and economic change in China, to date, *we have no systematic information on the impact of foreign investment on the decisions and practices of economic actors in China's transition economy.* In this study, I systematically analyze the effects that formal relations with foreign investors have on the economic practices emerging in China. I model the extent to which, controlling for other effects, formal relations with a foreign investor have predictive power for the decisions and practices Chinese firms are adopting in the reform era.

Relationships with foreign firms can take on many forms, from formal joint-venture relationships to cooperative licensing agreements to informal social networking. As a gauge of the organization's formal relations with foreign firms, I focus on whether an organization has a joint-venture factory [*hezi qiye*] with a foreign investor. I use the joint-venture investment because it is the most formal of the relations, as well as the most complex in terms of cooperatively working out the details of the joint-venture factory. Joint ventures involve the construction of a new organization (a separate legal entity) that is jointly owned by both the foreign and Chinese organizations.[34] As such, the process of constructing a joint venture requires the Chinese organization to work side by side with the foreign investor, hammering out the details of what is often a long-term relationship in a way that is not necessary in most licensing agreements or other types of less formal agreements. If there are effects of relationships with foreign investment partners, we will most likely see them here. Forty-eight of the firms in my study had at least one joint venture with a foreign partner, thus allowing for a controlled comparison between those firms that have formal joint-venture relations with foreign partners and those that do not.

ORGANIZATIONAL GOVERNANCE

I observe the effects of organizational governance in two ways, looking first at the characteristics of the organization's general manager[35] and then at the governance environment in which a firm is situated. The former is a measure of the organization's internal governance; the latter is a measure of the firm's relationship to the state. With respect to internal governance, I focus on the educational background of the organization's general manager. In prereform China, general managers of manufacturing organizations most often had backgrounds in engineering or some other technical skill, if they had any postsecondary education at all. In the reform era, general managers tend increasingly to have an educational background in business or economics, as was the case for 54 percent of the firms in my sample.

As for governance environment, that a firm is situated in the administrative hierarchy of the former command economy not only had profound effects for how the organization experienced the command economy but also for how it is experiencing the economic transition. I operationalize this effect in two ways. First, since firms under the jurisdiction of municipal bureaus are experiencing the transition much differently than those under the jurisdiction of municipal and district companies, I look specifically at the effects that location under these different levels of state administration has on firm practices. Second, because one of the issues for a firm's relationship to its state administrative office resides in the amount of administrative attention an administrative office can give to an organization, the size of the firm's jurisdiction is also, in some cases, critical. Therefore I also look at a firm's governance environment as a function of the size of the jurisdiction in which an organization is situated.

A Preview of What Follows

Through a combination of quantitative and qualitative data, I analyze the emergence and adoption of market strategies and firm structures in a sample of organizations in China's economic transition. Though I cover a diverse range of themes, the analysis has a logical order. I am interested in the organizational structures and constraints that lead to the adoption of institutions, and since different institutions have meaning for different levels of organization, I have selected examples of strategies and structures that are meaningful for the different levels of analysis. The logic of the study is the following: I begin with the intra-organizational changes that are transforming organizations in reform-era China; I then analyze the market practices and the dynamic of inter-organizational negotiations in the emerging markets of the transition economy. Finally, I address the extent to which the changes occurring in Chinese firms diminish the importance of *guanxi* as an institutional system in Chinese society.

Before I delve into the empirical realities of Chinese firms, chapter 2 sets the stage for the analyses that follow. In this chapter I describe some of the critical institutional changes occurring over the course of China's economic transition. I examine the premise that the institutional structure of state administration in China's prereform industrial economy has important consequences for the variety of ways that organizations experience the reforms in the transition era. I also highlight the changes that have been central to the reform of Chinese organizations from the perspective of Chinese managers.

Chapters 3 and 4 focus on the internal structure and labor practices of the firms in my study. Chapter 3 examines internal practices and arrangements in firms, including the existence of labor mediation institutions, Workers' Representative Committees, formal grievance-filing procedures, hiring practices, job descriptions, and promotion practices. Through an analysis of these new practices and structures in Chinese firms, the chapter explores the rise of formal rational bureaucracies in Chinese organizations. I argue that the structures emerging in Chinese firms are giving rise to a formal rational approach to management. Although clearly there are still elements of the old structures on which this new system is being built, the emergence of formal bureaucracies at the firm level sets the stage for a radical departure from the authority relations of the past. I also show that these formal rational structures are not purely symbolic: They have real consequences for organizational practices and worker unrest. The analysis in chapter 3 shows that foreign investment matters for the new institutional structures emerging at the firm level in China, and these new structures have substantive consequences for Chinese workers.

Chapter 4 focuses on a variety of labor arrangements in the firms, including wages, nonwage benefits, and labor contracts. A prominent theme in this chapter is the formalization of labor relations at the firm level and what these changes illuminate about organizational uncertainty. In particular, where labor contracts offer firms the opportunity to end lifetime employment, the institutionalization of labor contracts is primarily about organizational uncertainty in the economic transition. I show that firms in poor financial shape and those at the highest levels of China's industrial hierarchy are the most likely to put an end to the institution of lifetime employment on an organizationwide basis by placing all their workers on labor contracts. This indicates that firms in the upper levels of China's administrative hierarchy are experiencing a significant amount of uncertainty in the reform period and that they are organizing their labor arrangements accordingly.

The focus of chapters 5 and 6 is the project of market construction and the organizational decisions that reflect this process. The case of China's economic transition presents a clear example of the importance of states in the construction of markets, as the Chinese state is currently engaged in the construction of institutional arrangements and governance structures central to the construction of a market economic system. Yet, it is a mistake to look only at trends in productivity and profits to see where market reforms are having the greatest impact. In chapter 5 I look specifically at firms' price-setting practices. Autonomous price setting is central to the emergence of true markets, and in order to understand the extent to which true markets are emerging in China, we must understand the dynamics and practices surrounding price setting and price negotiation. Like many of the practices I analyze in this study, price-setting practices are fundamentally tied to a firm's position in the state administrative hierarchy and to formal relationships with foreign investors.

Chapter 6, which examines two specific strategies of firms in the economic transition, takes up the issue of emerging market constraints and the path dependence of the economic transition. The findings of chapter 6 show that although scholars have argued that market constraints are not being hardened for firms at the upper levels of China's administrative hierarchy, these firms are experiencing a high degree of uncertainty in the economic transition, an indication that support from the state is waning for these firms. As such, they are among the most likely to experiment with new economic strategies in the reform era.

Chapter 7 explores the negotiations between foreign and Chinese organizations and the way these negotiations shape the outcomes of joint-venture contracts and the emergence of a rational-legal system. The empirical case in this chapter is whether organizations have specified dispute arbitration clauses— stipulating arbitration at the Chinese International Arbitration Commission or out-of-country arbitration—in their joint-venture contracts. The specification of arbitration clauses in joint-venture contracts depends primarily on whether the foreign investor is from a Western country and on the Chinese firm's position in the state administrative hierarchy. The findings are discussed in terms of the light they shed on the rationalization of economic negotiations in China's economic transition. The implications of the analysis lead to a discussion of the relationship between foreign investment and the institutionalization of a rational-legal system in China and the ways that foreign investors attempt to create stable institutional systems in an institutionally unstable world.

Chapter 8 puts the previous discussions and analyses squarely in the context of Chinese society with a discussion of *guanxi*, itself an institutional system. Where several scholars have argued that *guanxi* is playing an increasingly important role in China's industrial economy, I argue that this Chinese institution is actually declining in importance in the reform era. While managers view relationships in general as important in market activity, the use of connections for accomplishing official tasks is giving way to the mechanisms being forged in the emerging formal rational-legal system. In other words, at least in the urban industrial economy, networks are still very important, but they are used less for the backdoor accomplishment of procedures [*houmen banshouxu*] and more for simply cultivating business relationships in emerging markets. This transformation is intimately tied to the construction of a formal rational-legal system at the state level. As with a number of other findings presented in this study, this transformation is also part of a path dependent process, as the extent to which organizations have embraced this change depends on their position in the state administrative hierarchy.

While in chapter 9 I recap some major themes presented throughout the text, in this concluding chapter I focus primarily on the implications of my study for the assessment of economic transitions, firm performance, and policy decisions relating to foreign investment and trade policies with China. With respect to the general implications of this study for research on economic transitions, the findings support recent research that has emphasized the path-dependent nature of market reforms. As China's transition moves forward, a process of marketization is indeed taking place, but the extent of the marketization is, at the same time, highly contingent on the institutional structure of state administration. The path-dependent nature of this transition also allows the case of China to fit well with the recent conclusions in research on comparative capitalisms, which argue that there is little convergence of capitalist forms in the world economy.[36] Market emergence and transformation are dependent on the preexisting institutional structures that were in place before the reform. Nevertheless, foreign investment plays a pivotal role in the types of decisions and practices Chinese organizations adopt and the ways they think about economic change.

With respect to the implications of this study for policy debates, I argue that although a number of scholars, pundits, and politicians have strong opinions about the relationship between economic development and human rights in China, few, if any, of these opinions are grounded in anything empirical about institutional change in China during the reform period. Policies, such as awarding China Most-Favored-Nation status, need to be based not on assertions or beliefs about the effect of trade and economic development on human rights in China but, rather, on empirical research conducted to examine how these aspects of life in China are interrelated. The issue is not whether the Chinese government will suddenly become legalistic as a result of economic development and trade with foreign countries. The state can produce any number of laws (it has already produced many) and set up any number of institutions that reflect rational-legal notions. But the mere existence of these new institutions does not tell us anything about whether they are meaningful for the lives of individuals; they tell us nothing about how the rights of individuals are changing in a real sense. For this type of information, we need to conduct research on the ways that broad institutional changes are meaningful at local levels. We need to look at how work environments and access to the formal institutions have changed for individuals over the course of the reforms. The study I present in these pages is relevant in two ways for the Most-Favored-Nation debate. First, the analysis shows a general trend toward formalization and the emergence of a formal rational system of authority at the organizational level. That individuals can now take grievances against organizational leaders to an arbitration institution external to the organization is a significant and tangible change with regard to individual rights—and as individuals become increasingly familiar with these rights, they are exercising them more and more. Second, the study shows a clear association between formal relationships with foreign companies and the emergence of these formal rational bureaucracies, as well as the use of other institutions such as the Chinese International Arbitration Commission. The perspective I present in the concluding chapter thus supports a position of engagement: Institutional change is not going to come from political pressure alone. Rather, it will come from negotiations over, and the actual use of, these new institutional practices in markets and in the workplace.

Concluding Remarks: Toward an Economic Sociology of Market Transitions

Economic sociology begins with the premise that there is nothing magical or transcendental about markets or economic principles. Markets do not exist in the abstract. They are social constructions that are shaped by the institutional, political, and cultural environments in which they are embedded. Economic actors enter these arenas as individuals (or organizations) who, themselves, are embedded in social relations and political and cultural contexts. One criticism of economic sociology has been that although its critique of neoclassical economic theory has merit—especially on empirical grounds—it must do more than simply critique the neoclassical economic model.[37] We must offer a positive theory of how markets are shaped and what economic actors actually do.

There are three elements of such a theory that must be applied in the study of economic transitions. First, institutions and history matter. The preexisting structures on which new market institutions are built have profound effects on how economic actors experience the construction of new markets. To a large extent, a society's history and institutional structure define the path it will take through periods of economic transition, regardless of what the architects of that transition have in mind. Arguments about the transcendental nature of markets or the adoption of existing (i.e., Western) models of market institutions make sense only in the abstract. Ignoring the importance of preexisting institutional structures and cultural contexts in the creation of markets is an invitation for chaos (see, e.g., Russia). Second, whether economic actors are rational profit maximizers is an empirical question of markets, not an issue to be explained away through assumptions. Neil Fligstein has argued that economic actors are just as likely to seek stability in emerging markets as they are to seek profits, and my research, especially the findings presented in chapter 6, offers compelling support for this position.[38] The point here is that economic actors make decisions for a variety of reasons, and we only weaken our analyses by making assumptions about rational action and some magical push toward efficiency. Third, the state is ever present in the construction and maintenance of markets. Nowhere in the world do markets operate independent of state action. In other words, the idea of a laissez-faire market economy is a myth or, at best, an imagined ideal. As Peter Evans so aptly puts it: "State involvement is a given. The appropriate question is not 'how much' but 'what kind.'"[39]

The case of economic transition in China shows the importance of each of these elements. The institutional and state elements of this theory actually blend together in the Chinese case, as I show that the institutional structure of state administration and, specifically, a firm's position in the administrative hierarchy of the former command economy have powerful implications for how that firm will experience the reforms. I also show that organizations and the managers that run them do not always behave in ways that can easily be explained by a rational profit maximization framework. I do not reject the notion that economic constraints matter for economic actors in the emerging markets of China's transition economy. Rather, I show specifically where, how, and why economic constraints matter; where, how, and why institutional history and state structure matter; and how and why economic actors make decisions in reform-era China.

Empirically, in the study of economic transitions, we need to shift our focus from standard economic indicators to the strategies, structures, and practices adopted by economic actors in transforming economies. In other words, we need to get down to specific cases of economic reform. The rapid economic transformation in China offers us a unique opportunity to explore the causal relationships among economic, institutional, political, and social forces in an important transforming economy. In what follows I cover a broad range of economic decisions and practices emerging over the course of China's economic transition. None of these individual changes can be taken alone as conclusive evidence about China's reforms. Taken together, however, the recurrent themes and patterns that stretch across the various decisions studied here offer compelling evidence of the institutional, political, and social factors that define China's reforms.

Two

Path Dependence in China's Economic Transition

> My concern here is not with some lingering traces of
> socialist ideology or with the reconstructive surgery that
> gives new anatomies to the old nomenklatura but with
> institutional legacies of the transitions themselves. . . .
> It is in the ruins that these societies will find the materials
> with which to build a new order; therefore, differences in
> how the pieces fell apart will have consequences for how
> the political and economic institutions can be reconstructed
> in the current period. In short, it is the differing paths of
> extraction from state socialism that shape the possibilities
> of transformation in the subsequent stage.
> *(David Stark 1992)*

> China's reforms are highly path dependent, in that before
> the reforms began its industrial hierarchies were already
> much more decentralized than those of the Soviet Union
> and vastly larger than those of the smaller communist
> countries. . . . Where previous work has tended to frame the
> analytic problem of transition economies either as the
> creation of well-functioning markets or as the rebuilding of
> economic institutions (and the establishment of property
> rights), the Chinese case suggests . . . that the same
> problems may be fruitfully recast in organizational terms,
> as ones of government administrative capacities and
> incentives for officials.
> *(Andrew Walder 1995a)*

IN THE STUDY of economic transitions, focus on the effect that preexisting structures and systems have on the course and trajectory of economic transitions has given rise to a perspective some scholars have referred to as "path dependence."[1] The central message of this view is that preexisting structures and conditions give rise to different paths through reforms. It makes little sense to think about universal blueprints for economic reforms or transcendental economic principles that exist independent of the culture and history of a given society. New institutions are built on the legacies—"the ruins," as David Stark puts it—of systems past, and these preexisting structures and systems necessarily influence the shape of the new systems that emerge in their stead.[2]

Preexisting institutional structures are central to the path of economic transitions in two ways. First, on a societal level, in order to understand the market organization of a given society, the analysis must be put in the context of these preexisting institutional structures. Countries as culturally similar as Taiwan and mainland China are bound to travel along different paths toward market economies, if only because their institutional histories are so very different. Second, at the firm and individual levels, preexisting structures also have an impact on the ways that different actors within a given society will experience economic reforms. Throughout this study I focus on a crucial institutional structure that gives rise to variation in firms' experiences in China's transition: the administrative hierarchy of China's former command economy. In China's transforming economy, this institutional structure determines a firm's proximity to the central government. As such, it shapes the opportunities and experiences of organizations in China's emerging marketplaces. The positions of organizations in this state administrative hierarchy are crucial for the resources they control, the connections they can rely on, and the political power they wield.[3]

In this chapter I present a view of China's economic transition that places this government structure at the center of the reforms. Essentially I argue that upper-level government offices are divesting themselves of administrative and economic responsibilities in the reform era, and they are pushing these responsibilities down the hierarchy of the former command economy. Firms directly under the jurisdiction of high-level government offices experience an extreme sense of being set adrift in the reform era, as they are forced to handle these administrative and economic details themselves. While some scholars have argued (based on slower rates of growth in productivity) that reforms are not being implemented in this sector of the economy, these upper-level firms *are* experiencing a great deal of market autonomy and uncertainty in the economic transition. Firms at lower levels of the former command economy are protected by lower-level government offices and thus experience more of a mixed economy, as the government offices above them help them navigate their ways through the economic reforms. These reform processes and, specifically, the institutional structure of state administration that preceded the reform era frame the research in the empirical chapters that follow. In my discussion in this chapter, rather than recounting all the major reform policies, I discuss the reforms in broad brush strokes, focusing primarily on those reforms the Chinese managers I interviewed emphasized as most important in the reform era.[4] The discussion in this chapter should thus be viewed as a loose framework for the empirical analyses that follow.

Administrative Rank in China

Several scholars of China's transition have attempted to incorporate institutional analyses into their studies of economic transitions, but few have successfully operationalized variables and studied the ways that institutional structures actually matter in the reform era.[5] Andrew Walder's work is an exception here, as his focus is primarily on the specific ways that state institutional structures shape organizational outcomes in the Chinese economy. As a result, Walder's work is much better equipped to deal with the larger questions of the economic transition—the emergence of market constraints (whether or not firms continue to receive money from the state)—than are individual-level studies that focus on the emerging private economy. Walder's (1992a) early work in this area focuses on the institutional and organizational structure of the command economy and the ways that this structure influenced organizational decisions and practices.[6] More recently Walder's (1995a) work on the economic transition also focuses on how variation across the state industrial hierarchy leads to different rates of growth, diverse models of enterprise management, and various fiscal and property rights arrangements in the transition economy. This industrial hierarchy, a vestige of the planned economy, is one of the most important factors shaping firms' experiences in the economic transition.

After 1949 in China, a complex administrative system of government organizations was set in place to mobilize firms and the individuals within them around directives issued from the central government. This system was an administratively decentralized governance structure that allowed the central government to promulgate policies down the hierarchy of government jurisdictions, relying on the local government offices to mobilize organizations (work units and neighborhood associations) and thereby people. Thus a decentralized institutional structure emerged from the ideological and production-oriented policies that the central government saw as most efficient for the management—and control—of the nation. The result of these policies was a "nested hierarchy" of government organizations spread throughout the country, each with jurisdiction over a smaller sector of the population. In industrial China, all organizations are directly under the jurisdiction of a specific governing organization at a specific level of this administrative hierarchy [*zhuguan bumen*]. An ideal typical view of the administrative structure of the government administrative hierarchy in urban industrial areas is presented in Figure 2.1. Yanjie Bian (1994a, 9) explains that "this administrative structure forms the hierarchy in which national resources and incentives are allocated from the central command to the various levels of local governments." He further points out that firms at different levels of this hierarchy had variable access to resources under the command economy: "Favors accrue to the higher levels of government jurisdictions and their subordinate work organizations."[7]

Studies of industrial China have been content to distinguish between types of ownership—state, collective, private—among industrial organizations,[8] but these distinctions are less revealing than the positions the organizations occupy in the administrative hierarchy. As Walder (1995a, 271–73) puts it:

> In terms of the definition of property rights . . . there is no fundamental distinction between state and collective enterprises. . . . Field studies have shown repeatedly throughout the 1980s that township and village industrial enterprises are owned and operated by local governments whose officials are deeply involved in virtually all major decisions regarding the hiring and compensation of managers, the establishment or closing of firms, the mobilization of investment capital, changes in production line, and marketing strategies. . . . *The most important way in which government ownership rights in state and collective sectors do differ is in the extent to which they are regulated by higher levels of government.* . . . What varies in this hierarchy is not the nature of government property rights but the composition and scale of industry and the degree to which government rights are attenuated by central regulations. (Emphasis added)

The important point here is that we need to look beyond distinctions of ownership type to the institutional structure of state administration and the ways that varying positions within this hierarchy influence organizational action. Resources, monitoring capacities, government connections, and other government responsibilities all vary with the levels of this administrative hierarchy, and these factors have a direct impact on organizational action in both the planned economy and the economic transition.

Government Administrative Offices That Oversee Chinese Firms

While the overall rank of a governing organization is important, there is another distinction that is critical with respect to governing organizations. Within the Chinese urban industry there are two types of administrative offices presiding over organizations: bureaus [*ju*] and administrative companies [*xingzheng gongsi*]. Municipal bureaus (along with ministries under the central government) tend to preside directly over large, asset-intensive organizations, whereas smaller industrial organizations tend to be under the control of administrative companies (municipal companies and district companies), the government offices at lower levels of the administrative ladder in urban areas.[9] There has been much discussion of the monitoring problems associated with larger fields of governance and the way such problems give rise to soft budget constraints and on the attenuation of property rights at the lower levels of

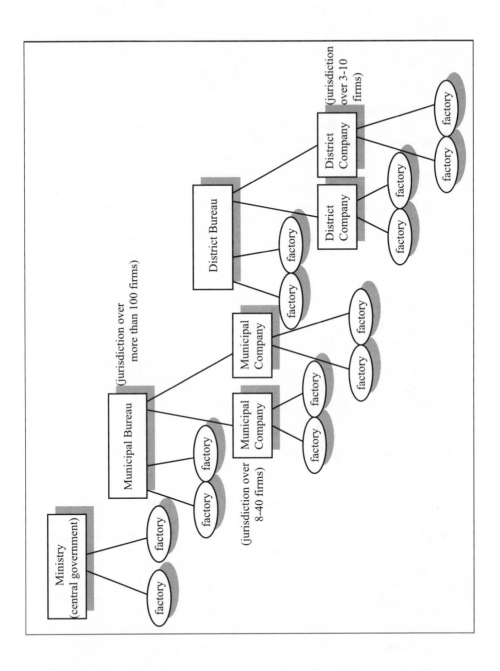

Ministry (central government)
— factory
— factory

Municipal Bureau (jurisdiction over more than 100 firms)
— factory
— factory

Municipal Company (jurisdiction over 8-40 firms)
— factory
— factory

Municipal Company
— factory
— factory

District Bureau
— factory
— factory

District Company
— factory
— factory

District Company (jurisdiction over 3-10 firms)
— factory
— factory

China's industrial hierarchy.[10] In my interviews with Chinese managers and officials, a different, albeit related, theme emerged that is directly related to state-firm relations in the economic transition: the administrative and economic responsibilities of governing organizations.

The administrative scope of a municipal bureau is quite large, as it must administer all factories directly beneath it (more than one hundred in the case of the electronics and chemicals sectors and more than four hundred in the case of the light-industry sector). A bureau is also responsible for representing its municipal sector in the negotiations that go on with the central government over resource allocations, and the like. Administrative companies are significantly different from bureaus in that their sole administrative function is to monitor the factories and organizations they control (usually somewhere between ten and twenty factories but sometimes as few as two factories for district companies). Before the economic reform, these differences in responsibility worked favorably for both government and factory at upper levels of the administrative hierarchy: Controlling many organizations brought in hefty revenues for the upper-level administrative offices, and favoritism (as well as high monitoring costs) increased access to resources for organizations directly under the upper-level offices.[11] The differences in responsibility are also reflected in the extent to which an administrative office had an active hand in controlling investment and development decisions. Under the command economy, bureaus played an active role in the planning and development of a given sector; directives came down from the central ministry [bu], but bureaus had a significant amount of influence over how they were implemented and carried out. The same was true for revenue flow in the opposite direction: Some share of revenues was always passed on to the central government, but municipal governments (of which municipal bureaus are a part) also had significant control over revenues and the redistribution of resources at the municipal level.

The situation for administrative companies was much different. In pre-reform times, these administrative offices were often referred to as "govern-

---

On opposite page:

Figure 2.1: Institutional Structure of State Administration in Urban Industrial China

Note: The hierarchy in municipal areas has two additional levels of control over factories: the Street Association, which is a subdivision of the district government, and some larger factories (usually textile factories) have control over smaller factories. Most economic organizations under Street Associations are in the service sector, so they were not relevant for the sampling conducted in this study. Note that this figure is an ideal typical representation of the organizational structure of industry in China and that there is considerable variation from bureau to bureau and company to company. For example, 110 factories are directly under the jurisdiction of the Electronics Bureau, whereas more than 400 factories are under the jurisdiction of the Light Industry Bureau. The numbers presented here are ranges derived from the firms included in my sample.

Source: Based on interviews with industrial managers and directors and government officials (see Appendix 2). See Walder (1992a) and Guthrie (1996, 1997) for a basic discussion of the "nested hierarchy" of the industrial structure.

ment funnels" [*zhengfu loudou*], as they did little more than siphon directives down to the firms under their jurisdictions and siphon revenues up to the municipal bureaus above them. A manager in the foods sector explained this administrative structure in the following way:

> Before, the company was just an administrative arm of the government. We called the company a "government funnel": What orders came down from the government were just funneled down to the factories underneath the company. (Interview 85*, 1995)

As "government funnels," the administrative companies were responsible for little more than carrying out the bureaus' directives of the planned economy and ensuring that the communist social order remained intact.

Changing State-Firm Relationships in the Economic Transition

Over the course of China's transition from a planned economy to a market system, the relationships between administrative offices (both bureaus and companies) and the factories they oversee have changed significantly, and these changes have varied by the level of a firm's government administrative office. My focus here is on the rearrangement of administrative and economic responsibilities across the hierarchy of the former command economy in the economic transition.[12] Within this general rearrangement, important changes in the state-firm relationship have occurred at three levels in the urban industrial economy: (1) on a macrolevel, economic responsibilities have been pushed down the hierarchy of the former command economy; (2) at the lower-level government offices, these administrative offices have themselves become much more economically oriented; and (3) at the firm level, as independent budgets and self-responsibility policies now define firm practices, economic constraints are beginning to matter in significant ways for Chinese firms.

Pushing Responsibilities Down the Hierarchy

The first change has occurred on a macrolevel, as administrative and economic responsibilities have been redistributed across the government industrial hierarchy. In essence, the economic and administrative responsibilities that used to lie in the hands of bureaus have been pushed *down* the hierarchy of the former command economy. Under the command economy, bureaus controlled production decisions, development plans, investment strategies, and so on, but in the economic transition, these responsibilities are being turned over to the organizations beneath them. This rearrangement of responsibilities has different consequences for factories directly under the jurisdiction of bureaus than it does for those under administrative companies. As Figure 2.1 represents, there is nothing between the bureaus and the factories directly under their jurisdictions, and as administrative and economic responsibilities are shifted down the hierarchy, the factories directly under the bureaus have been forced to handle these responsibilities on their own. As the bureaus divest themselves of administrative and economic responsibilities, these factories have been the most directly exposed to the market reforms, and among these firms there is an extreme sense of being set adrift by the state in the period of economic reform. The organizations under administrative companies, on the other hand, do not experience the same sense of abandonment. For these firms, there is a government office that lies between the bureaus and the firms, and as economic responsibilities are pushed down the hierarchy, the onus of these responsibilities falls primarily on lower-level government offices (municipal and district companies). These lower-level firms are being guided through the economic transition by the same government organizations that were nothing more than "funnels" under the planned system. Administrative companies help the firms under their jurisdictions develop long-term transitional plans, development plans, and strategies for survival in the emerging market economic system. Thus there is an important difference, in terms of how firms experience the economic transition, for firms located directly under the jurisdiction of bureaus and those located under the jurisdiction of administrative companies. And this difference has implications for the decisions and practices firms adopt over the course of the economic transition.

From Administration to Economics

A second major change in the industrial economy has to do with the nature of the administrative companies themselves: Over the course of the economic transition, government administrative companies—and recently bureaus— have slowly made the transition from administration economics [*xingzheng gongsi biencheng jingji danwei*]. These government organizations are still called administrative companies, but now the officials see themselves as being responsible for much more than passing down central government directives or doling out resources. Now the companies are responsible for the economic health of the organizations over which they preside.[13] One official in an administrative company explained this change in the following way:

> Before, we were just a government administrative institution [*zhengfu xingzheng jigou*]. But now, since about 1987 really, our company is an economic institution. Our job is to help the development of this sector through overseeing the development of the factories underneath our administrative company. All the factories underneath us are on independent budgets, but we decide the major economic things that are

going to go on with the factories underneath us. We decide the major development projects, how money will be allocated to help development, this kind of thing. We didn't have this kind of responsibility before. (Interview 80, 1995)

Even though these administrative companies are responsible for the survival and development of the factories underneath them, this does not mean that they hold property rights over the factories in terms of the rights of revenue extraction. The profits of the organizations below them are still ultimately left to the factory, and, for many of the cases, the only money sent to the center is in the form of value-added and income taxes [cengzhi, suode shui]. However, the companies do get a management fee [guanli fei], which is often based on factory profits.

Administrative companies are not only responsible for development, but, in some cases, they are also responsible for bailouts. As the primary social security system of Chinese society, it is often problematic to simply shut down losing firms (though this situation is changing, as I discuss below).[14] Most factory managers and directors maintain that they themselves are responsible for handling losses, but some will admit that bailouts still come from above:

We need to have our own money these days to invest and to cover any losses we have. In principle, we are supposed to cover these losses on our own. But, of course, if we can't cover the losses, we can sometimes get help from above. (Interview 90*, 1995)

However, not all government organizations can handle bailouts in the same way. The weight of the responsibility of covering losses increases with administrative rank. Although overall budgets increase with administrative rank, the number of organizations under a given administrative office's jurisdiction also increases with administrative rank. As a small subdivision of municipalities, district companies have a much smaller scope than municipal companies, which, in turn, have a much smaller scope than municipal bureaus. The more organizations for which a government administrative office has responsibility, the less likely the administrative office will be able to guarantee that losses will be covered; they are, in essence, dividing up a finite pie among larger groups of organizations. As we move up the ladder of administrative rank (see Figure 2.1), government administrative organizations are less likely to be able to guarantee that losses will be covered.

Bureaus are also making a transition from an administrative function to a focus on economics. Bureaus still preside over sectors of the industrial economy, but they do little in the way of administration at the firm level today. Some bureaus have even gone so far as to change their names to State-Owned Assets Management Companies [guoyou zichan jingying gongsi] and trim their administrative staff significantly. As one official explained:

The goal of this change is to transform the state, especially the bureaus, from an administrator to an investor. (Interview 101, 1995)

The nominal transformation of the bureaus, which was first experimented with in 1995 in Shanghai, emphasizes the extent to which administrative organizations—especially those close to the central government—are removing themselves from administrative and economic decisions. As the asset managers of the large-scale organizations in a given sector, bureaus still have some responsibility for bailing out faltering organizations. If their factories all shut down, the municipality will have a huge influx of unemployed workers, which will strain the urban economy. But in urban industrial sectors today, bureaus are increasingly selective about the factories into which they will sink resources. For the most part, as administrative—and, increasingly, economic—decisions are pushed down the hierarchy of the former command economy, firms are often left to fend for themselves in the open market.

Independent Budgets and Self-Responsibility

The third major change in the urban industrial economy is occurring at the factory level. Factories are now increasingly operating under the system of independent budgets or independent accounting systems [*duli hesuan*], and the meaning of this system has changed significantly since the reform.[15] Independent budgets did officially exist under the old system, but they had little more than nominal meaning in the command economy. This system has taken on a new meaning in the economic transition to allow organizations some degree of economic freedom in the developing markets and to allow the state to distance itself from the economic plans and practices of firms. If organizations were to seize opportunities to invest outside their production scope or to attract foreign investors from the outside, some degree of freedom was needed. The strategy was to pass the budgetary responsibilities down to the organization and, at the same time, allow firms to keep some of their profits (the amount often negotiable) for organizational development. Such projects range from internal factory developments, such as the upgrading of machinery, to outside investments. An organization's government office still holds the appropriate administrative fiat for large-scale investments (especially those involving foreign investors).[16] But the general result of independent budgets has been an increase in the economic freedom of firms in the marketplace.

Going hand in hand with the renewed emphasis on independent accounting policies is the system of "self-responsibility for gains and losses" [*zifu yingkui*].[17] Under this system, firms not only are allowed to keep extra earnings but are supposed to cover their own losses. If an organization is losing money and is getting no help from the government, the management must either borrow money from the bank—for which they often have to find another firm to underwrite—or borrow directly from another firm. Conversely, if an organization is making a significant amount of money, the majority of the earnings can be kept for future development and restructuring projects.[18] Organizations are allowed to keep a percentage of their profits every year as residual savings [*ziji jilei qian*] (literally, "own accumulation fund"), and they are allowed to use this money to search for additional development paths.[19] One Shanghai official explained the self-responsibility system in the following way:

> Organizations can't rely on the government to take out a loan or to bail out losses anymore. Previously the situation had many negative side effects. Even after the beginning of the economic reform, enterprises were often bailed out by the state, and this made for unequal market competition in many ways. First, these enterprises didn't have to worry about losses, so, in a way, this was unfair for other competitors. But being disconnected from losses has a downside, too. When you don't have to worry about losses, efficiency goes down. It's not really a good situation for anyone. . . . The situation we're trying to create now is like the family situation when the father pushes the son out on his own. In many ways, the government still helps in the management of affairs: It sends the director or the CEO to manage the company. But, in the end, the company is responsible for making a living. If it loses money, it is responsible for taking care of itself and surviving. (Interview 106, 1995)

It is interesting to note the extent to which this official's comments are imbued with both the logic of economics and that of gradualism in the institutionalization of the self-responsibility policy. On the one hand, the official recognizes the efficiency problems that arise from a system of soft budgets. On the other hand, the tentative language in his words "trying to create" and the family metaphor speak more to the gradualism and experimentation that has distinguished China's transition to a market economy.[20]

The independent budget and self-responsibility policies have fundamental implications for the transformation of the system in which "enterprises [had] no rights to profits deemed 'excess' by planning authorities, and they expect such profits to be expropriated."[21] In China today, nearly all individual factories keep some profits (unless they are part of a multidivisional firm[22]), and they are expected to plan their development (and survival) accordingly. Aggressive factory directors are rewarded through the successful development of their organization. Factory directors who are less aggressive or those who are overseeing losing organizations, though rarely under imminent danger of losing their jobs, are nevertheless threatened by the prospect of their organizations being cut off from funding and shut down, a situation that has been relatively widespread in some sectors (e.g., textiles in Shanghai). Factory directors are thus encouraged to pursue development opportunities that will allow them to optimize their factory production and to increase overall turnover and profit margins either through internal reorganization programs (e.g., management restructuring or machine upgrading) or through outside investments.

Still, independent budget and self-responsibility policies are, to some extent, flexible practices, and the discretion of bailouts and investment decisions are left up to the administrative office that governs a given organization. One manager in the foods sector explained the flexibility of the policies in this way:

> Of course, now everyone always says that organizations are responsible for their own losses [zifu yingkui]; this is the major change that came with independent budgets [duli hesuan] after the economic development. But of course in reality, if a factory is losing money, what the government does about it varies from case to case. It's really very complicated because we can't just close down factories and send the entire workforce home. There are definitely cases where the government is giving money to the factories to cover their losses. But now we are really beginning to understand that we have to let the successful factories develop and start shutting down the losing factories. For every factory that is losing money, the government is thinking: Is it worth it to keep this factory running? If they decide that it's not, then it's up to the factory to do it alone. (Interview 85*, 1995)

Some losing factories, however, are no longer receiving bailouts from the government but instead have to take out bank loans to cover losses. One factory manager in the chemicals sector was part of this latter group; he explained the situation in a way that reflects the hardening of budget constraints for some factories:

> We get nothing from the government anymore. If we lose money and our savings can't cover the losses, we have to take out a bank loan to cover the losses. It's either that or shut down. The government takes no responsibility for it anymore. We are completely responsible for losses. (Interview 95*, 1995)

Of the losing firms in my sample [N = 21], most were reluctant to disclose information on how shortfalls were being met. However, a few firms were forthcoming with this information: Overall, in my sample, two of the losing firms were borrowing money from the banks, two others were receiving money from the government, and one was getting funds from another firm. One of the sample firms from the chemicals sector was underwriting the bank loans for a chronic loser in the same sector. As the vice general manager of that organization explained it:

> Our profits are very good. But the No. 5 Factory loses money every year—a lot of money. And every year we have to borrow money from the bank for them; they can't borrow money themselves because they don't have a good financial standing with the bank, and the government isn't helping them anymore. But we can borrow money, so every year we borrow money and help them repay the amount they borrowed the year before. It's really not a good situation. . . . [But] we are a socialist

country and this is the way we do things. Otherwise . . . they will have to close down, and many people will be laid off and sent home. We can't have so many people losing their jobs. (Interview 98*, 1995)

This case reflects an interesting situation of a semi-marketized world where some firms have been set adrift by the state, while others are willing to help out losing firms as part of a larger socialist ideal. While markets may be emerging on some levels, certain attributes of the system still make it quite different from Western market systems.[23] This manager's commitment to a socialist ideology is also noteworthy. Such ideological commitments cut against the view that individuals will strive to maximize profits as soon as structural circumstances allow them to do so.

Thus while cutting off factories and allowing them to shut down was not a possibility in the past, today it occurs with increasing frequency. The theory of soft-budget constraints argues that too many social factors are involved in the organizational structure of upper-level industrial sectors and firms for them to be shut down, viewing the system as entrenched to the extent that there is "no plausible threat to 'close' a government jurisdiction that loses money."[24] The empirical realities of recent trends in China's economic transition question this idea. In late 1994 and early 1995 the Shanghai municipal government shut down the majority of the textiles sector (including the bureau) in Shanghai as a result of the sector's chronic losses. In my research on large industrial organizations in Shanghai, I encountered thirty-eight that had closed down [quxiao].[25] That the government is now willing to let firms shut down rather than continue to bail them out is compelling evidence that budget constraints are being hardened in the urban industrial economy. Some scholars have argued that the Enterprise Bankruptcy Law (PRC 1986d) has fallen short of its institutional goal of accountability and shutting losing firms down. For example, Wang (1992, 118) recently noted that, at least as of August 1991, "not one of China's state firms" had ever been declared "officially bankrupt." As I was not able to interview managers of the firms that had been shut down, it is impossible to say whether any of them were declared "officially bankrupt" according to the Enterprise Bankruptcy Law. For many of them, however, I was informed that they had been shut down [quxiao] because of losses [kuisile] (literally, "died of losses").

Other Critical Institutional Reforms

Taxation

Another significant institutional change that relates directly to resource availability for both firms and governing offices is in the area of taxation. Resource availability under the command economy hinged on the fact that administrative offices collected the revenues and were therefore in a position to extract excess revenues from large jurisdictions. In China today, however, this system of revenue extraction by the governing organization is increasingly a thing of the past. Three primary changes have begun to reform this earlier system. First, the extraction of revenues has been standardized in the taxation system [*li gai shui*] (i.e., governing organizations are no longer permitted to simply extract all "excess" revenues), a change that was first experimented with in 1980 and then implemented more widely with the Second Phase Profits Changed to Taxes Reform [*Dier Bu Li Gai Shui Banfa*] of 1985.[26] Second, now taxation is basically standardized—value-added tax, 17 percent of turnover; and income tax, 33 percent of net income, though a significant amount of negotiation over tax rates for individual firms does occur. Third, firms pay their taxes directly to the State Tax Administration office at the central level and finance offices in municipalities, instead of to their governing organization.[27] Tax breaks and subsidized loan repayment make the concept of standardized taxation less meaningful, and implementing these internal policies is often a problem (i.e., they exist on paper but vary in practice).[28] In my sample, seventeen out of eighty-one firms (21 percent) reported tax rates for 1994 that differed from the standard value-added and income tax rates, indicating that bargaining over taxation is occurring with some frequency. However, all these firms also reported that their taxes go directly to the Government Tax Bureau of the relevant district or municipality (not to their governing organization). Although governing organizations still have ways to extract revenues from firms, such as negotiations over profits and management fees [*guanli fei*], the key point here is that taxes are now being paid to a central office. Without the convenience of revenue extraction across a wide base of firms, the ability of governing organizations to skim or extract excess amounts of revenue is significantly reduced.

Declining Power of the Party as an Organization

A number of scholars have argued that the Communist Party organization (hereafter, the Party) is one of the "distinctive institutional pillars" of economic, political, and social life in communist societies.[29]

> Communist power has been founded upon a distinctive (Leninist) form of political organization, and a distinctive form of economic organization (the command economy, or Soviet-style central planning). This power has been distinguished by a comparatively high degree of political discipline and conformity within the Party-State apparatus, and in the apparatus' relationships with ordinary citizens.[30]

In the sections above I have described some of the ways the Chinese industrial economy is transforming, as economic and administrative responsibilities are redistributed throughout the hierarchy. However, fundamental changes in Party power also play an important role in the economic transition.[31] Although the Party still wields significant power, the Party as an organization in today's China plays significantly less of a direct role in the actual monitoring of social and political activity in Chinese firms than it did in the prereform era. Municipal bureaus are still filled with Party members, and these individuals continue to have general control over the major decisions and practices of organizations (i.e., factories) in urban China. But as administrative and economic responsibilities are pushed down the ladder of the former command economy, the direct role of the Party organization (and that of Party cadres within bureaus) in the structure of work-unit life has diminished.[32] Similarly, at the firm level, although many upper-level managers in factories are Party members, the Party as an organization has no direct role in the decisions and practices the firm adopts. In other words, while the Party may still have influence over the general policies that define the reforms, as an organization it has little direct influence over whether these reforms are implemented at the firm level.

Interestingly, in my interviews, individuals most often spoke of the Party not in terms of the Party organization's monitoring capacity or structuring of political and social life in the factory but rather in terms of Party membership as a path to individual political or administrative power. Some managers simply dismissed the importance of the Party:

> The Party mattered a great deal in China in the 1960s. But this is the 1990s. It really has little meaning today. (Interview 38*, 1995)

Others pointed directly to the relationship between Party membership and political and administrative power:

> The only meaning Party membership has today is that you want a high position or you want power. Most people who are in high positions in state-owned companies are Party members. But it really has no other meaning than this in China today. (Interview 14, 1994)

> Our factory director is a Party member. His position helps us get administrative things done more quickly. Actually most factory directors are Party members, I think. I'm not a Party member, and I think, because of that, I could never become a factory director. (Interview 34, 1995)

The critical point here is that although Party membership may still play a significant role in the rise of individuals to positions of power in government and factory administration, as an organization the Party does not significantly influence the structuring (or monitoring) of political and social life within the organizations.[33] Naturally, this is a complicated transformation, because, as the respondents pointed out, the directors of many large-scale organizations are themselves Party members, so there is still some connection between the Party and the structure of factory life. However, as general managers and factory directors are increasingly concerned with the firm's economic issues, there is little time or interest in spreading Party ideology within the firm. For example, where factories routinely used to have weekly Party "educational" meetings, none of the firms in my sample had these kinds of meetings anymore.

The Impact of Foreign Investment

The presence of foreign companies and foreign investment is another significant change in China's industrial economy. When foreign companies invest in a developing economy, particularly when their goal is long-term investment eventually to capture a share of the local market, they bring with them their own organizational models and ways of participating in markets. The presence of these foreign investors has an impact on the organizational forms and practices in the Chinese economy in two ways. First, as I argue in chapter 3, foreign organizational models are held up as exemplary in the Chinese economy, and Chinese organizations mimic the practices of these foreign investors. Second, as I show in chapter 7, foreign investors negotiate with their Chinese partners, pushing them to take seriously rational-legal institutions that are present in the institutional environments from which the foreign investors come. In both these cases, relationships with foreign investors specifically, and the presence of foreign investors in the Chinese economy more generally, have an impact on the structure of economic action in Chinese firms.

Concluding Remarks

Focus on the institutional structure of state administration will be a crucial part of the analysis that follows. The position of a firm's governing organization within the administrative hierarchy of the former command economy is a crucial variable for a wide spectrum of practices that firms are adopting over the course of the economic transition. Past research has shown the importance of this variable for firm practices in the command economy, and researchers have pointed to its salience in the economic transition. Yet, much more attention needs to be focused on the remnants of the command economy if we are to understand the path-dependent aspects of China's transition to a market economy. My central claim with respect to the structure of this administrative system is that administrative and economic responsibilities are being pushed down the hierarchy of the former command economy. In the planned economy, economic and administrative power resided only in the hands of the bureaus (at the municipal level) and ministries (at the central level). For firms directly under the jurisdiction of bureaus, directives were passed down in a direct line from bureau to firm; for firms under the jurisdiction of administrative companies, directives were passed down from bureau to firm through the administrative companies ("government funnels"). In the economic transition, as economic and administrative responsibilities are pushed down this hierarchy, the firms under the direct jurisdiction of bureaus experience the greatest sense of being set adrift. These firms are being forced to assume nearly all the administrative and economic responsibilities previously handled by bureaus. They were protected by the most powerful municipal governing offices in the command economy, and now they are being forced to take on all the responsibilities that the bureaus handled for them under the command economy.

Firms under the jurisdiction of administrative companies, on the other hand, have benefited from a "layer" of government bureaucracy: As administrative and economic responsibilities have been pushed down the hierarchy, the administrative companies have assumed a proactive role in guiding the firms under their jurisdictions through the economic transition. Administrative companies have helped firms adopt long-term development plans, such as organizational restructuring and investing in fixed assets, and, in some cases, administrative companies have begun offering bailouts to troubled firms under their jurisdictions. Ironically, it is the firms that were the most protected in the planned economy—those at the upper levels of the administrative hierarchy (e.g., firms directly under the jurisdiction of bureaus)—that are experiencing the greatest sense of uncertainty and abandonment in the most recent phases of the economic reform, while those furthest from the central government are experiencing a more partial or gradual reform. This not only affects the decisions and practices that firms at different levels of the hierarchy adopt, but it also has implications for theories which have predicted that budget constraints are remaining soft for firms at the highest levels of China's administrative hierarchy. The decisions and practices of firms at the upper levels of this hierarchy indicate that these firms' worlds have become inherently unstable, and they organize their actions accordingly. As the analyses in the following chapters show, these firms' decision patterns indicate that they are operating more like autonomous market actors than industrial firms at lower levels of the administrative hierarchy.

This set of transformations should not be mistaken for the disappearance of China's administrative hierarchy, however. Although some scholars have argued that the hierarchy of the command economy will be dismantled as market mechanisms are strengthened, I think it is a misreading of the economic reform to assume that such a paradigmatic shift lies in the near future.[34] Even though economic and administrative responsibilities are being pushed down the hierarchy, the hierarchy itself is far from disappearing. The state maintains a majority stake in most of the organizations across all sectors and still holds the power of administrative fiat at the level of bureau and ministerial offices.

These particular state functions are even in place in sectors where the bureaus have been replaced by State-Owned Asset Management Companies [*guoyou zichan jingying gongsi*]. Thus even in those sectors where we would expect the greatest withering of the hierarchy, we still see a state that controls the vast majority of industrial assets (managed by the new asset management companies—the former bureaus), that still has the power to hire and fire general managers of large factories, and that still holds administrative fiat to control large investment development projects.

The question before us now is this: *What differences do these institutional changes actually make for economic decisions at the firm level?* Ultimately we must direct the analysis of institutional change in China toward the empirical reality of what is actually going on in Chinese firms. The changing systems described above are significantly different from those of the command economy, and if the differences are significant and real, we should be able to observe manifestations of the new market structure in organizations' economic practices. A systematic look at some of the firms' responses in the economic transition is necessary to understand the meaning of the reforms for economic actors in China's emerging marketplaces.

Three _____

Formal Rational Bureaucracies in Chinese Firms: Causes and Implications

> One of the central problems in organization theory
> is to describe the conditions that give rise to
> rationalized formal structure.
> *(John Meyer and Brian Rowan 1977)*

SINCE THE LATE 1980s, firms in China's industrial economy have been rushing to establish formal rational bureaucracies. In this chapter I explore the economic, political, and institutional factors that influence firms' decisions to adopt several different practices that can be defined as formalized organizational structures.[1] My central concern is the rationalization of Chinese firms and the movement away from a top-down, particularistic model of authority relations in the workplace.[2] I argue that Chinese firms are adopting rational structures not for reasons of efficiency but because they perceive these systems as the types of structures that market-savvy organizations adopt.

Specifically, in this chapter I explore the institutionalization of several newly emerging formal organizational systems and procedures: *formal organizational rules, job descriptions, grievance-filing procedures, mediation committees, Workers' Representative Committee meetings, promotion tests,* and *new worker hiring procedures.* I show that the emergence of rational institutions at the firm level is dependent primarily on the educational background of the general manager, the sectoral location of the organization, and whether the firm has a joint venture with a foreign company. The significance of the general manager's educational background suggests that professionalization is a factor in the economic conception of management that is emerging in Chinese firms. The importance of sectoral location suggests that firms mimic the practices of other organizations close to them, creating a trend of isomorphism within industrial sectors. The significance of a joint-venture partnership suggests that foreign investment matters for the organizational structures emerging in China's economic transition. Chinese firms that have close working relationships with foreign partners mimic and adopt Western-style structures to give the appearance of a "modern," market-savvy organization.[3]

Formalizing Firm Structure in China's Economic Transition

While the state has constructed a number of broad, sweeping institutional changes that indicate the emergence of a rational-legal framework on a macro level, it is important to explore the extent to which a formal rational system is emerging at the firm level.[4] In the literature on organizations, formalization refers to the extent to which "rules governing behavior are precisely and explicitly formulated and . . . roles and role relations are prescribed independently of the personal attributes of individuals occupying positions in the structure."[5] The formalization of an organization, in other words, refers to the systems, rules, and structures that are set in place in an organization to govern behavior in a rational way. Studies of formalization at the organizational level examine issues ranging from internal labor markets and job structure to incentive and remunerative practices to more theoretical explorations of what formal institutions represent and how they diffuse across organizational fields.[6] Research on formalization is diverse, yet a common theme throughout the literature is the study of the forces that give rise to organizational complexity and formal rational institutional structures. This line of inquiry is important for understanding China's economic transition because, during this transition, industrial organizations are undergoing extensive transformations and the nature of these changes and what they mean for individual workers need to be examined. Past research has shown that the organizational form of prereform China was based on a clientelist model where personal relationships (between managers and workers) dominated the firm structure.[7] Inasmuch as a wave of formalization is sweeping across organizations, it is important to explore the extent to which this clientelist system is giving way to a more formal rational organizational system. The analysis presented here will have implications for scholarship which suggests that China remains an informal, network-based system throughout the economic reforms.

Organizational scholars have taken a number of different approaches to the study of institutional structures and practices within organizations.[8] Researchers arguing from the rationalist perspective assume that organizations adopt formal practices and systems to enhance the firm's ability to carry out objectives and the overall efficiency of the firm. As Gouldner (1959, 100) puts it, "the rational model implies a 'mechanical' model, in that it views the organization as a structure of manipulable parts, each of which is separately modifiable with a view to enhancing the efficiency of the whole." Formalization is a rational process enacted by management or the leadership of the organization to make social relationships and social processes within the organization stable and predictable.

As I noted in chapter 1, the institutional view of organizations differs from the rationalist approach to organizations in significant ways. Where formal structures are adopted for rational and functional reasons in the rationalist conception, institutional theory posits that formal structures within organizations are adopted for reasons of legitimacy, as organizations attempt to respond to normative pressures, political mandates, or economic uncertainty. In many cases, organizations are not adopting practices for reasons of efficiency, but rather, they are simply mimicking the practices of other successful organizations they observe. Several studies have shown strong evidence that organizations respond to their institutional environments by setting up internal structures that fit with the rules and constraints of the social and political settings in which they are embedded.[9] Institutional environments may be defined by the state or any number of normative and cultural systems. Formal organizational structures are adopted by organizations not for reasons of functional efficiency or the goal of maximizing profits but as a response to the social and political pressures they face.

In the discussion that follows I argue that the formalization of organizations in China's economic transition fits more clearly with the institutional perspective on organizations than with rationalist theories. Internal structures in Chinese firms are most often adopted not because of a rational-profit maximization or for functional reasons but because they represent a type of legitimacy that is in line with the ideals and organizational models held up as exemplary in the economic transition.

Organizational Structure in Prereform China

Before we examine the processes and causes behind these organizational changes, let us briefly consider the type of organizational structure that existed in prereform China. If "modern" Western factory relations are based on "independence, contract, and universalism," factory relations in prereform China were much more "traditional" in that they were based primarily on "dependence, deference, and particularism."[10] Walder's (1986a) study on the structure of the work unit in prereform China revealed an organizational system that emphasized political and social relations in the firm, and the workers' dependence on supervisors, on management, and on the Party. Inasmuch as formalization implies the creation of a system of roles and relations that are not dependent on personal relations and personal attributes, organizations in the prereform Chinese system were decidedly not formalized. The relationships between workers and supervisors were particularistic, and supervisors had considerable discretion over processes in the workplace: "The discretion of supervisors, relatively unrestrained by enforceable regulations and contracts, [was] quite broad . . . [supervisors had] considerable ability to influence the promotions, raises, and, more importantly, the degree to which a worker and his or her family may enjoy the many nonwage benefits and advantages potentially supplied by the enterprise."[11] In other words, supervisors within organizations made decisions about worker advantages and advancement based on personal relations and personal decisions, unrestrained by formal rules or routinized decision-making systems. To what extent is the economic transition ushering in a new model of organizational structure in China? To what extent is the "institutionalized clientelism" of prereform China breaking down in the period of economic reform? And if in some cases it is breaking down, how does this transformation affect the lives of Chinese workers?

Changing Organizational Structure in the Reform Era

Organizational Rules

One practice that is changing the internal structure of organizations in the period of economic reform is the adoption of written organizational rules.[12] In the prereform period, written organizational rules were rarely a part of the work environment. Party organs and Party propaganda conveyed rules of conduct (based on Party ideology), and individuals followed the directives of work-group leaders in work units. In the economic transition, firms are, at least symbolically, becoming more formalized with respect to procedures and structures within the firm. Common themes touched on by many managers I interviewed who had implemented organizational rules centered on order in the firm and the stability that organizational rules provide for worker-manager relations. As one manager in the electronics sector explained:

> We have our own organizational rules [*zijide changgui*]. Every enterprise needs to have these. Otherwise too many problems may arise in areas where the rules are not clear. (Interview 49*, 1995)

Another manager, also in the electronics sector, discussed the issue in a similar way:

> We have our own organizational rules in addition to the official Labor Law. If you don't have your own rules, worker-management relations are confused and messy [*luan*]. After new workers come in, the first thing we do is introduce them to all the special rules of our organization. (Interview 54*, 1995)

One manager pointed directly to the growing autonomy of firms in the economic transition as the central factor underlying the emergence of written organizational rules across organizations:

> The years from 1990 to 1992 were really the important years for the internal systems and rules of our organization. These were years of significant change for the organi-

CHAPTER 3

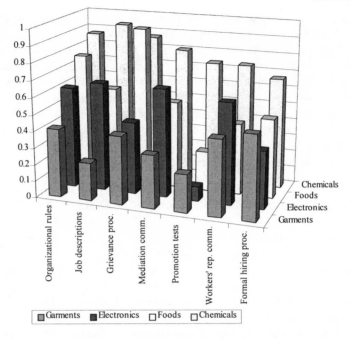

Figure 3.1: Proportion of Firms That Have Institutionalized Various Formal
Organizational Structures in Four Sectors in Industrial Shanghai, 1995

zational rules and the way we did things. Until 1990 everything was simply based on
the state allocation system [*guojia fenpei zhidu*]. But when the government stopped
operating by this system, we had to come up with our own ways of organizing
workers and making rules. Now we are very developed in this area. (Interview 53*,
1995)

Figure 3.1 shows that among the sectors represented in my study, firms in
the chemicals sector in Shanghai are the most likely (relative to the other sectors analyzed in the study) to have formal organizational rules, and firms in the
garments sector are the least likely to have them.

Job Descriptions

Job descriptions are also important for the transformation of the Chinese
workplace. Similar to organizational rules, job descriptions formalize the work
environment, clearly defining job responsibilities and thereby diminishing the
particularistic nature of labor relations as they were defined in the prereform
era. Much as Dobbin et al. (1993) studied the institutionalization of job descriptions as an indicator of formalizing and standardizing worker relations in

U.S. organizations, I view the emergence of job descriptions as part of an emerging formal rational system in Chinese firms. One manager explained the emerging system of job descriptions in his organization, saying:

> Over the last few years we have developed detailed job descriptions and job training for every job in the organization. Every time workers are transferred to a new job, we put them through training and have them study the job description. This is very important. (Interview 63*, 1995)

Another manager stated that the main factors driving the emergence of job descriptions were worker safety and general order in the firm:

> We have many areas that are very developed in terms of job descriptions and job training. We have extensive formal job descriptions for every job, and we also have special training for every job. Most of this centers on safety education, but we have it for every job whether they need safety education or not. Everyone must go through this before they start working. (Interview 64*, 1995)

Another manager linked the evolution of job descriptions to the emergence of the contractual system:

> Our job descriptions and raise systems all really started to become formalized in 1992 when we had all our workers sign contracts. With people signing contracts, we had to make sure that all the rules and procedures were clear so everyone could understand them. (Interview 55*, 1995)

Here again, organizations in the chemicals sector are more likely to have institutionalized job descriptions than organizations in any other sector.

Grievance-Filing Procedures and Mediation Committees

Many organizations have also begun institutionalizing some form of grievance-filing procedures and grievance institutions, such as mediation committees. It makes sense to address these two changes together, because when managers discuss grievance-filing procedures the conversation often turns to the specific institutions that support such procedures. Grievance-filing procedures constitute a fundamental shift away from the old system, because workers in many organizations now have guidelines for addressing inequities in their work situations. Just as the National Compensation Law[13], for the first time since the founding of the PRC, allows individuals the institutional opportunity for some form of legal recourse against the state, grievance-filing procedures in firms allow individuals to challenge the traditional and particularistic authority relations on which the communist system has been based. Individuals are now able to invoke rational-legal institutions that transcend the institutionalized patron-client relations of decades past. These formalized structures afford individual workers the power to take complaints about treatment or inequities through a process patterned after rational-legal systems. As one manager described the situation:

> For workers' grievances we have a mediation committee. Now we try to keep everything very official and legal with the workers. The labor relationship is now a kind of legal relationship [*laodong guanxi shi yizhong falu guanxi*]. (Interview 64*, 1995)

An official from the Labor Bureau described these changes more systematically:

> In China today there are four main ways for laborers to file grievances and solve problems. First, there is the face-to-face discussion of problems [*shuangfang ling jieshou*]. Second, there is the labor mediation committee [*laodong tiaojie weiyuanhui*] in the enterprise. Both these approaches should be set up institutionally in the work units. But I think some enterprises have set them up in an acceptable way and some have not set these systems up at all. Outside arbitration is the third type of dispute resolution now available for laborers [*laodong zhongcai weiyuanhui*]. The fourth method of dispute resolution is taking the matter to court. The first two methods of dispute resolution can be skipped if the worker doesn't want to go through with them. But if the worker ultimately wants to take a case to court, he or she must go through arbitration before going to court. Unfortunately we don't have a department in the Labor Bureau that specifically handles labor cases in the court system yet [there is one for arbitration]. But we are working on this. There is also another method of dispute resolution called the administrative mediation [*xingzheng tiaojie*]. But this method is outside the city jurisdiction and doesn't ultimately lead to the courts. (Interview 57, 1995)

Not surprisingly, some factory managers indicated that the mere existence of internal grievance-filing procedures and institutions in the firm does not guarantee the elimination of particularistic authority relations:

> Our factory has an internal mediation committee. But the problem with this institutional structure for the workers is that it usually tends to side with the factory and the factory director. It is unlikely that workers can get a fair trial from the mediation committee. (Interview 131*, 1995)

Two points are relevant here. First, for some organizations these new institutions are likely more symbolic than substantive.[14] Nevertheless, even if these new institutions do not fundamentally alter the authority relations extant in the Chinese workplace, they do establish a system that undercuts, to some extent, the legitimacy of the old system. Laws and other institutions often begin as symbolic structures before a legal culture emerges to support these institutional shifts. In some organizations we are probably observing the first phase of this process. Second, as I discuss in greater depth below, these internal institutions take on greater strength when they are considered in the context of external institutions that serve a similar purpose. For example, each district has a Labor Arbitration Commission [*laodong zhongcai weiyuanhui*], which is under the jurisdiction of the Labor Bureau. These commissions offer workers a rational-legal institutional system outside the firm that allows them to take their complaints to another level if they are displeased with how their own organizations handle grievances. One manager in the garments sector described the situation in his firm in this way:

> Our organization does not have a mediation committee. . . . [As a result] some workers from our factory have applied to the Labor Arbitration Commission. This has only begun happening in the last two years, though. We have a Labor Law now in China, and people are being encouraged to protect themselves through their own power and rights. (Interview 105*, 1995)

Figure 3.1 shows that organizations in the foods sector are more likely to have institutionalized these formal rational structures than organizations in the other three sectors.

Workers' Representative Committee Meetings

Workers' Representative Committees [*zhigong daibiao dahui*] (WRC) are another organizational change of the reform era. These committees are set up to allow workers to participate as a collective voice in the organizational reforms accompanying the economic transition. Although most organizations now have WRCs, some still have not established them:

> We don't have a Workers' Representative Committee or official Workers' Representative Committee meetings. There's really no need for us to do these things. We are a very small organization [150 active and 200 retired employees]. We just have an informal meeting among all the older workers in the factory and the factory directors and anyone else who wants to attend. If there are any major issues or problems in the factory, we try to work them out at these meetings. But we don't have a set time to have the meetings nor do we have an official committee. (Interview 120*, 1995)

Although there is little variation on whether organizations have WRCs (98 percent, or seventy-nine out of eighty-one organizations in the sample have them), the significant issue with respect to WRCs is whether organizations have institutionalized meetings (and regular meeting times) in which these committees can participate in organizational changes.[15] For organizations that take this institution seriously, meeting times are often firmly set at two, three, or, in a few cases, four times a year. In these meetings, general managers listen to workers' complaints regarding the structure of the organization, and they present new changes that the organization will undergo in the coming year. Some organizations go so far as to vote on organizational changes at the WRC general meetings, but this is uncommon. Others have no meetings at all for the WRC and thus have failed to provide a forum for the committee to have any impact on organizational structure. In one such case, a manager in the electronics sector explained:

> We don't have a set number of times that the Workers' Representative Committee meets every year. Maybe, on average, they meet about once a year, but it really depends on what issues arise during the course of the year. If something important arises, we'll call a meeting; some years we might not have a meeting at all. (Interview 131*, 1995)

By sector, organizations in foods and chemicals are the most likely to have institutionalized this form of worker participation.

Promotion Tests

The institutionalization of promotion tests in firms in the economic transition is an important area of inquiry, not only because it relates to the overall formalization of the organization but because it bears directly on how individuals are rewarded in the organization. In the prereform system, individuals were rewarded according to behavior and especially activism with respect to the Party. In the economic transition, managers increasingly consider issues such as job skill, work ethic, and worker efficiency. In many organizations, workers now advance through a formal promotion system, rather than by currying favor with superiors.

Despite these changes, some managers still speak of promotion decisions as being determined by the subjective decisions of supervisors and managers in the factory. As one manager in the garments sector explained:

> Promotions are decided based on behavior, attitude, and management aptitude if we are trying to decide whether to promote a worker to the management level. The factory director talks to the Workers' Representative Committee and the Labor Union to make sure that everyone agrees on whether a worker should be promoted. Then he makes the promotion decision. (Interview 105*, 1995)

Some managers speak of the process as being somewhat institutionalized, yet ultimately connected to subjective decisions:

> For promotions we have a selection and educational system. The task of two people in our managerial office is to observe workers on the job. If their behavior [*biaoxian*] and attitude [*taidu*] toward work is good, and if they are hard-working, then they are selected to attend our factory's management school. Then if they do well in the management school, they are chosen for a promotion. (Interview 60*, 1995)

A final group of managers speaks of highly institutionalized practices, including tests, for promotions in their organizations:

> Promotion decisions are our own matter; they have nothing to do with our administrative office. There are really two kinds of promotion. One is promoting workers from one working level to the next within the factory. This is a simple matter. We just give workers the promotion tests when they have been here for a certain amount of time. If they pass, they are promoted. The other kind of promotion is more complicated because it has to do with promoting workers to management and administrative positions. These promotion decisions are based more on what the management office thinks of the worker's behavior, working attitude, and ability [biaoxian, gongzuo taidu, nengli]. (Interview 82*, 1995)

Figure 3.1 shows that organizations in the chemicals sector are the most likely to have institutionalized this organizational practice.

Formal Hiring Procedures

Another aspect of the formal rational bureaucratic systems emerging within Chinese firms involves hiring practices. In the planned economy, hiring was based on state assignment of jobs. In urban areas, the Labor Bureau simply divided the workforce among the available work units in a given area. In the mid-1970s, at the end of the Cultural Revolution, 95 percent of urban jobs were state-assigned.[16]

Over the course of the reforms, the state has gradually removed itself from this administrative responsibility, and firms increasingly make hiring decisions independent of state control. Of the organizations in my sample, forty-five (56 percent) reported making hiring decisions fully independent of the Labor Bureau's control. Although the Labor Bureau no longer has complete control over an organization's hiring decisions, a significant number of firms in industrial Shanghai (44 percent) still rely, to some extent, on the state with regard to hiring practices. However, even in those organizations that do not exercise full control over their hiring decisions, the Labor Bureau's influence is significantly less than in the prereform period. In my analysis of the organizational determinants of formal hiring procedures, I use only the subsample of organizations that exercise full control over their hiring decisions. One manager in the electronics sector explained the shift from state allocation of jobs to a situation no longer controlled by the Party-state apparatus:

> There are two approaches to hiring procedures: putting an ad in the paper or going through the Labor Bureau. We usually go through the Labor Bureau . . . Connections [guanxi] and introductions are really not very important in the hiring process today.

Especially in Shanghai, they are not important at all. In the past, connections were very important. But today this has changed a great deal. Since the economic reform, it really never happens anymore. (Interview 45*, 1995)

Another manager had a similar view of the diminishing state control over labor markets:

We have no set procedures for hiring workers. It used to be that the government arranged everything in terms of employment. People couldn't just float around. Now it's more complicated. . . . Of course, connections [guanxi] are still important in hiring decisions. It always matters who you know and whom you have connections with. . . . But hiring is now based on the talent market [rencai shichang] more than anything else. You just put an ad in the paper and select the best employee from all the respondents. The Labor Bureau really has no people anymore; most of the time we just go straight to the talent market to find workers. (Interview 39*, 1995)[17]

Whereas the first manager's organization was, to some extent, still under the control of the state bureaucracy with respect to labor, the second manager's firm operated independently.

Managers also vary on the extent to which they think connections matter in hiring decisions in Shanghai today:

We don't rely on the Labor Bureau at all anymore for finding new workers. In 1975 we started our own school, and we get most of our workers from there. But if we need other workers who, for some reason, we can't find in our own school, we go to the talent market [rencai shichang]. . . . People used to be able to come in through connections. But this kind of thing happens less and less now. Today our corporation keeps very close control over job searches. We want the best workers with the most skills and abilities. Starting this year our corporation has a rule that all hiring has to be approved directly by company management. (Interview 94*, 1995)

For hiring new workers, our organization always follows procedures; we never allow people to be introduced into the organization or to rely on connections to get a job. We are very strict about this. I think that every organization might differ in this area, but ours is especially focused on not relying on connections to get things done .(Interview 95*, 1995)

One government official in Shanghai saw the emergence of formalized hiring procedures as being closely tied to market constraints and an increasingly competitive marketplace where organizational performance matters:

There are several ways to get new workers now. Sometimes firms will go to one of the labor services companies [laodong fuwu gongsi]; there are so many of these now. Every district and even every street committee definitely has this type of service. Sometimes organizations will also still rely on the Labor Bureau to help find workers. But now they go to the specialist schools to look for workers more than anything else. It is more and more important today that firms get workers who are well-trained and can do the work in the factory well. It's a very important part of market competition to have workers who can do their jobs well. This is the main reason we don't really allow workers to come in through connections or introductions anymore. It's just too much of a waste if we don't hire the best person for the job. (Interview 106, 1995)

Figure 3.1 shows that firms in the electronics sector are most likely to have institutionalized a formal hiring procedure, while those in the chemicals sector are least likely to have adopted this practice.

I turn now to a multivariate analysis of the organizational determinants of the adoption of these various organizational practices. Table 3.1 presents the organizational characteristics associated with the adoption of each of these organizational practices.[18] While Figure 3.1 suggests that the chemicals sector is the most institutionalized sector in Shanghai, the multivariate model shows that this is not the case when controlling for other organizational factors. If anything, net of other effects, location in the foods sector is a more significant predictor of the adoption of several formal structures. The institutionalization of written organizational rules in Shanghai's industrial firms is dependent on three factors. There is a significant positive relationship between the existence of organizational rules and whether the firm has a joint venture with a foreign partner, whether the general manager has a background in business or economics, and, net of other effects, whether the firm is in the foods sector. The analysis presented in Table 3.1 does not reveal much with respect to the institutionalization of job descriptions—only that, net of all other effects, organizations in the garments sector are significantly less likely than those in each of the other three sectors to have institutionalized job descriptions. The determinants of grievance-filing procedures are similar to those of organizational rules: Firms that have joint ventures with foreign companies, those with general managers who have backgrounds in business or economics, and those in the foods sector are significantly more likely to have institutionalized grievance-filing procedures. In addition, whether or not the organization lost money in 1990 is negatively associated with the adoption of grievance-filing procedures in these industrial sectors. Controlling for all other effects, organizational size is significantly associated with the institutionalization of the mediation committees, and this organizational structure is also significantly correlated with location under the jurisdiction of a municipal company, that is, a middle-level governing organization in China's urban industrial economy (see chapter 2, Figure 2.1). The institutionalization of Workers' Representative Committee meetings is negatively associated with losses, an organization's employee ratio, and location under the jurisdiction of a municipal bureau. In other words, organizations that have performed poorly and those that have burdensome employee ratios (more retired workers per active worker) have been less likely to

TABLE 3.1

Logistic Coefficients for the Internal Structure of Organizations in Four Industrial Sectors, Shanghai, 1995

Independent variables	Org. rules (written)	Job descriptions	Grievance procedures	Mediation committee	Worker's rep. committee mtgs.	Promotion test	Formalized hiring procedure[b]
Organizational variables[a]							
Chemicals	1.59	4.56**	1.37	1.04	1.06	−1.72	−.03
	(.61)	(2.13)	(1.42)	(1.71)	(1.36)	(1.12)	(.49)
Foods	1.71**	1.58**	3.89***	.90	−.46	−1.59**	−.02
	(.83)	(.75)	(1.24)	(.77)	(.72)	(.74)	(.34)
Electronics	.90	2.23**	−.50	.19	.71	1.60	−.30
	(.98)	(1.03)	(1.03)	(.93)	(.92)	(1.11)	(.44)
Active employees (ln)	.42	.28	−.13	.90**	−.04	−.20	.02
	(.46)	(.46)	(.48)	(.45)	(.44)	(.41)	(.33)
Organizational health	.15	.71	.14	.39	.54	−.08	.003
	(.25)	(.59)	(.22)	(.46)	(.34)	(.15)	(.08)
Employee ratio	−.16	.17	−.35	−.19	−.50**	.38*	.33*
	(.20)	(.22)	(.22)	(.21)	(.23)	(.21)	(.19)
Losses, 1990	−.76	−.01	−2.01**	−.39	−1.60**	1.37	−.16
	(.78)	(.72)	(.89)	(.74)	(.77)	(.88)	(.30)
Joint venture	1.55*	.75	2.83**	.06	1.63**	−.85	.58*
	(.82)	(.72)	(1.04)	(.73)	(.75)	(.76)	(.33)
Governance variables							
GM w/ bus./econ. backgrnd.	1.84***	.73	1.31*	.03	.21	−.13	.96***
	(.66)	(.62)	(.73)	(.63)	(.60)	(.65)	(.34)
Municipal bureau	−1.47	−.99	−.29	—	−1.75*	−.66	−.58
	(1.06)	(1.00)	(.96)		(.77)	(1.80)	(.55)
Municipal company	—	—	—	1.36**	—	—	—
				(.68)			
Constant	−3.60	−3.86	−.38	−5.57**	.66	1.80	−.67
	(2.52)	(2.53)	(2.59)	(2.48)	(2.42)	(2.22)	(3.00)
χ^2	33.29***	33.55***	46.65***	36.14***	29.55***	34.56***	33.80***
No. of cases	81	81	81	81	81	81	45[b]

Note: See Appendix 4 for discussion of variables. Numbers in parentheses are standard errors. * $p < .1$ ** $p < .05$ *** $p < .01$ (two-tailed tests). Variables in bold are statistically significant.

[a] Reference category for sector is garments.

[b] Model is based on the subsample of organizations that make hiring decisions independent of the Labor Bureau.

TABLE 3.2
Ordinal Logit for the Overall Institutional Structure of
Organizations in Four Industrial Sectors, Shanghai, 1995

Independent variables	B	S.E.
Organizational variables[a]		
Chemicals	2.87**	1.16
Foods	1.83***	.60
Electronics	.03	.74
Active employees (ln)	.36	.33
Organizational health	.21	.22
Employee ratio	−.17	.15
Losses, 1990	−1.24**	.59
Joint venture	1.18**	.58
Governance variables		
GM w/ bus./econ. backgrnd.	1.22**	.50
Municipal company	.74***	.28
Pseudo R^2		.25
No. of cases		81

Note: See Appendix 4 for discussion of variables. B is the effect of the coefficient; S.E. is the standard error.   ** $p < .05$ *** $p < .01$ (two-tailed tests). Variables in bold are statistically significant.

[a] Reference category for sector is garments.

institutionalize channels for democratic participation in the organization. The institutionalization of promotion tests is positively associated with location in the foods sector, negatively associated with location in the electronics sector, and negatively associated with a firm's employee ratio. Finally, employee ratios, joint-venture relations, and a general manager's background are all significant predictors of the likelihood that an organization will have institutionalized formal hiring procedures.

Table 3.2 presents an analysis of the determinants of the overall institutionalization of Shanghai's firms.[19] The results in this table lend support to the picture given in Table 3.1: net of all other effects, organizations in the foods and chemicals sectors are significantly more institutionalized than those in other sectors. Organizations that lost money in 1990 are significantly less institutionalized than other firms. Those that have a joint venture with a foreign firm are significantly more institutionalized than those that do not. Firms that have a general manager with a background in business or economics are more institutionalized. And organizations under the jurisdiction of municipal companies are significantly more institutionalized than firms at other levels of the industrial hierarchy. In the following sections of this chapter I examine several of the significant organization-level findings that, according to Tables 3.1 and 3.2, are driving the process of formalization in Chinese firms: tightening fiscal constraints, isomorphic effects within sectors, a firm's position in the state hierarchy of the former command economy, the general manager's background, and joint-venture relationships.

The Causes of Organizational Change

Tightening Fiscal Constraints

The findings presented here show that fiscal constraints are tied to the approaches organizations take to make their way through the reforms. Organizations that are faltering in the economic transition are significantly less likely to adopt strategies that reflect a desire to transform the existing structures of their workplaces (shown by the significantly negative effect of losses in Tables 3.1 and 3.2). Two things are going on here. Even though I argue in this book (chapters 2, 4, and 6) and elsewhere (see Guthrie 1997, 1998b) that market constraints are in fact playing a role for organizations throughout China's transition economy, the concept of a soft-budget constraint has by no means been eliminated. Organizations that are losing money in the economic transition are those that have been least able to adapt to the harsh realities of the market economy. Many of these perennial losers continue to be bailed out by the state, primarily through "loan" subsidies, or by other organizations (see, for example, the discussion in chapter 2 of Shanghai's No. 5 Factory). Locked in a pattern of losses and bailouts, as long as these organizations can count on a bailout coming from somewhere, they have little impetus to transform the internal operations of their workplace. Second, irrespective of bailouts and budget constraints, these organizations are simply less in tune with the processes and demands of the market economy. In other words, they are less cognizant of the workplace transformations that are necessary in the transition from a command to a market economy.

One might argue that there is an endogeneity problem here: Performance is not an indicator of institutional change, but institutional change is a predictor of performance. Although things may operate in both directions, throughout this study I generally argue for the former perspective for two reasons. First, since most of these organizational changes were adopted in the late 1980s and 1990s in Chinese factories, it is unlikely that they can be linked in a causal way to balance-sheet reports from 1990. Second, it is also unlikely that organizational changes could have such an immediate effect on performance. The more probable scenario is that losses are an indicator of a general inability to adapt to the demands of China's emerging markets, and organizations that are unable to adapt to market demands are less likely to transform their work environments in significant ways. In either case, according to the parameters examined here, faltering organizations are significantly less likely to transform the firm's internal structures in the economic transition.

Isomorphism within Sectors

Institutional theory posits that organizations adopt formalized institutional structures as a way of seeking legitimacy in the marketplace. The specific organizational practices and structures that firms adopt are based on examples of practices and structures that other organizational actors in the marketplace employ. Because organizations seek legitimacy by adopting organizational practices employed by other organizations, there is a tendency toward isomorphism in the marketplace—that is, organizations come to resemble one another. DiMaggio and Powell (1983) developed this theoretical perspective by exploring the specific mechanisms by which institutional isomorphism occurs across organizational fields. They identified mimetic, coercive, and normative isomorphism as three distinct ways that organizations adopt similar practices and ultimately come to resemble one another over time.

Evidence of isomorphism within sectors in industrial China comes from the fact that for the specific organizational practices analyzed above, several of the sector effects are significant, controlling for other organizational characteristics.[20] Net of all other organizational characteristics, firms in the foods sector are more likely than those in other sectors to have institutionalized organizational rules, grievance-filing procedures, and promotion tests. Overall, organizations in the foods sector tend to adopt more of these organizational structures (see Table 3.2). With respect to job descriptions, organizations in the garments sector are significantly less likely to have institutionalized job descriptions.

Although it seems clear from the net effects displayed in Tables 3.1 and 3.2 that organizations in the same sectors adopt similar sets of internal structures, the deeper question is what mechanisms exist to make organizations in these fields isomorphic. In other words, what remains unclear in the data is whether it is mimetic, coercive, or normative forces that make organizations within these sectors isomorphic with respect to specific organizational practices. Mimetic isomorphism arises from uncertainty in the marketplace and from the tendency for firms that are experiencing uncertain market environments to imitate other organizations near to them.[21] As firms make their way through the reforms, the sense of being set adrift by the state has created a great deal of uncertainty for many organizations. Firms become isomorphic in this rapidly changing (uncertain) market environment, because "organizations tend to model themselves after similar organizations in their field that they perceive to be more legitimate or successful."[22] Firms look to successful organizations near them and model their own organizational structures on the practices that appear to be central to the practices of successful organizations. It should be noted here that although this approach to market uncertainty may be rational, the model of action is one that is fundamentally at odds with the assumption of rational profit-maximizing decision makers in organizations. Organizations adopt strategies they *perceive* to be successful or legitimate, and this decision-making criterion is often completely divorced from a clear understanding of what these practices will mean in terms of efficiency.

Coercive isomorphism refers to any situation, formal or otherwise, in which pressure is exerted on an organization to adopt a given set of practices. The most obvious examples for such pressure are government mandates in the form of policies, laws, or regulations. In my research and interviews I came across no sets of laws or policies that targeted specific sectors with respect to the organizational decisions and practices examined in this study.[23] In other words, there are no visible state mandates that can explain the reasoning behind why organizations in the foods sector are more likely to institutionalize organizational rules, grievance-filing procedures, or promotion tests. However, there are broad governance structures that have significantly altered the institutional environments in which all firms are situated. The Labor Law (PRC 1994) and the Labor Arbitration Commissions are two governance structures that have had the largest influence on firms' institutional environments and, by extension, the internal practices firms adopt in the period of economic reform. For example, chapter 10 of the Labor Law, entitled "Labor Disputes," is specifically devoted to describing the process laborers are legally entitled to follow should a dispute arise in the workplace. The law explains the rights of the worker to take disputes to outside arbitration (the district's Labor Arbitration Commission) should she or he be unsatisfied with the manner in which grievances are being handled within the organization. It is extremely plausible that these institutional shifts have exerted pressure on organizations to alter their internal structures, much as changing institutional environments in the 1960s in the United States forced U.S. organizations to alter their internal structures by experimenting with job ladders, employment tests, job descriptions, and the like.[24] It is possible that sector effects of organizational practices in China are reflections of variation in how much these broader institutional changes (the Labor Law, the Labor Arbitration Commissions) are taken seriously in the respective sectors.

Position in the Industrial Hierarchy: Municipal Company Governance

As coercive isomorphism is tied to political influence, coercive mechanisms may also come into play in the case of China when governing organizations pressure firms under their jurisdictions to adopt a given set of practices. The analyses presented above show that the level of government administration is a factor in the institutional structure of organizations in the reform period: firms under the jurisdiction of municipal companies are significantly more likely than those at other levels of the hierarchy to institutionalize mediation committees, and, according to Table 3.2, they are considerably more institutionalized overall. Organizations under the jurisdiction of municipal bureaus are significantly less likely than those under the jurisdiction of municipal and district companies to institutionalize Workers' Representative Committee meetings.

Although the political nature of these effects would place the issue in the category of coercive isomorphism, inasmuch as isomorphic mechanisms "are not always empirically distinct," coercive isomorphism may also run over into mimetic isomorphism in the practices and decisions of governing offices.[25] At the lower levels of the state administrative hierarchy, governing offices are acting more like corporate entities (similar to a holding company) with respect to the firms under their jurisdictions.[26] These governing offices are acting less like government agencies and more like holding companies in that their main concern is not regulatory action as much as it is the economic success of the firms they oversee. These levels of state administration (municipal bureau, municipal company, and district company) act, in some ways, like crosscutting organizational fields. Organizations and government offices view other firms and governing offices at the same level in the administrative hierarchy as their peer group. Scale and scope of industry vary with position in the administrative hierarchy, and firms at a given level in the hierarchy compare themselves primarily to other firms of similar scale and scope. It is also natural for firms to compare themselves to other organizations in similar administrative positions, because the budgetary situations of these firms with respect to the command economy were often similar.[27] These governing bodies, which are paying close attention to the organizations under their jurisdictions, are guiding their firms to adopt internal structures that reflect a formal rational-legal system. Thus organizations at the same levels of the administrative hierarchy (in other words, organizations in the same politically defined organizational field) become isomorphic with respect to one another through a combination of mimetic and coercive mechanisms.

The General Manager's Background

Organizations that have general managers with an education in economics or business are more likely than other organizations to adopt formal organizational rules, grievance-filing procedures, and formal hiring procedures, and they rank higher on the overall institutionalization scale. Fligstein (1987, 1990, 1996b) argues that CEOs of organizations interact with their institutional environments in defining the strategies and structure of the organizations they run. In periods of uncertainty, the individuals who rise to leadership positions in organizations are those who can offer solutions to the problems the organizations face. The solutions that leaders of organizations adopt become conceptions of control that then define viable solutions to the ways organizations are run. The governance of an organization—the conception of control under which the organization operates—is crucial for the decisions and practices that organizations adopt, and it is also vital for the broader conceptions of how organizations should be run in a given organizational field. Successful conceptions of control often stretch beyond the confines of individual organizations, becoming institutionalized within the organizational field as a legitimate way to operate organizations. The background of the CEO is relevant in this process because the conceptions of control that leaders bring to their organizations are often closely related to their backgrounds and training.

In China, a conception of control is emerging that bears directly on the internal structure of organizations. This conception of control is oriented toward the economic management of firms, but, more important, it is also a formal rational conception of control. General managers in Chinese organizations who were trained in business or economics or both are guiding organizations to adopt a set of formal rational institutions that reflect a new set of authority relations in the workplace. With respect to American capitalism, it makes sense to talk about more specific conceptions of control within the larger rubric of capitalism (e.g., sales, legal, and financial conceptions of control) as Fligstein (1990, 1987) has. In China, however, the distinctions are positioned more broadly between socialist management styles—and the particularistic authority relations embedded in that type of system—and a formal rational management style where authority is less particularistic, more impersonal, more dependent on formalized institutions. This newly emerging conception of control in China marks a fundamental shift from the type of authority relations described in previous analyses of factory life in prereform China.[28]

In addition, it is likely that general managers with similar educational backgrounds are heavily influenced by the professionalism occurring in educational venues. In DiMaggio and Powell's (1983) discussion of institutional isomorphism, normative pressure, the third mechanism by which organizations become isomorphic, is grounded primarily in professionalization and education: "Universities and professional training institutions are important centers for the development of organizational norms among professional managers and their staff."[29] Managers learn the theories and norms of organizational strategies and structure in the material that is taught in the classroom as well as through the informal networks that develop in educational settings.[30] The significance of general managers with business and economic backgrounds in the institutionalization of grievance-filing procedures, organizational rules, and formal hiring procedures (as well as overall institutionalization) suggests that these managers are grounded in a similar understanding of organizational structure and economic strategy in the economic transition. They were trained in similar settings and have analogous views of the types of organizational structures that should emerge in the period of economic reform. It is also likely that many of these managers are tied into common networks of organizational leaders. Leaders may be more apt to have relationships with other leaders of similar backgrounds. These types of networks would not be surprising in the relatively small organizational fields of industrial Shanghai.

The Effects of Foreign Investment

Organizations that have joint-venture relationships with foreign companies are significantly more likely to have organizational rules, grievance-filing procedures, and WRC meetings, and they are considerably more "institutionalized" overall than organizations that do not have a joint-venture relationship with a foreign company. From the popular rhetoric of "getting on track with the international community" [*gen guoji jiegui*] (see chapter 7) to more concrete institutional changes such as the Company Law (PRC 1993), the Chinese government is leading an economic transition that clearly places a premium on Western-style organizational practices and systems. As one manager in the foods sector explained:

> I think the most important thing that we understand about linking up with the international world has to do with "getting on track" [*jiegui*] with Western management systems and practices. For the most part, now we do things very much the way you do them. The management system of our company is very much like the systems you have in the West [*gongsi guanli zhidu xianzai gen xifang yiyang*]. (Interview 85*, 1995)

Another manager in the chemicals sector linked the issue directly to negotiations over joint ventures:

> The ideas we now have about profits are similar to the ways Western companies think of them. In the past, this was not the case at all. We must be able to talk about these issues in contract negotiations or joint-venture negotiations with foreign companies. So we have to understand the way the international world does things. (Interview 93*, 1995)

From the perspectives of these and other managers with whom I discussed this issue, China's Modern Enterprise System [*xiandai qiye zhidu*] is very much about adopting management strategies that are in line with the business practices of the international world.

The effect of joint-venture relationships on the internal structure of Chinese organizations arises in two ways. The first is related directly to the process of mimetic isomorphism described above. Managers in Chinese organizations perceive Western-style management practices and organizational structures to be more oriented toward profits, efficiency, and successful bureaucratic structure. The obvious place for managers to look for models of how successful international organizations are structured is through their joint-venture relationships. Contact with foreign managers exposes Chinese managers to foreign management practices through observing how the joint ventures are set up and through discussions and negotiations with their partner managers. Through this contact, these Chinese managers can better model their organizations after foreign organizations.

A second, more important part of the joint-venture effect has to do with *attracting* foreign investment. Virtually all Chinese enterprises strive to land joint-venture contracts. Joint-venture contracts mean both material and intangible gains for Chinese enterprises. Materially, joint ventures often mean the possibility of technology transfer (depending on the contract negotiations) and an infusion of capital.[31] Technology is often the most important immediate gain the Chinese enterprise stands to accrue through a joint venture, and often a basic part of the agreement centers on the transfer of technology to the Chinese organization. There are also other intangibles: With joint venture contracts come prestige, access to international markets, and contact with foreign companies and foreign-style management practices. As a result, Chinese firms engage in a number of practices to attract foreign investment and to establish relationships with foreign partners. Many of the practices these firms adopt are related to the intra-organizational practices analyzed above. As one manager in the chemicals sector explained:

> Changing into a company is a very important part of the economic reforms happening in China. Actually, we are already like a fairly large company. In the international way of looking at things, a factory or an enterprise is a production-oriented organization; a company, though, contains within it the production, the management, and possibly several other subsidiaries. . . . We are becoming a company to meet up with the international perspective on these things. It's a kind of linking up with the international world [*yizhong guoji jiegui*]. *If a foreign company comes to China and wants to invest, who are they going to look for? They are going to look for the organizations with the most progressive and most Western ways of management and organization.* We know that companies are the principal types of organizational systems in the West, and now the better factories and enterprises in China are becoming companies. *It's a way of acting the way the foreign companies act, so they will see what kind of organization we are.* (Interview 98*, 1995)

As this manager indicates, Chinese organizations adopt formalized institutional practices not only to appear legitimate in the state's eyes but also for legitimacy in the eyes of foreign investors.[32]

Chinese industrial firms are building internal bureaucratic structures through the adoption of a number of different formal organizational practices. These trends are grounded primarily in isomorphic tendencies within sectors, the emergence of a formal rational conception of firm governance, and an impact of foreign investment through joint-venture relationships. Thus Chinese firms are responding to the economic models they see present both within their sectors and through their partnerships with foreign companies.

But Do Formal Rational Bureaucracies Matter?

Formal Rational Bureaucracies and Hiring Practices

In China today, a new type of bureaucracy has begun to emerge at the organizational level, and this bureaucracy includes formal hiring procedures, as I showed in the first half of this chapter. The discussion thus far, however, does not reveal to what extent, if any, these structures are meaningful for the practices and environments within organizations. Are these structures anything more than symbolic? Do they have meaning for authority relations in the firm or for organizational decisions and practices in the realm of labor relations?[33] To address these crucial questions, I now turn my attention to two examples in which these emerging bureaucracies in Chinese industrial firms are affecting organizational practices and the experiences of workers within the organization. In this section I demonstrate that as these bureaucratic systems develop within individual organizations, hiring practices are moving away from the use of connections toward a more formalized set of rational bureaucratic procedures. The evidence I present here runs counter to arguments by scholars who emphasize the network aspects of Chinese society, such as Yanjie Bian, who asserts that "in the years to come . . . *guanxi* . . . will prevail in manipulating job placement and job mobility processes" in China.[34] I suggest that the emergence of formal rational bureaucratic structures at the firm level is having significant implications for the rationalization of hiring decisions in reform-era China.

During the early and mid-1980s the state was establishing a number of broad institutional changes that were pushing administrative and economic responsibilities down the hierarchy of the former command economy, putting these responsibilities in the hands of firms themselves and, in some cases, the administrative companies that presided over them (see chapter 2). As these institutional changes were new in the mid-1980s, and especially given that no other organizational bureaucracies and hiring procedures existed to replace state control in this area, it is not surprising that organizations relied on institutional systems that were familiar to them, namely, connections. However, with the new autonomy afforded industrial organizations by the receding state and the new more formalized institutional policies forged at the state level, organizations (and the administrative companies presiding over some of these newly independent organizations) have begun to build their own bureaucracies. And these bureaucracies are based, at least symbolically, on formalized rational processes. The empirical question for the reforms is the extent to which these formalized rational structures in organizations have implications for Bian's prediction that connections will continue to dominate in manipulating job placement and hiring processes.

Bian's (1994b) argument is basically that the use of connections in hiring decisions varies with the state's bureaucratic strength: When state bureaucratic control was strong, the use of connections to secure jobs was at its lowest; as direct state bureaucratic control has withered in the reform period, the use of connections to secure jobs has increased. Although the evidence and analysis Bian presents are convincing, his study assumes that government bureaucracy is the only type of bureaucracy that will possibly control hiring practices in urban China. While it is true that the receding state bureaucracy coincided with a rise in the use of connections to secure jobs in urban China (as Bian shows), it does not necessarily follow that state bureaucracies are the only bureaucracies that will inhibit the use of connections in hiring practices. Even if state bureaucracies continue to recede, it does not necessarily follow from the evidence that the use of connections will continue to be the dominant system in job allocation and hiring practices. If a new type of bureaucratic system were to arise in China—for example, a formal rational bureaucratic system within organizations—this new bureaucratic system may very well reduce the importance of connections in hiring decisions and job allocations. In fact, Bian does note that his findings are not only connected to the receding state bureaucracy but also to the lack of formalized internal organizational bureaucracies. According to Bian (1994b, 979; emphasis added), "By the late 1980s, *because of a lack of* advertising and *formal hiring procedures, guanxi* became the predominant means of channeling individuals to work units." This statement implies that emerging formal hiring procedures would, like government bureaucracies did in the past, alter the prevalence of connections in hiring practices and labor market processes. In fact, this is exactly what is occurring in urban industrial China today.

I showed in Table 3.1 that formal hiring procedures are dependent primarily on whether an organization has a joint-venture relationship with a foreign company and on the background of the organization's general manager. More important than what determines whether an organization will have formalized hiring procedures, however, is whether these *procedures* matter for how organizations actually engage in hiring *practices*. In a set of questions separate from my discussions with managers about the formal structures of their organizations, I discussed the ways that managers make hiring decisions. Table 3.3 presents the determinants of whether organizations allow individuals to be hired through *guanxi*.[35] In the model presented in Table 3.3, the presence of a

TABLE 3.3

Logistic Coefficients for the Determinants of the Use of Connections [*Guanxi*] in Hiring Decisions in Four Industrial Sectors, Shanghai, 1995

Independent variables	B	S.E.
Organizational variables[a]		
Chemicals	2.32	1.64
Foods	.85	.68
Electronics	−2.33*	1.38
Active employees (ln)	1.16	1.07
Organizational health	−1.73**	.81
Employee ratio	1.13**	.19
Losses, 1994	−.36	.58
Joint venture	−.54	.62
Formal hiring procedures	−3.57**	1.61
Governance variables		
GM w/ bus./econ. backgrnd.	1.19	.74
Municipal bureau	1.89	1.18
Constant	−2.19	5.57
χ^2	33.94***	
No. of cases	45	

Note: See Appendix 4 for discussion of variables. B is the effect of the coefficient; S.E. is the standard error. * $p < .1$ ** $p < .05$ *** $p < .01$ (two-tailed tests). Variables in bold are statistically significant.

[a] Reference category for sector is garments.

formalized hiring procedure (the dependent variable for this practice in Table 3.1) is viewed as an independent variable with respect to hiring practices.

The results of this analysis show that organizations in the electronics sector are significantly less likely than those in other sectors to allow connections to factor into a hiring decision.[36] Although organizations in this sector are no more likely than other organizations to have institutionalized formalized hiring procedures, nevertheless they are significantly less likely to allow workers to enter the organization through connections. Organizational health is negatively associated with the use of connections in hiring decisions, whereas a healthy employee ratio is positively associated. Most important for this model, however, is the effect of formal hiring procedures on whether an organization will consider connections in a hiring decision: Formal hiring procedures exert a strong negative effect on the likelihood that an organization will allow connections to be considered as part of the hiring decision. In other words, the formalized hiring practices that organizations adopt *do* matter in the overall rationalization of the labor hiring process.

To place these findings in the context of cultural and network-based views of Chinese society, I have shown here that a new type of intra-organizational bureaucracy is emerging in China. This bureaucracy is arising for a number of reasons, and it has real implications for the rationalization of labor relations and labor market processes. One part of this intra-organizational bureaucracy is the formalized hiring procedures being adopted by firms that have increasing autonomy over labor market decisions. These procedures are more than just symbolic, as intra-organizational bureaucracies, specifically formal hiring procedures, inhibit the use of connections in hiring practices in industrial organizations in Shanghai today. Thus, where Bian predicts that connections will dominate labor processes in the future, I argue that the extent to which this is true depends on the new types of organizational forms that emerge over the course of China's economic transition. If current trends are any indication, contrary to Bian's predictions, formal rational bureaucratic systems within organizations may diminish the importance of connections in China's labor market processes.

Formal Rational Bureaucracies and Worker Discontent

Another way of examining the substantive meaning of firm level institutional environments is by examining their effect on worker discontent.[37] Data on worker discontent, however, are difficult to measure and even more challenging to come by. The study of worker discontent is particularly appropriate for the current period of China's reform because several critical reforms (external to the organizations) are providing options for workers to file grievances that are supported by state institutions; one such institution is the Labor Arbitration Commission [*Laodong Zhongcai Weiyuanhui*].

The Labor Arbitration Commission (LAC) is an institution under the jurisdiction of the Labor Bureau. Each urban district and county has an LAC. The emergence of the institution of labor arbitration in China is directly related to the issues of the economic transition and the emergence of a market economy. An official in the Labor Bureau, who now oversees the Labor Dispute Office in the LAC, explained this relationship as follows:

> The need for arbitration in China grew as we moved away from the planned economy. In the planned economy everything was fixed and decided by the government. No one could be fired from his or her job, and everyone was secure. In the early 1980s we started to move into a market economy. With this came the labor system reform [*laodong zhidu gaige*]. One of the big problems of the labor system under the planned economy was that organizations had lifelong commitments to taking care of the workers in their organization. This became a big problem, because it made it very difficult for the organizations to compete with other private and foreign organiza-

tions that had much less overhead and fewer responsibilities. As we moved into the market economy, we had to create a system in which organizations could take care of themselves; we had to stop the system in which every time individuals were hired, they were the organization's lifelong responsibility. The first significant change in this area was the introduction of the labor contract. With labor contracts, for the first time organizations were able to hire someone for a limited amount of time—one, three, or five years. This began in 1986; actually the rules were first issued in 1986, but they were not passed into law until 1987. At the same time, as we were introducing contracts that allowed organizations only to hire workers for a fixed amount of time, we realized that the labor relationship would become far more complicated with this change. We realized we would need a way to settle labor disputes. So in 1987 we also formed the first Labor Arbitration Commission. (Interview 57, 1995)

The emergence of the LAC is grounded in a number of legal and institutional changes of the reform period. The document that first defined these changes was the State-Owned Enterprises Labor Dispute Resolution Temporary Rules [*Guoying Qiye Laodong Zhengyi Chuli Zhanxing Guiding*], which was adopted by the State Council in 1987. Although this document dealt only with dispute resolution in state-owned organizations, the 1993 People's Republic of China Labor Dispute Resolution Regulations [*Zhonghua Renmin Gongheguo Qiye Laodong Zhengyi Chuyi Tiaoli*] expanded the rules to include all types of labor relationships. Over the course of this period, the issue of labor disputes was slowly transformed from "one that protected organizations to one that also protected the laborers; by 1993, labor arbitration was really viewed as a protection law for all laborers" (Interview 57, 1995). In addition to further standardizing labor relationships, the Labor Law also further solidifies the position of the LAC as an institution for labor dispute resolution: Chapter 10 of the Labor Law is fully devoted to labor disputes and the use of the LAC. These institutional and legal changes establish arbitration as a formally supported legal structure in the governance of labor relations in reform-era China.[38]

The Labor Arbitration Commission has two sections: one is the arbitration court [*zhongcaiyuan*], and the other the labor section [*zhuanzi laodong bumen*], which primarily handles labor disputes. One group within the labor section is made up of volunteer workers, and the other is ruled by the presiding official. The volunteer system, of course, depends on the participation of workers. The labor union at each organization submits names of individuals to occupy these voluntary positions, and the LAC chooses workers from this list.[39] Three groups are represented in the labor arbitration process: The government is represented by the Labor Bureau [*laodongju*]; the worker, by the organization's Labor Union [*gonghui*]; and the organization, by the Economic Commission [*jingji weiyuanhui*] in the Central Economic Administrative Unit [*zhonghe jingji guanli bumen*]. Actually this government unit only represents state-owned organizations; if the dispute involves a private company, a separate government department represents the organization.

Basically three types of problems go through the LAC. The first relates to disagreements over contractual issues surrounding firing [*kaichu*] or quitting [*cizi*]. The second type of dispute relates to salaries, insurance, and benefits. The third type of problem relates to vacation days and work leave. Three different sections in the commission each handle one of these three types of disputes. The greatest problem area for applications to the LAC is contractual disputes [*hetong zhengyi*], which, as of 1995, comprised more than 50 percent of the applications to Shanghai's LACs. Most often the problem arises because people have signed contracts and the work unit is not adhering to the terms of the contract; these cases are usually decided in favor of the workers.[40]

The state has created this system, in conjunction with the Labor Law, as an institutional structure to help facilitate due process in the workplace. According to an official in the Labor Bureau:

> Our main focus in creating this process is to build a legal system [*jiancheng falu zhidu*] that will make all labor relationships the same. If there is a problem, we want all resolutions to be simple and straightforward. (Interview 57, 1995)

Yet, individual firms still decide how they structure their organizations internally; thus how organizations treat their workers on a daily basis varies. One tangible method of inferring how workers are treated in a particular organization is in whether anyone within the organization has ever applied to the LAC for dispute resolution. In my survey of organizations in Shanghai, I attempted to capture this variation among firms.[41] One manager addressed the issue in this way:

> We've had people apply to the Labor Arbitration Commission. We lost every time. Usually the problem was that we wanted to fire someone or end the labor relationship, and the worker didn't want to end the relationship. They had all signed labor contracts, and, in our opinion, they had violated the terms of the contract. But the Arbitration Commission didn't agree. (Interview 64*, 1995)

Other managers depict situations in which no workers have applied for outside arbitration for dispute resolution:

> No one in this factory has ever applied to the Labor Arbitration Commission. We don't really have too many serious problems that arise here. . . . For one thing, we have our own mediation committee in the factory [*ziji neibu tiaojie hui*]. But I think the more important reason is that everything in our factory is equal. For instance, although the workers only make, on average, about 6,000 RMB per year, this is about the same amount earned by the general manager, myself [the vice general manager], and all the other managers. The workers know we are working hard to make things better for everyone. (Interview 110*, 1995)

TABLE 3.4

Logistic Coefficients for the Determinants of Whether Any
Employees Have Ever Applied to the Labor Arbitration
Commission for Organizations in Four Industrial Sectors,
Shanghai, 1995

Independent variables	B	S.E.
Organizational variables[a]		
Chemicals	−.74	.66
Foods	−.63	.52
Electronics	−.03	.50
Active employees (ln)	.76*	.40
Average age of employees	−.19**	.09
Average salary of employees (ln)	−.60	.93
Employee ratio	−.65**	.32
Losses, 1990	−.58	.41
Organizational rules	.25	.40
Mediation committee	−.70*	.42
Governance variables		
GM w/ bus./econ. background	.35	.38
Municipal bureau	.05	.46
Constant	6.07***	.35
χ^2	21.64**	
No. of cases	81	

Note: See Appendix 4 for discussion of variables. B is the effect of the
coefficient; S.E. is the standard error. $* p < .1$ $** p < .05$ $*** p < .01$
(two-tailed tests). Variables in bold are statistically significant.

[a] Reference category for sector is garments.

Another manager had this to say:

> No one from our factory has ever applied to the Labor Arbitration Commission.
> There was one person planning to do so some time last year. But, in the end, that
> person went through our own mediation institution [*ziji tiaojie jigou*], and we re-
> solved the problem. (Interview 103*, 1995)

It is interesting that both these managers view the mediation institution within
their organizations as a factor in whether employees apply for external arbitration. This view is tested systematically in the multivariate model.

Table 3.4 presents the determinants of whether any employees within a
given organization have ever applied to the LAC for dispute resolution. In this
model I include two variables that I have not included in other analyses
throughout the book: the average salary of employees in the organization and
the average age of workers. Average salary is included because workers in

organizations that pay lower wages may be more likely to be discontented with their work situations, and discontented workers are probably more likely to raise disputes with the organization. The employees' average age is a crude proxy for dissatisfaction and a sense of entitlement: Young workers, who have grown up in the age of legal reforms, may have a greater sense of entitlement in the economic transition and, as a result, may be more likely to raise disputes and apply for outside resolution. Because they were raised in the age of reforms, individuals from younger generations may also have a better understanding of the legal and institutional changes occurring over the course of the economic transition. In addition, in this model I include dummy variables to account for specific formal structures in the firm: "Organizational rules" indicate whether the firm has institutionalized formal rules in the economic transition; "mediation committee" indicates whether the firm has an internal mediation institution within the organization.

The results in Table 3.4 show that the size of the organization increases the likelihood that an individual will apply to the LAC for dispute resolution. An organization's employee ratio is negatively associated with whether an employee ever applied to the LAC for dispute resolution: The more retired workers there are per active worker (yielding a low value in employee ratio), the more likely that a worker will have taken a case to outside arbitration. In other words, the heavier the economic burden for a given organization, the more likely it is that workers will be dissatisfied to the point of applying for outside arbitration. Although employees' average salary in an organization is not related to the pursuit of outside dispute resolution, the average age of employees is significantly related to whether an organization's workers will have taken cases to the LAC. The younger the employees' average age in the organization, the more likely that individuals within the organization will have taken a dispute to outside arbitration. As I mentioned above, I interpret this finding to be indicative of the ethos and experience of the younger generation of workers in urban China in two ways. First, the majority of individuals in this younger generation of workers were completing their education during the economic transition. They were also just beginning work at that time. Thus this younger generation of workers is extremely aware of the legal and institutional changes brought about by the reforms, much more so, at least, than the older workers are. Further, younger workers are more exposed to the legalistic ways of thinking about labor relations, and they have less conditioning and experience in the types of authority relations that defined labor relationships in the prereform period.

Second, and more important, younger workers are more apt to have formalized relationships with the firms in which they are employed (for discussion, see chapter 4). In virtually all the firms surveyed for this study, the factories place their young workers on labor contracts, guaranteeing nothing to the young employee beyond the period of the contract. Older workers, whose years with the organization predate the economic transition, are often protected from labor contracts and formalized labor relations. As a result, younger workers are far more likely to view the labor relationship through a formal, rational-legal lens. When disputes arise, these younger workers readily invoke the institutions that are within the legal purview of dispute resolution. At the same time, in part as a result of the formalized nature of labor relations within the younger generation and in part as a result of less time spent in a given organization, these younger workers have not developed the personal ties to the organization and to management that the older generation have.

Finally, the existence of a mediation committee within an organization significantly *decreases* the likelihood that individuals within the firm will apply for outside dispute resolution. This is an important finding because it shows that these institutional structures within firms are more than symbolic. When a firm has its own mediation committee, individuals first seek to resolve disputes in the institutional structure already in place in the organization. As with the negative association between formal hiring procedures and the use of connections in the hiring process, the effect of an internal mediation committee on the likelihood that employees will apply to the LAC indicates that the internal bureaucracies emerging in firms in China's economic transition have real consequences for how organizations operate.

Concluding Remarks

In a recent interview reported in the *New York Times*, a plaintiff involved in a suit against his wife's work unit exclaimed, "Doesn't a work unit have to heed national law? We want an explanation. We are just protecting our rights."[42] Such sentiments mark a radical departure from the authority relations of the past. Institutional changes such as the National Compensation Law and the Labor Law create a framework in which individuals can file grievances with higher authorities.[43] With the creation of these rational-legal systems, individuals, for the first time in the history of the PRC, can receive their day in court. Recent estimates of the number of cases brought before Chinese courts has grown from about 13,000 in 1990 to an estimated 100,000 in 1997; lawsuits against the government specifically have risen over 12,000 percent.[44] These cases include individuals suing their work units, the police, and a variety of other government agencies.

In this chapter I have examined some of the ways that formal rational structures and mentalities are penetrating the firm environment. If the system of the past was based on particularistic authority relations that amounted to a system of personalized patron-client relations, the current system in China is evolving toward one in which formal rational-legal structures are emerging at the state level, and new forms of formal rational bureaucracies are emerging at the firm level. Organizational rules, job descriptions, grievance-filing procedures, mediation committees, workers' representative committees, promotion tests, and formal hiring procedures all constitute the firm-level structures of these emerging formal rational bureaucratic systems.

The existence of these new institutional systems within organizations does not, on its own, constitute evidence of a dramatic shift away from the enduring elements of the prereform system. These emerging firm-level institutions could be little more than a symbolic attempt to compete for foreign investors. Indeed, research in institutional theory has argued that institutional structures are often more symbolic than practical. If firms are adopting these institutional structures, but the structures are having little impact on how authority relations are organized at the firm level, that would lend support to the view that, even in the reform era, elements of the communist system will endure.[45] However, if these firm-level bureaucratic structures are in fact transforming the ways that authority relations are constructed at the firm level, the implications of these changes for the enduring elements perspective should perhaps be considered more fully. The pertinent question then is how meaningful these changes are for decisions and practices of and within organizations.

The analyses above test some of these associations empirically. In two particular cases I have shown that firm-level institutions are significantly associated with changing practices of the firm and of individuals within the firm. In one case I have shown that there is a significant relationship between formalized hiring procedures and firms' actual hiring practices. Firms that have institutionalized formal hiring procedures are significantly less likely to allow connections to influence their hiring decisions. Bian (1994b) has argued that as state bureaucracies recede, the use of connections will increasingly dominate hiring practices. However, although Bian's evidence shows this to be the case for the late 1980s, I argue that this period was more likely one of transition between bureaucratic systems than a harbinger of the type of system that would emerge in China in the long run. In the 1980s state bureaucracies were in the early stages of recession. The receding state bureaucracy left in its wake an organizational void and considerable chaos over how processes such as labor market practices should be handled. The result was that managers allowed connections and networks to factor significantly into labor market decisions and practices. However, as the state was divesting itself of bureaucratic power and responsibility, firms were constructing their own internal bureaucracies. As these bureaucratic systems within firms have become more formalized and more developed over the course of the reforms, they have influenced firms' decisions in terms of labor market practices.

In a second case I have shown that the existence of an internal mediation committee within an organization significantly reduces the likelihood that workers in that organization will file grievances with external mediation institutions (namely, the district or municipal Labor Arbitration Commission). The implications of this association are important on two levels. First, the emergence of the LAC as an institution in China has significantly changed the rules of authority relations in Chinese society. In the past, workers had no recourse for filing grievances over inequities (real or perceived) in the firm. Although their relationships with managers may have played a role in their fates within the firm, it was virtually impossible for workers to challenge the decision-making power of managers and Party elites. In China today, discontented workers can take grievances to an external institution set up for the sole purpose of protecting workers' rights. In conjunction with the Labor Law, the Labor Arbitration Commissions provide a forum in which workers can challenge authority relations. Not only are authority relations becoming more formalized and less particularistic, but they are also becoming more equitable with respect to the distribution of power between workers and management. Second, it is important to note whether people are actually making use of institutional shifts such as the LAC and, if they are, how this relates to institutional structure and changing authority relations at the firm level. According to officials in the Labor Bureau, applications to bring cases before the LAC have risen steadily since 1987, and the number of applications in 1994 rose 150 percent from that in 1993.[46] But, more important, evidence in this chapter shows that the institutional structure of firms in China is significantly associated with the likelihood that individuals will apply to the LAC. In firms that have dramatically altered the structure of authority relations in the organization by providing forums for mediation, these changes are significant enough that workers do not feel the need to apply for external mediation of these decisions. The central message in both these cases is that the emerging bureaucratic structures in firms are having a significant impact on the ways firms operate in the economic transition. Both practices relate to the emergence of rational-legal institutional structures within organizations and a general formalization of labor relationships.

As a final note, I would like to return to the theories of formalization and organizational change. The emergence of formal rational bureaucracies in Chinese workplaces fits more clearly with the institutionalist perspective on formalization than with rationalist or efficiency theories of organizational structure. Institutional theory predicts that organizations adopt institutions for reasons of legitimacy and that this logic does not necessarily adhere to the model of action described by neoclassical and efficiency theories of organizations. Organizations exist in institutional environments, and the decisions and practices they adopt reflect the norms, cultures, and pressures of these environments. They adopt decisions and practices that are less associated with issues of efficiency and productivity than with ideas about what these decisions and practices mean in a cultural and normative sense. Sectoral effects that are significant, net of a number of other organizational characteristics, suggest a mechanism of mimicry at the sector level; the background of a firm's general manager indicates that professionalism and an economic conception of the firm are emerging as factors in new approaches to firm management. Most important, however, are the significant effects of joint-venture relationships on the adoption of new institutions at the firm level. It is likely that Chinese firms are mimicking the practices of foreign firms, adopting the practices they observe in other successful firms. Firms may also be adopting these practices for reasons of legitimacy in the eyes of potential foreign partners in order to attract foreign investment. While Chinese firms may be embracing Western-style structures with the long-term goal of becoming more efficient, they are adopting these specific institutional structures because they are *perceived* as being efficient based on the success of Western companies, not because of a rational calculus of profit maximization. Such motives raise questions about rationalist theories of organizational structure and fit closely with notions set forth in institutional theory and economic sociology.

Four

Changing Labor Relations in the Period of Market Reform

> Despite the importance of organizations for stratification
> . . . research on stratification—at least until recently—
> generally ignores organizations. Instead, most studies of
> earnings differences focus either on (a) differences between
> individuals (e.g., as in the status attainment tradition in
> sociology or the human capital framework in economics) or
> (b) differences between societies or large geographic
> units. . . . Earnings differences are generated at multiple
> levels: at the organizational level; within organizations due
> to characteristics of occupations, jobs, and individuals; and
> between organizations due to industrial differences,
> patterns of unionization, and other contextual variations.
> *(Kalleberg et al. 1996)*

> Of course, the simplest thing would be to put everyone on
> contract and not be responsible in the long term for anyone.
> But it's actually not so easy to do this. The labor contract
> system really only started in 1990 [for us]. Virtually all
> workers who started working after this time have been put
> on contracts. But what do we do with workers who have
> been with our company for so many years of their lives? It's
> not fair just to say to them now: "OK, now you have to sign
> a contract." It's complicated, and we have to look at it on a
> case-by-case basis. We have to take care of the workers
> who have been with us for so many years of their lives.
> *(Industrial manager; Interview 41*, 1995)*

IN CHAPTER 3 I showed that a combination of economic and institutional factors matter for the adoption of various organizational structures. In this chapter I extend that argument to an analysis of changing labor relationships in the transition era. I focus on two central issues of the economic transition with respect to labor relations: remuneration and the redefinition of the labor relationship through emergence of the labor contract [*laodong hetong*], an institution that, in effect, marks the end of the socialist institution of lifetime employment.

In the first case, benefits and pay are central to labor arrangements and organizational survival because, inasmuch as benefits and pay are tied to incentives, a central question for firms is how an enterprise should remunerate employees in a market economy. Command economies are typically known for keeping wages low, while offering a range of living benefits that are tied to the workplace. As wages have risen over the years of economic reform in China, enterprises have staggered under the burden of anachronistic policies of extensive workplace benefits. How the dispensation of wages and benefits is changing in the reform era is a central issue of the reforms.

In the second case, lifetime employment, as the defining feature of the work unit under the planned economy in China, was the very essence of the labor relationship that existed between enterprises and workers. Workers entered their work unit, and, from that moment on, the work unit was the social system that dispensed their salary, housing, medical insurance, and any other benefits the unit might offer. This relationship would extend through the worker's retirement. With tightening fiscal constraints, lifetime employment has exacerbated the burdens of workplace benefits, and redefining the labor relationship has become a central issue for the industrial reform. Many broad institutional changes have emerged to redefine the labor relationship, including the new pension system, [*yanglao jin*], the Labor Law [*laodongfa*], and the existence of Labor Arbitration Commissions [*laodong zhongcai weiyuanhui*]. However, as I have emphasized in previous chapters, to truly understand the gravity and meaning of these broader institutional changes, the analysis must focus on how these changes are actually shaping the experiences of workers and environments at the firm level.

Wages and Nonwage Benefits in Transition Economies

Many studies have examined economic transitions through the use of individual-level data on wages and income.[1] Based on changes in individuals' income, certain inferences have been made about how individuals are now experiencing labor markets and economic opportunities. Many of the studies in this area share in common the desire to extend their analyses of wages to theoretical and substantive conclusions about the institutional changes and the forces at work in economic transitions from socialism to capitalism. However, although wages are a critical indicator of changes in social and economic structure in transitional periods, this type of data is limited in a few important ways. The main problem here is that individual-level data rarely reveal directly how broader institutional structures affect wages. Scholars often can only make crude guesses or inferences about broader institutional variation from the individual-level changes that are observed. For example, while Peng (1992, 198) concludes that "property-rights theorists may have overemphasized the relationship between types of property ownership and the behavior of firms, including the wage determination process," his data are unable to test the effect of government administrative rank, a factor other scholars have convincingly shown to be linked to remuneration across Chinese urban industrial organizations.[2] In China's transition economy, the institutional structure of state administration is central to the ways that property rights are exercised at least as much, if not more so, than distinctions between state and collective ownership; thus, to draw conclusions about property rights, research on remuneration should control for this variable.[3] Similarly, Xie and Hannum (1996, 37) attempt to connect their findings to broader institutional issues such as labor markets (or the lack thereof) and property rights, and they see their results fitting with theories "that give primary attention to institutions as agents of stratification in socialist and reforming socialist economies." Yet actual data on these institutional effects are barely addressed in Xie and Hannum's analysis.[4] In a sociological study of economic transitions, we need to be able to observe specific differences across the institutional environments in which the units of analysis are situated. Despite the strengths of individual-level data on income, collection of data at the individual level often makes it difficult to connect this type of data to the broader organizational and institutional environment. To some extent, what is needed is an analysis positioned to deal with larger questions of institutional environments in order to examine changes in the distribution of wages (and nonwage benefits) in China's economic transition. We need an approach that complements these individual-level analyses, one that explores more explicitly institutional environments and industrial structure, issues that studies based on individual-level data are unable to illuminate.

Walder's (1992a) study on the redistributive mechanisms of the planned economy points us in the right direction in this area of research. Walder's central interest is in what organizations' remunerative practices (in terms of how they distribute nonwage benefits) can tell us about the institutional environments in which firms are situated (in the command economy). Walder's work in this area is important because instead of focusing on income at the individual level, he emphasizes the organizational level and the ways that institutional structures affect organizations' abilities to reward workers. Discussion of the topic at the organizational level draws attention to the mechanisms that constrain the distribution of wealth for organizations. Bian's (1994a, see especially chap. 7) study of wages is also able to link the effects of organizational, industrial, and political institutional structure to income at the individual level. Thus he is able to show the effects of such organizational variables as bureaucratic rank, size, and location in various sectors. Both Walder's and Bian's studies, while beginning with individual-level survey data, are careful to take into account firm structure and a firm's position in state administrative hierarchies. Both these studies also raise intriguing questions: Do the same mechanisms that are important for the distribution of benefits at the organizational level (analyzed by Walder) affect wages? Will an analysis of both wages and nonwage benefits at the organizational level show similar patterns across the indicators or will the distribution of wages be significantly different from that of nonwage benefits? In the first part of this chapter I examine remuneration as a function of organizational and institutional variables by observing the average wages that organizations paid to their workers in 1994 and the nonwage benefits organizations offered in the reform era.

Wages

The logic of a command economy virtually requires what Walder refers to as a "frozen wage structure."[5] Naughton (1995) discusses the economic structure of command economies, pointing out that control of income is very important for the structure of the command economy. Markets are artificial or, in many cases, virtually nonexistent in a command economy, and "a rough balance must be struck between household demand for consumer goods and their supply."[6] Because the state controls prices and (theoretically) supply, it must also control household income, which mediates demand. The state is not always able to make this balance work, and the result is a "shortage economy."[7] This general structure of the command economy was complemented by "Maoist asceticism," which held wages remarkably constant in prereform times.[8]

Thus, as the state was in close control of wages and household income throughout the prereform period, this control over wages was intimately tied to control over enterprises and over the industrial economy more generally. With the beginning of the economic reform, changes in wage distribution came quickly. The "self-responsibility" and profit-retention policies allowed firms to raise workers' wages, and in many cases, especially in the early years of reform, enterprises did just that.[9] There were two reasons why enterprises raised wages (usually in the form of bonuses) rapidly in the early part of the economic reform. First, bonuses were the primary incentives through which firms could tap individual motivation, a centerpiece to the rhetoric of Deng Xiaoping's economic reforms. Second, and more important, in the early years of the reform enterprises were still operating under soft-budget constraints, and by increasing bonuses they were often able to evade the new accounting regulations that would tax higher base wages.[10]

Not surprisingly, as organizations have tried to keep up with the rising cost of living in urban areas, the rapid increase in wages has become an economic constraint for them.[11] As one manager in the foods sector explained:

> The responsibilities of state-owned organizations are heavier than most, and it is hard for us to keep up with the rise in costs. Over the last few years our costs have

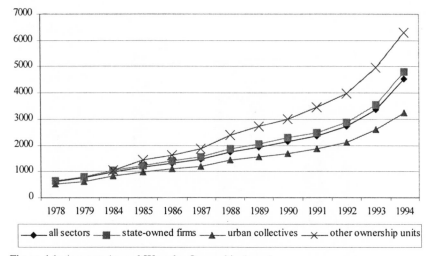

Figure 4.1: Average Annual Wage by Ownership (yuan)
Source: Zhongguo tongji nianjian (Statistical yearbook of China), 1995

been rising much faster than our production. Three years ago the average annual salary for our workers was around six thousand to seven thousand RMB. Last year the average salary was closer to ten thousand. We have had to increase salaries to keep up with the rising cost of living in Shanghai. But our production has not kept up with the rising costs. . . . Our profits have been going down steadily every year. Last year we just about broke even. (Interview 84*, 1995)

As the economic transition has progressed—and as economic constraints began to play a more serious role in the decisions of organizations—wages have become intimately tied to organizational constraints.

Figure 4.1 shows that average annual wages have risen from about 600 RMB in 1978 to 4,538 RMB in 1994, an increase in overall wages of more than 600 percent. In addition, real wages (cost-of-living adjusted) have risen at an average annual rate of 5.4 percent since 1978. The figure also shows that, over time, there is increasing variation in remunerative practices across different organizational types. Wages in urban collectives tend to be lower than average wages in state-owned organizations, which are generally lower than wages in privately owned and joint-ventured organizations.[12]

What can we learn about changes in wage distribution from the sample of firms I have engaged for this study? Changes in wage distribution in industrial Shanghai will give us some insight into the factors associated with changes in remunerative practices more generally in China's economic transition. The institutional and economic changes of the economic transition leave us with several questions regarding the distribution of wages. First, from the

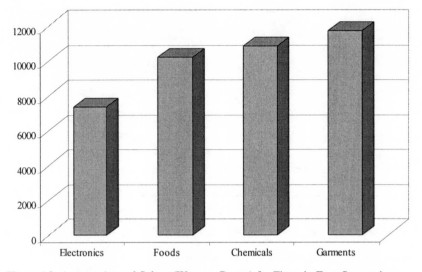

Figure 4.2: Average Annual Salary (Wages + Bonus) for Firms in Four Sectors in Industrial Shanghai, 1995

perspective of tightening fiscal constraints and increasing factory responsibility discussed earlier (chapter 2), we can predict that wages are also somewhat dependent on the organization's economic well-being. Figure 4.1 indicates that wage differentials are somewhat dependent on organizational types in terms of property rights (collectives vs. state-owned). This is also a testable hypothesis with respect to wages in the economic transition. Walder's (1992a) work on the distribution of benefits under the command economy has illuminated the importance of government administrative rank. In the analysis below I address each of these issues.[13]

Figure 4.2 shows the average wages for the organizations in my sample by sector. It is apparent from the figure that organizations in the electronics sector pay considerably lower wages than organizations in other sectors of Shanghai's industrial economy. This is not surprising given that the electronics sector was often cited by my interviewees as among the most troubled sectors in the reform era, and a higher percentage of organizations in the electronics sector reported losses in 1994 than did any of the other sectors represented in my study.[14] Although location in the electronics sector has a significant, negative effect on wages even controlling for other organizational effects, I will show that a number of other organizational and institutional parameters also matter in the dispensation of wages by organizations.

For the sectors included in my study, the results presented in Table 4.1 show that a combination of economic constraints and political factors matter for the wages organizations give their employees in the economic transition.[15] Be-

TABLE 4.1

Ordinary Least Squares Coefficients for the Determinants Average Annual Salary (ln) in Four Industrial Sectors, Shanghai, 1995

Independent variables	B	S.E.
Organizational variables[a]		
Chemicals	−.06	.15
Electronics	−.39**	.13
Garments	.05	.13
Active employees (ln)	−.04	.05
Employee ratio	−.03	.03
Organizational health	−.02	.27
Losses, 1990	−.22**	.10
Products exported, 1990	−.003**	.001
Joint venture	.40***	.10
State-owned	−.01	.11
Governance variables		
GM w/bus./econ. backgrnd.	.02	.15
Municipal company	.15*	.08
Constant	9.37***	.28
R^2		.39
No. of cases		81

Note: See Appendix 4 for discussion of variables. B is the effect of the coefficient; S.E. is the standard error. * $p < .1$ ** $p < .05$ *** $p < .01$ (two-tailed tests). Variables in bold are statistically significant.

[a] Reference category for sector is foods.

sides location in the electronics sector, poor economic performance (as indicated by losses in 1990), the percentage of the products the organization exported in 1990, the existence of a joint-venture relationship, and position in the state administrative hierarchy are all tied to wages. The effect of poor economic performance on wages suggests that tightening fiscal constraints are having an impact of organizational decisions in the urban industrial economy. Organizations that are performing poorly in the economic transition have struggled to make ends meet and, as a result, have raised wages at a slower rate than have other firms. The effect of a firm's export market shows that the types of markets in which organizations are engaged has an impact on the wage structure of workers in the organizations. Organizations that are exporting a significant portion of their products often have their workers operating on piece-rate rather than fixed-rate salaries, which often turn out to be lower than the latter. In addition, organizations seeking to capture a share of a given export market have added incentive to keep costs low, as their success in the export markets often depends largely on their ability to deliver products to an international contractor for the lowest price. Organizations that have joint-venture relations with foreign partners pay their workers more because, at least in part, the managers of these organizations have direct contact with management practices from market economies. They are thus likely to have a clearer sense of the link between incentives and productivity. It may also be that joint-venture relations are an indirect proxy of economic strength and that the joint-venture effect on wages is tied to economic strength. It should be noted, however, that the joint-venture effect is significant net of other indicators of economic health, indicating that the joint-venture relationship has some other significance above and beyond its tie to a firm's economic health. Finally, consistent with the findings presented in chapter 3, organizations under the jurisdiction of municipal companies in Shanghai appear to be aggressively pursuing organizational change in a number of different ways, including changing their employees' incentive structures.

The findings presented here show that economic constraints, a firm's position in the institutional hierarchy of the former command economy, and the models of organizational management to which Chinese firms are exposed all influence a given organization's wage structure in the reform era. Where Bian (1994a, 171) found that "state ownership and bureaucratic rank are significant predictors of both bonuses and salaries," I present a picture that is different in subtle ways. In my sample of firms, state ownership is not a significant predictor of wages, and bureaucratic rank does not increase wages in a monotonic fashion. Instead, organizations at specific levels of the state hierarchy are institutionalizing changes in similar ways, as are those exposed to foreign models of organizational management.

Nonwage Benefits

Nonwage benefits are also a crucial part of remunerative practices in socialist societies, especially in the case of China. Walder's (1992a) analysis of the distribution of nonwage benefits under China's planned economy showed that remuneration under the old system depended on variation in resource dependence at different levels of state administration.[16] Walder found that the administrative rank of a firm's governing organization was a critical factor in the distribution of nonwage benefits across organizations and thus was critical as a mechanism of stratification in the planned economy.

Walder's institutional perspective points the direction for an analysis of nonwage benefits in the transition era. Two issues are of particular interest here. First, inasmuch as Walder's study is based on individual-level data, are there any other crucial structural and economic factors that contribute to *organizational* decisions in these realms?[17] Does an organization's economic situation matter for the distribution of nonwage benefits? In other words, do profit

TABLE 4.2

Logistic Regressions for the Determinants of Housing Benefits Offered by Organizations in Four Industrial Sectors, Shanghai, 1995

Independent variables	B	S.E.
Organizational variables[a]		
Chemicals	−1.54	2.10
Electronics	−2.77*	1.45
Garments	−1.70*	.97
Active employees (ln)	.98	.68
Employee ratio	−.70*	.39
Organizational health	.56	.62
Profit margin, avg. 1990–1994	−.11*	.06
Losses, 1990	−2.39*	1.34
Joint venture	1.24	.90
Governance variables		
GM w/ bus./econ. backgrnd.	−.44	.87
Municipal bureau	4.08**	1.77
Municipal company	2.23**	1.08
Constant	−3.67	3.50
χ^2	63.09***	
No. of cases	81	

Note: See Appendix 4 for discussion of variables. B is the effect of the coefficient; S.E. is the standard error. * $p < .1$ ** $p < .05$ *** $p < .01$ (two-tailed tests). Variables in bold are statistically significant.

[a] Reference category for sector is foods.

margins, losses, and general economic health matter for the distribution of benefits across organizations in the economic transition? Second, inasmuch as Walder's study is about the distribution of nonwage benefits under the pre-reform system, it gives rise to several questions about the economic transition. Is administrative rank as important in the economic transition as it was under the old system? In the economic transition, is the distribution of housing significantly different from other benefits, as Walder found to be the case under the command economy?

In Tables 4.2 and 4.3, we again see that a combination of economic constraints and political institutions matter for the decisions organizations make in the reform era. First, Table 4.2 shows that, net of other organizational effects, there is sectoral variation on the likelihood that an organization offers housing in the transition era: Organizations in the electronics and garments sectors are significantly less likely than those in the foods sector to offer the benefit of housing. Profits and losses are both tied to the likelihood that an organization will offer housing. The loss effect is fairly straightforward, the clearest evidence that economic constraints matter for organizational decisions regarding the benefits they offer their workers in the transition era. Housing is an expensive benefit, and if an organization has been struggling to survive in the economic transition (as indicated by whether it lost money in 1990), it will be significantly less likely to offer this benefit. If economic constraints do matter, the negative association between an organization's profit margin and the likelihood that the organization will offer housing is somewhat enigmatic—given that losses reduce the likelihood of housing, we would expect that profits would increase that likelihood. However, the effect of an organization's profit margin is not only one of economic comfort but also an indicator of an organization's approach to the economic reforms. The organizations that are performing the best in the transition economy are those that have undertaken aggressive changes in the structure and operations of their workplaces; they have adopted organizational strategies and structures that most clearly reflect market economic principles. One way these aggressive developers have cut costs is through the elimination of expensive benefits such as housing.

An organization's employee ratio is negatively associated with the likelihood that the organization will offer housing. In other words, the more retired workers an organization has, relative to its active employees, the more likely the organization is to offer housing to its employees. This is also somewhat counterintuitive: As the employee ratio is one facet of an organization's economic burden, we would expect that housing benefits would vary in a positive way with an organization's employee ratio—the more healthy the organization is on this parameter, the more likely it would be to have resources for housing. However, benefits such as housing are not only based on economic considerations; they are also based on institutional and political factors in the organization. With respect to the employee-ratio effect, the organizations that have a large number of retired employees tend to be the older state-run organizations that were the model of the socialist work unit established under Mao.[18] These organizations usually offered their employees some form of housing benefits, and that institution has carried over into the reform era. In addition, organizations that have a large number of retired employees have greater responsibility with respect to their workers overall, and housing is one of the ways they compensate their employees.

Consistent with Walder's argument about housing benefits in the prereform era, Table 4.2 shows that organizational policies on housing benefits in reform-era China vary according to a firm's position in the administrative hierarchy of the former command economy. The higher a firm sits in the administrative hierarchy, the more likely it is to offer the benefit of housing.[19] However, where Walder argued that the significance of a firm's position in the hierarchy for the benefit of housing reflected greater access to state resources for upper-level firms in prereform China, it is likely that other factors are present in today's China. Later in this chapter, and again in chapter 6, I introduce evidence that resources have been significantly tightened for firms at the upper levels of China's administrative hierarchy, particularly those under the jurisdiction of municipal bureaus. And if upper-level firms are being cut off from access to state resources, as other data in this study indicate, it would be simplistic to assume that the significance of bureau governance for firms is simply a function of continued access to state fiscal resources. One surely important element here is the path dependence of institutions, systems, and structures at the organizational level. Once a given structure is set in place in an organization, that structure becomes an inextricable part of the organization; similarly, once a given cluster of benefits is associated with employment in an organization, these benefits become tied to the workplace. For a number of reasons—from employee expectations to the fact that an organization owns real estate—organizations do not simply cut off the benefit of housing when fiscal resources are tightened, and organizations that offered a given benefit in the past are significantly more likely to offer that benefit today.

The results presented in Table 4.3 are similar to those regarding housing, with a few important additions. In terms of overall benefits offered, organizations in the chemicals and electronics sectors offer significantly fewer benefits than those in the foods sector. The number of benefits an organization offers varies with size, with larger organizations offering more benefits than smaller ones. It is interesting that although the presence of a joint venture is not a significant predictor of housing benefits, it is a significant predictor of the total number of benefits an organization offers. It is unlikely, though, that we are observing a causal effect here, as many of the benefits we are seeing have a history that predates joint-venture relationships. It is clear, however, that joint-venture relationships, while they have given rise to higher salaries, have not curtailed the socialist institutions of work unit benefits. On the contrary, organizations with joint-venture partnerships are likely to raise wages *and* continue to offer benefits to their employees. Finally, we see more evidence here of the notion that general managers who are schooled in business or economics or both are transforming the internal organization of the workplaces they oversee. While these general managers are institutionalizing formal rational structures in the workplace (chapter 3), they are also aggressively cutting costs by eliminating extensive workplace benefits.

Workplace benefits are dependent on a combination of economic constraints and the institutional structure of state administration. That economic constraints are beginning to shape the workplace environment says important things about the progress of the economic transition. Organizations are no longer simply drawing funds from state coffers, and, as fiscal constraints are tightening in the transition era, they are beginning to make decisions that account for these fiscal constraints. However, the institutional history of workplace benefits also matters here, as organizations that were most favored in the

TABLE 4.3

Ordinal Logit for the Determinants of the Total Number of Benefits
Offered by Organizations in Four Industrial Sectors, Shanghai,
1995

Independent variables	B	S.E.
Organizational variables[a]		
Chemicals	−2.41***	.89
Electronics	−3.36***	.88
Garments	−.49	.60
Active employees (ln)	2.06***	.40
Employee ratio	−3.92**	1.64
Organizational health	.50	.83
Profit margin, avg. 1990–1994	−.06**	.02
Losses, 1990	−1.07	.67
Joint venture	2.03***	.63
Governance variables		
GM w/bus./econ. backgrnd.	−1.18***	.49
Municipal bureau	.76***	.27
Municipal company	.96***	.33
Pseudo R^2		.37
No. of cases		79

Note: See Appendix 4 for discussion of variables. B is the effect of the
coefficient; S.E. is the standard error. ** $p < .05$ *** $p < .01$ (two-tailed
tests). Variables in bold are statistically significant. Benefits included in the
dependent variable are housing, medical coverage for family members,
medical clinic, childcare, kindergarten, retail shop, commuter bus, and
library.

[a] Reference category for sector is foods.

command economy remain significantly more likely to offer benefits such as
housing in the reform era.

In the next part of this chapter, I turn my attention to a new institution in the
transition economy, the labor contract, which marks a fundamental shift in
employment relations. Organizational practices regarding this institution also
show the complex interplay between economic uncertainty and the institutional structure of state administration.

Labor Contracts

While changes in benefits are reshaping organizations in China, the nature of
the labor relationship itself also provides a fundamental shift in the structure of
the workplace. Under the command economy, the state all but guaranteed em-

ployment.[20] As a document from the State Council put it in 1983: "The current system of employment in China, under which the majority are permanent workers, in practice operates as a kind of unconditional system of life tenure" (PRC 1983a).[21] Workers were assigned to work units by the Labor Bureau, and from that point on, the work unit was responsible for dispensing income, benefits, and retirement pay for the rest of the worker's life. In different periods, especially in the late 1970s, a small fraction of the population was classified as "waiting for employment" [diaye], but for the most part, the state still fulfilled its promise to find employment for everyone.[22] Although, by 1980, state sector jobs had become more competitive than ever before (only 37 percent of workers were assigned jobs in state enterprises [guoyou qiye]), still 80 percent of workers were assigned jobs in either state enterprises or collectively owned enterprises [jiti qiye] in that year.[23] Once jobs were assigned, except in rare cases of disciplinary firing and even rarer cases of layoffs (which were often followed by reassignment to another enterprise), the job assignment was for life. This is not to say that workers never changed jobs or resigned from a given enterprise. But once they were assigned to a work unit, except in exceptional circumstances, workers had the option of staying at that organization for life.

The emergence of labor contracts in China marks an important turning point for the socialist system created under Mao. Labor contracts began a new system in which enterprises are only responsible to workers for as long as the contract specifies. If the enterprise and individual sign a one-, three-, or five-year contract, the enterprise is only responsible for the worker for that period of time and is under no obligation to renew the contract at the end of that period. The enterprise also has no obligation, at the end of a contract period, to continue to pay workers income or benefits. One manager in the chemicals sector explained the gravity of this change:

> The labor situation has changed tremendously over the last few years. . . . I think that probably the most significant change is that now we have everyone on labor contracts. Now if workers violate the terms of their contracts, they can be fired. . . . We've never had this type of labor relationship before. (Interview 103*, 1995)[24]

The labor contract was officially introduced in 1986 with Document 77 and Decree 99, both promulgated by the State Council.[25] These documents explicitly define three types of contracts: the fixed limited-term contract [guding qixian laodong hetong], the nonfixed limited-term contract [wuguding qixian laodong hetong], and the per-project work limited-term contract [yixiang gongzuo wei qixian laodong hetong].[26] Although these institutional arrangements officially emerged in 1986, experimentation with labor contracts dates back as early as 1983, as defined by the 1983 State Council Notice for Trial Implementation (PRC 1983a). Following the 1986 documents, the legitimacy of the labor contract was further enhanced by the Enterprise Law (PRC 1988a,

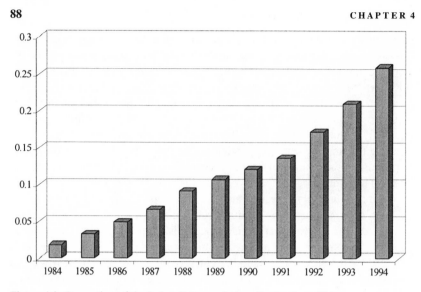

Figure 4.3: Proportion of the Labor Force on Labor Contracts in China
Source: *Zhongguo tongji nianjian* (Statistical yearbook of China), 1995

chap. 3, art. 31), which states that "the enterprise shall have the right to employ or dismiss its staff members and workers in accordance with the provisions of the State Council." Though such a statement does not sound extreme with regard to enterprise rights in market economies, turning over the rights of hiring and dismissing workers to the enterprise was radical in the context of China's recent institutional history. Other institutional changes, such as the establishment of the unemployment and social security funds, set up to protect workers in the event their organization would dismiss them in the "reoptimization" movement, have also given legitimacy to the use of labor contracts.[27]

Figure 4.3 shows that the proportion of the industrial labor force on labor contracts has risen steadily and significantly since 1984. In 1984, 1.8 percent of the labor force, or 2,090,000 individuals, were on labor contracts.[28] By 1994, about 26 percent of the labor force, or 38,390,000 individuals, were on labor contracts. By sector, the labor contract has been most readily adopted in manufacturing, where 41 percent of workers were on labor contracts in 1994.[29]

In the sections that follow I address two questions. The first focuses on what the rise and adoption of the labor contract tells us about the empirical reality of economic transition in China: Which firms are adopting the labor contract in China, how are they using it, and why? The second question centers on the implications of this study of economic models of decision making surrounding institutional arrangements and institutional change: What does the case of the labor contract in China tell us about models of economic behavior in industrial societies, especially with respect to economic transitions from socialism to a more market-oriented system?

Retired Workers, Factory Burdens, and Labor Contracts in Shanghai

In industrial organizations many factory managers see the issues of lifetime employment and the overemployment that came with state distribution of labor as *the* central challenges of industrial reform. As the state distributed labor irrespective of enterprise need under the command economy, enterprises now are paying the price with bloated workforces that outstrip the needs of the enterprise in terms of running machinery and the enterprise's general production capacity. One manager in the chemicals sector explained his factory's situation:

> We have 676 workers and more than 200 retired workers, so our economic burden is very heavy. Actually, this issue is one of the biggest problems China is having right now in terms of the economic reform. Enterprises have always been set up to take care of their workers as one of their primary functions. So [under the old system] workers would just be distributed to the factories whether they were needed or not. . . . This is the problem with state-owned enterprises. Not only do we have 200 retired workers to care for, but we also have 2 or 3 workers doing the task 1 worker could do. It's impossible to be competitive with that kind of responsibility. We have a joint venture [a factory investment with a foreign partner] that is doing really well. It has 100 workers, and they produce about the same amount that our factory produces every year. How can we compete with them when we both have the same volume of production and turnover, but they are paying salaries and benefits for 100 workers and we are paying for almost 900 workers. It's impossible. (Interview 99*, 1995)

This manager's main complaint was about overemployment and the trouble it poses for market competition. Managers see their organizations as unable to compete in the market when they are struggling against organizations that have workforces (and therefore overhead) that are significantly less than those of the state- and collectively owned organizations in China's economy. The manager's reference to the joint venture expresses the issue of competition explicitly: They are producing the same amount as the joint-venture factory in which they have invested, yet they are paying an overhead of roughly six times what the joint venture is paying.[30] Another manager in the electronics sector connected this issue to development:

> The biggest problem that our state- [and collectively] owned enterprises have is retired workers. We are taking care of so many people in comparison with the number other private companies take care of. We can't compete with them in terms of development. They take all their profits and put them back into the company; we have to use all our profits to take care of workers who are no longer working here.

And many of these retired people are even working at other companies, but they still come here every month to get their pay. (Interview 41*, 1995)

As economic and administrative responsibilities are placed more directly on enterprises (through independent accounting and self-responsibility systems), the enterprises themselves, not the state, are responsible for using revenues to cover income, benefit, and the organization's retirement costs. If factories have to spend all their income on overhead, there is little left over for development projects that could cover anything from the upgrading of machinery to diversification investments.

These issues and perspectives bear directly on the labor relationship between the work unit and employees. Industrial officials in China posit that the labor contract was set forth as an institution to protect workers in the emerging market economy. As one official in the Labor Bureau put it:

> The purpose of the contract is to set up an institutional system that protects the workers. (Interview 31, 1995)[31]

The argument here is that as the state turns more direct control of administrative and economic decisions over to enterprises, the workers will need institutional guarantees and protections in lieu of the state's direct action on their behalf. However, although this view may be the state's official line on the labor contract, managers have a variety of opinions on the purpose and function of contracts. Many managers view them as a way of institutionalizing a legalistic and formalized relationship between the enterprise and the worker, which protects the organization as much as it does the worker. As a manager of an organization in the electronics sector explained:

> The labor contract highlights a very important change in the conduct of both workers and the organization. If a worker is acting against the contract [*weifan hetong*], we can just fire that worker. If we, as management, act against the contract, the worker can take us to the Labor Arbitration Commission. It's really a two-sided approach to the labor relation. (Interview 55*, 1995)

Other managers point out more directly that the labor contract's function as an institution is quite complicated. One manager, also from the electronics sector, explained:

> The establishment of contracts with workers is very complicated in China today. Contracts are useful for protecting both the worker and the employer. For both, once there is a contract, there can be no confusion about what is expected of the worker and what the employer is allowed to demand. It is good for the worker because the employer cannot exploit the worker. But it is also good for the employer. It used to be that once an organization hired a worker, that organization had lifelong responsibility for that worker. So bringing on a worker was a long-term financial commitment. The organizations had no choice about this. But now the iron rice bowl has

been broken, and an organization can decide how and when it wants to hire workers. The contracts allow us to control how long we employ workers. (Interview 37, 1995)

A manager from the foods sector discussed the complexity of the issue in a similar way:

We have many retired employees because we are an old company. All the people who were with the company and retired before we had labor contracts are the company's responsibility for as long as they live. The contracts are set up partly to offer protection for workers. But they also help to protect the factories. Under the old system, if someone worked for a factory, the factory was responsible for the well-being of that individual for as long as she or he lived. Now, because contracts specify a fixed amount of time for a worker to be hired, enterprises are protected from this type of lifetime commitment. (Interview 78*, 1995)

Thus the labor contract benefits both the worker and the factory. For the worker, an institutionally secure system replaces the void left by the state's retreat in its direct handling of employment matters. As administrative and economic responsibilities are handed over to the enterprises, a system is being established that allows workers to see their rights specified explicitly in a contract. The contract binds the factory to uphold its end of the bargain for the time specified. Other new institutions, such as the Labor Arbitration Commissions constructed in the late 1980s, help support the institutional guarantees specified in labor contracts. But, as the managers quoted above have indicated, the enterprise also enjoys direct benefits from this institution. The labor contract protects organizations by allowing them to hire workers for a finite period of time. They can bring in new workers—or transform their relationships with old workers—under an institutional guarantee that protects the factory from the economic burden of lifetime employment.

How organizations are approaching this change varies considerably, and my analysis below illuminates the organizational factors behind the decision to implement this fundamental shift in the labor relationship. My interviews reveal a distinction among organizations with regard to labor contracts: some have put all their workers on labor contracts (in other words, have implemented the labor contract on an organizationwide basis); others have put only some of their workers on labor contracts (have not implemented the labor contract on an organizationwide basis). The analysis that follows deals primarily with the former, that is, those organizations that have adopted labor contracts for *all* their employees.[32] Why have some organizations implemented the labor contract—and thus ended lifetime employment—throughout the organization, whereas other have only incorporated this change in a piecemeal fashion? What does this tell us about the shifting nature of labor relations in China's economic transition? How do these changes fit with other models of economic action surrounding institutional agreements?

Institutionalizing the Labor Contract in Shanghai's Industrial Firms

It could be that some organizations simply conform to the institutional practice of putting workers on labor contracts but actually view the contract as doing little to alter the organization-employee relationship. As one manager in the chemicals sector described:

> We've had 100 percent of our workers on labor contracts since 1993. But I'll tell you something about the labor contract: It really doesn't mean much for state-owned factories. State-owned enterprises are still state-owned, and they are still this country's social security system. As long as that's the case, we can't just let workers go or fire them. And as long as we still have to keep workers on no matter what—unless they do something really bad, but this rarely happens—labor contracts will have little meaning. Little really has changed since we started making workers sign labor contracts. It's just a procedure we do. (Interview 99*, 1995)

This manager's view of the labor contract as being largely symbolic and procedural is noteworthy. In cases such as these, adoption of the labor contract does not have the same meaning as in firms that see the contract as fundamentally altering the labor relationship. To control for this possibility, managers were asked the following question: "Can workers in your organization who are on labor contracts be fired [at the end of the contract or in cases of extreme transgression]?" If the manager answered no, this indicated that the labor contract was not a meaningful institutional change in the organization.[33]

Figure 4.4 shows the institutionalization of the labor contract on an organizationwide basis by sector. In the chemicals sector, 100 percent of the organizations surveyed had institutionalized the labor contract on an organizationwide basis. The foods sector is similar to the chemicals sector in that nearly all (90 percent) of the firms surveyed had institutionalized the practice organizationwide. Use of the labor contract in the garments and electronics sectors are different from that in the foods and chemicals sectors. Firms in the garments and electronics sectors have only gradually institutionalized the labor contract organizationwide, and, by 1994, still fewer than half the firms surveyed in these sectors had institutionalized labor contracts throughout their organizations.

Table 4.4 shows once again that a combination of economic and institutional factors influence this significant transformation of employment relations in China. From an economic perspective, both organizational health and a firm's employee ratio are negatively associated with a firm's decision to institutionalize labor contracts on an organizationwide basis. In other words, the poorer the organization is faring economically in the transition era and the more burdensome its employment situation, the more likely it is that the organization will place all its employees on labor contracts. That firms in poor

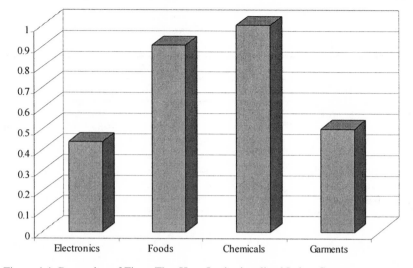

Figure 4.4: Proportion of Firms That Have Institutionalized Labor Contracts on an Organization-wide Basis in Four Sectors in Industrial Shanghai, 1995

economic shape are more likely to institutionalize labor contracts for all employees supports the idea that some firms are using labor contracts as a form of protection against the economic burdens of lifetime employment. Lifetime employment of large workforces (both active and retired workers) is among the greatest burdens enterprises are experiencing in the economic transition, and organizations in poor financial shape are barely able to stay afloat precisely because of labor costs. Thus, when the institutional opportunity to end lifetime employment arose, firms began to take advantage of this opportunity in accordance with their economic health. Firms in better shape financially have not implemented the labor contract throughout their enterprises, allowing some workers to remain as lifetime employees. Consistent with this finding, the employee ratio, the variable that assesses the impact of the retired labor force on an organization's decisions regarding the labor contract, shows a significant negative effect in this model. The negative association between this variable and the organizationwide adoption of the labor contract indicates that firms with healthier (less burdensome) employment ratios are less likely to take advantage of this institutional change and completely shift the nature of the labor relationship.

Net of other effects, firms under the jurisdiction of a municipal bureau are about *forty* times (exp[3.67] = 39.25) more likely to institutionalize labor contracts than those at lower levels of the hierarchy. This finding suggests that organizations at the upper levels of China's administrative hierarchy are experiencing the reforms in significant ways and are experimenting with various market practices to deal with the uncertainty of their reform experiences. Based on evidence of slow gains in productivity, Walder (1995a) hypothesized

TABLE 4.4

Logistic Coefficients for the Decision to Place 100 Percent of Employees on Labor Contracts for
Organizations in Four Industrial Sectors, Shanghai, 1995

	Model I		Model II		Model III	
Independent variables	B	S.E.	B	S.E.	B	S.E.
Organizational variables[a]						
Chemicals	37.31	41.90	38.88	31.56	27.75	41.36
Electronics	−5.67***	1.49	−5.47***	1.70	−4.80***	1.37
Garments	−2.61***	.99	−2.49**	1.00	−2.59***	.95
Active employees (ln)	−.60	.64	−.47	.63	−.17	.51
Employee ratio	−.06**	.03	−.05**	.02	−.03	.02
Organizational health	−.12*	.07	−.13*	.08	.09	.70
Profit margin, avg. 1990–1994	−.03	.05	−.03	.05	.01	.05
Losses, 1990	.09	1.10	−.29	1.14	.28	1.01
Joint venture	1.40	.80	1.37	.91	1.38	.88
Governance variables						
GM w/bus./econ. backgrnd.	−.21	.80	.10	.81	−.12	.70
Municipal bureau	3.67**	1.60	1.25**	.57	—	—
Municipal company	1.60	1.28	.72	.65	—	—
Jurisdiction size (ln)	—	—	—	—	.64*	.33
Constant	6.36*	3.75	7.98*	4.37	4.18	3.10
χ^2	45.15***		40.18***		41.46***	
No. of cases	81		75[b]		81	

Note: See Appendix 4 for discussion of variables. * $p < .1$ ** $p < .05$ *** $p < .01$ (two-tailed tests).
Variables in bold are statistically significant.

[a] Reference category for sector is foods.

[b] This model omits those firms (N = 6) for which the general manager asserted that individuals could not be
fired even though the organization had instituted the labor contract for all workers. Thus Model II is based on a
sample size of N = 75 instead of N = 81.

that reforms have not been enacted in the upper echelons of China's industrial
hierarchy, specifically arguing that "at the higest levels of the hierarchy of
government . . . the response to the new [financial] incentives has been relatively muted" (p. 270).[34] In other words, weak economic indicators imply a
lack of reform. If we look beyond economic indicators, however, we see a
different picture: Firms at the upper levels of the hierarchy are the most likely
to adopt new institutional changes of the reform era. I argue that the firms that
had the most access to resources under the command economy are now experiencing uncertainty in the market, an indication that budget constraints are
being hardened and that the market reform is becoming a reality for organizations at all levels of the administrative hierarchy.

   Where the economic variables indicate that firms experiencing economic
uncertainty in the transition are more likely to make use of labor contracts on

an organizationwide basis, the governance variable suggests that firms at the upper end of the administrative hierarchy are experiencing a type of administrative uncertainty.[35] Firms at this level are being forced to handle virtually all administrative and economic responsibilities in the reform era, which has created a great deal of uncertainty for these firms. In response to this uncertainty, they adopt practices to help stabilize their economic and administrative position in the reforms. The greater sense of being set adrift by the state at this level of the hierarchy has given these firms cause to embrace the market reforms more fully than their counterparts at lower rungs of the hierarchy. Model II in Table 4.4 excludes the six organizations that had implemented the labor contract organizationwide yet did not see the change as having a major impact on the labor relationship (i.e., they did not believe the labor contract allowed them to end lifetime employment). This model reproduces the results given in Model I, thereby raising confidence in the findings and argument presented here.

As I asserted in chapter 2, part of the variation in levels of governance boils down to the number of organizations over which a government office has jurisdiction. The more firms under a given governing office, the less administrative and economic resources that governing office can offer each firm under its jurisdiction. This is partly why firms under the jurisdiction of municipal bureaus are experiencing the greatest sense of uncertainty in the transition era: With the rapid changes of the economic transition, municipal bureaus simply do not have the administrative resources to help guide all the firms under their jurisdictions through the reforms. Model III in Table 4.4 examines the association between the institutionalization of the labor contract and governance as a function of the size of the jurisdiction in which a firm is situated. The model shows that the larger the jurisdiction, the more likely an organization will be to institutionalize labor contracts on an organizationwide basis. In other words, the more firms with which a given organization has to compete for administrative and economic resources from state administrative offices, the more likely that firm will end the institution of lifetime employment. Those under the largest jurisdictions have the greatest sense of being set adrift by the state, and they are taking advantage of institutional changes that allow them to ease the economic and administrative burdens of the reform era.

Fairness, Loyalty, Socialist Ideals, and Economic Decision Making

The results presented above suggest that, like enterprises in other transition economies, Chinese organizations that are experiencing uncertainty adopt new institutional practices to help them deal with those uncertainties.[36] In the case described above, firms experiencing extreme uncertainty in China's transition take advantage of a new institution forged at the state level that allows them to end lifetime employment. For reasons of economic uncertainty, firms in poor financial shape in the economic transition are more likely to adopt labor contracts throughout the firm; similarly, firms that have onerous burdens of retired workers are more likely to institutionalize labor contracts organizationwide. In administrative uncertainty, organizations under the jurisdiction of municipal bureaus, compared to municipal or district company governance, which are protected by attentive lower-level administrative offices, are more likely to implement labor contracts across the firm. As economic and administrative responsibilities are shifted down the hierarchy of the former command economy, firms at the upper levels of the administrative hierarchy are experiencing the reforms most directly. As a result, these firms are embracing an institution that marks the end to the socialist institution of lifetime employment.

At this point I have provided evidence for why firms are adopting the labor contract as an institutional change. However, the situation also begs the opposite question: Given that the labor contract offers organizations the possibility of ending lifetime employment—a prospect that can only have positive economic results for firms—what would be the incentive not to take full advantage of this institutional change? In other words, why would an organization not seize the opportunity to implement the labor contract throughout the firm? Why would a firm allow some workers to stay on as permanent, lifetime employees?

The first clear distinction regarding the decision not to implement labor contracts has to do with workers' ages and tenure (which are highly correlated) in an organization. New workers—particularly young, new workers—are almost always the first to be put on contract. This is especially true for workers who have been hired after the organization began using labor contracts. Older employees who were part of the organization before the institution arose are most often the ones allowed to stay on as long-term employees when the organization has decided not to adopt contracts across the organization. As one manager in the electronics sector expressed it:

> We have about 20 percent of our employees on labor contracts. Of course, the new people all sign the contracts; this is now a requirement for new employees working here. But the older workers are not the same as the newer ones; they are not in the same situation. They have been here a long time, and it's not really fair to just say, "Now you have to sign a three- or five-year contract." We're having them sign contracts a few at a time. (Interview 63*, 1995)

These comments not only point to the distinction between old and new employees with respect to labor contracts but also indicate the reasoning behind the distinction. Basically, two factors come into play in firms' decisions not to implement labor contracts organizationwide. The first has to do with loyalty and past patron-client relationships. Scholars have argued that factors such as loyalty and monitoring costs must be figured into the equation of labor relations.[37] That the Chinese system was one of patron-client relations in prereform times has been well documented.[38] In return for loyalty and reduced monitoring requirements, patrons reward clients with contractual outcomes that benefit the worker. Where firms can afford to do so, they reward past loyalty and honor these past relationships. If they are not constrained economically, organizations view it as improper simply to break off what has been a long-term patron-client relationship when it becomes institutionally possible. Thus, if they can afford to do so, organizations reward the loyalty and clientelism of past relationships retroactively. As one manager in the electronics sector put it:

> There is a historical reason for this way of doing things. For our older workers who haven't yet reached retirement age, people in their fifties who are starting to get old and tired, it's really not fair to put them on contracts. Many of them have been working for this factory for twenty or more years; they have spent most of their lives working for this factory, but they just haven't reached retirement age yet. Suddenly to put these people on labor contracts would be cruel. Suddenly they would have no retirement security; that would be very unfair to them. . . . It's no way to treat people who have been working for you for so long. (Interview 130*, 1995)

As the words of this manager make clear, the relationship and the feeling that the older workers have given years of loyalty to the organization factor into the decisions surrounding changes in the labor relationship (see also the second epigraph at the beginning of this chapter). Note that this reasoning is not only about incentives and efficient labor arrangements for older workers, as rationalist and efficiency theories would explain economic decisions such as long-term contracts. These managers speak of *fairness* and acceptable *ways of treating people*, sentiments that do not fit with rational profit-maximizing conceptions of economic action.

Second, in the case of China, not only does loyalty matter for maintaining labor relationships most favorable for the worker, but socialist ideology and a sense of equity also play into the economic equation of labor relations and contractual outcomes. Although enterprises are experiencing a market economy and the constraints this system places on them, managers still speak the socialist language of doing what is "right for the workers" and making decisions that are fair. They talk about a commitment to a socialist system that takes care of their workers, even as the government sets forth new institutions that are reflective of a market economic system. As one manager in the garments sector explained:

> We only have about 50 percent of our workers on labor contracts, because about half our workers came over from the original factory. All the workers who were already employed in the old factory were not put on labor contracts, and all the newly hired workers were. Many of these old workers are nearing retirement age, and they have

been working for the factory for many years. It wouldn't be fair suddenly to put them on contracts, just before they are about to enter retirement. . . . It is a heavier burden for our factory, but in these kinds of situations we have to do what's right for the workers. So we only put the new workers on labor contracts, and those who have been here for a long time and are expecting retirement benefits will still get them. (Interview 115*, 1995)

One manager's tone approached that of defiance in the face of the government mandate that enterprises comply with the state-mandated change of adopting contracts throughout the enterprise:

We have the new workers who have come into the factory over the last few years sign contracts. But there is no need, no reason, for the older workers to sign contracts. The older workers were already here for many years before we ever started this labor contract policy. It really wouldn't be fair for us to make them sign contracts just like the new workers. Then they would feel that they've been working here for all this time, and now the factory is saying they can stay only for a fixed amount of time. But the government has this rule that all workers are supposed to sign labor contracts. Since we think it's not fair for the older workers, we only follow this rule for the newer workers in the factory. Our older workers are staying on as permanent employees! (Interview 120*, 1995)

The language of fairness to workers and the desire to take care of workers who have given years of their lives to the enterprise indicate that, for those enterprises that choose to allow some workers to stay on as permanent employees, there are factors in the economics of decision making that extend beyond economic measures and outcomes. When organizations can afford to, they reward loyalty and patron-client relationships that were in place before the economic reforms. Some managers also maintain a focus on the socialist system and on that system's commitment to take care of workers, choosing to continue to support workers in the name of socialist ideals.

Concluding Remarks

The findings presented here on wages and nonwage benefits support the contention that organizational studies can enhance our understanding of the processes at work in the economic transition and the critical economic and structural factors on which these processes hinge. The results support the argument that just as the rank of a firm's governing organization was important for remuneration in prereform China, it remains important in the economic transition. At the same time, results also show that several other organization-level variables are important in the decisions firms make about wages and nonwage benefits, and the importance of economic variables for these decisions indicates that firms are responding to economic constraints and taking a market-oriented approach to survival.

In a number of ways, the more interesting findings regarding changes in labor relations come with the analysis of labor contracts. Labor contracts in industrial China mark the end of a socialist institution that has been the hallmark of the Chinese work unit system: lifetime employment. The analysis presented here emphasizes economic and institutional factors in the implementation of labor contracts across industrial organizations. First, the decision to adopt labor contracts throughout the organization, ending lifetime employment for all workers in the firm, is a function of the economic burdens the firm faces. Organizations in more difficult economic situations are significantly more likely to adopt labor contracts across the organization, thus making use of the institutional opportunity to end lifetime employment. Second, the decision to implement labor contracts on an organizationwide basis is a function of the level of government administration that presides over a given enterprise, as organizations under municipal bureaus are significantly more likely to institutionalize labor contracts organizationwide than are firms at lower levels of the administrative hierarchy.

Considered together, these findings point to two types of uncertainty for organizations in the economic transition: economic uncertainty and administrative uncertainty. With respect to the former, firms that are struggling to survive in the economic transition adopt practices reflective of the economic uncertainty they are experiencing. Taking advantage of a new institution constructed at the state level, these firms institutionalize labor contracts throughout their employee ranks, effectively ending lifetime employment for all workers in the firm. Similarly, firms that are positioned at the upper levels of China's administrative hierarchy are significantly more likely to end the socialist institution of lifetime employment across their establishments. As I describe in chapter 2, large industrial firms under the jurisdiction of municipal bureaus are currently experiencing the greatest sense of being set adrift by the state, and, as a result, they are encountering a great deal of uncertainty in the economic transition. With less government support (and less ability to count on funds from state coffers), they are also experiencing a kind of administrative uncertainty and, as a result, are more likely to take advantage of the institutional reforms that allow them to end lifetime employment. Like their economically weak counterparts, these firms adopt strategies that help them stabilize their market position. The adoption of labor contracts across firms is a form of enterprise self-protection: Firms more likely to place all their workers on labor contracts are experiencing some degree of uncertainty in the emerging Chinese markets, and they place all their workers on contracts as a way of protecting themselves against the burden of lifetime employment. Despite the fact that these firms have shown slow gains in productivity, reforms are being enacted at this level of the economy in meaningful ways.

An organization's decision to retain some workers as permanent employees also speaks to such issues as loyalty, conceptions of fairness, maintaining clientelist relationships established before the reform period, and the socialist ideology of supporting workers. Previous research made clear the centrality of clientelist relationships as an institution in prereform Chinese organizations. In many ways, given the centrality of those relationships in factories before the economic transition, it is not surprising that the patron-client relationships that were forged under the old system would not be swept away by new market institutions. In the views of many managers I interviewed, there is still significant commitment to the relationships that were formed under the old system. Managers spoke of fairness, rewarding workers' commitment to the firm, and the ideals of what is right in a system that looks first to protect workers. In some cases, they also spoke in defiance of the idea that they should accept the government mandate to incorporate these market-oriented institutional changes and thereby disavow the relationships that were forged over many years before the economic reform. In organizations that are not constrained economically, the commitment to these clientelist relationships appears to be the crucial factor in the survival of a socialist institution that places a major burden on firms, and those organizations that have the economic luxury of allowing their older workers to avoid contracts do so. In other words, organizations that are *not* experiencing uncertainty reward loyalty instead of maximizing profits. In this example of economic decision making, firms' market practices belie the logic of the basic assumptions behind transition theories that are grounded in a neoclassical understanding of markets and market action. Sachs's convergence theory, which assumes that actors the world over will respond in a like manner to the shock therapy of immediate and radical institutional change, and Nee's emphasis on actors' rational pursuit of profits in unleashed markets cannot account for economic decisions that precisely make no sense from a profit-maximizing perspective. The resilience of relationships and ideologies that preceded the reforms play a crucial role in the decision making of managers in reform-era China.

Five _____

The Politics of Price Setting in China's Transition Economy

> There is in every society or neighbourhood an ordinary or
> average rate both of wages and profit in every different
> employment of labour and stock. This rate is naturally
> regulated. . . . The natural price, therefore, is, as it were, the
> central price, to which the prices of all commodities are
> continually gravitating.
>   *(Adam Smith 1789)*

> Adam Smith's flash of genius was his recognition that
> prices that emerged from voluntary transactions between
> buyers and sellers—for short, in a free market—could
> coordinate the activity of millions of people, each seeking
> his own interest, in such a way as to make everyone better
> off. It was a startling idea then, and it remains one today,
> that economic order can emerge as the unintended
> consequence of the actions of many people, each seeking
> his own interest. The price system works so well, so
> efficiently, that we are not aware of it most of the time.
>   *(Milton and Rose Friedman 1979)*

THE NOTION THAT, in a free market, prices will gravitate toward a natural or equilibrium state is a central tenet in classical economic theories of markets. Price mechanisms efficiently organize economic activity by transmitting information and pushing producers to adopt the most cost-effective methods of production.[1] An economic sociology of markets, beginning with White (1981), contends that price-setting practices are fundamentally social, as economic actors make decisions according to the social networks and institutional environments in which they are embedded. The case of China supports the notion that emerging price-setting practices in China's economic transition are both political and social.

If the existence of a price mechanism is central to the social and economic structure of markets, a central issue in the transition from a command to a market economic system is the ability to set prices independent of state control. Yet, in research on economic transitions, surprisingly little attention has been paid to the dynamics of actual price-setting practices of economic actors in the marketplace. As I have argued in earlier chapters, there is tension between the desire to test hypotheses about the emergence of market mechanisms and the use of data on individual-level income or aggregate data on productivity. Because changes in market mechanisms will not *necessarily* lead to changes in income or productivity (though it is often assumed they will), it is difficult to see how these changes can be taken as concrete evidence of the "transition from redistribution to market mechanism."[2] Concrete information on what economic actors do in the face of changing market organization can bring us much closer to understanding the ways that economic actors are responding to changing institutional conditions. For example, information on whether industrial organizations are free to set prices independent of state control—and how they go about setting prices given that freedom—is more directly related to the emergence of market mechanisms.

In this chapter I look directly at the ability of Chinese industrial organizations to set and negotiate prices independent of state control. Essentially I show that while organizations are increasingly able to set prices on their own, this change depends on a firm's position in the administrative hierarchy of the former command economy and whether firms have formal relations with foreign partners. Firms at the upper levels of the hierarchy are significantly more likely than those at lower levels to set prices on their own, indicating that these firms are experiencing the most autonomy surrounding pricing in the economic transition. They are also significantly more likely to set prices according to a rationalized pricing formula, indicating that these firms have moved the furthest along the road toward economic rationalization. Firms positioned at lower rungs of the hierarchy are still operating under the government's thumb, as the government offices to which they report are still in considerable control of these firms' decisions in the transition economy. The significant effects of formal relations with foreign joint-venture partners show that Chinese organizations that have foreign partners are significantly more likely to set prices independent of state control, and they are significantly more likely to set prices according to a rationalized pricing formula. I interpret these effects as an indication that even in the realm of something that has been as fundamentally political as price reform, Chinese organizations are influenced by the models of foreign organizations they observe up close in the marketplace. In China's economic transition, price-setting practices are fundamentally political and social.

Price Setting

A critical issue in transitions from command to market economic systems is the freedom for economic actors to set and negotiate prices independent of state control, especially for large industrial organizations. Several important works in the field of economic sociology define the important role pricing plays in the social construction of markets. White's (1981) work on the social construction of markets focuses primarily on cost and valuation, but price must also play an integral role in this process: firms' observations of other organizations' actions and decisions are a part of the process of market construction, and price setting is one critical observable within the marketplace. Eccles and White (1988) carry this discussion further, arguing that price is a socially constructed phenomenon and is intimately tied to authority structures. Fligstein's (1996b) discussion of markets and market institutions also begins with a definition that views a price mechanism at the center of production markets, which are structured around dynamics of power and control. Thus an economic sociology of markets makes clear that we must deal with the emergence and structure of a price mechanism if we are to understand the social construction of markets. Yet, studies of individual-level gains in income, the emergence of entrepreneurship, or changes in productivity across sectors of the economy tell us nothing concrete about the emergence of a price mechanism or even the freedom of market actors to set prices independent of state control. If we want to say anything about the emergence of a "market mechanism" or the transition from hierarchies to markets, we should be able to say something about price-setting practices that operate independent of state control. Few empirical studies of China's transition have addressed this issue.[3]

In prereform China all price setting in large industrial organizations was controlled by the state through the administrative hierarchy of the command economy. Reforming pricing would prove to be a central issue in the economic transition. A study of market transition must be able to account for the politics of price setting and price reform at the firm level. The extent to which a pricing system has been implemented in China has varied across sectors and organizations and may vary by the type of government control. In order to draw conclusions about the shift from the hierarchy to the market, we must observe changes in the practice of price setting at the firm level.

Price reform has followed the course of gradual reform, laden with politics, experimentation, and piecemeal implementation. Government control of pricing began to change officially with general reforms in 1979 and then more specifically with the October 1984 Reform Declaration. Implementing a market pricing system may not have been a central part of the financial rationalizing system being promoted by Zhao Ziyang, but it was an important issue that was on the table for many years of the reform and was often advocated by Zhao himself. The "price reformers" certainly saw the issue as crucial to the success of the reforms, and even if the "enterprise reformers" were antagonistic to the idea, the liberalization of prices was a central issue to the debates raging between these two reform-minded groups. But if the debates over price control and liberalization were pivotal to the reforms, progress on the issue was slow. By the end of 1984 factor prices were still unreformed, and product prices had still not yet been realigned.[4]

In 1985 policy making began to turn toward the ideas of the enterprise reformers, as the government adopted the dual-track system of the reform.[5] This approach encompassed many specific policies, but the essence of the dual-track approach was the following: Enterprises would operate across two separate spheres of economic activity, one being the planned sector of the economy and the other the market sector. As a result, enterprises remained part of the planned economy on one level, but they were also permitted to sell goods produced above and beyond the plan at open-market prices. It was at this point that true market prices began to emerge and enterprises were permitted to begin setting their own prices, if only for goods produced outside the plan. However, as central government officials began to recognize that they "could not control outside-plan prices," market price quotations "began to appear in official journals."[6] This development was an interesting one because, while the state was recognizing its limits in price control, these "official" journals of market price quotations are produced by the state. Thus, even in the liberalization of pricing, we see the heavy hand of the state in "suggesting" prices through official journals.

The years since 1985 have seen many pendulum swings between liberal and conservative reforms. As late as 1992–93 once again a push came toward fully dismantling price controls and allowing market-controlled prices.[7] But on the whole, the years since 1985 have taken enterprise production further away from the plan and allowed enterprises to operate in an increasingly marketized setting.

Price-Setting Practices in Shanghai

The extent that price control was still occurring in the mid-1990s at the level of individual organizational units is an empirical question of the reform, one that I set out to answer in my study of organizations in Shanghai. How, in China's transition economy, do price-setting practices vary in terms of sector, position in the administrative hierarchy of the former command economy, and organizational type? If there has been price liberalization in some part of the economy, how are firms setting their prices? Further, how are firms viewing prices once they are set; are they viewing them as fixed and unmalleable or are they negotiating with other organizations over final prices? To get the answers to these issues, I discussed with managers whether their organizations set prices for *all* products of the organization. I had to frame the discussion in this way in order to discover whether organizations are operating *fully* independent of state control, which is what my research aimed to uncover. For organizations that the state still controls in this realm, the dual-track system allows for some degree of economic freedom, but these firms are operating differently from those that are making decisions fully independent of the state. For organizations that reported having full control over pricing, I further discussed with managers how they went about setting their prices.

The ways that managers responded to these issues can roughly be divided into three general categories. First, there is the category of organizations that still do not set their own prices, despite sixteen years of economic reforms; for these organizations, the state continues to set and/or control prices. The governance structures that define the rules of the emerging markets vary, to some extent, by sector, and also according to the idea that some products are more closely linked to people's survival than others. As one manager explained:

> Some sectors depend on a government pricing system. This happens most often in sectors that affect people's lives directly, like foods. But these days the government pays little attention to products that do not have a direct effect on people's lives. (Interview 36*, 1995)

A manager in the chemicals sector described his firm's situation in the following way:

> In this sector [pesticides] there is still some government control of prices. For the products that are under government control, we can't go over the price limit [*xianzhi jia*], so we usually just set our prices at the limit. But for products that are not under price control, we usually try to set prices according to the market price. (Interview 103*, 1995)

From these statements it appears that sectors in which products may have an effect on people's livelihoods—whether staple foods are cheap enough for people to buy or whether farmers are able to acquire pesticides at reasonable rates—are the ones that are still under state control in the realm of price setting. As I will show below, however, the situation is more complex than simple variation across sectors.

The second cluster of organizational practices with respect to the issue of price setting forms around the practice of setting prices independent of state control yet with little in the way of a formulaic method of determining what these prices would be. Managers in this group of organizations reported that they simply rely on "the market" to determine the prices of their products [*kan shichang ding jiage*]. The organizations that rely on "the market" for price setting may be free of government control over pricing, but they lack well-developed or systematic ways of thinking about how prices should be set. A manager in the electronics sector described his firm's reliance on "the market" for price setting as follows:

> There is no official influence in this sector for price setting. We often bargain with our customers, but we are really guided by the market in terms of price setting. The market is crucial for price setting: Now many factories produce the same product, and quality is about the same everywhere. If one factory offers the product much

cheaper than everyone else, that factory will get the most business. So we all have to pay attention to one another and compete for business. (Interview 36*, 1995)

While this organization's approach to price setting does not reflect a sophisticated understanding of input prices and other external costs that might figure into the construction of a systematic price-setting procedure, the manager is clearly aware of one of the critical factors that produce instability in markets: "the tendency of firms to undercut one another's prices."[8] A price mechanism is directly related to this type of instability, and that this manager has linked these issues indicates that marketlike situations are emerging in the electronics sector. Another manager in this sector said of price setting in his firm:

Our price setting is completely based on the market. We just look at the market price for our products and try to set a similar and competitive price. This kind of focus on the market for price setting also has a lot to do with our attitude toward "getting on track" [*jiegui taidu*]. We are really getting on track with the international world in many ways. (Interview 53*, 1995)

"Getting on track with the international world" [*gen guoji jiegui*] is an acceptable (and fashionable) way of saying that Chinese firms are adopting Western-style institutional systems (see chapter 7 for further discussion). This manager sees market-driven pricing systems as a part of this process.

Organizations in the garments sector also generally rely on the market for price setting, but because of the nature of this production market, the process differs somewhat from that in other sectors. Most firms in the garments sector work on a contractual basis, producing a set number of products that had been contracted by another organization. With this situation, the pricing typically is prearranged, based on the bidding involved in landing a contract with a garment retailer.

Our price setting is simply based on bidding. We offer a price to our customers, and then they usually offer us a much lower price. So we are actually always negotiating prices; we really have no set way of deciding prices at all. (Interview 107*, 1995)

The third category of organizational responses to the question of independent price setting was one in which firms set their own prices (no government control) and also had relatively sophisticated systems and formulas for determining their prices. For these types of firms, pricing was most often based on a complex formula that accounted for several inputs (e.g., cost of labor, cost of resources, taxes, cost of management fees) and a predetermined profit margin. As a manager in the electronics sector explained:

We decide our prices in two ways: One way is based on the average prices in international and domestic markets; the other is based on a formula that accounts for cost of labor, cost of resources, overall cost of production, and an 8 to 10 percent profit margin. (Interview 60*, 1995)

Another manager in the electronics sector articulated the following organizational outlook in response to the question of price setting:

> We really set our prices quite low. We base the price on the cost of materials and labor and then add a small amount for profit. But I never want to be too hard-nosed about making money [literal translation: "black-hearted"—*zhuan qiande hua wo conglai buyao xin tai hei*]. We just want to make enough money so that the factory can survive. So we set our prices very low. . . . [Pointing to a TV in the room:] How much do you think that TV would sell for in America? Probably about $100–$150, right? We sell it to our Hong Kong distributors for about U.S.$28. We could sell it for a lot more, but we're not trying to make so much money off our products. (Interview 130*, 1995)

This manager's organization had the freedom to set prices on its own, and the manager had a relatively sophisticated understanding of inputs and pricing. Interestingly, however, here again we see the importance of social and political context on Chinese managers' views of economic processes: Cutting against the assumption of profit-maximizing actors, this manager explicitly tried to *avoid* maximizing profits for his firm. Far from the desire to maximize profits, this manager seems far more focused on survival and little beyond. The use of the term *black-hearted* to describe profit maximization is a revealing commentary on where some managers feel the economic reforms are headed.

These managers' responses to concrete questions about price-setting practices highlight a number of important issues for China's transition economy. First, there is still some degree of state control in the realm of pricing, and it is apparently—at least according to the managers' perceptions—closely tied to the production of staple goods. Economic stability has, over the course of the reforms, been one of the state's primary concerns in the reform process. China's reform process has been gradual throughout, and the realm of pricing is no exception. Second, the rhetoric of "getting on track" with the international community is a ubiquitous theme in discussions of various aspects of China's transition economy. Many of the decisions and practices that firms are adopting in the reform era are often framed in terms of their relation to this catchall phrase. Clearly there are strong economic reasons for price reform; autonomous pricing is probably the most basic of transcendental market principles that we can point to. Yet, even this aspect of markets does not stand outside the notion that "we are doing what Western firms do" (which is essentially what *gen guoji jiegui* implies). Third, even firms for which state controls have been removed are not rushing to maximize profits, as shock therapy accounts of transitions would predict. Shock therapy and convergence accounts of economic transition operate from the assumption that economic actors will have one response to the removal of state controls. However, the suggestion that profit maximization is a "black-hearted" practice suggests that institutionalization of a capitalist ideology may take time, and notions of profit maximization are not going to leap immediately onto the scene the moment economic actors are given the freedom to control their own economic destiny. Culture, socialist ideology, and politics are all also part of the equation of how economic actors evaluate their situations, and the empirical realities of reform—especially what some managers have to say about it—in China bear this out.

Analyzing Pricing-Setting Practices

What factors are important for the liberalization of pricing at the organization level? First, the extent to which the liberalization of pricing has occurred at the organization level has varied, not surprisingly, by sector. The prices of foods, particularly staple goods, continued to be controlled much later than other products. Also, the prices of upstream industrial goods such as steel and inputs such as petroleum and coal continued to be under government price control, a fact that contributed to the problems of chronic losses in these economic sectors. Second, as is so often true with the Chinese case, variation in levels of government administration and tension between central and local governing plans and policies were influential in the liberalization of prices in the economic transition. The tension between central and local plans was supposed to have been attenuated by the view in Beijing that local plans were "guidance plans . . . noncompulsory targets."[9] The reality, however, was that local plans and policies were much more compulsory than they were guidelines. Inputs are still, to some extent, allocated by local governments, which ties production more closely to local plans than to central plans. Organizations rely on their local governments for inputs, and how they alter their production quotas and schedules in the economic transition is therefore closely tied to local governments and local control. The issue of variation in local control and the tension between central and local policies also extends to the realm of pricing: "Local governments imposed varying degrees of price controls even on outside-plan transactions."[10]

Beyond sector and geography, however, I will show below that two other crucial factors influence organizational practices in the realm of pricing. First, position in the state administrative hierarchy matters for whether firms have the autonomy to set prices on their own. Firms at higher levels of the administrative hierarchy—especially those directly under the jurisdiction of municipal bureaus—are significantly more likely to be free of government control in the realm of price setting. In other words, the politics of state structure and the structure of the former command economy matter for how the reforms are progressing on this critical issue. My findings here indicate that processes of marketization and hardening budget constraints are, in fact, occurring at the upper levels of China's administrative hierarchy. Second, association with for-

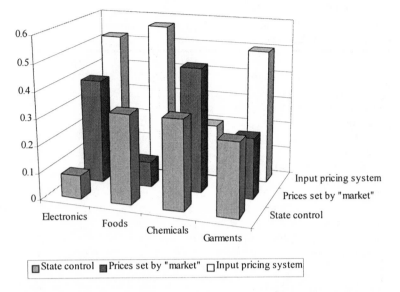

Figure 5.1: Proportion of Firms Using Various Price-Setting Practices in Four Sectors in Industrial Shanghai, 1995

eign organizations (through joint ventures) has an impact on the emergence of autonomous price-setting practices across organizations. This association indicates that the market practices of Chinese firms are, at least in part, dependent on contact with organizations from advanced market economies. The manager who articulated the link between pricing and "getting on track" with the international community suggests this association; the analysis below will show that, more than simply a rhetorical statement, this association exists systematically across industrial organizations in Shanghai.

Figure 5.1 shows the proportions of firms by sector engaged in different price-setting practices. Less than 10 percent of firms in the electronics sector were still under the state's control in setting prices, while more than 30 percent of firms in the foods and chemicals sectors were unable to set prices autonomously. Just less than 30 percent of firms in the garments sector were under state control in setting prices. Overall, less than 10 percent of the organizations in the foods sector are setting prices according to "the market," and among firms that have the freedom to set prices, only 14 percent are relying on "the market." The sector in which the highest proportion of firms sets prices according to the market is chemicals: Overall, just under half the firms in this sector set prices according to the market, and among firms that are free to set prices, the figure is 70 percent. Interestingly, the chemicals sector has the smallest proportion of firms setting prices based on an input cost formula; the foods sector has the highest proportion of firms setting prices this way.

TABLE 5.1

Logistic Coefficients for the Practice of Independent Price Setting by
Organizations in Four Industrial Sectors, Shanghai, 1995

	Model I		Model II	
Independent variables	B	S.E.	B	S.E.
Organizational variables[a]				
Chemicals	−1.68*	.91	−1.40	.95
Foods	.91	.80	1.28	.92
Garments	.05	.96	.43	1.03
Active employees (ln)	−.004	.33	−.27	.37
Employee ratio	−.01	.02	−.02	.02
Organizational health	−.13	.15	−.13	.17
Profit margin, avg. 1990–1994	.04	.03	.03	.04
Losses, 1990	−.24	.77	−.52	.84
Products exported, 1990 (%)	.01	.01	.01	.01
Joint venture	1.58**	.71	1.39*	.72
Governance variables				
GM w/bus./econ. backgrnd.	—	—	.54	.56
Municipal bureau	—	—	.56**	.27
Constant	−.31	2.42	−.82	2.64
χ^2	17.82*		22.78**	
No. of cases	81		81	

Note: See Appendix 4 for discussion of variables. B is the effect of the coefficient; S.E. is the standard error. $* p < .1$ $** p < .05$ (two-tailed tests). Variables in bold are statistically significant.

[a] Reference category for sector is electronics.

Table 5.1 presents a systematic view of independent price-setting mechanisms in the organizations selected for this study. Model I shows that, net of other effects, location in the chemicals sector has a significant negative association with a firm's ability to autonomously set prices, as compared to location in the electronics sector. This is not surprising, given that this sector is one of the high-state-control sectors selected for the study (see Appendix 1 for discussion). The firms under state control for price setting in the chemicals sector were most often those involved with the production of pesticides. Pesticides occupy a position in an organizational field that overlaps with production in the foods sector: If prices of pesticides were free of state control, they could have an impact on food prices. It is interesting, however, that location in the foods sector does not have a significant relationship with state control over price setting, controlling for other factors, despite conventional wisdom to the contrary (see quotes above).

The only other organizational variable that matters, according to Model I, is whether the firm has a formal relationship with a foreign partner (in the form of a joint-venture investment), which has a significantly positive effect on the firm's ability to set prices free of state control. Organizations with joint-venture partners are about five times more likely than those without such partners to be setting prices independent of state control. I interpret this result to mean that firms exposed to the market practices of economic actors from foreign market economies are likely to be influenced by the systems and practices that exist in those market economies. The Chinese firms observe the decisions and practices of their foreign partners, and they recognize the benefits of such market practices as independent price setting. These firms are likely to put pressure on the state to amend the governance structures to fit more with the institutional structures they see available in the market environments of other economic systems. In some ways, extended contact with foreign entities has a positive impact on the emergence of the institutional structures that will define China's emerging market economic system.[11]

Model II adds variables of governance to the equation with significant results. Controlling for all other factors, a firm's location under the jurisdiction of a municipal bureau governing organization has a significantly positive effect on whether the firm will have the freedom to set prices independent of state control. This association fits well with my general argument that administrative and economic responsibilities are being pushed down the ladder of the former command economy (see chapter 2), and this transformation has considerably different implications for organizations at different levels of this administrative hierarchy. While scholars have argued that reforms have been enacted the least for firms at the upper levels of China's industrial hierarchy (based on slow gains in productivity),[12] if we look at the actual practices of firms at this level of the hierarchy, we see that these firms are living in increasingly marketized worlds. As I outlined in chapter 2, as administrative and economic responsibilities are pushed down the hierarchy of the former command economy, firms directly under bureaus are affected differently than organizations positioned at lower levels of the hierarchy because they are not protected by another layer of government bureaucracy. As bureaus divest themselves of administrative responsibilities, the firms directly under their jurisdictions are forced to take over more of the responsibilities of the transition economy. Organizations at lower rungs of the hierarchy, however, are still being controlled by government offices.

Firms at the upper levels of China's industrial hierarchy are operating under governance structures that increasingly resemble those of market economies. They have increasing autonomy over decisions and practices in the emerging markets of China's transition economy. Firms at lower levels of the hierarchy, on the other hand, are under the jurisdiction of municipal and district companies, and these administrative companies still wield significant control over the decisions and practices of the firms under their jurisdictions. The findings presented here add another layer of evidence to the view that significant reforms are taking hold in the upper levels of China's administrative hierarchy.

In addition, however, Walder's (1995a) view of "local governments as industrial firms" fits well with the perspective I present here. Walder's argument is that state governing units at lower levels of the industrial hierarchy (especially in rural areas) are able to keep tighter control over firms under their jurisdictions. In this sense, these governments are actually acting like holding companies or multidivisional firms. I argue that this is also true in urban industrial sectors: Administrative companies keep closer control over firms under their jurisdictions than municipal bureaus do. This tighter control amounts to different governance structures, different conceptions of control, and, ultimately, different practices that firms are free to adopt in the economic transition.

The distinction between bureaus and administrative companies as governing organizations, to some extent, lies in the size of the jurisdiction: Bureaus have direct control over many firms, whereas administrative companies have control over relatively few firms. It could be that price setting is a problem of monitoring in that the larger the jurisdiction in which a firm sits, the more likely it is to act independent of state control, an argument I have developed elsewhere.[13] However, in a model run with jurisdiction size as the governing effect, this governance variable was not significant, suggesting that while bureau governance matters, it is for reasons other than the number of firms in a given organization's jurisdiction.[14]

In sum, net of all other effects, firms under the jurisdiction of municipal bureaus are significantly more likely to be setting prices independent of state control. This is an important finding in two ways. First, this result indicates that firms at different levels of the administrative hierarchy are being treated differently in terms of the autonomy they experience in the economic transition. Compared to firms under the jurisdiction of municipal and district companies, organizations under the jurisdiction of municipal bureaus are significantly more likely to have direct control over pricing practices. I argued in chapter 2 that firms under the jurisdiction of municipal bureaus are experiencing a greater sense of being set adrift by the state, whereas firms under local government offices are being controlled in ways more akin to the command economy. The findings presented here support this argument. If price setting is an integral ingredient of marketization, firms under higher levels of the government are experiencing marketization to a greater extent than those at the lower levels of the hierarchy, at least with respect to this practice. Second, the lack of significance of the size of a firm's governing jurisdiction indicates that the effects of different levels of the administrative hierarchy are not simply a function of how many other organizations a firm's governing office has to watch over. For the autonomy given to firms over the practice of price setting, different levels of state administration have allowed firms under their jurisdictions freely to handle this market activity at different rates.

For those firms that *are* setting prices independent of state control, it is interesting to explore the approaches various firms take in deciding their

TABLE 5.2

Logistic Coefficients for Approaches to Price Setting
(1 = input/cost formula; 0 = "market sets price") for Organizations
in Four Industrial Sectors, Shanghai, 1995

Independent variables	B	S.E.
Organizational variables[a]		
Chemicals	−1.09	1.09
Foods	3.43**	1.41
Garments	1.51	1.08
Active employees (ln)	−.02	.49
Employee ratio	−.03	.02
Organizational health	−.16	.19
Profit margin, avg. 1990–1994	.11*	.06
Losses, 1990	−.24	1.14
Joint venture	1.84*	1.08
Governance variables		
GM w/bus./econ. backgrnd.	.13	.71
Municipal bureau	1.70*	.99
Constant	−1.24	3.34
χ^2	23.38**	
No. of cases[b]	61	

Note: See Appendix 4 for discussion of variables. B is the effect of the coefficient; S.E. is the standard error. * $p < .1$ ** $p < .05$ (two-tailed tests). Variables in bold are statistically significant.

[a] Reference category for sector is electronics.

[b] Model is based on the sub-sample of organizations that set prices independent of state control.

prices. Which firms set their prices based solely on "the market," and which set their prices based on a formula that accounts for inputs, costs, and a profit margin? Table 5.2 presents a systematic view of the approaches firms take to setting prices. The population of firms for this particular discussion is made up of those firms that were setting prices independent of government control (i.e., those that were still under government control for price setting were factored out). Therefore, instead of a population of eighty-one firms, as in most of the other analyses presented throughout this study, sixty-one firms are included in the analysis presented in Table 5.2.

Location in the foods sector has a significant effect on the likelihood that a firm will institutionalize a complex pricing system. With considerable state control over pricing in the foods sector, prices remain relatively low in this sector. As a result, firms that are located in the foods sector operate at relatively slim margins of profit. Thus there is pressure to rationalize prices in order to be certain that the firm will not be losing money based on the input prices and labor costs that arise from production. Besides this structural pressure, there may also be an isomorphic effect operating here, where firms mimic practices adopted by successful firms in markets.[15] A significant positive association also exists between the complex pricing systems and profit margins, indicating that firms with larger profit margins are more likely to be setting their prices in more complex formulas. Here again, results are tentative because the causality may run in both directions: It is as likely that firms with more institutionally organized market strategies are making more money as it is that higher profits lead to more institutionally organized price-setting strategies. Nevertheless, the positive association here is an interesting one, as firms that are doing better in the economic transition tend to be those with more institutionally advanced price-setting mechanisms and strategies. It may be that firms with institutionally advanced pricing systems are more organized overall in terms of production strategies and therefore are better able to deal with the independent administrative and economic responsibilities they have in the economic transition.

Formal relationships with foreign organizations (through joint-venture partnerships) have a positive effect on the institutionalization of complex pricing systems, further evidence of the rationalizing effect that contact with foreign capitalist organizations has on Chinese firms. Location under bureau governance also increases the likelihood that a firm will adopt more complex price-setting practices, as organizations under the jurisdiction of municipal bureaus are more than five times as likely to use a complex pricing system than are firms at lower levels of the industrial hierarchy. As I asserted above, organizations under municipal bureaus have been given significantly more autonomy in the market reform than have other firms in the economic transition, especially relative to organizations under municipal and district companies. Firms in this sector of the economy are no longer protected or closely administered by the organizations presiding over them; they have, for the most part, been left to find their own paths in the economic transition. This lack of protection and administrative attention offered by state agencies has led to a greater market orientation and more institutional advances in market institutional realms such as price setting. Administrative companies, on the other hand, have kept closer control over firms under their jurisdictions both economically and administratively. As a result, there has been less of a push for those organizations to develop institutionally advanced market practices in the economic transition.

Negotiating Prices

In addition to discussions over methods of price setting, I also discussed with managers whether their organizations negotiated prices [*shangliang jiage*] with customers or whether prices were fixed once they were set. In some ways, the practice of negotiating prices with customers may say even more about which firms are making their way into the market economy. These firms are truly going to the market and bargaining with customers to make a sale. Like all other practices, however, there is variation on what organizations actually do regarding this issue.

Among firms that set their own prices, some indicated that they do not negotiate prices at all. As one manager in the foods sector explained:

> Our prices are set based on the cost of resources, the cost of labor, a profit margin, and a management fee. We never negotiate prices with our customers. They're set, and that's the final price. (Interview 88*, 1995)

Other managers painted similar pictures:

> We really don't negotiate prices with customers. We try to make the quality of our products as good as possible and compete openly in the marketplace. We want to rely on these aspects of production, so we really don't change prices for anyone. (Interview 49*, 1995)

Some managers seemed to think that negotiations were not necessary, as his firm's price-setting practices were "fair":

> We set the prices ourselves. There is no state control of the prices in this sector anymore. . . . Really we don't negotiate prices with customers. We try to take the customer's needs and costs into account when we are setting the price. And I think we set very fair prices. (Interview 99*, 1995)

> We almost never negotiate prices. It could be possible that a company would tell us that our price is too high, and, if it is a big customer, maybe we might consider it. But our prices are really fair, so we never really negotiate. (Interview 68*, 1995)

Some managers indicated that they do negotiate prices with customers, albeit reluctantly. One manager in the chemicals sector said:

> We negotiate prices with customers—especially larger customers—when we need to. It's a complicated problem; we try to set a fair price from the beginning, one that takes into account our customers' situations. But we also need the business, so we will negotiate prices if we have to in order to keep customers, especially larger customers. (Interview 103*, 1995)

Some organizations seemed to make exceptions only for "old customers" [*lao kehu*]:

> We never negotiate prices, except with old customers. Since China became a market economy, the prices have never stopped changing. So we just produce our products and set the prices based on our costs. (Interview 71*, 1995)

Finally, some managers framed the issue in terms of competition, apparently willing to negotiate prices because markets in China are becoming increas-

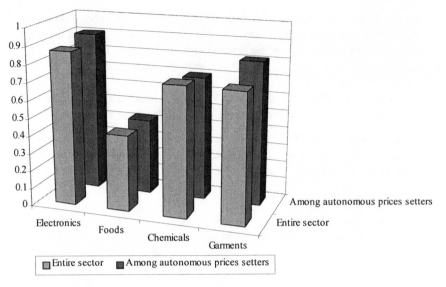

Figure 5.2: Proportion of Firms That Negotiate Prices with Customers in Four Sectors in Industrial Shanghai, 1995

ingly competitive and they can ill afford to lose business to other players in the market:

> We negotiate prices with customers often. Market economies are competitive, and we need to compete. (Interview 60*, 1995)

> We negotiate prices with customers if they want to. In the market economy now, we have this competition problem [*jingzheng wenti*]. If we can't compete in terms of price, we won't be able to do the volume of business we need to do. So sometimes we have to negotiate. (Interview 59*, 1995)

The link here between the "competition problem" (note again the negative view of market imperatives) and negotiation indicates that struggling firms view price negotiation as a way of ensuring sales.

Figure 5.2 shows the variation by sector of whether firms negotiate prices with their customers. Overall, by industry, the electronics sector has the highest proportion of firms that negotiate prices with customers; the foods sector has the lowest proportion. These proportions are not surprising given that the fewest number of firms in the foods sector have the autonomy to set their own prices. The trends are basically the same among firms that are free to set prices within each of those sectors.

Table 5.3 presents multivariate analyses of the factors that contribute to the organizational decision to negotiate prices with customers. In this analysis, although one might think that the only relevant population of firms is that

TABLE 5.3

Logistic Coefficients for the Practice of Negotiating Prices with Customers for Organizations in Four Industrial Sectors, Shanghai, 1995

	Model I		Model II	
Independent variables	B	S.E.	B	S.E.
Organizational variables[a]				
Chemicals	−.27	1.19	.52	1.44
Foods	−.48	1.07	−.76	1.05
Garments	1.19	1.23	.75	1.22
Active employees (ln)	−.01	.48	−.22	.53
Employee ratio	−1.27	2.01	−.35	2.06
Organizational health	.27	.22	.46	.37
Profit margin, avg. 1990–1994	.01	.04	.02	.04
Losses, 1990	.64	.91	.67	.94
Products exported, 1990 (%)	−.002	.01	.001	.01
Joint venture	−.65	.85	−.37	.84
Gov. control of pricing	−1.84*	.95	−1.51	.94
Input pricing system	−.66	.88	−.62	.90
Governance variables				
GM w/bus./econ. backgrnd.	−.02	.68	.11	.66
Municipal bureau	2.83**	1.34	—	—
Municipal company	1.70*	.86	—	—
Jurisdiction size (ln)	—	—	.91**	.36
Constant	1.64	3.36	.82	3.43
χ^2	27.47**		29.81**	
No. of cases	81		81	

Note: See Appendix 4 for discussion of variables. B is the effect of the coefficient; S.E. is the standard error. * $p < .1$ ** $p < .05$ (two-tailed tests). Variables in bold are statistically significant.

[a] Reference category for sector is electronics.

which is already setting prices independent of state control, this is actually not the case. In fact, of the firms in my sample that were still operating under some level of state control in setting prices, more than half (55 percent) reported negotiating prices with customers. Model I shows that there is a strong political element to the organizational practice of negotiating prices with customers. Controlling for several organizational variables, whether a firm operates under state control of pricing has a statistically significant negative effect on the likelihood that an organization will negotiate prices. This is not surprising, as firms that are under the state's control in price setting are experiencing less marketized worlds and thus are less likely to take the step of haggling over prices with customers. A firm's position in the hierarchy of the former command economy also matters for the likelihood that it will negotiate prices with customers. Firms under the jurisdiction of municipal bureaus are about seventeen times more likely (exp[2.83] = 16.95) than those under district companies to negotiate prices with customers; those under municipal companies are about five and a half times more likely (exp[1.70] = 5.47) than their counterparts under district companies to negotiate prices. The ability to negotiate prices with other firms in the economic transition indicates that firms are operating in open markets in which they have the freedom to barter and haggle with customers. The higher a firm is in the administrative hierarchy of the former command economy, the more likely it is to be approaching market practices in this fashion.

The monotonic increase in likelihoods across the two administrative levels suggests that what we are observing here is not a qualitative difference between bureaus and administrative companies but, rather, a difference in governance styles that increases with administrative rank. I argued in earlier chapters that one factor influencing governance at difference levels of the administrative hierarchy is the size of the jurisdiction. Administrative organizations that have jurisdiction over more firms simply have less ability to keep track of the specific decisions and practices of the firms under their jurisdictions. If the effects we are seeing here are a function of the size of the jurisdiction in which a firm is situated, we should see effects of a firm's jurisdiction size on the practice of price negotiation similar to those of municipal bureau and municipal company governance. Model II affirms this view, as the larger a firm's jurisdiction, the more likely it is to negotiate prices with customers. The more firms a given organization's governing office has to watch over, the more likely it is that the organization will adopt this practice. This suggests that price reform is, at least to some extent, related to the administrative capacity of governing organizations. Administrative offices that are dividing their attention among only a few firms (as district companies are) are much more likely to control the activities of the firms under their jurisdictions, forcing them to adhere to prices as they were originally set. This picture fits with the idea of tight-fisted control over pricing at lower levels of the administrative hierarchy presented earlier in this chapter.

Concluding Remarks

Inasmuch as price mechanisms are a central part of market economic systems, the ability to set and negotiate prices independent of state control is a fundamental part of transitions from command to market economies and the emergence of a market mechanism. Despite the centrality of this issue for economic transitions, studies in sociology and economics that rely on income or aggregate measures of productivity are silent on the topic. Returns to education and entrepreneurship and changes in productivity reveal nothing about the freedom for large-scale economic actors to set and negotiate prices as they please. Further, while there have been significant in-depth accounts of China's dual-track system, to date we have surprisingly little evidence on how individual firms are actually dealing with the setting of prices. In this chapter I have focused directly on firms' practices surrounding the setting and negotiation of prices.

Under the command economy, firms simply followed state directives on production and sales. State administrative offices (usually bureaus) controlled inputs and outputs, and the state had full control over prices. In the economic transition, the liberalization of prices has been a central theme in the reforms. Now some firms themselves are responsible for setting prices fully independent of state control. Because this is a possibility that did not exist in the prereform period, the patterns of change in this realm are fundamentally linked to the economic transition. Thus the patterns we observe with respect to price setting reveal realities of the transition itself. The results presented in this chapter show that price-setting practices depend primarily on joint-venture relationships with foreign firms and a firm's position in the administrative hierarchy of the former command economy. The significance of a firm's position in the administrative hierarchy emphasizes the path-dependent nature of price setting and the emergence of market freedoms in China's transforming economy. In reform-era China the type of economy emerging and the ways that individual actors will experience this economy depend on the institutional structures that preceded the reforms and the economic practices to which firms are exposed through their economic networks.

In her review of Guo's (1992) study of price reform in China, Krug (1994) argues that although Guo presented an insightful and textured discussion of the fact that prices in China's transforming economy are as often determined by ad hoc procedures as by a rationalized set of decisions, he missed the fundamental point that political relations among firms and their governing organizations are a crucial piece of the price-reform puzzle. My position on this issue is the same as Krug's: The politics of reform and the institutional structure of state administration extend even into the realm of pricing. While bureaus are divesting themselves of control over the enterprises under their jurisdictions, more locally positioned governing offices are controlling the firms under their jurisdictions more like bureaus did in the command economy.

The significance of a formal relationship with a foreign company indicates that Western-style market practices are the most common among firms that observe these practices up close in the market transition. These practices are not transcendental or natural, and firms must have some context from which to draw them; indeed, they must have some set of concrete practices which they can observe and on which they can model their own practices. It is also interesting in this context to note the variety of views managers have of the emergence of price autonomy in reform-era China. Managers of organizations that have not adopted market-based price-setting practices view the process with skepticism. References to the "black-hearted" practice of profit maximization and the "competition problem" advance the notion that even with the loosening of state controls, the market mentality, which neoclassical models seem to posit as a natural human proclivity, is not simply lurking below the surface, waiting to emerge at the first opportunity. These managers live in a world that, until recently, has been defined by the institutions and ideology of socialism. Getting their minds around market-driven processes is not simply a matter of loosening state controls. It requires a reorientation toward and a rethinking of economic practices at a fundamental level.

Six

Economic Strategies in the Face of Market Reforms

> The overall strategy of a firm reflects, at any given point in time, important organizational facts. . . . Any decision to fundamentally alter the deployment of internal resources represents a major structural change. These kinds of changes do not occur often; when they do, they provide us with an opportunity to examine the conditions under which actors can alter their social structures.
>
> *(Neil Fligstein 1991)*

MARKET DECISIONS and strategies of organizations in transition economies illuminate important, often hidden facts about the nature and meaning of broader institutional changes of economic reforms. In this chapter I examine two specific strategies adopted by firms in the emerging markets of China's industrial economy. Like in the preceding chapters, my focus here is on the decisions firms are making in China's emerging markets and the implications those decisions have for understanding China's reforms and for theories of economic transition more generally. As I have argued in previous chapters, individual-level data on changing mechanisms of stratification do not tell us directly about such crucial issues as the market practices of economic actors in the economic transition or the hardening of budget constraints; such data, therefore, cannot answer the larger questions of marketization. On the other end of the spectrum, studies that employ aggregate data on productivity across sectors and regions as indicators of reforms are blind to the specific ways that economic actors' social worlds are changing. Without direct observations of economic decisions, these studies have assumed that reforms have not been meaningfully enacted in large state-owned urban industrial firms (i.e., those at the upper levels of the administrative hierarchy). The strategies explored in this chapter are the adoption of the Company Law and the adoption of a diversification strategy, and the analyses of these practices tell a different story about reforms in the upper levels of the economy. Analyses of these strategies support the notion that the state's institutional structure plays a significant role in both market strategies that firms are adopting; moreover, significant changes are reaching the state sector. Foreign investment is also an important factor in

the strategies that firms are adopting in China's transition, as firms are significantly influenced by the presence of a joint-venture partnership in the adoption of the Company Law.

As I asserted in my discussion of labor contracts and price-setting practices,
a process of marketization is occurring in urban industrial China, but it is a
process that is contingent on the institutional and organizational structures that
preceded the reforms. Firms are experiencing a world where market constraints are emerging, but the extent to which the firms are set adrift in the
market depends on their position in the state administrative hierarchy. Firms at
the highest levels of the hierarchy are significantly more likely to experiment
with a number of different strategies and practices in the economic transition.
However, these changes are hidden from studies that have focused exclusively
on standard economic indicators. Part of the analysis in this chapter is in direct
dialogue with studies suggesting that firms in the upper reaches of China's
administrative hierarchy are still being protected from the reforms. The analysis I present here shows that we need to view the strategies of firms—that is,
the specific ways that firms are responding to reforms—as being equal in importance to data on productivity and economic gains.

Beyond Economic Performance in Transition Theories

One problem with many of the studies on economic transitions is that there has
been a lopsided focus on the cases where productivity, changes in economic
performance, and entrepreneurial activity are taking place. In these analyses,
the focus for economic transition is on "the pursuit of power and plenty by
economic actors in society."[1] Even for scholars who are not focused on entrepreneurship, the studies begin with the puzzle of explaining the compara-
tively rapid gains in industrial productivity in rural China. For these studies,
the evidence of economic transition begins with performance and the economic arrangements that have led to gains in productivity. For example,
Walder, who has addressed many of the institutional questions of China's
reforms directly, bases his analysis on variation in aggregate measures of productivity. His hypothesis that "many of the predicted problems associated with
. . . soft budget contraints should be prevalent" at upper levels of the administrative hierarchy is grounded primarily on the observation that the township
and village public sectors have experienced significant gains in industrial performance (productivity) while the urban industrial sector has developed at a
much slower rate in terms of productivity.[2] However, based on this evidence,
can we be sure that fiscal constraints are not being tightened for large-scale
urban industrial enterprises? Hard-budget constraints will not *necessarily* lead
to performance gains, and therefore slower rates of change in these areas cannot be taken as evidence that budget constraints are not being hardened in the

urban industrial economy.[3] The debate thus far has been guided by a logic that is overly focused on efficiency and performance outcomes: Reforms—loosely defined as a tightening of fiscal constraints and an introduction of market economic practices—will breed efficiency, and if we observe a lack of economic efficiency (measured in productivity), then we can assume that reforms have not been enacted. A lack of efficiency means a lack of reform. However, it could also be the case that reforms are being enacted, but economic actors are failing to adapt to the necessities of market environments.

Gauging the extent of the economic transition as a function of aggregate gains in industrial performance and entrepreneurial activity ignores the fact that economic reforms may be taking hold, but this may be true irrespective of productivity, profitability, or entrepreneurial activity. But where else would we look for indicators of the reforms? Economic sociology provides us with some tools for answering this question. If reforms are happening in areas of the economy that are not growing, it is safe to assume that there will be a great deal of uncertainty for firms that formerly dipped—without limits—into state coffers. And past research has shown that organizational actions and decisions are often adopted in response to uncertain market and institutional environments.[4] An empirical examination of organizational actions in the face of uncertainty is a necessary supplement to studies based on aggregate increases in productivity or vitality of the private sector in analyses of economic transitions. The decisions and strategies of firms in the transforming economy can take us much further in understanding the impact of reforms than inferences from aggregate measures of productivity. If it is true that reforms are not being enacted at the upper levels of the industrial economy, if large-scale state-owned firms are indeed still being protected from the reforms, we would expect these firms not to be adopting new economic strategies of the reform era. The question is not whether these firms are being more productive in the reform era; rather, the more basic issue is whether firms are doing things differently than they were before the reforms.

Fligstein's (1996b) "markets as politics" theory offers several critical insights for the study of societies engaging in the political project of market construction and transformation. In Fligstein's view, the state, large-scale organizations, and the preexisting institutional structure of the economic system all become important factors in the political project of market construction. Fligstein's perspective also offers a framework for understanding economic action in unstable markets. According to Fligstein, actors are not necessarily the rational profit maximizers that classical economic models have posited them to be. Actors may still be rational, but what they do is strive to create stable worlds. Fligstein's view of market action is not a matter of rational action in worlds of perfect and imperfect information; rather, the focus is on linking survival and profit-maximizing strategies in one general model of market action. For dominant actors in the market, the drive for stability usually amounts to profit-maximizing strategies of market domination (and thus a stabilization of their dominant position). But for "challenging" actors whose positions are not inherently stable or dominant in the market, their worldviews may lead to strategies of stability that do not always make profit-maximizing sense. The point here is that stability strategies and profit-maximizing strategies are both legitimate forms of economic activity observable in the marketplace, and a theory of economic decision making must be able to account for both. This wide-angle view of economic activity is critical for making sense of the processes of marketization that are occurring in the Chinese urban industrial economy, especially at the upper echelons of the administrative hierarchy. In reform-era China, as legally standardized accounting systems are set in place and the state attempts to standardize taxation and begin the process of hardening budget constraints (see chapter 2), this state-induced crisis has caused firms to respond in various ways as they seek stability in the market.[5]

In China's economic transition, budget constraints are being hardened, albeit gradually, and high-level governing organizations can no longer incur the cost of blindly supporting the organizations beneath them. Lower-level administrative offices, on the other hand, are having an easier time managing resources and protecting the interests of the firms they control; they are also having an easier time offering administrative support and long-term development strategies to the firms in their jurisdiction. In chapter 2 I discussed several of the state-level institutional changes that have given rise to this "state-induced crisis." In the following sections I analyze two emerging economic practices that organizations are adopting in response to the state-induced crisis; both strategies are closely linked to the institutional structure of state administration that preceded the reforms. I break from the approach of other organizational studies in that I do not begin with the economic assumption that growth in output, performance, and profitability are the most fitting indicators of tightening fiscal constraints. In fact, focusing on these types of indicators may cause us to miss many things going on in the economic transition, particularly in cases of faltering firms. Both strategies I analyze below illuminate this fact.

The Company Law

In chapter 1 I argued that state-level institutional changes—policies and laws—in and of themselves are not meaningful measures of reforms; they are only significant to the extent that economic actors incorporate them into their worlds. One institutional change that allows us directly to observe the interaction between a state-level institution and organizational responses to incorporating this change is the Company Law. Adopted by the National People's Congress on December 29, 1993, the Company Law provides the first legal basis in the history of the PRC for private, collective, and state enterprises to exist as autonomous legal entities. It is an institutional change that continues the process of separating enterprises—both legally and operationally—from the state redistributive system of the former command economy. Yet, although the law now exists in China, there is still considerable variation as to whether organizations have chosen to incorporate this change into their daily operations.

Analysis of the move to adopt the Company Law illuminates the ways that firms think about the legal and institutional changes of the economic reforms, what these changes actually mean for firms in the economic reform, and the structural factors that give broad institutional changes meaning for different economic actors. In exploring what the Company Law means for individual firms, the language of "adopting" the Company Law is perhaps somewhat misleading. This is because factories do not simply adopt the law; they actually have to apply to the Economic Commission [*jingji weiyuanhui*] to become companies. Thus the process has a political component: Factories must apply to the municipal government, and the government must approve their applications. One could argue that the state plays an important role in who becomes a company and that a factory's decision to apply to become a company has little to do with the process. However, all the organizations in my study except one met the minimum requirements (in terms of turnover) to become a company (Company Law, chap. 1, art. 23), and, in practice, few applications are turned down. On the whole, managers spoke of the decision to apply to become a company as being very much an individual firm's choice, having little to do with the state selecting firms to apply. The state is involved in the approval process, but that comes after the factory has chosen to apply for company status. One manager explained his factory's situation:

> Right now we are still following the Enterprise Law. But we plan to switch over to the Company Law this year. We want to expand our operations. We want to become a company. (Interview 97*, 1995)

Inasmuch as the Company Law now exists in China, it is economic actors that decide whether they will incorporate this law into their daily practices. I view the process of choosing to become a company and then going through with the application process all as part of the adoption of the Company Law.[6] Once firms have applied for and received the approval to change from an enterprise to a company, they have, in effect, adopted the Company Law. In the discussion that follows I first briefly explore the implications of the Company Law as a state-level institutional change. Second, I explore the meaning of this law from the managers' perspective. Third, I examine the factors that influence firms to apply for the status of company and thereby adopt the Company Law.

A Brief History of the Company Law

Several scholars have emphasized the political nature of the construction of new laws in postreform China, as well as in other transforming societies.[7] The Company Law marks a fundamental shift in the organization of China's industrial economy, as Chinese organizations can now apply for the status of limited-liability company [*youxian zeren gongsi*] or limited-shares company [*gufen youxian gongsi*] and thus assume the mantle of independent legal entities. Yet, despite the interesting characteristics of the Company Law as a state-level institutional change of the economic transition, and despite the fact that this law is a critical part of China's transition to a "socialist market economy" and the emergence of the "modern enterprise system," relatively little research has been done on the Company Law.[8] In addition, there has been little research on how legal changes, such as the Company Law, affect the decisions and practices of individual economic actors.

As far as PRC laws go, the Company Law is actually a fairly long document with 11 chapters and 230 articles. The first article of the law clearly lays out its statement of purpose: "This law has been constructed and set in accordance with the needs of constructing a modern enterprise system [*xiandai qiye zhidu*], widening the scope of company organizational behavior, protecting the company, protecting the shares and legal profits of shareholders, safeguarding the social economic order, and advancing the development of market socialism" (chap. 1, art. 1). This is an interesting statement in that it covers a wide range of issues from organizational scope and behavior to more systemic issues of "advancing market socialism." It points to the fact that the law is both specific in its application for individual organizations and broad in its implications for institutional change in China's current project of market construction. The law is set, in theory, to protect individual stakeholders in organizations and to help engender a broader legal and institutional system across the market socialist economy. This situation is indicative of the challenge and predicament in which the Chinese state currently finds itself: When the economic system was nothing more than a command economy, the system was simple, direct, and completely dependent on the decisions bureaucrats made for enterprises. Currently, as the system becomes increasingly complex, operating increasingly independent of the state, the government finds itself in the apparent contradiction of being forced to protect individual stakeholders while trying to maintain the aspects of the system that make it decidedly socialist. Institutionalizing the contradictions—and some solutions to those contradictions—through legal channels has been a critical part of China's path through the reform period.

The first major change brought about by the Company Law is that an organization can now officially be a "legal entity" [*faren*] (chap. 1, art. 3). As one Shanghai official explained:

> The old concept of "legal entity" [*faren*] is not the same concept of legal entity specified in the Company Law; that is, the "legal entity" of the Enterprise Law is not the same as the legal entity of the Company Law. Legal entities should have independent power. But the enterprises were actually all controlled by the government, whereas the legal entity of the Company Law actually has true autonomy [*duli quanli*], and this has made a real difference in our ability to conduct certain economic matters. (Interview 106, 1995)

Thus the first step to broadening the scope of economic action, according to the Company Law, is to establish that an enterprise that assumes the status of company is an autonomous organization responsible for its own economic development and stability. Huang and Zhou (1994) point out that this idea of legal entity covers a wide scope of organizational responsibilities, ranging from deeper responsibility for knowing, understanding, and following laws to taking responsibility for all internal institutional structures within the organization. In addition, when organizations become official legal entities, the self-responsibility and independent budget policies (see chapter 2) take on much stronger meaning for these organizations.

Many of the reform-era Chinese laws "borrow extensively from Western legal doctrines, concepts, procedures, and terminology,"[9] a fact readily apparent in an inspection of the Company Law. The first eighteen articles of the law, which comprise the first chapter, establish what a company is in general, what different types of companies exist (limited-liability companies [*you xian zeren gongsi*] and limited-shares companies [*gufen you xian gongsi*]), and the fact that the Company Law (as opposed to the Enterprise Law) will be the legal governing body for these organizations. The next chapter (arts. 19–72) focuses on the specific institutional arrangements and issues that are central to the formation of a company. This covers the minimum production turnover an enterprise must have to become a company (500,000 RMB), all the internal issues for which the company's institutional rules must be set, several specific rules regarding shareholders (if any exist other than the state), several articles on the formation and responsibilities of a board of directors, other management issues, and workers' salaries and benefits. Chapters 3 and 4 (arts. 73–158) address the limited-stock company and the particulars that surround this type of company. Chapter 5 (arts. 159–173) addresses issues of bonds and debentures; chapter 6 (arts. 174–181) deals with financial affairs (including suggestions on how the company ought to divide up residual profits); chapter 7 (arts. 182–188) deals with company mergers and breakups; chapter 8 (arts. 189–198) deals with bankruptcy and dissolution; chapter 9 (arts. 199–205) is specifically devoted to the institutional structure of foreign companies;

chapters 10 and 11 (arts. 206–230) discuss the legal responsibilities that go along with the Company Law and with being a company.

Compared to the Enterprise Law[10], which has only sixty-nine articles and is relatively simple in its presentation of organizational structures, the Company Law lays out a complex legal system for building what the authors of the law believe is the "modern enterprise system" [*xiandai qiye zhidu*]. Whereas the Enterprise Law strongly emphasizes maintaining the state-enterprise relationship as part of the planned economy (see arts. 55–57), the Company Law focuses squarely on the autonomy and market orientation of the company. Clearly the company is viewed as a critical element of the socialist market economy. And as Huang and Zhou (1994, 5) point out in their discussion of the Company Law: "Building a socialist market institutional system is the main goal of China's reform."

Having briefly laid out the law's content and structure, I now turn to an analysis of the adoption of this law by firms in Shanghai. I focus on managers' views of the law's meaning and importance and what these perceptions tell us about the political and social meaning of the Company Law in the period of economic transition. Which organizations are adopting the Company Law? What do managers of different organizations think about this law? Does the adoption of this law reveal an aggressive stance toward development? How does a firm's sectoral location, economic health, and position in the industrial hierarchy affect the adoption of the Company Law?

Adopting the Company Law

In Shanghai today there is considerable variation with regard to whether organizations have applied to become a company. Managers' responses range from having little idea of what the Company Law is to being extremely excited and knowledgeable about adopting this law. For those who knew little about the Company Law, one could argue that these managers simply had not been exposed to the law and were not adequately equipped to incorporate the law. But the types of organizations these managers ran were in many ways consistent with an overall lack of knowledge about or interest in the economic reforms. And this is precisely the point: Certain organizations in the economic reforms are less knowledgeable about the reforms, are less interested in the reforms, or are choosing—or being guided in—different directions vis-à-vis the reforms. It is useful to examine who these managers are, what types of organizations they run, and how these organizations relate to other firms in the transition economy.[11]

For some managers, interest in the legal changes of the reforms reflects more rhetoric than anything else. As one manager said:

> State-owned organizations like ours pay close attention to all the laws that come out of the government. The Company Law, the Labor Law, these will all be very important for us. (Interview 30, 1995)

But when I asked more directly if he had even read the Company Law, he said:

> Actually no. You may be more familiar with these laws than we are. I didn't realize the Company Law was out yet.

I had a similar encounter with a government official in Wuhan shortly after the Company Law had been promulgated:

> OFFICIAL: These laws [the Company Law, among others] are very important for us. We pay very close attention to them.
>
> GUTHRIE: Have you and others in your office read the Company Law then?
>
> OFFICIAL: It's not out yet.
>
> GUTHRIE: Uh . . . I'm pretty sure it is. I think it was adopted in December of last year, and it was actually promulgated in July of this year.
>
> OFFICIAL: Really? I don't think that's right. I'm pretty sure it's not out yet. Are you sure? (Interview 11, 1994)

In fact, the law had been promulgated four months earlier, and officials in some departments had copies of it on hand at the time of this interview. For individuals such as those quoted above, there seemed to be some interest in legal change, at least rhetorically, but they had little substantive knowledge of or interest in the laws themselves. They were much more interested in simply parroting the line about the importance of the new laws of the economic transition.

Some managers, however, did not even go this far. One manager in the garments sector said:

> I'm not exactly sure what the Company Law is. But I have heard about it. I don't think it has anything to do with us really. (Interview 107*, 1995)

Displaying a lack of knowledge of the application process and that any factory can apply to become a company, one manager in the electronics sector said:

> The Company Law has no meaning for us. We're a factory not a company, right? (Interview 39*, 1995)

Another manager in the electronics sector saw the division between factory and company in a similar way:

> The Company Law has very little relevance for us. Factories are in the category of enterprises. The scope of companies is larger than that of enterprises. The Company Law was set forth to organize the structure of companies. Factories will continue to be organized by the Enterprise Law. (Interview 36*, 1995)

These individuals all drew a distinction between the scope of what their enterprises do and what companies do. Yet, they expressed no interest in developing in the direction of becoming a company in the future. Other managers simply expressed exasperation at trying to keep up with all the laws emerging in the reform. A manager in the electronics sector expressed this exasperation and lack of knowledge, saying:

> I'm not so sure about [the Company Law]. I think our work unit focuses on the Enterprise Law. Maybe we still pay attention to the Enterprise Law. But I've heard that maybe the Company Law is more important now. The government is working on these laws right now. It's all very confusing with so many laws coming out at once. (Interview 53*, 1995)

One manager responded in a weary tone that reflected her lack of interest in trying to keep up with all the changes:

> Yes, yes, [we follow] the Company Law or the Enterprise Law, or whatever . . . whatever the state says we should be following these days. (Interview 110*, 1995)

In contrast to these managers' lack of knowledge or interest in the Company Law, some managers expressed a clearer understanding of the Company Law and the legal changes accompanying the economic reforms. A manager in the electronics sector described his organization's view:

> Right now we focus on the Enterprise Law more than the Company Law. The Company Law just came out in July of last year. This is a broader law than the Enterprise Law, so it could also include us. But we have followed the Enterprise Law for a long time, so right now it's just simpler to use that as our guide. (Interview 60*, 1995)

A manager in the foods sector said something similar:

> Now we are still going by the Enterprise Law. I think we will be switching over to the Company Law sometime in the future, but we haven't gotten to that point yet. (Interview 76*, 1995)

For these managers a thread of understanding of the Company Law ran throughout the interviews. Although they saw their organizations as not quite ready for the transition between enterprise and company, they seemed to be familiar with both the Enterprise and the Company Laws and with the process of transition between the two.

Another category of responses to these issues came from firms I considered to be more aggressive developers. All the firms in this category were very familiar with the laws, what their implications were, and the administrative process that links them, and they all had made the decision to pursue company status. They all had either already become companies or were applying for that status at the time of the interview. One manager in the chemicals sector explained his factory's situation:

> Currently we are still following the Enterprise Law; we are still an enterprise. But we have already applied to become a company and should get the approval later this year. The change will not be so great for us because we have really been acting like a company for several years, really since 1986. (Interview 97*, 1995)

Another manager in the chemicals sector described a similar situation for her factory:

> Although we are currently applying to be a multidivisional company [*jituan gongsi*], we are still following the Enterprise Law until the approvals for this change come through. Right now we are just waiting. (Interview 95*, 1995)

Another manager put this process in the context of the firm's relation to the bureau, its governing organization, and the greater autonomy and economic responsibilities the firm itself will be taking on with company status:

> This year we are applying to become a company. . . . After we become a company we will be completely de-linked [*tuogou*] from the bureau. Right now, even though we are an independent legal entity, the de-linking is not complete; we still have a kind of special relationship with the Chemicals Bureau because they are our government administrative organization. But after we become a company this will change completely. . . . It has been a long process in getting to this point. . . . Now we are just waiting for the approvals to come from the Economic Commission. (Interview 97*, 1995)

It is interesting to note the anticipation with which this manager spoke of his organization's imminent separation from the state. It is also worth noting, however, that several of the general managers who expressed excitement about becoming a company, when pressed, had a difficult time articulating how things would change for their organization. Often they would simply respond by saying something along these lines:

> Uh . . . I guess our scope will be much bigger [*guimo bijiao da*] when we are a company. . . . And we'll be more powerful. (Interview 96*, 1995)

Other firms that had already completed the application process expressed fairly extensive knowledge of what the Company Law meant for them. One manager in the foods sector explained his firm's situation:

> In 1986 business in our factory really started picking up. Before, we were a planned economy. But after the economic opening, our factory was one of the earliest to integrate a market economic approach. The year 1986 is actually when our profits really started picking up. Then last year we applied to have our factory changed from an enterprise to a company. So now we are under the Company Law, and our scope of business is much wider. It's really a much better situation for us in terms of development now. (Interview 82*, 1995)

This manager, like several other of the "aggressive developers" in my survey, saw his organization as incorporating an official institutional change that simply gave a label, credence, and legitimacy to the aggressive market actions his company had been carrying out since the mid-1980s. One manager in the chemicals sector, whose organization had already been awarded the company status, seemed annoyed that the club was not more exclusive:

> Being a company has no meaning right now. Everybody is applying to become a company; it's really chaotic [*luan*]. Every single little enterprise or store with three workers is a limited company now. It should be an indicator of scope of production, scope of business, subsidiary divisions, and some other things. But now it's just really chaotic. (Interview 105*, 1995)

Another manager in the chemicals sector, whose organization had not yet applied to become a company, expressed the same concern over the substantive meaning of this institutional change:

> Right now there are many enterprises applying to become companies, and they can't even tell you the real differences between being an enterprise and being a company. They might tell you that their scope will be larger, but that's an obvious and sort of meaningless change. The real changes are much more important and more subtle. But so many enterprises are just following the trend and applying to become a company so they can put out a new sign [*gua yige xinde paizi*] with a new name. They think that changing their name will make them a new and different organization. . . . Our enterprise is eventually going to apply to become a company, but we're going to make sure we are ready for this change and that we understand all the differences that being a company will bring us. (Interview 100*, 1995)

This manager presented a more sophisticated understanding of the dynamics behind this institutional change than most. His view of the rush to become a company as a symbolic exercise (changing the organization's name, changing titles, hanging up a new sign) with little substance gets at the mechanisms and dynamics that lurk below the surface of many changes occurring in organizations throughout China. Organizations are rushing to adopt new structures and organizational forms not because they are substantively better or more efficient—in fact, many managers cannot even articulate what the changes will be, let alone why they will be more efficient—but because they are *perceived* to be more efficient, part of what it means to be a "modern" enterprise.

In sum, among the managers I interviewed for this study, there were a variety of responses to this state-crafted institutional change of the economic transition. These responses ranged from a complete lack of interest in or knowledge of the law to a deep knowledge of the law and a desire to incorporate and take advantage of this institutional development. It will help to place these managers' views on the Company Law in a broader context of the organizational characteristics that increase the likelihood that a firm will attempt to

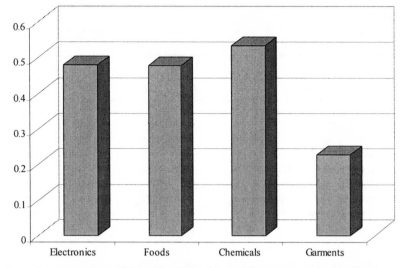

Figure 6.1: Proportion of Firms That Have Adopted the Company Law in Four
Sectors in Industrial Shanghai, 1995

become a company. Thus the analysis below is about which firms are more
institutionally aware of the changes occurring at the state level. It will also
illuminate which types of organizations are developing more aggressively, attempting to take on the status and responsibility that goes along with becoming
a company.

Figure 6.1 shows the adoption of the Company Law across sectors in Shanghai. The electronics, foods, and chemicals sectors all have a higher rate of
adoption than the garments sector.

Table 6.1 basically shows two significant findings, both consistent with several of the findings presented in earlier chapters. First, controlling for other
effects, firms that have relationships with foreign companies are significantly
more likely to apply for company status. Firms engaged in relationships
with—and therefore under the influence of—foreign partners are more likely
to pursue economic strategies which the state has defined as "modern enterprise systems." Two things are probably going on here. First, firms that have
applied to become companies are likely to be aggressive developers. One factory manager in the chemicals sector described his firm's adoption of the Company Law as only the most recent strategy in an extended period of enterprise
restructuring and "aggressive development" [*jijide fazhan*]:

> The actual change [becoming a company] was not so great for us, because we have
> been developing and really operating like a "company" for a long time already;
> really since the mid-1980s. (Interview 98*, 1995)

TABLE 6.1

Logistic Coefficients for the Adoption of the Company Law by Organizations in Four Industrial Sectors, Shanghai, 1995

Independent variables	Model I		Model II	
	B	S.E.	B	S.E.
Organizational variables[a]				
Chemicals	−.80	.51	−.69	.49
Electronics	−.83	.47	−.65	.43
Garments	−.48	.45	−.47	.44
Active employees (ln)	.15	.37	.32	.36
Organizational health	−.02	.08	−.04	.08
Profit margin, avg. 1990–1994	.05	.03	.04	.03
Products exported, 1990 (%)	−.01	.01	−.01	.01
Joint venture	.63*	.36	.68**	.34
Governance variables				
GM w/bus./econ. backgrnd.	−.38	.29	−.37	.29
Municipal bureau	1.50*	.90	—	—
Municipal company	.44	.38	—	—
Jurisdiction size (ln)	—	—	.16	.22
Constant	−2.13	2.48	−3.89*	2.21
χ^2	20.37**		17.71*	
No. of cases	80		80	

Note: See Appendix 4 for discussion of variables. B is the effect of the coefficient; S.E. is the standard error. * $p < .1$ ** $p < .05$ (two-tailed tests). Variables in bold are statistically significant.

[a] Reference category for sector is foods.

Similarly, firms that are developing aggressively and successfully during the economic transition may be more apt to have landed joint-venture contracts. Aggressively developing firms are more attractive joint-venture partners, as foreign companies are likely to prefer working with organizations that are successfully navigating their way through the period of reforms. In one sense, the presence of a joint-venture relationship may be a proxy for aggressive and successful development of a firm in the period of economic reform.

A second interpretation of this result is that an organization with a joint-venture relationship with a foreign partner may be more likely to pursue company status because of institutional influence. It should be noted in the results above that a firm's decision to adopt the Company Law is not significantly related to the firm's profit margins or its overall organizational health, variables that would presumably be proxies for aggressive development. Not only are these other effects insignificant, but the effect of a joint-venture relationship is significant independent of these factors. Thus the stronger interpretation of the joint-venture effect is probably that a foreign partner provides a Chinese firm with up-close examples of how foreign firms operate. The "modern enterprise system" is, in many ways, a rhetorical stand-in for Western-style management practices. Firms that are exposed to the concept of the "modern enterprise system" through contact with foreign companies and through setting up a joint-venture company with a foreign partner are more likely to see the institutional advantages (real or perceived) of broadening the organization's scope of operation and becoming an independent legal entity. In chapter 3, I discussed the notion that firms may adopt practices which other organizations have adopted because, in the search for market success, organizations mimic practices of successful organizations. Such mimetic mechanisms may also be in operation here, and they may work across societal and cultural boundaries. When a firm has extended contact with a foreign organization and when the firm works with a foreign partner to set up a joint-venture company, the Chinese firm is exposed to company systems from other market economies. When the state promulgated the Company Law in 1994, the firms with foreign partners had the clearest sense of what a company was and what the advantages of being a company would be. The result is that contact with foreign partners increases the likelihood that the Chinese firm will adopt the newly emerging Chinese version of the "modern enterprise system."

The second finding that emerges from Table 6.1 is that location under a municipal bureau has a statistically significant positive effect on a firm's decision to adopt the Company Law, increasing the likelihood by more than four times ($\exp[1.5] = 4.48$). In China's economic transition, various conceptions of control are emerging at different levels of the administrative hierarchy. These various interpretations of control are functions of the relative responsibilities and monitoring capacities of government administrative offices, which vary across the levels of the government hierarchy.[12] Bureau offices, with jurisdiction over many enterprises, do not have the administrative resources to monitor and offer administrative advice or help to the firms in the large organizational fields under their jurisdictions. Consequently, firms under municipal bureaus experience a greater sense of being set adrift in the economic transition. They are thus encouraged—or they feel the impetus—to pursue economic strategies on their own. Adopting the Company Law and thereby broadening the scope of action in China's growing markets is one such strategy that firms, especially those under bureaus, are taking. Firms under the jurisdiction of district companies, on the other hand, are more closely monitored by their government organizations (relative to those under bureaus), and these firms are offered a significant amount of administrative help and attention in the economic reform. Therefore, when the opportunity arose to apply to become a company and adopt the Company Law, these organizations under the jurisdiction of administrative companies felt less need to pursue this increasingly trendy institutional change.

Firms under the jurisdiction of municipal bureaus are significantly more likely to pursue (or be pushed to pursue) company status and adopt the

Company Law, whereas firms under district companies are less likely to follow this route. One could argue that the different levels of governance simply pursue different sets of rules and practices, and firms under municipal bureaus are more likely to adopt the Company Law just because governance structures in the organizational fields under bureaus allow them to do so. However, there are no formal rules or articles in the Company Law itself or in the "Company Law Implementation Procedures" that indicate an explicitly different set of rules for organizations at various levels of the municipal administrative hierarchy. In addition, while my perspective is that different conceptions of control—informed by different scopes of responsibility, burdens, and monitoring capacities—are adopted by governing organizations at different levels of the administrative hierarchy, one could also argue that firms under bureaus are more apt to get approvals because of government connections or because the government is selecting firms under the jurisdiction of bureaus to become companies. Probably both things are going on. Firms under bureaus are more likely to adopt aggressive development strategies and seek the status and economic advantages that go along with becoming a company because of the sense that they are being set adrift by the state. At the same time, as the bureaus push administrative and economic responsibilities down the hierarchy, firms under their jurisdiction are encouraged to develop and broaden their scope of independence. Bureaus want to reduce their responsibilities to firms under their jurisdiction and thereby push those responsibilities onto the firms themselves; forced to deal with increased responsibilities themselves, firms under bureaus adopt an aggressive stance toward development, which encompasses incorporating institutional changes that further allow for and facilitate this aggressive independent development.

Model II introduces an important test to help us interpret the results of Model I. If the effect of bureau governance is an issue of government resources (administrative and fiscal), then there should be a relationship between the size of the jurisdiction and whether a firm adopts the Company Law.[13] If there is a difference between the way organizations under government bureaus are governed compared to the way organizations under administrative companies are governed, then we should see the significance in the dummy variables but not in the size of the jurisdiction. The model shows that the size of a firm's jurisdiction does not increase the likelihood that the firm will adopt the Company Law. These results indicate that there are significant differences in the conceptions of control and the ways that firms under the jurisdiction of bureaus are governed relative to firms under administrative companies, as I have suggested above.

In sum, by viewing the adoption of the Company Law as an economic strategy in the reform, I have shown evidence for two types of institutional effects at the firm level surrounding a specific state-level reform. First, there is the effect of the presence of a joint venture. Chinese firms are exposed to the perceived advantages of operating as a company through contact with a for-eign partner and through observing the structure of the joint-venture entity. In attempting to become more like their foreign partners, they are significantly more likely to adopt institutional reforms such as the Company Law. A second institutional effect is indicated by the significance of a firm's position in the government administrative hierarchy. This effect is likely to have a more polit-ical line to it as organizations located at different levels of the administrative hierarchy experience different conceptions of control by their respective gov-ernment offices. As I have argued in chapter 2, organizations at structurally similar positions vis-à-vis the state have a great deal in common in the eco-nomic transition. Where some studies have argued that reforms have not been enacted in the upper levels of China's industrial hierarchy, the analysis I pre-sent here indicates that organizations at the upper levels of China's industrial hierarchy are, at least in some ways, among those firms that are the most en-gaged in the changes of the reforms. If the organizations in this economic sector are not becoming more productive, it is not for lack of trying. This argument will be developed further in the discussion on diversification below.

Service-Sector Diversification

That economic and administrative strategies are being placed squarely on the shoulders of the firms themselves is reflected not only in aggressive develop-ment strategies (as in the adoption of the Company Law) but also in the pursuit of survival strategies and economic practices that are more closely related to losses or a poor economic performance. In this section I discuss the issue of firms' reactions to unstable market situations through an analysis of their deci-sion to adopt a diversification strategy.[14] Following theories in economic soci-ology, I view the adoption of a diversification strategy as an indication of a firm's desire to create a stable world, and organizations using this strategy are those that have limited access to the state's administrative and fiscal resources in the economic transition.[15] That the firms adopting this strategy are those in the upper levels of the administrative hierarchy further indicates that signifi-cant changes are occurring in this part of the economy.

Firms often adopt alternative economic strategies in the face of uncertainty. Diversification is one such strategy that firms in China's economic transition have adopted to create stability and spread out risk. Other studies in economic sociology point to the utility of analyzing diversification strategies for under-standing firms' economic and political situations.[16] In the case of China, the adoption of a diversification strategy is, for several reasons, a good place to begin for achieving an understanding of the structural conditions emerging in the current urban economic reform. First, whether organizations choose to diversify is likely to be tied to the economic hardships they are facing, the extent to which fiscal constraints are being tightened, and the degree to which the state is continuing to protect certain organizations in the economic transition. An analysis of economic strategies, as well as the economic, structural, and governance factors that drive them, will yield the clearest picture of China's economic transition. The second advantage of this variable, not unrelated to the first, is that this specific type of diversification is an entirely new practice that has emerged over the course of the economic transition. Diversification into the service sector is, by definition, intimately tied to the economic changes of China's transition economy, as it emerged during and as part of the economic transition.[17] It is therefore appropriate to view this strategy as intimately tied to the economic, structural, and governance changes occurring in the economic transition.

Troubled firms have several possible survival strategies from which to choose in the economic reform: They can receive protection—in the form of bailouts—from the state; they can borrow money from the bank (though this is becoming increasingly difficult in the reform era); or they can borrow from other firms. Another survival strategy that many managers see as an option in the face of the reforms is that firms can spread out risk by investing in the low-risk, fast-return markets of the service-sector economy [*disan chanye touzi*]. This type of investment has become a quick-return capital investment strategy that allows organizations to invest earnings outside of their own industrial sector into the rapidly expanding service sector. Yet, with significant variation on the adoption of this strategy, opinions on the utility of this practice differ considerably. One manager in the electronics sector explained the utility of investments in the service sector, saying:

> This is the only way we are making any money. Investments in this sector are very good because we can make a quick return on any investment at a relatively high rate. We don't need to wait for a product to be produced and then for the market to decide if it is going to sell. We just make money through investing in services. As soon as you invest, you can start making money. . . . Now we are trying to run the factory but at the same time make money to support the organization through our service-sector investments. (Interview 43*, 1995)

Another manager in the foods sector described the decision to invest in the service sector in similar terms, emphasizing the extent to which this was a market strategy of spreading risk:

> We want to continue to develop and invest in other areas and markets. In China right now the service sector is a great opportunity for investment. It is also important because you have to protect yourself; if you concentrate too much on one product or in one sector and that market starts to become weak, there's nothing you can do. You won't be able to adapt to the market changes, and the enterprise will die from the losses [*kuisile*]. We have a saying in business: When the east is dim, the west is light [*dongfang bu liang, xifang liang*]. This means that if things aren't happening in one

area, they may still be happening in another area. So if you spread yourself out and invest in many different areas, it's a way of protecting yourself; somewhere there is bound to be light. That's the main reason investment in other areas is very important. (Interview 72*, 1995)

Though not about the diversification of product lines, this understanding of diversification investments relates to studies of "classical" diversification strategies that view firms as choosing to enter industries that are expanding rapidly in an attempt to spread risk through investments.[18] Despite the positive spins that many managers gave this market strategy, equally strong dissenting opinions were voiced. As another manager, also in the electronics sector, explained:

In Chinese business we have a saying: Every sector is like a mountain [*ge hang ru ge shan*]. This means that just because we have made it to the top of one sector, we may not necessarily be successful in another sector. That is like climbing an entirely different mountain. Our company understands the electronics sector very well, but that does not mean we would understand the hotel or restaurant industry in the same way. Maybe we would fail terribly at it. So we just stay in one sector. (Interview 38*, 1995)

To understand the organizational characteristics associated with this practice, the service-sector diversification variable was included in the data by asking general managers whether their organization has service-sector investments—besides a factory store in the organization.[19] The interviewees were further asked to specify the percentage of the organization's turnover derived from these investments. For the purposes of this discussion, however, investment in the service sector was simply coded dichotomously as yes or no.

Adopting the Service-Sector Diversification Strategy

Figure 6.2 shows the proportions of firms that have adopted this strategy by sector. Firms in the electronics sector are significantly more likely to adopt this strategy than are those in other sectors.

Table 6.2 presents the determinants of a firm's strategy to adopt this diversification strategy. Model I shows that organizational size has a significant positive association with the decision to diversify into the service sector. A firm's overall organizational health has a significantly negative association with the adoption of this strategy. The healthier an organization is, the less likely it is to diversify; the more troubled an organization is, the more likely it will adopt the diversification strategy. This finding supports the notion that service-sector diversification is an economic strategy adopted by firms that are struggling to survive in China's emerging markets. Service-sector diversification is not about profit maximization but, rather, is about economic uncertainty, and firms

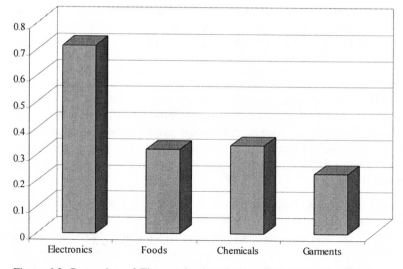

Figure 6.2: Proportion of Firms Adopting the Service-Sector-Diversification Strategy in Four Sectors in Industrial Shanghai, 1995

adopting this strategy are seeking stability by investing in the fast-return markets of the service-sector economy. If diversification were a strategy associated with profit maximization, we would expect to see stronger firms also adopting the strategy as part of an overall development strategy. But, as the results above show, it is the weakest firms, those in the most tenuous positions economically, that are turning to diversification.

Questions may be raised, however, about the direction of causality among these associations given the data employed in this study: Did firms adopt the diversification strategy because they were economically weak, or did they become economically weak because they diversified? If the latter were true, my assertion that service-sector diversification is a tactic adopted by firms experiencing uncertainty in China's markets would appear tenuous.[20] Model II addresses these concerns. The year 1990 preceded the time when virtually all firms had adopted service-sector diversification.[21] If diversification is indeed a strategy that economically weak firms are adopting—as opposed to one that is making firms economically weak—we should see results for the year 1990 in Table 6.2 that are similar to those presented in Model I. As Model II shows, the results for the 1990 associations are similar to those of 1994: Firms that were in poor economic health in 1990 were more likely to adopt the diversification strategy over the next four years.

Model III, which introduces the effects of the administrative level of a firm's governing organization, reveals that organizational health still has a significant negative association with the dependent variable, net of all other effects, indicating that poor economic health increases the likelihood that a firm will adopt

TABLE 6.2

Logistic Coefficients for the Adoption of Diversification Strategy by Organizations in Four Industrial Sectors, Shanghai, 1995

	Model I		Model II		Model III		Model IV	
Independent variables	B	S.E.	B	S.E.	B	S.E.	B	S.E.
Organizational variables[a]								
Chemicals	−.79	1.00	.04	1.07	−.63	1.18	.16	1.25
Electronics	.86	.83	.93	.94	.62	1.04	1.24	1.14
Foods	.51	.73	.54	.85	.63	.79	1.83	1.02
Active employees (ln)	.83**	.34	1.19	.41	.42	.40	.18	.43
Employee ratio	−.04	1.78	.41	2.00	−.61	2.05	−.15	2.29
Organizational health	−.29*	.16	—	—	−.40*	.21	−.53**	.24
Organizational health, 1990	—	—	−1.13**	.53	—	—	—	—
Profit margin, avg. 1990–1994	.04	.04	.03	.04	−.003	.04	−.04	.04
Losses, 1990	.09	.78	.29	.84	−.45	.93	−1.13	1.09
Joint venture	.28	.70	.36	.76	−.09	.78	−.10	.88
Governance variables								
GM w/bus./econ. backgrnd.	—	—	—	—	1.36**	.67	1.23*	.74
Municipal bureau	—	—	—	—	2.96***	.96	—	—
Jurisdiction size (ln)	—	—	—	—	—	—	1.59***	.44
Constant	−5.72**	2.47	−8.22***	2.88	−3.87	2.77	−6.94**	3.08
χ^2	20.39**		27.34		35.09***		46.22***	
No. of cases	81		73		81		81	

Note: See Appendix 4 for discussion of variables. B is the effect of the coefficient; S.E. is the standard error.
* $p < .1$ ** $p < .05$ *** $p < .01$ (two-tailed tests). Variables in bold are statistically significant.
[a] Reference category for sector is garments.

the diversification strategy. The bureau governance variable also has a significantly positive effect: Location under a municipal bureau increases an organization's likelihood of adopting the diversification strategy by almost twenty times (exp[2.96] = 19.30). These findings support my general argument that large-scale organizations under municipal bureaus are directly experiencing tightening fiscal constraints. If the situation were otherwise, if budget constraints were still remaining soft in the upper levels of the administrative hierarchy, what would be the incentive for organizations at these levels to seek profits and spread out risk through diversification? In addition, it is interesting to note that the general manager's background matters for the likelihood that a firm will adopt this strategy, as firms with general managers who have a background in business or economics are about four times more likely (exp[1.36] = 3.90) to have adopted this practice. Similar to the findings presented in chapter 3, this result shows that managers who have backgrounds in business or economics or both (as opposed to engineering, technical training, or no training at all) are significantly more likely to experiment with new economic strategies in the reform era. In sum, diversification into the service sector is one way of dealing with uncertainty in the marketplace, and economically weak firms, those under the jurisdiction of municipal bureaus, and those with economically minded general managers are all likely to experiment with this strategy.

Finally, Model IV shows the effect of organizational governance as a function of jurisdiction size. The significantly positive association of jurisdiction size (the number of firms a governing office oversees) helps to interpret the other models and lends support for the thesis set forth here that government responsibility is critical in the availability of economic and administrative resources and the subsequent strategies that organizations adopt. Jurisdiction size is positively associated with diversification, meaning that the more factories a given firm's government office oversees, the more likely it is that the firm will adopt a diversification strategy. As government jurisdiction increases in size, so, too, does the tendency to seek external incomes increase. Bureaus oversee many factories—usually somewhere between one hundred and four hundred—so they have heavy administrative responsibilities, especially in the economic transition. Therefore, as budget constraints become hardened for all organizations (governing and economic), the resource pool they can offer to organizations beneath them becomes more a function of the number of organizations competing for resources than a function of the gross value of budgetary resources. Organizations beneath bureaus, then, are forced to seek other paths to stability. This explains the positive effect of bureau governance in the preceding models. The situation for district companies is quite different. Although their overall budgets may still be smaller, the number of organizations competing for economic and administrative resources is somewhere between two and ten. Thus there is a greater chance that these offices will have slack resources or redistribute resources among firms under their jurisdictions. It should be noted that a substantial increase in the chi-square statistic is evident in this model compared to the other models in Table 6.2. Since the only factor that distinguishes this model is the substitution of jurisdiction size for bureau and municipal company governance, we should take seriously the explanatory power of jurisdiction size with respect to the practice of diversification.

Uncertainty in Chinese Markets

Following the argument to which I alluded in my discussion of labor contracts, the results presented in Table 6.2 indicate that both economic uncertainty and administrative uncertainty are emerging in the markets of China's transition economy. Economic uncertainty is fairly straightforward: Organizations that are struggling economically are likely to seek stability by investing assets in the quick-return markets of China's rapidly expanding service-sector economy. The evidence of economic uncertainty in Chinese markets indicates that significant changes are occurring in the urban industrial sector in the economic transition. That productivity has not risen as rapidly in urban industrial areas as it has in rural areas has been taken as evidence that reforms are not being implemented in China's urban industrial areas and that firms in that sector are still supported by state funds.[22] Yet, weak firms in this sector of the economy are seeking alternative paths to economic stability. If reforms were not being enacted, if firms were still supported by state funds, what would be the incentive for an organization to spread risk and invest in quick-return markets? A look at the strategies and practices of firms in China's transition economy indicates that, in fact, market reforms are taking hold in this part of the economy: increasingly firms are being set adrift, and they can no longer count on state bailouts in situations of economic hardship. This implies that although aggregate measures of productivity in the upper levels of China's administrative hierarchy seem to indicate that reforms are not being enacted in this economic sector, in fact firms are starting to act under marketlike constraints— economically weak firms face uncertain futures. And these firms are embracing the practices of market actors, that is, they are adopting the survival strategies of spreading out risk and seeking fast returns in alternative markets.

Though related to economic uncertainty, administrative uncertainty is somewhat more complicated. As with economic uncertainty, the driving force behind administrative uncertainty is the enactment of reforms. But the reforms have had a different impact on firms at different levels of this administrative hierarchy. An examination of the mechanisms behind administrative uncertainty requires an exploration of the relationships among individual firms, the responsibilities of and constraints on governing offices, and how these responsibilities and constraints are changing in the economic transition.

Government Responsibilities

Tightening Fiscal Constraints for Administrative Offices

What are the mechanisms behind the administrative uncertainty that firms under municipal bureaus experience in China's transition economy? Location under a municipal bureau significantly increases a firm's likelihood of diversifying, whereas district and municipal company governance decrease the likelihood of diversification. There are two principal reasons why governance at different administrative levels matters so much for diversification.[23] First, while we know that the number and scale of enterprises increase with higher administrative levels, I emphasize the fact that in the economic transition, economic responsibilities grow with administrative rank precisely because of the larger scale and scope of sectors under higher-level administrative offices (see chapter 2). In China today, as the project of market transition continues and accounting, taxation (state revenue extraction), and legal institutional systems become codified and solidified, the revenue bases of government organizations are constricted. Under the planned economy, governing organizations simply extracted revenues from the organizations under their jurisdictions. In the economic transition, as a result of the Profits to Tax Reform [*li gai shui*], firms are required to pay taxes to the government and no longer have to turn profits over to their governing organization.[24] Many governing organizations still collect a management fee [*guanli fei*], and some still collect a portion of firms' profits. However, if the core of the planned economy lies in the fact that firms turned revenues over to their governing organizations and this money was redistributed to firms in the jurisdiction, the fundamental transformation of that system has been set in motion over the course of the economic reforms.

The result of these policy changes of the reform is that government organizations cannot continue to cover the costs for all the firms under their jurisdictions. With less money coming in from those firms under their jurisdictions and with a finite amount of money coming from city and central governments, governing organizations have a limited amount of fiscal resources to draw from. And the more firms these governing organizations have to watch over—with potentially more firms to bail out—the more constrained fiscal budgets of governing organizations become in the economic transition. For governing organizations with jurisdiction over many firms (e.g., between one hundred and four hundred for municipal bureaus; see Figure 2.1)—which in the past relied on the revenues from many firms for their overall budgets—the change has been extreme. These organizations no longer have access to the revenues of a large group of firms, and thus their access to excess fiscal resources has been reduced significantly. For governing organizations with jurisdiction over a few firms (e.g., between three and ten for district companies; see Figure 2.1), tightening fiscal constraints have much less of an impact: In the planned economy, these governing organizations only drew their budgets from a small group of firms, and, to some extent, their budgets were constrained under the planned economy (they were also turning the majority of their revenues over to the bureaus). In addition, these organizations simply have fewer firms to guide through the economic transition and potentially fewer organizations to bail out in the case of financial difficulties.

The second reason for the adoption of a diversification strategy is an outgrowth of the first: Whereas bureaus controlled sectors in the planned economy, in the period of economic reform, administrative and economic responsibilities are being pushed down the hierarchy to administrative companies and to firms themselves. The individual factories under bureaus experience the most uncertainty in this newly marketized world, because they are left alone to succeed in the market or to make their case for resources from the state along-side all the other firms in the same position in their jurisdiction. Those under administrative companies, however, are protected from the do-or-die market system, and they are also monitored by a governing organization much more closely than the isolated factories under the bureaus are. If it becomes clear that a factory underneath an administrative company is heading for a shortfall, the bureaucrats of the district or municipal company can afford the time and attention to help the organization reorganize and restructure. Further, administrative companies can offer bailouts, because, although their overall budgets are substantially smaller than those of bureaus, they also have significantly fewer responsibilities in terms of the number of organizations they watch over and guide through the economic reform. In addition to bailouts, they can offer long-term development strategies and general attention that cannot be offered by the bureaus, which are now quite selective about which firms they protect in the economic transition. The overall effect is that budget constraints *are* being hardened in the urban industrial economy, but this is a process that is mediated by the economic responsibilities government offices incur. The larger the economic responsibilities of the governing organization, the greater the extent to which firms are left to fend for themselves in the market economy.

Monitoring, Information, and Development Plans

Government responsibility is not only about fiscal resources. Issues of monitoring and information are also intimately tied to government responsibility and the changing structure of the administrative hierarchy in the economic transition. Accounts of monitoring and information have emphasized the monitoring problems that come with "layers" of bureaucracy.[25] According to this view, where local governments in townships and villages have direct control over the firms under their jurisdictions, the administrative companies that control firms in urban areas simply add another layer of bureaucracy between the firm and the municipal bureau and, in effect, become barriers to the upward flow of information. Consequently, while local governments are better able to monitor the few firms under their jurisdictions (because they have direct contact and control over the firms), higher levels of governments in urban areas not only have more firms to monitor but there are also more levels of bureaucracy to distort the information required for close monitoring and control. Monitoring, then, is about both the size of the jurisdiction and the layers of bureaucracy through which information is filtered in the monitoring process.

Under the old system and in the early period of the reform, it is true that companies simply added an additional layer to the bureaucracy. But this view requires modification for the current situation in China's urban industrial economy. In the past, as the heads of sectors, bureaus exercised significant administrative control over their sectors, and the companies simply acted as the government "funnels" [*zhengfu loudou*]. As described above, administrative and economic responsibilities in the economic reform have been pushed down the administrative hierarchy of the former command economy. Today, companies perform the same functions that were formerly the bureaus' responsibilities. Rather than acting as an extra layer of bureaucracy, the administrative companies act as the direct representatives of the state in guiding the firms under their jurisdictions through the economic reforms. Bureaus also have direct control over some firms, and they are also basically responsible for guiding these factories through the reform. But the disparity between the number of firms under each is significant (see Figure 2.1), and this directly affects the amount of administrative attention the respective levels are able to offer the firms under their jurisdictions. Therefore, at this stage in the economic transition, the monitoring capacities in urban areas are less about layers of government bureaucracies and more about a simple comparison of the size of a given jurisdiction. District and municipal companies are now far more like the local governments that Walder (1995a, 266) described as having "a greater ability to monitor firms," while bureaus are much less able to offer administrative guidance and attention in the economic reform.

So how does this account fit with the fact that firms under district companies are less likely to diversify than those under bureaus are? The answer again lies in government responsibility, but the resource in question with respect to monitoring and information is administrative rather than fiscal. As administrative responsibilities are pushed down the hierarchy of the former command economy, administrative offices with smaller jurisdictions are able to offer direct attention and long-term development plans to the firms beneath them. The ability of district companies to keep track of and attend to the development issues of firms under their jurisdictions is heightened by the fact that they have fewer firms to attend to. In my sample, the majority of firms under district companies reported having significant and frequent contact with their governing organization, whereas those under municipal bureaus most often asserted that the bureaus had neither the time nor the administrative staff to attend to their development needs. This is especially true today given the extent to which bureau administrative staffs are pared down as bureaus prepare to make the transition to State-Owned Asset Management Companies [*guoyou zichan jingying gongsi*]. With no more than ten factories to watch over, administrators in district companies are often able to guide the firms through the economic reform with long-term development and organizational restructuring plans. A manager in the foods sector attributed his factory's rapid development over the last few years directly to decisions that the factory's district company had made:

> In 1990 things really started to develop quickly for our factory. Our district company changed many things and helped us develop a lot. They made us into a limited public-shares factory [*gufen youxian gongchang*] and formed a board of directors, and we started thinking about how to develop within this sector aggressively [*jijide fazhan*]. Since then, we have made many changes within our organization that reflect our market orientation. I think, maybe, you will find that our organization is quite different from many that you will see in China. (Interview 74*, 1995)

As this manager indicates, the long-term restructuring programs—a product of close monitoring by the company—come directly from the district company's administrative help and attention. Bureaus, on the other hand, simply do not have the administrative resources to take an active interest in long-term restructuring programs for firms under their jurisdiction in the economic transition. So while fiscal resources are tightened for firms under both levels of government, firms under bureaus experience a greater sense of being set adrift in the market than do those under municipal and district companies. This sense of uncertainty in the market is the reason why firms under bureaus are the most likely to adopt strategies of spreading out risk through investment in fast-return markets.

In short, the larger financial and administrative responsibilities of municipal bureaus (relative to municipal and district companies) have two consequences. First, they are unable to guarantee bailouts for shortfalls; second, and more important, they are less able to help the organizations underneath them pursue aggressive development programs. As the factory director whose firm had just been converted into a public-shares factory indicated (see quote above), the type of development strategies that district companies are creating for the organizations below them have more to do with fundamental changes in the organizational structure than with quick returns. With only a few organizations under their jurisdiction, these companies have the resources and administrative time to focus attention on long-term development plans for the organizations they control. Thus organizations under district companies have less need to seek stability through diversified investment, as their worlds are stabilized by the close attention of their governing organizations. Organizations directly under bureaus, on the other hand, do not derive stability from their governing organizations, because bureaus do not have the time or resources to help restructure losing organizations into more successful organizational forms. With considerably more independence, these organizations do what they can to ensure that budgets will be met. They seek market stability by spreading themselves out across different sectors and searching for fast-return capital investments.

Concluding Remarks

Firms have many specific economic strategies that are relevant for understanding the economic transition. The two explored in this chapter are the adoption of the Company Law and service-sector diversification. The Company Law, an institution the state created during the reform era, is fundamentally tied to the economic transition. It is an institution that was designed for the express purpose of creating a "modern enterprise system" [*xiandai qiye zhidu*]. The impact this law has on firms in the economic transition, how they decide to incorporate it, and the meaning it has for them will also reveal information for interpreting the social and structural forces at work in the economic transition. The results presented here again show that joint-venture relationships and location under the jurisdiction of a municipal bureau significantly increase the likelihood that firms will adopt the Company Law.

Service-sector diversification is, by its very nature, part of the transition from the planned economy to a market system. Before the economic reform began in 1978–79, a competitive service sector was virtually nonexistent. Over the last few years, it has become one of the fastest growing sectors of the Chinese economy. Suddenly, in the Chinese economy, there is a sector that offers fast returns on capital investments. Whether organizations take advantage of the growth in this sector is a question that has implications for how organizations are making their way through the economic transition. If organizations are investing in this sector, we might see them as adopting a development strategy whereby they seek stability in markets through diversifying into the service sector. Organizations that are not adopting this strategy are choosing instead to approach development through long-term organizational restructuring. The reason for this difference has to do with the types of government administrative organizations that are above these factories. While Walder's (1992a) work shows that the availability of slack resources increases with administrative rank in the urban industrial redistributive economy, the evidence presented in this chapter shows a reversal of these trends under the economic reform. Slack resources may increase with administrative rank but so do administrative and economic responsibilities. One should not underestimate the difference in the amount of attention a municipal bureau—with several hundred factories and companies under its jurisdiction—and a district company—with about ten organizations beneath it—can pay to organizations under their respective jurisdictions. Material resources—in the form of bailouts—are not the only story here: Companies can offer direct attention to creative, long-term development strategies to the organizations underneath them, whereas bureaus have little time to deal with such details. Organizations that are set adrift react to the new uncertainty by adopting strategies that allow them to spread out risk through investment in fast-return markets.

Consistent with the findings of previous chapters, the analyses in this chapter show that the Chinese economy is a system that is highly contingent on the state's preexisting institutional structures and the politics of market construction. Overall, state control still allows for variation on governance patterns and strategies, especially in a nested organizational hierarchy like China's. Large organizations that are under bureaus seek means to create stable economic worlds, which include development strategies that organizations under district companies are less likely to seek. The question for the future will be this: Which approach allows for more stability and longer-term economic growth? The answer to this question may indicate much about the selection process that will ensue as China's economic reform continues.

The findings also show that managers' decision-making processes with respect to the Company Law and service-sector diversification do not reflect the decisions of rational profit-maximizing managers. In adopting the Company Law, many managers have little sense as to what the changes will mean substantively. Others recognize the process of adopting the Company Law as being purely symbolic—hanging up a new sign and giving directors new titles—amounting to little more than a cosmetic makeover for the organization. My analysis here also shows that organizations with formal relations with foreign partners are significantly more likely to adopt this practice, suggesting that Chinese organizations mimic the models that are available to them in the marketplace. The dynamics of service-sector diversification differ from those behind the adoption of the Company Law, but the questions this strategy raises for neoclassical assumptions of rational profit-maximizing economic actors are also fundamental. In this case, economic decision making is driven by economic uncertainty and a sense of being set adrift by the state in the reform era. Instead of worrying about maximizing profits, firms that are experiencing administrative and economic uncertainty are striving to create stable worlds. In light of this evidence, it is not surprising that firms in this economic sector are not becoming more productive. Instead of upgrading old machinery, they are investing fiscal resources in the fast-return markets of the service-sector economy. Economic and administrative uncertainty lead to economic decisions that are guided more by the pursuit of stability than the pursuit of profits.

Seven

Institutional Pressure, Rational Choice, and Contractual Relations: Chinese-Foreign Negotiations in the Economic Transition

> In old China due process of law, sanctity of contract, and private enterprise never became the sacred trinity that they became in the capitalist west.
> *(John King Fairbank 1992)*

> China's international economic relations . . . have grown in complexity, and former attitudes toward trade disputes may have to change. . . . Veteran China traders who assume that disputes will be resolved in the traditional manner should realize that this new milieu will change the behavior of Chinese firms.
> *(Stanley Lubman and Gregory Wajnowski 1993)*

> Our country is developing laws to get on track with the international community [*gen guoji jiegui*]. Our investment approaches now are using law to protect both sides. Market economics is a system that relies on law. We are now seeing that this is completely different from the planned economy.
> *(Manager, electronics sector; Interview 54*, 1995)*

THROUGHOUT THIS STUDY, I have modeled the effects of formal relationships with foreign investors on various organizational outcomes. In this chapter I take that analysis one step further, focusing on the structure and dynamics of Chinese-foreign relationships and negotiations. My aim is to look beyond the individualized decisions organizations are making in terms of internal structure or market strategies, focusing instead on the inter-organizational negotiations that are an integral part of the reforms. The question I seek to answer is this: What are the dynamics of inter-firm negotiations between Chinese firms and foreign investors, and how do these investment negotiations affect the rationalization of economic transactions in China's transforming economy? Through an analysis of the specification of arbitration clauses in joint-venture contracts, I show that a firm's position in the state administrative hierarchy matters for the institutional practices it adopts in the economic transition. I also show that foreign (particularly Western) investment matters for the extent to which rational-legal institutions are taken seriously by economic actors in China. Institutional pressure from on-the-ground negotiations with foreign investors from Western-style market economies plays a significant role in types of rational-legal institutions emerging over the course of China's economic transition.

Getting on Track

The government of the PRC has always been a well-oiled propaganda machine, and, recently, widely disseminated rhetoric relating to the economic transition, institutional change, and the emergence of a rational-legal system has centered on the imagery of "getting on track" with the international community [*gen guoji jiegui*]. Literally, the term *jiegui* refers to a piece of metal that links two railroad tracks together. A popular term in China today, *jiegui* is a metaphor for integration into the international economy, evoking imagery of getting on track (with the international/Western world), bringing tracks together (Eastern and Western), and moving forward (in terms of development). When a manager hears the term *jiegui*, the conversation invariably turns to the international community and creating an institutional environment in China that is more reflective of that community. Some managers see the issue as integrally tied to the emergence of a market economy (see quote at the beginning of the chapter), whereas others frame the issue in terms of its relation to foreign investment in China:

> In my opinion *jiegui* means opportunity. Now that we are developing the same types of legal and institutional systems as foreign enterprises and countries, we can talk on the same level with them. We can all agree about how things should be done. And if the foreign firms are comfortable, they will invest here. *Jiegui* really helps develop investment for China. (Interview 56*, 1995)

While the term *jiegui* is often invoked rhetorically, representing an attitude toward the economic transition and the general construction of institutional systems that will make China more like other advanced market economies, it is also often tied directly to specific institutional changes in the economic transition. For example, in one of my interviews, a manager employed the language of *jiegui* to discuss changing contractual practices and, specifically, the emerging institution of arbitration:

> The area of contractual arbitration is really an important change with respect to Chinese society. We're all very careful with contracts now. We always have con-

tracts with other companies, especially when we establish a joint venture with a foreign investor. The contracts also often specify that if there is a problem, it will be handled by arbitration. This way both sides can feel that if a problem does arise, it will be resolved in a way that is fair to both parties. In this area we are really getting on track with the international community. (Interview 53*, 1995)

A Chinese lawyer working in the China International Economic and Trade Arbitration Commission (CIETAC) explained the issue in similar terms:

Arbitration is a kind of linking up with the international community. It makes the investment environment more acceptable for companies that want some kind of fair guarantees that they will be protected. Now in China, we are all doing many legal things that are the same as those in the international world. (Interview 91, 1995)

In this chapter I explore a set of relationships and an institution situated at the center of the process for which the Chinese term *jiegui* is a metaphor. This process is about the ways that Chinese economic actors navigate globalizing markets and the extent to which rational economic practices matter in these increasingly international markets. It is about embracing systems that will make foreign investors feel at home in the new institutional environments of China's emerging markets. I focus on the specification of arbitration clauses in foreign-Chinese joint-venture contracts, which play an increasingly important role in the contract negotiations between foreign investors and their Chinese partners. As I explore the emerging institution of arbitration in Chinese contractual practices, it will be useful to think about this institutional change in the context of the government's goal of "getting on track" with the international community and what the implications might be of linking rational contractual practices to this state-defined goal. Foreign negotiations and the institutional outcomes that emerge from these negotiations are an important part of defining the course of China's economic transition, and it is therefore useful to study the course of the economic transition from this perspective.

For several reasons, examining the structure of contracts between foreign and Chinese economic actors—and, more specifically, the specification of arbitration clauses within these contracts—is an appropriate way to begin exploring China's course of "getting on track" with the international community. First, as I have pointed out in earlier chapters, a true understanding of economic transitions must focus not on state directives and policies but on how these directives and policies are incorporated into economic actors' social worlds and daily practices. An exploration of contractual practices will allow us to examine the negotiations between organizational actors in the marketplace and to test theories and models of institutional change. Second, inasmuch as foreign investment is an important part of China's economic transition, the study of arbitration clauses in joint-venture contracts focuses directly on how foreign and Chinese firms come together to negotiate institutional outcomes in the economic transition. Finally, although a system of arbitration has existed in the PRC since 1954, only over the course of the economic transition has this institution taken on a meaningful role in Chinese markets. The issue of arbitration, then, allows us to explore a Western-style, rational-legal institution that is becoming increasingly important in China's transforming economy.

In the following sections I first set forth some ideas about models and theories of institutional change in transforming economies. I then present a brief history of arbitration in China. Finally, I offer an analysis of the specification of arbitration clauses in joint-venture contracts.

Studying Institutional Change in Transition Economies: Economic Negotiations and the Rise of a Rational-Legal System

Studies of economic transitions often present findings on the outcomes associated with the economic transition and infer backward to the structural and economic forces that give rise to these changes. The logic of this research tack is the following: Research begins by theorizing a link between outcomes and institutional change; then, by observing the outcomes, scholars draw conclusions about institutional change. There are two problems, however. First, although analyzing changes in individual or household income or in productivity confirms theoretical propositions, it does not give us an empirical view into the dynamics of institutional change. Studying the ways that economic actors deal with specific institutional changes and the extent to which their decisions are tied to the institutional environments in which they are embedded can take us much further in this pursuit. Second, the focus of the analysis is overwhelmingly on outcomes (i.e., the effects of institutional change) rather than on the causes and dynamics of change. We need to focus here on what economic actors do—and the social, political, and institutional factors that drive these decisions—rather than how much money they make as a result.

In addition, the implicit assumption in many studies is that the institutional changes driving the economic reforms are vaguely based on the state's decisions regarding the liberalization of the economy.[1] However, although the state is certainly responsible for many of the institutional and policy changes in periods of economic reform, equally important are the ways that economic actors incorporate broad institutional changes into their daily decisions and practices and the economic, social, and normative pressures they experience that drive them to take these state directives seriously. A state-driven model of economic transition does not address questions of the social factors behind decision-making processes in periods of economic reform.[2] The macro view of rational institutional change endows the state with complete power over the process of economic transition and institutional change and misses the point that economic transitions are often the result of negotiations among economic actors in emerging marketplaces. Economic negotiations are central to the type of market economy that will emerge in transforming socialist societies. If the extent to which economic actors view and adhere to institutional changes varies, how does this variation occur? Do economic actors adhere to institutional changes on the basis of cost-benefit analysis, as rationalist theories of economic action would posit, or do cultural or institutional forces also play a significant role in the economic actors' decisions surrounding new institutions and policies? Further, while many studies add to our understanding of individual and organizational effects in economic transitions, few deal with the broader questions of what a market transition means for the rationalization of an authoritarian society.[3] As markets assume a growing presence in the organization of economic activities, will a rational-legal system emerge to replace the top-down authoritarian system that characterizes command economies? An entire set of questions is left untapped here by studies focusing on changes in income and productivity. These questions lead us back to issues, first examined by Max Weber, regarding the structure of capitalist systems, their relationship to rational-legal institutions, and whether the two are inextricably intertwined.[4]

The lack of development in contract law and other rational-legal institutions in old China has been well documented.[5] The underdevelopment of rational-legal institutions was further exaggerated under the communist regime, where the rule of administrative fiat and government control became the effective law, and any remnants of a rational-legal system were purged shortly after the communist takeover.[6] Over the course of China's economic transition, as economic autonomy begins to flourish and contracts—along with a host of new legal institutions—begin to emerge, important social changes relating to both markets and a rational-legal system are also beginning to surface. As a result, important questions regarding the relationship between capitalism, contracts, and rational-legal institutions to support contractual agreements have suddenly become pertinent to the China experience. Economic actors—how they view and respond to these changing institutions—stand at the center of these social transformations.

Societies in transition from planned to market economies provide a remarkable opportunity to observe firsthand the role of individual actors, institutional environments, and the state in the emergence of particular market economic systems. A number of important questions guide research in this area: If Weber was right about the relationship between rational capitalism and a formal rational-legal system, will formal rational-legal structures accompany the transition toward capitalism that many countries are currently making? What will be the processes of individual decision-making and inter-firm negotiations behind the emergence of rational-legal institutions? Will organizations behave according to a rational calculus, or will normative and cultural factors play a role in inter-firm negotiations that give life to different institutional systems? Finally, what role does foreign investment play in this process? In the international economy emerging in the world today, institutional change and the appearance of formal rational systems must be viewed in the context of global markets and international organizations. Study of institutional change must consider the influence of organizational actors from different cultural and institutional settings and backgrounds. Through an analysis of the structure of joint-venture negotiations and the contracts that eventually result from these negotiations, I provide some answers to these questions.

Contractual Negotiations in China's Transition Economy

Contractual negotiations are a fitting place to begin exploring the emergence of a rational-legal institutional framework because the contracts reflect explicit choices on which the parties have agreed in terms of their reliance on a rational-legal system. An organizational analysis is also fitting for this type of study because organizations undertake significantly large economic transactions (relative to petty agricultural entrepreneurs, for example), so issues of negotiation and the ways that outcomes will be regulated are much more salient in an analysis of organizations than they are for an analysis of petty entrepreneurs in economic transitions.[7] The joint-venture relationship between foreign companies and Chinese firms is an interesting situation to begin an exploration of the rationalization of contractual practices because this relationship, by its very nature, involves negotiations between organizations from different cultural and institutional settings (i.e., foreign and Chinese organizations).

Since 1978, foreign investment and the contracts that define these investments have increasingly become a central part of development in China's economic transition.[8] Adopted in July 1979, the PRC's Joint Venture Law allowed foreign organizations to become a part of China's economic transition:

> With a view of expanding international economic cooperation and technological exchange, the People's Republic of China shall permit foreign companies, enterprises, other economic organizations or individuals (hereinafter referred to as "foreign joint venturers") to establish equity joint ventures together with Chinese companies, enterprises, or other economic organizations (hereinafter referred to as "Chinese joint ventures") within the territory of the People's Republic of China, on the principle of equality and mutual benefit and subject to approval by the Chinese Government.[9]

Since that time, contracts and investments have risen substantially in China over the course of the economic transition. Figure 7.1 shows the number of

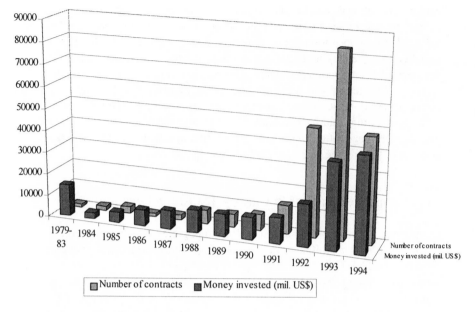

Figure 7.1: Foreign Investment
Source: *Zhongguo tongji nianjian* (Statistical yearbook of China), 1995

contracts and the amount of money invested by foreign investors over the course of China's economic transition. As the figure shows, there has been extreme growth in this area since 1990. In 1993 more contracts were signed and more capital promised than ever before. As the figure suggests, foreign investment is becoming an increasingly important part of China's economic transition.

The Negotiation of Institutional Outcomes

My view of the structure of contracts begins with the negotiations between economic and political actors. These negotiations set the stage for and help construct the institutional environment that will define an investment agreement. Economic actors enter a negotiation over an economic agreement. They define the terms of that agreement, and they define the types of institutional systems on which they will rely to define the agreement. Two parties that know and trust each other might rely on a handshake to seal an economic agreement; parties that do not know each other might push toward a more formal rational-legal approach to an economic agreement. How economic actors make these agreements and the institutional structures on which they choose to rely help define the institutions that are salient in periods of economic reform. If the overwhelming practice in China is to rely on connections and trust to seal agreements, this will have a significant impact on the direction of the economic reforms and the type of economic system that eventually emerges. The negotiations between economic actors over these economic agreements are a central part of the engine that drives the process of institutional change.

The Players

In a study of contractual negotiations, it is useful to begin by identifying the players that enter into the negotiations. An empirical example may help to illustrate the parties involved and their principle concerns in the China case.[10] In 1991 DuPont opened an agricultural chemicals plant in Shanghai. Somewhat naive to the dangers of technological pirating in Third-World development, DuPont executives assumed that in an international market such as Shanghai's, the company's venture would be protected by the same contractual and patent laws that are implicit in virtually all Western business negotiations. When local entrepreneurs infiltrated the company, copied one of DuPont's herbicide formulas, and started a rival company to produce it, DuPont found that Chinese courts would not protect the intellectual property rights of its products.[11] In 1994, on the brink of embarking on another joint venture in China, DuPont used what bargaining power it had to pressure government officials to set forth policies that would safeguard against the recurrence of a similar incident. DuPont's chairman, Edgar Woolard, met with Chinese President Jiang Zemin to discuss formal policies that would protect foreign investors. The short- and long-term effects of this meeting are unclear. However, DuPont's approach is indicative of a broader change that may have far-reaching implications for the organizational and institutional structure of Chinese society. It is unlikely that Woolard was able to extract any guarantees from President Jiang. However, if many foreign organizations begin to assert such demands and constraints on investment ventures, the ability to influence the outcomes of such demands may become contingent on the capital that a given organization brings to the negotiating table. As DuPont's second investment in China was estimated at U.S.$16 million, the government organizations may have been interested enough in assuring the investment that they were willing to accommodate some of DuPont's demands or at least offer stronger guarantees that contracts would be upheld and intellectual property protected.[12] In China today, the state, foreign firms, Chinese firms, and their governing organizations negotiate over the structure of joint-venture agreements and the institutional systems that will support those contracts. All these organizations have interests in entering negotiations over the rules of the organizational fields and seeing the rules come to an acceptable outcome for all parties involved.

As this example indicates, in the negotiations over joint-venture contracts and relations in China, at least four economic actors are involved in this bargaining relationship. First, there is the Chinese firm. For a foreign company to set up a joint venture in China, it must have a Chinese partner.[13] Second, there is the foreign company seeking to invest in China. Third, there is the governing organization that has direct authority over the Chinese organization (see Figure 2.1). Often, negotiations over a joint-venture investment project are conducted as much with the Chinese firm's governing organization as they are with the firm itself. Peripherally, there is also the state administrative office that makes approvals on investment in a given area: Municipal bureaus and central ministries most often make the approvals for projects in any given sector.[14] Foreign organizations, Chinese enterprises, and Chinese government organizations bring different commodities, expectations, demands, and bargaining tools to the negotiating table. They struggle and negotiate over the rules that define the organizational fields in which they are operating.

In the joint-venture relationship, each organizational body entering the negotiation over a project has something to offer: The foreign organization offers economic—fiscal and technological—capital, as well as access to international markets. The Chinese firm often offers a site on which a joint-venture entity can be established, access to local markets, and connections with officials in the firm's governing office. Connections with government officials are among the most valuable bargaining chips a Chinese firm has to offer. If the firm has either direct connections with individuals in the municipal bureau or if the firm's governing office has individuals with connections in the municipal bureau, the firm can promise influence over the approval process as part of its contribution to the investment. As such, firms directly under the jurisdiction of municipal bureaus are in the strongest bargaining position with respect to this issue, because the office of approvals and their governing organization are one and the same. Finally, the Chinese government has administrative fiat over the approval process, and, in a broader sense, the government has the regulatory power to institutionalize the rules that would protect the interests of foreign investors.

For both the foreign investors and the Chinese government, there are also trade-offs and much to lose. The foreign firms risk the capital (fiscal and technological) they invest. A failure of profitability and net loss on the investment and security of intellectual property are risks that a foreign company undertakes when investing in China's developing markets. The Chinese government, on the other hand, risks the sovereignty that it has protected since the founding of the PRC. If a foreign organization is able to define a venture contract that is considered to be too profitable for the foreign party, the state views the foreign control of the market as a loss of sovereignty to foreign encroachment.[15] Foreign investment is needed for China's development, but many state officials remember too well the century and a half before the Communists took power in 1949, when foreign powers in China had robbed the country of its sovereignty and its dignity.

Rational, Institutional, and Cultural Models of Contractual Negotiations

Throughout the analyses presented in this study, I have employed competing frameworks derived from rationalist, institutional, and occasionally cultural notions of social structure and social change. Each of these frameworks leads to different predictions with respect to the analysis of contractual negotiations. Based on the underlying assumptions that actors make strategic choices for rational reasons, in a rationalist framework we would expect the specific assets that each party brings to the negotiating table to define the outcome of the negotiation in a straightforward manner.[16] On the foreign side, we would expect that contractual protection in economic relationships between Chinese firms and foreign investors would vary with the value of the contract. Economic actors investing large sums of money in China will have greater bargaining power as they are bringing more to the bargaining table. They will therefore have a better ability to push for an institutional outcome that allows for the greatest amount of protection against disputes. On the Chinese side, organizations that are under the jurisdiction of government offices in the upper levels of China's administrative hierarchy will have more bargaining power as they come to the negotiation armed with more power, connections, and influence over approval processes than organizations under lower-level government offices. These upper-level firms may be able to negotiate for institutional outcomes that would favor the Chinese organization in a dispute situation.

From the institutional perspective, organizations are subject to the institutional pressures of the environments in which they are embedded. In other words, there is more to understanding an organization's bargaining position than assuming that the organization is trying to maximize its position from a rational calculus point of view. Organizations may make rational decisions, but structures and practices may be adopted for reasons other than profit maximization or efficiency. Organizations enter negotiations and attempt to secure provisions that are reflective of the types of institutional pressure they receive in their own institutional environments. They try to secure provisions that are symbolically meaningful in the organizational field in which they are situated. From an institutional perspective, in joint-venture contract negotiations, we would expect to see organizations negotiating not primarily according to the value of their investment or the size of the contract, but rather, their bargaining position should reflect practices that are seen as the most legitimate in the institutional environment from which they came.

A cultural framework is similar to the institutional view in that both reject the notion that economic actors act solely on the basis of a rational calculus of profit maximization. Neither view argues that economic actors do not make rational decisions, but both argue that specific aspects of economic actors' social environments are influential in the decisions of actors in the marketplace. Economic actors' cultural backgrounds have significant influence over the economic decisions they make in the marketplace. A cultural theory of economic negotiations is embedded in a number of accounts of economic and legal change in China.[17] These studies argue that the path of economic reform in China is shaped by Chinese culture. Culture defines the ways that economic actors adapt to economic and institutional changes, and it defines the overall path of the reforms for a given society. With respect to the issue we are exploring in this chapter, we should expect that culturally discernible lines would inform the position organizations take on contract negotiations. We should be able to observe a pattern of decisions that reflect uniformity among Asian or Chinese economic actors or both.

An Emerging Rational-Legal Institution: Arbitration Clauses in Joint-Venture Contracts

In 1954 the PRC's first arbitration commission, the Foreign Economic and Trade Arbitration Commission, was formed as an institution to resolve trade disputes between China and Soviet bloc trading partners. Created by the China Council for the Promotion of International Trade, the institution remained virtually dormant for twenty-five years. In 1980, in the wake of a host of economic reforms, the institution was changed to the China International Economic and Trade Arbitration Commission, or CIETAC. Following the PRC's Joint-Venture Law (PRC 1979a), which for the first time allowed foreign parties to invest directly and set up ventures in the PRC, the role of CIETAC was expanded to handle more than simple trade disputes. The commission would now handle disputes between foreign investors and their Chinese partners. While the central body of the arbitration commission sits in Beijing, in 1989 CIETAC set up branch offices in Shanghai and Shenzhen.[18]

Firms setting up joint ventures in China have three options regarding dispute resolution: Chinese courts, CIETAC, and third-country arbitration. In basic terms, disputes settled in a Chinese court favor Chinese partners, whereas disputes settled at CIETAC or in a third country are more likely to give foreign investors and their Chinese counterparts equitable consideration.

As one expatriate lawyer, who had been working on foreign investment in China from his Hong Kong office for many years, explained:

> Many contracts that are signed between Chinese and foreign firms have dispute resolution provisions in them. There are a couple of alternatives for these provisions. The disputes can be taken to a Chinese court or it can go to CIETAC or to a third country for arbitration. Usually if there is no specified resolution provision, the dispute goes de facto to the Chinese court. This is a big problem for foreign firms that are expecting to get objective decisions on disputes. Most of the Chinese courts are staffed by people who have no legal background at all. And many of the judges are PLA [People's Liberation Army] officers. They go through some minimal legal training, and then they are turned loose. A dispute goes to a Chinese court, and the foreign firm hopes to get an objective decision. But why should that happen? You have ex-military people who have done nothing but carry out the orders of the government all of their lives, running the courts and making decisions on disputes. Without a doubt they are most apt to be influenced by the opinions of the people in Chinese organizations. Furthermore, there is no requirement in China to give any reason for why a given decision was made, no requirement of citing precedent, and no requirement that a record of how the decision is made be kept. So what we try to do for our clients is come up with alternatives to the Chinese court system, such as arbitration. (Interview 26, 1995)

With a notoriously poor record on the education and legal training of judges, the majority of which are retired PLA officers, stories of corruption in the Chinese courts abound.[19] There is a bias against foreigners and anyone outside a given locality that may take cases to the local Chinese court for resolution.[20] Finally, a Chinese judge is not required to cite the legal backing for a given ruling, making it very difficult to contest a court decision.

These weaknesses in the Chinese legal system make dispute resolution a central part of contract negotiations. The way a dispute will be resolved—in the Chinese legal system or in another arbitration institution—becomes a point of the negotiation that both sides would like to have fall in their favor. As the expatriate lawyer also pointed out (see quote above), the type of dispute resolution and the structure of the contract in general are the result of a process of negotiation between foreign and Chinese organizations:

> What you see in the forging of these contracts and the specification of dispute resolution is a type of organizational negotiation between China and foreign investment organizations. (Interview 26, 1995)

Contractual practices, from this point of view, are not only about the emergence of a formal rational-legal system, but they also reflect the influence of negotiations with foreign investors and the general institutional pressures of the international markets. They are about the extent to which China is "getting on track" with the international world.

However, while the specification of arbitration clauses in joint-venture contracts is becoming a common practice, it is still by no means a uniform one. In my sample of firms, of the forty-eight organizations that had joint ventures, twenty-five, or 52 percent, had specified arbitration clauses in their venture contracts. One manager in the chemicals sector put the issue simply enough, saying:

> In this country, if there is a problem we follow the Chinese law; we go to the Chinese courts. That's how we do things in China. But we really haven't had the kind of problems that make this an issue. (Interview 90*, 1995)

Another manager, also in the chemicals sector, explained:

> We have a joint venture with a Hong Kong company. . . . Of course, we signed an extensive contract with the HK Company when we were setting up the venture. Everyone takes contracts very seriously now. . . . [But] we really had no need to specify arbitration or dispute resolution in CIETAC. We and the HK company agreed that the Chinese courts would suffice if a serious problem arose. (Interview 97*, 1995)

Many of the managers in organizations that did specify arbitration clauses in their joint-venture contracts view the issue simply as one of bargaining power.

> We have a joint venture with Sony of Japan. For this sector, it is a pretty large JV investment. The project is about 140 million RMB [U.S.$17.5 million] and employs about sixteen hundred workers. . . . The Japanese invested 70 percent of the money, and we only invested 30 percent. We spent a lot of time negotiating the details of the contract, especially on matters like arbitration and what would happen if there was a contract dispute. But because the Japanese invested 70 percent of the project, they really had much more power to decide how they wanted to arrange these things. In the end, we agreed to have the third-country arbitration in Singapore. I think everyone was happy with this in the end. . . . Now we are just completing the negotiations on another JV deal with a Korean company—also a 70/30 Korea/China venture— and in that venture we have also agreed to have arbitration of disputes go to Singapore. It just made sense to do the same thing with our Korean partner that we did with our Japanese partner. (Interview 131*, 1995)

Although these statements make the issue appear somewhat straightforward, full consideration of the factors surrounding the specification of arbitration clauses in joint-venture contracts yields a considerably more complicated picture. As I argue below, an organization's position in the state administrative hierarchy, economic issues, and the institutional environment in which the investing organization is situated come together to influence the structure of joint-venture contracts and the emergence of a rational-legal system in this realm. Before we explore a quantitative analysis of contractual practices, we must first consider the meaning of arbitration for state organizations.

Arbitration Clauses and State Sovereignty

Arbitration may be specified as the form of dispute resolution, through an arbitration clause in the joint-venture contract. The "model" arbitration clause, according to CIETAC's Arbitration Rules, released in 1994, reads:

> Any dispute arising from or in connection with this contract shall be submitted to the China International Economic and Trade Arbitration Commission for arbitration which shall be conducted by the Commission in Beijing or by its Shenzhen Sub-Commission or by its Shanghai Sub-Commission at the Claimant's option in accordance with the Commission's arbitration rules in effect at the time of applying for arbitration. The arbitration decision and award is final and binding upon both parties. (CIETAC 1994)

Third-country arbitration clauses can be specified in the contract by substituting the site of arbitration for CIETAC in the model clause. The arbitration clause is meaningful in a contract because it binds the parties to dispute resolution in a specific arbitration institution should a dispute arise (see also Article 26, PRC 1988b). In the absence of an arbitration clause, dispute resolution generally falls on the Chinese legal system. Arbitration can be chosen after a dispute arises, but inasmuch as both parties must agree on arbitration, it is unlikely, especially if the culpable party is Chinese, that both parties will agree to arbitration when the courts so strongly favor Chinese organizations. Thus arbitration clauses are an important point of negotiation in the *formation* of joint-venture contracts.

For foreign investors in China, the institution of arbitration offers a form of dispute resolution with a process and outcome that is considerably more calculable than dispute resolution in the Chinese legal system. From the Chinese perspective, many economic actors realize the necessity of offering an institutional option such as arbitration to foreign investors. Nevertheless, in some ways the specification of arbitration clauses in joint-venture contracts chips away at Chinese sovereignty over investments that are occurring within Chinese borders. Even though the largest body of individuals on the arbitration commission from any one country comes from China (five out of fifteen), two-thirds of the individuals on the commission represent interests other than China's. For the first time since the founding of the PRC, foreign parties have input on decisions that affect Chinese internal affairs. Enforcement still lies in the hands of Chinese authorities. But for a country that only a few years ago operated fully on the institution of administrative fiat, turning over the power of decision making to a third country or to an institution that is comprised of both Chinese and foreign representatives is somewhat problematic.

Chinese courts are a different story. Mostly run and controlled by individuals who are untrained in the law and who are also agents of the state, the

Chinese legal system lies much closer to the rules of administrative fiat. Former PLA officials, who have been following and protecting state interests throughout their careers, now carry out the protection of those interests in the legal system.[21] It is logical to assume that, all things being equal, a Chinese organization would prefer that disputes be handled in the Chinese legal system rather than an international arbitration institution. It could be argued that the state has an interest in the development of CIETAC because this alternative is an important part of attracting foreign investment. However, the existence of the institution as a symbolic structure that will attest to the rationality of the system and attract foreign investors does not predicate the state's preference in having disputes resolved at this institution. The reality is that as the state enters negotiations over the structure of joint-venture contracts, the specification of clauses that define the international arbitration institution (or a third country) as the milieu where disputes will be resolved, by definition, diminished the state's sovereignty over the joint-venture projects for which these clauses are specified.

The analysis that follows begins with the assumption that negotiations between economic and political actors over the structure of contracts matter for the process of institutional change over the course of China's economic transition. It also begins with the assumption that dispute resolution in the Chinese legal system favors Chinese organizations, whereas dispute resolution in international arbitration forums are less favorable to Chinese organizations. Thus Chinese organizations will prefer dispute resolution to occur in the Chinese legal system, whereas foreign organizations (in many cases) prefer that disputes be taken to institutions of international arbitration. Although some scholars have provided extensive descriptions of arbitration in China, general discussions of dispute resolution with a focus on mediation institutions, and extensive discussions of contracts in China, research has not addressed the question of what organizational characteristics give rise to variation in the practices relating to these institutional changes.[22] The analysis below will address this issue directly.

Which Organizations Have Joint-Venture Contracts?

Before we examine the specification of arbitration clauses in joint-venture contracts, it is useful to first examine the determinants of these contracts. Table 7.1 presents the determinants of whether an organization will have a joint venture with a foreign partner. Results show that, controlling for other effects, organizational size has a significantly positive effect on the likelihood that an organization will have a joint venture with a foreign partner. Larger organizations are more likely to have set up joint ventures with a foreign partner than smaller firms. This is not surprising, because foreign partners typically search for or-

TABLE 7.1

Logistic Coefficients for the Determinants of Whether an
Organization Has a Joint Venture with a Foreign Partner,
Four Industrial Sectors, Shanghai, 1995

Independent variables	B	S.E.
Organizational variables[a]		
Chemicals	5.23	14.39
Electronics	.93	.75
Foods	.95	.61
Active employees (ln)	1.21*	.69
Organizational health	.43	.78
Profit margin, avg. 1990–1994	.19***	.07
Losses 1990	1.27**	.50
Products exported (%)	.03**	.02
Governance variables		
GM w/bus./econ. backgrnd.	.23	.39
Municipal bureau	.88*	.60
Constant	−1.88	14.85
χ^2		56.18***
No. of cases		81

Note: See text and Appendix 4 for discussion of variables. B is the effect
of the coefficient, S.E. is the standard error. * $p < .1$ ** $p < .05$ *** $p < .01$
(two-tailed tests). Variables in bold are statistically significant.

[a] Reference category for sector is garments.

ganizations that have a large revenue base, as this is some measure, albeit a
crude one, of the organization's market position. Larger firms have larger revenues, so they are often the likely targets of foreign firms seeking joint-venture
partners in China.[23] Organizations that export a larger percentage of their products are also more likely to have a joint venture with a foreign partner. This
result is related to the political process surrounding joint-venture approvals in
China. Although foreign firms would most often prefer to capture Chinese
markets, Chinese officials and politicians would like to reserve those markets
for Chinese firms. Nevertheless, China's development requires foreign investment, especially for the development of technology and capitalist-oriented
management systems. This conflict of interests has given rise to a political
compromise: Foreign investors can set up joint ventures and thereby capture
some portion of the market, but the joint-venture company is also required to
export some percentage of its products. Thus the export ratio (the ratio of
production designated for export to that designated for sale in China) becomes
part of the negotiation process that involves the state and the foreign partner.
As export ratios are a part of the negotiation over joint ventures, foreign firms

are likely to look for Chinese partners that have experience with exporting products. In addition, if the state administrative office that is responsible for approvals (usually the municipal bureau) is uncomfortable with the foreign partner's demands for a low export ratio, the contract will probably not be approved.[24] The result is that factories that already export some portion of their products are attractive joint-venture partners. These companies can help navigate the complexities of exporting products from China. In addition, another explanation behind the significance of the percentage of a firm's products that are made for export may be that firms with more export products have a better understanding of international quality and standards. Through dealing with international customers and international markets, these firms may be better positioned to know how to deal with foreign companies that are seeking a Chinese joint-venture partner.

Interestingly, profits *and* losses are both significantly associated with joint ventures. These findings do not contradict each other, as both are significant for different reasons. Profits are associated with joint ventures because, as noted above, foreign companies tend to seek Chinese partners that occupy a strong market position. The most successful Chinese firms usually have joint ventures with foreign companies; in fact, it is an anomalous situation when a successful Chinese organization does not have at least one joint-venture partner at this time in China. In my sample of firms, of the sixteen strongest organizations (in terms of profit margins), 75 percent have at least one joint venture with a foreign partner. When foreign companies come to China seeking a joint-venture partner, the firms that have been the most successful on their own are viewed as the best potential partners for new ventures.

Based on this line of reasoning, it would seem that the firms that were losing money would be the least likely to land joint-venture contracts with foreign partners. However, there is another element to joint-venture partnerships. As I noted above, government organizations have significant bargaining power when it comes to joint-venture negotiations. This is especially true among the upper-level government offices (e.g., the municipal bureaus), which make the approvals for many of the joint ventures in their urban areas (all projects under U.S.\$30 million for most large cities). In industries that are set to develop rapidly in the future in China, foreign investors, in an effort to secure a strategic market position, will often take on a partnership with a Chinese firm that is not faring well in the economic transition. With the power of administrative fiat over approval processes, high-level government offices can often force foreign partners to choose the partner the governing office wants them to choose rather than the best partner in the market. When government offices select firms for foreign partnerships, they often select weak or losing Chinese organizations in the hope that a foreign partnership will help the firm develop a more efficient Western management style. Government officials often refer to this negotiation tactic as "marrying off" the troubled firms under their jurisdictions. In reality, these firms still remain under their jurisdictions, but the hope is that with profits coming in from a successful joint venture and the influence of Western management systems, the government organization will have to worry less about these organizations.

Finally, location of a firm at the upper levels of China's industrial hierarchy has a significant association with the likelihood that the organization will have a joint venture with a foreign partner. This association, again, is grounded in the positions these upper-level government organizations occupy in approval processes and the influence they may wield over other political situations. Foreign companies that are investing in China often strive to align themselves with government organizations that have the greatest amount of influence over the politically driven situations they may encounter in the economic transition. For example, the municipal bureaus hand down most approvals for joint-venture projects. Very large projects (U.S.$30 million and above) also have to receive approvals from the sector ministry of the central government in Beijing; but projects of less than U.S.$30 million fall under the sole jurisdiction of the municipal bureaus. It is not surprising that foreign companies strive to set up ventures with firms directly under the jurisdiction of these bureaus. Despite the fact that these bureaus still, to some extent, hold the stewardship for the entire sector (even though economic and administrative responsibilities have been distributed down the hierarchy), they naturally favor the organizations directly under their jurisdictions (see Figure 2.1). It is these organizations for which the bureaus are first and foremost responsible. So ventures that are set up with firms under the direct jurisdiction of the bureaus are likely to have a powerful political ally that can help with approvals of joint-venture contracts or product approvals when they are necessary. The firms directly under the jurisdiction of bureaus are also more likely to have strong personal connections in the bureau offices. Approvals for ventures set up with organizations at the upper levels of this administrative hierarchy are not only more likely to happen, but they are also likely to happen faster.

The Structure of Joint-Venture Contracts

For this part of the analysis, while the sample of firms is still the stratified random sample of firms surveyed for this research project, only forty-eight firms (out of eighty-one) in the sample had joint ventures with foreign companies. Therefore the analysis that follows is based on the sub-sample of forty-eight firms that had at least one joint-venture contract with a foreign company.[25]

Figure 7.2 shows the variation in the specification of arbitration clauses in joint-venture contracts by sector. Immediately evident from Figure 7.2 is that the electronics and chemicals sectors have significantly higher proportions of

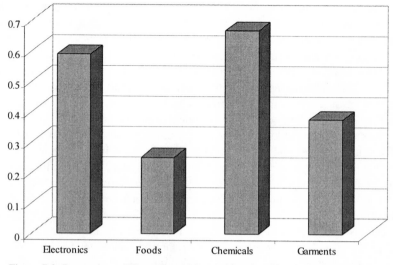

Figure 7.2: Proportion of Firms Specifying Arbitration Clauses in Joint-Venture
Contracts in Four Sectors in Industrial Shanghai, 1995

firms specifying arbitration clauses in joint-venture contracts than the foods
and garments sectors.[26] It could be argued that sectors which are more technology intensive focus more directly on issues of intellectual property rights, and
joint-venture contracts in these sectors are more likely to end up with arbitration clauses as a result. Or it could simply be that foreign parties in these
sectors are more concerned with establishing some form of recourse if intellectual property rights are violated. However, as the analysis below shows, this is
a simplistic view of the emergence of this institutional change.

Table 7.2 shows the associations among several organizational variables
and the specification of an arbitration clause in the first joint venture the organization set up with a foreign partner. From Model I, it appears that the data
support the rationalist approach to contract negotiations. Three findings en-
dorse this view. First, there are statistically significant negative effects of a
firm's position under the jurisdiction of a municipal bureau and a municipal
company, compared to a district company, on the specification of arbitration
clauses. This means that the higher a Chinese firm is in the administrative
hierarchy, the less likely a venture with that firm is to have an arbitration clause
in the joint-venture contract with a foreign partner. Bureau governance has a
larger negative effect than municipal company governance, and both have significantly negative effects compared to firms under the jurisdiction of district
companies, which are lower in the administrative hierarchy than both.[27] I interpret these results to mean that organizations at higher levels in the administrative hierarchy have more bargaining power and therefore have more influence

TABLE 7.2

Logistic Coefficients for the Specification of Arbitration Clauses in Joint-Venture Contracts by Organizations in Four Industrial Sectors, Shanghai, 1995

Independent variables	Model I		Model II		Model III		Model IV	
	B	S.E.	B	S.E.	B	S.E.	B	S.E.
Organizational variables[a]								
Chemicals	.03	1.01	−1.46	1.60	−.48	1.14	−.55	1.43
Electronics	1.20	.34	−.03	1.27	.43	1.10	−.25	1.52
Foods	−.55	.34	−2.00	1.45	−.99	1.37	−1.12	1.71
Active employees (ln)	1.51*	.84	2.32*	1.39	2.05	1.31	2.75	1.69
Organizational health	−.03	.14	.04	.24	.16	.20	.28	.27
Profit margin, avg., 1990–1994	.03	.05	.02	.08	.04	.08	.04	.09
Products exported (%)	.003	.02	.001	.03	.02	.03	.01	.03
Governance variables								
GM w/bus./econ. backgrnd.	−.19	.52	−1.08	1.07	−.79	.98	−1.23	1.18
Municipal bureau	−3.47**	1.38	−4.59**	2.96	−2.88*	1.62	−3.03*	1.86
Municipal company	−2.72**	1.20	−2.94*	1.62	−1.44	1.42	−1.87	1.67
Nature of joint-venture contract								
Value of contract (ln)	.66*	.39	.33	.56	.60	.54	.37	.64
Western partner	—	—	3.09***	1.17	—	—	—	—
Chinese partner (Singapore included)	—	—	—	—	−1.90**	.76	—	—
Chinese partner (Singapore excluded)	—	—	—	—	—	—	−2.78***	1.06
Constant	−22.35**	8.93	−22.75*	13.53	−25.29	16.39	−26.50**	12.86
χ^2	24.34**		41.62***		36.73**		43.02***	
No. of cases	48		48		48		48	

Note: See Appendix 4 for discussion of variables. B is the effect of the coefficient; S.E. is the standard error. * $p < .1$ ** $p < .05$ *** $p < .01$ (two-tailed tests). Variables in bold are statistically significant.
[a] Reference category for sector is garments.

over the structure of the joint-venture contract. Chinese organizations are usually not able to offer much in the way of fiscal or technological resources to a contract. Often they can offer such bargaining chips as a factory site and personnel. However, one valuable commodity the Chinese organization can bring to the negotiating table is connections to government offices. When Chinese organizations have direct connections to bureaus and ministries, they are in a position to have some degree of influence over the approval process and future administrative details (e.g., product approvals) that the venture might face. Given that government approvals decide the fate of a joint-venture contract, connections with approval offices are valuable commodities. The firms directly under the jurisdiction of municipal bureaus are in the best position with respect to this issue. These firms have a direct relationship with the municipal bureau, the organizational body that will approve or reject a joint-venture contract at the municipal level for a given sector. These firms thus have direct relations with the government organizational body that makes many of the final administrative decisions for a given sector. In some cases, it may be the promise of speeding a joint-venture contract along through the approval process that deters a foreign organization from pushing for arbitration clauses in joint-venture contracts; in other cases, it might be the promise of help with product approvals or securing a factory site at a good land price. This bargaining chip—the promise of connections with government officials in high-level government offices—is significant enough that the firm is able to dissuade foreign investors from pushing for the specification of arbitration clauses in joint-venture contracts.

Most important for the rationalist view of contract negotiations, there is a significant positive effect of the value of the joint-venture contract on the likelihood that a contract will have an arbitration clause. Earlier I hypothesized that the value of the contract will increase the likelihood that an arbitration clause will appear in the contract, because the foreign investor will be more likely to push for institutional protection for larger investments. The larger the contract, the more the foreign investor will want to push for an institutional protection that will have a rational calculable outcome should a dispute arise. For many foreign investors, the Chinese legal system does not offer a forum for dispute resolution that will yield a rational or predictable outcome. Foreign investors push harder for protections for larger investments. Therefore, according to the results presented in Model I of Table 7.2, the size of the investment increases the likelihood that an arbitration clause will appear in the joint-venture contract.

However, Models II–IV show that there is more to the specification of arbitration clauses than the value of the contract. While bureau governance continues to be significant in Models II–IV, the significance of the value of the contract disappears when we control for the location of the foreign investor. That the significance of the value of the contract disappears when we control for other factors indicates that the rational negotiation perspective explains less about the decision-making processes for the companies that are bringing the sizable investments to China. On the other side of the negotiating table, however, controlling for all other factors, position in the state administrative hierarchy continues to matter for the specification of arbitration clauses in contracts (at least for the firms located under the direct jurisdiction of a municipal bureau). I interpret this result as an indication that a rationalist approach is relevant for negotiations from the Chinese side, whereas the negotiations from the side of the investors must be explained more in terms of institutional and cultural factors. I will return to this argument below.

Models II–IV show that whether a foreign partner is from the West or Asia or specific Chinese societies (Hong Kong or Taiwan) has a very strong effect on the likelihood that there will be an arbitration clause in the contract. The value of a joint-venture investment is significantly correlated with the investing country, so the significance of the value of the contract in Model I is a spurious effect; the more important variable is the location of the foreign partner.[28] Model II shows that there is a strong positive effect of the foreign partner being from a Western country on the likelihood that a joint-venture contract will have an arbitration clause; the Western investor is contrasted to investors from Asian countries in this model.[29] This means that a company from a Western environment setting up a joint-venture contract with a Chinese partner is significantly more likely than its Asian counterparts to push for the specification of arbitration clauses in the contract irrespective of the contract's value. Models III and IV show that joint ventures set up with partners from Chinese countries are significantly less likely to have arbitration clauses specified in the contracts than ventures set up with partners from any other country (Western countries, Korea, and Japan comprise the reference category). Model IV excludes Singapore from this sub-sample, showing that the effects are even more extreme when we consider only investors from Taiwan and Hong Kong.

Support for Rational and Institutional Theories

Overall there is support for both rationalist and institutional approaches to understanding contract negotiations. Foreign investors typically provide fiscal resources and technology for joint ventures; the Chinese side can provide connections to government offices that can influence approval processes. For a rationalist model of institutional change to make sense, we would expect that contractual outcomes would vary as a function of these parameters. The size of the contract (value), what sector the venture is located in (high technology or not), and the Chinese firm's position in the state administrative hierarchy all should matter for the structure of joint-venture contracts. There is strong evidence across all the models that the Chinese partner firm's position in the state administrative hierarchy has a significant influence over the structure of joint-venture contracts, at least with respect to dispute resolution. Location under the municipal bureau, the organizational body that approves all contracts and handles other issues such as product approvals, has a strong negative association with the specification of arbitration clauses in joint-venture contracts. In other words, firms that have direct connections to municipal bureaus are likely to end up with contracts that allow for dispute resolution favorable to the Chinese party (i.e., no arbitration clause). These firms are likely to be able to offer promises of a speedy approval process and political support for the project from a powerful governing office if it becomes necessary. The other side of the rational bargaining view is not supported by the full models, however.

While the value of the contract is positively associated with the specification of arbitration clauses (Model I), these results disappear when we control for the location of the foreign investor, indicating that other institutional forces are influencing the economic decisions of foreign investors.

The results show a strong positive association between whether a company is situated in a Western institutional environment and the likelihood that the company will negotiate for Western-style dispute resolution clauses in joint-venture contracts. This result is true net of several other factors, including the value of the joint-venture contract. This suggests that Western investors are subject to institutional pressures that give them cause to push for arbitration clauses in joint-venture contracts. Investors situated in market economies that are structured around tenets of a rational-legal system are likely to feel the most comfortable when they can define rational-legal institutional support to protect their investments. While Chinese courts cannot yet be trusted to re-solve disputes in a way that will yield calculable outcomes, CIETAC and third-country arbitration are much more likely to do so. Companies that are used to a rational-legal system and predictable outcomes are likely to feel the most comfortable investing in China if they can secure institutional guarantees that will allow for this same type of security. As a result, companies from this type of institutional setting that are investing in China are likely to push for arbitration clauses in joint-venture contracts. Similarly, countries operating within weak institutional environments, such as Taiwan and Hong Kong, will be less likely to push for clauses in contracts that reflect rational-legal guaran-tees. As a Taiwanese investor in China explained:

> Taiwanese people only understand and focus on the use of law about 60 percent as well as Westerners do. Americans are more legalistic that the Taiwanese, so when they [Americans] come here to invest, they rely heavily on the laws and legal institu-tions. They are always putting arbitration clauses in their contracts and trying to do things very legalistically. Taiwanese, on the other hand, don't totally trust law; and if you put a Taiwanese businessperson together with a Chinese businessperson, who trusts the use of law even less, there is very little chance that they will focus on the use of laws and legal institutions when they are making some kind of business agree-ment. I think you will find that fewer Taiwanese joint ventures are using arbitration clauses that specify [CIETAC] in their contracts. (Interview 134, 1995)

My data bear out this Taiwanese investor's predictions, as only one firm that had a joint venture with a Taiwanese organization had arbitration clauses in the contract.

A cultural view of economic transition argues that cultural differences de-fine the types of capitalism that emerge in given parts of the world, and there have been many proponents of this belief. This is especially true within the literature on economic transitions that view the economic changes in China as the result of Chinese-style capitalism. While some cultural differences may affect whether a country will specify an arbitration clause in a joint-venture contract, the models presented above do not strongly support this view. If this were the case, we would expect to see all firms with a given cultural background to be pushing for contracts to be structured in similar ways. Models III and IV test this issue. Model III shows that when we select for all foreign investors from Chinese societies (Taiwan, Hong Kong, and Singapore), there is, in fact, a strong negative relationship between location in a Chinese country and arbitration clauses. However, if we separate the Singaporean companies out and look only at joint ventures with companies from Taiwan and Hong Kong, as I have in model IV, we find that the size of the negative coefficient becomes even larger. This suggests that Singapore companies are not negatively associated with arbitration clauses. In fact, of the two firms in the data set that had joint ventures with companies from Singapore, both had arbitration clauses in their contracts. But of the twenty firms that had joint ventures with companies in Taiwan or Hong Kong, eighteen did not have arbitration clauses in their contracts. With respect to the Singapore joint ventures, there are not enough cases to make any sweeping claims. However, if the data show trends in either direction, it is that joint ventures with Singapore companies tend to specify arbitration clauses in the contracts, whereas ventures with companies from Taiwan and Hong Kong do not. I interpret these results to indicate that Chinese culture is not as much a factor in the specification of arbitration clauses in joint-venture contracts as is the institutional history of the country in which the foreign firm is embedded.

Concluding Remarks

While studies on China's economic transition often look at issues such as changing income distribution or changes in organizational productivity, in this chapter I have focused on the negotiations among organizational actors and the institutional outcomes that emerge from these negotiations. On a general level, the issues I have raised in this chapter are directed toward questions of the relationship between capitalism and a rational-legal system. Weber viewed a rational-legal system as a necessary part of the rise of capitalism in the West. An interesting question for the study of economic transitions is to what extent the construction of markets in transforming socialist societies will give rise to a rational-legal system to support those markets. If a rational-legal system is becoming important in economic transitions, who are the organizational actors who play a role in these institutional changes?

The evidence presented here paints a nuanced picture of the relationship between the emergence of a rational-legal system and the emergence of markets and capitalism in China. Legal proceedings in China may still be far from an institutional system of calculable outcomes, but the state has created the foundation for an institutional environment that allows for dispute resolution that is more dependent on rational-legal institutions than on the capricious decisions of administrative fiat. From CIETAC to the numerous legal changes that have defined China's economic transition, the state has constructed the framework for institutional change and market transformation in the economic transition. However, I have argued here that broad institutional changes only matter to the extent that they are adopted and employed by economic actors in the emerging marketplaces of China's transition economy. The findings of this chapter show that organizational actors are incorporating institutional changes that are meaningful for the emergence of a rational system with calculable outcomes, but this change is contingent on a firm's position in the state administrative hierarchy and the investing firm's country of origin.

If a rational-legal institutional system is emerging to support market activity in China, this change appears to be happening in ways and for reasons that were not anticipated by Weber's theory and cannot be explained by economic convergence theories. Weber's theory leads us to believe that market transactions require the foundation of a rational-legal system simply because market actors require predictable outcomes when dealing with other market actors who are unfamiliar to them. In the case of China, however, it appears that market actors from different institutional environments view this issue differently. Market actors from Taiwan and Hong Kong appear content to continue relying on personal relations to organize their business relations. However, market actors from Western countries, Japan, and Singapore are pushing for a more rational-legal institutional system. In other words, the empirical experience of China's economic transition indicates that, over time, a rational-legal system will emerge to support market transactions in China, but not because, as Weber predicted, there is anything inherent in the structure of capitalism. A rational-legal system will emerge in China because foreign investors, many of whom are from the West, are an important part of China's development. And investors situated in highly institutionalized (in a rational-legal sense) environments are pushing for institutions that make them comfortable with the prospect of investing in a developing system such as China's.

Eight

The Declining Significance of Connections in China's Economic Transition

When people rely on "*guanxi* practice" for procedural matters [*kao guanxi xue ban shouxu*], as they did in the past, society becomes very messy [*luan*]. In the old system, if you wanted to get procedures done, you had to make sure you knew people in the right places; you had to try get procedures passed by relying on the people you knew. You had to talk to many people, and the process always took a long time. It wasn't always certain that you would know the right people to take care of the procedures. But now it's all very clear. You just follow the laws and make sure that you follow all of them closely. Things happen much more quickly today.

(Industrial manager, Shanghai; Interview 53*, 1995)

In markets, *guanxi* is really important. But I think it's strange that so many people think *guanxi* is so different in China than in other places. Whenever I'm in Europe, people always ask me about this. The last time I was in Europe, when people started asking me about *guanxi* in China, I asked them, "You mean to tell me that Europeans don't rely on friends and connections to do business? I don't believe it. I don't believe it's possible anywhere." I told them that I don't think it matters what country you're doing business in; everyone relies on connections to do business. Otherwise you wouldn't do much business. For example, I had a great time talking to the businesspeople I met the last time I did market research in Europe. We were like old friends by the end. Now, when I want to buy machinery parts, they will be the first people I call. If they don't have what I need, I'll ask them to suggest some people they know and trust who do. There is nothing special about China in this way of doing business. But this kind of *guanxi* is different from relying on *guanxi* to carry out procedures and going around the law [*i.e., guanxi xue*]. Using connections in that way is illegal; but there is nothing wrong with using *guanxi* to do good business.

(Industrial manager, Shanghai; Interview 72*, 1995)

A STUDY OF institutional structures and economic practices in China's transforming society must not eschew a discussion of *guanxi* (connections/social relationships) and the social structures and arrangements that system implies. Like systems of rational-legal institutions or formal rational bureaucracies, *guanxi* is itself an institutional system that shapes the decisions and practices of economic, political, and social action. And the extent to which this system is being transformed in the reform era has many implications for the present and future of China's transition. In chapter 3 I argued that the emergence of formal rational bureaucracies at the firm level in China has had an impact on the ways that firms operate in the reform era, indicating specifically that these bureaucracies have implications for the use of *guanxi* in hiring decisions. In this chapter I focus more generally on the institution of *guanxi*, questioning the notion that social networks and the use of these social networks to accomplish economic and procedural tasks are becoming increasingly important in China's economic transition. I take seriously the views of managers and government officials on this matter, and, based on the their perspectives, I construct an argument about the transformation of *guanxi* in the economic transition.

This discussion has implications for the assumptions we make about political and economic reform in China. In a recent *New York Times* article, Seth Faison introduced to the public the notorious Chu Shijian, former general manager of the Red Pagoda Cigarette Company in China. Faison's articles are always meticulous, revealing a deep understanding of the social and political mores of Chinese society, and this article is no different. However, the article does argue from a puzzling position that is indicative of the China field more generally: China watchers are obsessed with the notion that the Chinese system is fundamentally built on connections and corruption, but the evidence for these views often reflects a society in transition more than one that is implacably corrupt. Inasmuch as Mr. Chu is an example of rampant corruption in China, Faison's article is about the extent to which corruption, connections, and irrationality are an integral part of the Chinese economic system today. Faison points out that the Chinese economic system "remains stubbornly old-fashioned, is wide open to so much corruption that success almost inevitably leads to financial shenanigans that can spoil any chance of efficiency or genuine profitability."[1] Indeed, he notes that "corruption is so endemic in China's businesses that no one can accurately see where it begins and ends." Yet, the central fact that should be taken away from the account is this: *Chu Shijian is in jail for corruption.* Though Faison simply glosses overt this point, the article could just as easily be written about the fact that corrupt general managers are being disciplined, and some are, in fact, landing in jail. Faison also notes that hundreds of company executives were disciplined for corruption in 1997, though naturally the focus here is on the *speculation* that "thousands more have gone unpunished" rather than on the *fact* that disciplining high-level managers is a radical departure from the early years of the economic transition.

No one would argue that corruption does not exist in China's transition economy; nor would anyone assert that political connections and networks do not play a role in economic decision making in the new economy. However, it is somewhat mystifying that regardless of the state's progress in rationalizing economic systems, China scholars seem so much more likely to view these changes as illuminating the places where change has not yet occurred rather than viewing them as the steps toward a rationalizing system that they are. In another, more academic example, Mayfair Yang's evidence for the importance of *guanxi* in the urban industrial economy amounts to corrupt deals that were *abandoned* because of government regulations against them and accounts from managers predicting a declining role of corrupt practices as the economic transition progresses. Yet, these examples are taken as evidence of the strength and resilience of *guanxi* in China's economic transition.

Whereas many China scholars view *guanxi* as a deep-seated cultural fact of Chinese society, I view it as an institutionally defined system that is changing in stride with the institutional changes of the reform era. While a number of scholars have argued that social networks (*guanxi*) and the use of these social networks to exchange gifts and favors (*guanxi xue* or *guanxi practice*) are increasing in importance in China's transition, I present a different picture, at least with respect to the urban industrial economy.[2] Essentially I argue that *guanxi* and *guanxi practice* are increasingly viewed as distinguishable institutions in the economic transition. And while *guanxi* is often embraced as an important facet of business, a clear distinction is made between "establishing good business relations" [*gaohao shangye guanxi*] and using social relations to take care of procedures [*kao guanxi xue ban shouxu*] in economic and political situations. These "backdoor" practices [*houmen*] are increasingly taboo for large urban industrial firms. In China today, powerful economic actors pay more and more attention to the laws, rules, and regulations that are part of the emerging rational-legal system. Many managers of large industrial organizations increasingly view *guanxi practice* as unnecessary and dangerous in light of new regulations and prohibitions against such approaches to official procedures. Like many of the findings presented throughout this study, changes surrounding *guanxi* are tied to the state's institutional structure, as attitudes toward *guanxi* and *guanxi practice* depend on a firm's position in the state administrative hierarchy. Attitudes toward *guanxi* also vary with a number of organizational factors ranging from the background of the firm's general manager to whether the organization has a joint venture with a foreign company.

In short, of the two types of *guanxi* that help shape action in China today, one lies in conflict with the rational-legal system emerging at the state level, whereas the second type of *guanxi* is often viewed as a necessary part of the market reforms. Whereas some scholars assume that *guanxi* is a cultural fact that dominates Chinese society, I view it as highly dependent on the institutional environment in which it is embedded. Contrary to the views of other scholars on this issue, I argue that *guanxi practice* has withered in the reform era as a result of the emerging rational-legal system at the state level and formal rational bureaucratic structures emerging at the firm level. Understanding how the system of *guanxi* interacts with the rational-legal system and formal rational bureaucratic structures is important for understanding how this system is changing in the reform era, and it is also important for understanding the reforms more generally.

Research on *Guanxi* and *Guanxi Practice*

Recently I published an article in *The China Quarterly* on the fate of *guanxi* in China's transition economy.[3] In the first half of that article, I wrote an extensive review of Mayfair Yang's seminal book on *guanxi*, *Gifts, Favors and Banquets: The Art of Social Relationships in China*.[4] Though important in positioning my own argument on the changing nature of this social institution, I will not reconstruct that review here. I will, however, recount the highlights of that discussion.

Yang's analysis of *guanxi* is based on a distinction between social relationships (*guanxi*) and the *use* of those social relationships to manufacture "obligation and indebtedness" (*guanxi xue*).[5] In other words, social relationships are distinguishable from the institutional system of exchange through which they are commodified. In my review of her argument, I raised three issues. First, I argued that Yang's ethnographic data do not support the argument that the importance of *guanxi practice* has "increased at an accelerated rate" for "all types of commercial transactions."[6] Yang gives two examples of the presence of *guanxi practice* in the urban industrial economy, and, in both examples, we see managers who are actually pulling back from the use of *guanxi practice*.[7] Second, I argued that despite the fact that she distinguishes between *guanxi* and *guanxi practice* early on in her analysis, her argument about the growing importance of *guanxi practice* can only be accomplished by blurring the distinction between the two concepts. Her examples of *guanxi practice* in the economic transition often come across as nothing more than friendships and the cultivation of business relations. But the cultivation of friendships and business relations is nothing particular to the Chinese economy, as a number of scholars have pointed out that social relations influence economic relations and decisions in many societies.[8] In blurring the distinction between *guanxi* and *guanxi practice*, we lose the sense of what is particularly Chinese about the institution in question. As the economic transition progresses, there seems to be less and less of the complex web of obligations and debt—at least in the commercial economy—that China aficionados have come to know so well.

Finally, in a related vein, I argued that Yang's discussion makes the mistake of comparing ideal typical notions of market economies with empirical observations of the Chinese economy.[9] Social relationships are unquestionably important in Chinese society. But does the presence of these relationships in economic decision making distinguish Chinese society from other market economies? Only the strictest neoclassical economist would argue that social relations do not play a role in economic decision making. The question for the China case is whether social relations play a significantly different role in the Chinese economy than they do in advanced capitalist economies. I argue that in China's urban industrial economy, this gap is diminishing. While Chinese managers do view social relationships as important in market economies, they see this view as very different from one that embraces the "crooked" ways of *guanxi practice*.

Ultimately Yang makes a claim that is similar to Bian's view of Chinese social structure and the changing scope of state control. Both these scholars argue that Chinese society is structured around "web[s] of social relationships."[10] They both maintain that the Chinese state is receding and that individuals are increasingly turning to these social relationships to accomplish official and economic tasks. My argument, however, is that the state is in the process of constructing a rational-legal system at the state level and formal rational bureaucracies at the firm level. Since the beginning of the economic reforms—actually since the end of the Cultural Revolution—the state has been receding from direct control over the social and economic spheres. At the same time, the state has been constructing rational-legal structures that, once set in place, will regulate the economy in new ways. In the early stages of this process, however, before any of these new rational-legal structures could take hold, there was a growing sense of an organizational void left by the receding state. It was during this period that people began to turn to institutions such as *guanxi* and *guanxi practice* to accomplish tasks. However, while Bian and Yang predict a trend that continues in this direction, the late 1980s and early 1990s marked a new phase of the reforms.[11] By the 1990s the rational-legal structures that were being constructed at the state level were beginning to have some regulatory strength, and they were beginning to shape the ways that individuals acted in social and economic realms. As we will see below, this later period has had a profound impact on perspectives and activity in the urban industrial economy.

In the discussion that follows I will present three issues: first, a reformulation of the situation of *guanxi* and *guanxi practice* in urban industrial China; second, the ways that managers in urban industrial China in 1995 conceived of *guanxi*, on the one hand, and the use of connections to accomplish procedural and bureaucratic tasks (i.e., *guanxi xue*), on the other; and, third, a systematic analysis on organizational factors that are associated with managers' views of these issues. I should emphasize here that this discussion is about the urban industrial economy per se. While my view of *guanxi practice* in the economic transition—with respect to the urban industrial economy—diverges from Yang's, my discussion intentionally does not address other parts of her argument. It may be that *guanxi practice* is becoming an increasingly important part of the *minjian*, or private sphere, that Yang describes. I make no claim about this.[12] Rather, my discussion focuses specifically on the situation of *guanxi practice* in the urban industrial economy.

The Bifurcation of *Guanxi* and *Guanxi Practice* in the Urban Industrial Economy

In China's urban industrial economy, there is a growing distinction between *guanxi* and *guanxi practice* in the country's economic transition, and this distinction has implications for how economic actors view and employ these two institutions in the reform era. Several scholars implicitly, if not explicitly, distinguish between *guanxi* and *guanxi practice* (i.e., *guanxi* versus *guanxi xue*): *guanxi* implies social relations, whereas *guanxi practice* implies the *use* of these social relationships to make exchanges, accrue debt, or accomplish tasks.[13] The two institutions are intimately related, as the gift transaction and the gift economy are based on the network of social relationships; nonetheless, there is a clear distinction between them. This distinction is one that is growing in China's economic transition, especially for large-scale economic actors in the urban industrial economy. And in addition to this growing distinction between the two institutions, economic actors in the urban industrial economy are increasingly distancing themselves from the "deviant" or "crooked" ways of *guanxi practice*.[14] At the same time, however, many economic actors view relations [*guanxi*] as distinguishable from the gift economy [*guanxi xue*], and they view the former as critical for market economies and successful business practice. An official explained the distinction between social relations and the gift economy in this way:

> When you speak of guanxi there are really two kinds. There is the deep [*shen*] guanxi, which is usually what people are referring to when they talk about *guanxi practice* [*guanxi xue*] or using *guanxi* to get special treatment. Then there is another kind of *guanxi* that is not deep and really only refers to people understanding one another, knowing one another as acquaintances. In the past, the first type of *guanxi* was perhaps very important. But today, with the opening of China, the deeper *guanxi* is much less important. *Guanxi* today usually just means that you know people and understand them. For taking care of procedural matters, *guanxi xue* is much less important than it used to be for actually getting things done. It is possible that connections could make things more convenient, or allow things to get done more quickly, but really nothing beyond that. (Interview 40, 1995)

A manager in the electronics sector made a similar assessment of the distinction between *guanxi* and *guanxi practice*:

There are basically two kinds of *guanxi*. The first kind, which I mentioned before, has to do with using connections to get things done and to get advantages. This is happening much less now, and the government really discourages it. In my opinion, this isn't the way we do things in China anymore. The second kind of *guanxi* is natural in society and in a market economy. If two firms are both selling the same product, the most important things by far are the quality and the price. But if the quality and price of our products are about the same, of course it will help if you've been doing business with the customer for a long time. If the customer has been doing business with one of us for a long time or if he or she knows one of us better than the other, that customer is going to trust that person more. Relationships are always important in these situations. This is a kind of *guanxi*, but it is not the kind of *guanxi* we had before. (Interview 55*, 1995)

The importance of this distinction is increasing in the urban industrial economy for two reasons. First, the state monitors large industrial organizations far more closely than individual actors in the economy. Given that the official discourse surrounding *guanxi practice* is negative, it is not surprising that large-scale industrial organizations are more careful about the extent to which they engage in this institution. Industrial managers are increasingly careful to keep on state regulations surrounding economic practices, and they act in accordance with these regulations.[15] Second, as the economic transition progresses, China's markets are becoming increasingly competitive. There are very real economic incentives and constraints against favoring social ties over the economic imperatives of quality, price, and the feasibility of a given project. Add to this the fact that self-responsibility policies [*zifu yingkui*] and other aspects of hardening budget constraints mean that firms can no longer count n the state to bail them out. The result is that economic actors in China— particularly large-scale economic actors—are forced to entertain business decisions that make the most economic sense. They can ill afford to make decisions based on social relations if these decisions make less economic sense than those based on an assessment of economic factors (price, quality, efficiency, etc.).[16] The competitiveness of industrial markets and the state's (relatively) close monitoring of large-scale industrial and commercial organizations make these economic actors shy away from the "deviant [and inefficient] winds" of the gift economy.[17]

In addition to markets becoming increasingly competitive, the very existence of markets changes the meaning and significance of *guanxi* in China's transition economy. In China today, emerging markets and the transition from a command to a market economy allows actors the freedom to make economic choices in an open market. If one element of *guanxi practice* for industrial managers under the command economy was the necessity of gaining access to distribution channels (input and output), which state officials controlled under that system, in China's transition economy officials have no such control over the distribution of resources and products. In many sectors, an open market increasingly controls the flow of goods. This change has profound implications for the transition away from a focus on *guanxi practice* to a more general focus on *guanxi* as business relationships. Industrial managers no longer need to curry favor with state officials to overcome bottlenecks or gain access to resources, and, as a result, they do not view *guanxi practice* as an important part of decision making in China's industrial economy. They do, however, view general relationships forged with potential business associates (potential suppliers and customers) as being an important part of gaining a competitive advantage in the markets of the transition economy. In the analysis that follows I will discuss managers' views of these issues, and the organizational and institutional characteristics associated with variation in managers' perceptions of the importance of *guanxi* and *guanxi practice*.

Empirical Evidence from Shanghai

In the empirical part of this chapter, I explore the changing system of *guanxi* in the economic transition as it relates to the urban industrial economy. I focus primarily on the views of industrial managers regarding this issue.[18] I also present data on the extent to which changes in the system of *guanxi* and perceptions of these changes are associated with various organizational and institutional characteristics.

In China today, the emergence of a rational-legal system, at least officially, has undeniably begun. The state is implementing the broad-based institutional changes that define the transition away from personal power and the use of particularistic relations to accomplish procedural and official tasks. This is a complex transition because the state is implementing these changes on top of systems of *guanxi* and *guanxi practice*, which, after a history of more than two thousand years, have become very routinized in Chinese society. An expatriate lawyer explained the changing role of *guanxi* in China today:

> There are two things going on right now. There is a basic rationalization of the system and the creation of a legal infrastructure that supposedly makes people accountable for the things they do. But, at the same time, the old system is still in place. The people who are in power now are the same people who were in power before. And if you have good *guanxi* with them and a reason why you need an exception or an exemption from the law, you lobby and find someone you know, and eventually you get what you want. These connections, this system of *guanxi*, do make a difference at the end of the day. A great example is the joint-venture approval process. All of these laws and regulations are laid out, and in order to get an approval, you do need to make sure that all of the points of the process are legally correct. But the

ministries will also look at the project and say, "Who is behind this project? Is the project good for China? Is it good for what we are trying to do right now?" Those details are just as important as the legal details. Approvals are based on *guanxi* and lobbying as much as anything else. (Interview 26, 1995)

I should note here that while connections and *guanxi practice* may still be important in procedural processes, according to this lawyer's perspective, the fact that today you have to "make sure that all the points of the process are legally correct" is already a radical departure from the system of the past. Although the transition between these two systems is and will continue to be a slow and incremental process, the very existence of a rational-legal system at the state level is an important first step in defining and shaping economic and social action in China. However, as I have emphasized at several points throughout this study, more important than the construction of state-level institutional changes is how economic and social actors view and act on these changes. One Chinese lawyer emphasized that the construction of a rational-legal society relies on changes that run much deeper than the construction of rational-legal structures at the state level:

The most difficult part is changing the way people think. You Americans, as you grow up, become used to a legalistic way of thinking. You know the laws and you understand them. But this is not the case with the Chinese. We have grown up knowing one thing: Always listen to your leader. Changing the way people think about these things is the most difficult task of a developing nation. It takes a great amount of time; many things must be changed for a significant amount of time before people will start to think in a different way. (Interview 29, 1995)

A government official made a similar point about the distinction between official laws and how people view them:

We are not a completely legalistic society yet. We have many of the laws that we need to be a society that relies on laws to do things. But the legal way of thinking is not really ingrained in the way people think and act yet. We have laws on intellectual property rights and anticorruption laws. The problems right now are enforcement and just getting people to think in the ways these laws indicate we should. But I believe that as we keep developing with the international world, we will continue viewing laws as more and more important. The laws are set up to help us get away from personal influences on the system. The Cultural Revolution was one person's mistake, and it took the entire country in a different direction. So laws are helping us get away from the type of system that allows this kind of personal influence to have such an impact. Right now the law is not natural to us; many people don't know many of the interpretations of the laws the way perhaps you do in America, especially the common people who know relatively little about laws. But this is changing. The first step is to get people to understand that they can use laws to protect themselves. Once this starts to happen, people begin to see the use of the law and they will start using it more and more. This is one reason why the Labor Law is so important: Beyond the protections it institutionalizes for laborers, it also gives people a reason to learn about a law and see what relying on a law can do for them. So this law, in particular, will have an impact wider than just its own area; it will have an impact on the way people think of laws in general. . . . In China today, people relying on connections to get things done [*kao guanxi xue*] is still somewhat of a problem. But we are solving this problem. In the future, *guanxi* will be less and less important, and laws will be more and more important. . . . I think the United States must have some problems with people using connections, too. (Interview 65, 1995)

Central to the views of these informants is that a legalistic culture runs much deeper than the simple construction of laws. The existence of laws on paper does not necessarily imply that social and economic actors in the society will understand or view the laws as important in their daily lives. All three of the above informants view this type of transition as an incremental process that will occur in China over a significant period of time.

Nevertheless, despite the fact that it will take "a great amount of time" to change social patterns and ways of thinking at the individual level, important changes have already begun with regard to legal institutions. In the urban industrial economy, managers of large industrial firms voice many issues and concerns surrounding the general fate of *guanxi*, the use of *guanxi practice*, and the role of *guanxi* in business and markets in China's transforming economy. In my survey of industrial firms in Shanghai I discussed these issues with managers focusing, first, on their views of *guanxi practice* and, second, on their views of the general use of *guanxi* in markets and business. Managers' answers to questions surrounding *guanxi* and *guanxi xue* varied significantly. From the outset, in the urban industrial economy this distinction between *guanxi* and *guanxi xue* is every bit as important as Yang found it to be in the private economy (see quotes above). As soon as I raised the question of *guanxi* in interviews, many managers immediately cautioned: "*Guanxi* and *guanxi xue* are two separate things, and you should think of them separately. Which one are we talking about?" I will discuss the two issues separately, first discussing *guanxi practice* and second discussing *guanxi* as social relations.

Using Connections to Get Things Done: Managerial Views of Guanxi Practice

Views on *guanxi* practice in the urban industrial economy can basically be broken into two general categories: those that see *guanxi practice* as withering in the urban industrial economy and those that see *guanxi practice* as becoming more important in the urban industrial economy. Among the group that view *guanxi practice* as a withering institutional system in the urban industrial economy, there are basically two views of the forces that undergird this process of change. Briefly, these are the legal and institutional changes occurring at the state level and the competitive forces that arise in a market economy. Legal and institutional changes have an impact on *guanxi practice* as the state constructs a rational-legal system by which procedures are to be carried out in the official sphere. As these legal and institutional changes are taken more seriously in society, economic actors alter their behavior. This varies across the economy, as small, individual actors, who often are not monitored closely by state offices, may ignore these official institutional changes and continue relying on their own networks and systems for accomplishing tasks in the official sphere; large, powerful actors in the industrial economy, who are often under the state's watchful eye, may be more likely to take official institutional changes seriously. Competitive forces that arise in a market economy make economic actors take institutional changes seriously because there is an emphasis on selecting the best service, product, or project, irrespective of personal relations. When personal relations no longer matter in the equation, the institutional changes meet with less resistance, as there is no competing set of criteria on which to make decisions.

One official who emphasized the legal changes that are influencing the use of *guanxi practice* in the urban industrial economy explained:

> In recent years there has been some improvement in relying on connections to get things done [*kao guanxi xue*]. But it still has a big influence on the way we do things, on the investment environment, on many things. We have two thousand years of history behind this way of doing things. It would be silly to expect that in fifteen short years, because of a few laws, this way of doing things would just go away. . . . The main reason things have improved in this area, though, is that the government is educating people in laws and the legal ways they are doing things now. We also have a number of laws that discourage people from using *guanxi* to carry out procedures [and operating through corrupt practices]. Then there is also the National Compensation Law [*guojia peishang fa*], which guarantees that people will be compensated for the things that the government does wrong. We all know and understand these laws, especially in the bigger, more open cities. Shanghai is a modern city. Our current legal thinking is part of a modern way of doing things. We pay much closer attention to laws and legal procedures now than we did five or ten years ago. (Interview 61, 1995)

While this government official clearly sees the process of change as an incremental one, he also sees a diminishing importance in *guanxi practice* and an increasing importance of China's emerging legal system. A manager in the electronics sector voiced a similar view:

> Relying on connections to get things done [*kao guanxi xue*] still exists, of course. But it is not a serious situation anymore. It's a situation that is changing, becoming less

and less important. China is changing in many significant ways. I don't mean that it doesn't exist anymore, though. There are still situations where people do things this way. . . . Laws have become a very important part of doing things in China today, especially in organizing the market. In order to control the competition in the market, the government has introduced all kinds of laws, to order the market and society. . . . I think these laws and orders are really making the investment environment here much better. We're linking up with the international community [*gen guoji jiegui*]. The linking-up attitude is especially having a huge impact on our organization. (Interview 59*, 1995)

There are three central points to these informants' views on the fate of *guanxi practice* in China's urban industrial economy. First, *guanxi practice* is still an acknowledged institutional system that shapes the decisions and practices of organizational actors. Second, although it is still an important institutional system in China, it is one that is *decreasing* in importance, albeit in an incremental fashion that will likely occur over a long period. Third, the major force in the diminishing importance of *guanxi practice* is the rational-legal system that is being constructed at the state level.

Other managers, however, believe that the emerging legal structures make the use of *guanxi practice* obsolete for industrial organizations in China today. As one manager put it,

Guanxi has little bearing on whether a project will be approved. The most important thing is to follow the official and legal procedures. If you don't follow the procedures and laws, no project will be approved; the only way to get a project approved is to follow these rules. (Interview 36*, 1995)

Another manager echoed this view:

For official procedures, *guanxi* is less important today than it ever has been. Mostly this is because laws are more important now than ever before. Of course, knowing people helps you get things done. This is true in everything. But laws are by far the most important thing today. In 1994 the government came out with the Anti-Corruption Competition Law [*fandui buzhengdang jingzheng fa*]. This law clearly specifies that you can't use *guanxi practice* to get things done. The laws in China today are very clear on these points. (Interview 55*, 1995)

For these managers, the emerging rational-legal system in China has already rendered the practice of *guanxi* somewhat obsolete. Some managers seemed to take honest offense at questions of *guanxi practice* in China today:

Guanxi has nothing to do with procedures today. Perhaps it mattered for getting things done in the 1960s and 1970s. But this is the 1990s. *Guanxi* has nothing to do with it. . . . In Chinese we have a saying: "Friends are friends and business is business." In reality, *guanxi* and business are two separate things. You keep them apart. Of course, as you do business with different individuals, you get to know them, you get to understand them, and maybe you eventually become friends with them. But how is that different from anything anywhere else in the world? The difference between doing business and personal connections is that you can leave business partners behind, but you can't leave friends behind. If you're speaking specifically of the method of conducting affairs through connections [*guanxi xue*], it has little to do with today's China. We follow procedures the way they should be followed. And we do business with people we know, or we get to know people we do business with. Either way, there is no real place for *guanxi xue*. Not in China today. . . . Of course, good relations are important. Everyone should treat one another well, and, in business, you should always try to develop good relations with people you meet. But if an investment is in the approval process and, for example, the feasibility study is not done well or does not convey good results, then approvals should not be sought through *guanxi xue*. This is not the way to do business, and it is happening less and less in China today. Of course, there are situations where someone proposes a really good project and it gets overlooked. Maybe in this situation it makes sense to call someone you know and ask them to look at your proposal again. But what we should focus on is the law and procedures and getting the process right. (Interview 38*, 1995)

A second oft-cited reason for the declining importance of *guanxi practice* revolves around the competitiveness of China's emerging market economy. In a competitive market environment, there is pressure to select projects that will succeed in the market. Successful economic projects mean income for economic actors and an increasing tax base for municipal and central governments. Under the command economy, the state was covering all costs for firms, and efficiency and competitiveness on the open market were not considered to be important considerations. Further, as the state continues to tighten fiscal constraints and to force organizations to take responsibility for their own economic situations, competition among firms increases. With rising competition, rising quality, and rising efficiency, bureaucrats are increasingly likely to consider the viability of a project over personal connections. Informants discussed the issue in a variety of ways:

Guanxi has changed a huge amount in the economic reform. In the past, *guanxi* was really important in the business world. But now quality, price, speed, and production seem to be all that matter. This is really the greatest achievement of the economic reform. It used to be that an individual could control and influence a situation through her or his connections. Now the power of connections [*guanxi quan*] has really been eliminated, especially for cadres. Everything has been standardized and equalized. This is really a big improvement over the past. (Interview 44*, 1995)

We still have to get approvals from above for projects and changes. But usually to get these approvals, the government looks at the content of the project and not much else. *Guanxi* really has no role in it. . . . In my opinion, *guanxi* is somewhat important in markets. But *guanxi* is really just a reflection of yourself. Look at the quality of your product, look at the price; if you are good in these areas, people will want to work with you, they will want to cooperate with you, and your *guanxi* will be good. You'll form good relationships with customers. If you are bad in these areas, all the connections in the world cannot help you succeed. (Interview 50*, 1995)

Yes, of course we have this. But this is not a good way of doing things. Now it is much better than it used to be. *Guanxi* really has no place in doing things today. What do people rely on to get things done? Their economic and competitive strengths. If you have a good competitive future and you follow the laws, these are the most important things. You have no need for *guanxi*. Now aren't we doing market economics? If you have a market economy, you have to have competition. This is the most important thing in the market by far. . . . *Guanxi* is not very important in doing business either. The market in China is huge now. We have investors from Hong Kong, Taiwan, the United States, Singapore all coming here to invest in the market. Do you think they are coming because they have connections. They have no connections here. They are coming because the market is big. And now success for everyone depends on the quality of their products and the service of their production. Their success and failure will be based on whether they can compete, not on who they know. (Interview 80, 1995)

All these informants argue that competitive forces of the emerging market economy are driving economic and political actors to focus on quality and service instead of the norms of the institutional system of *guanxi practice* when making decisions in the period of economic reform.

However, this view of the economic transition should be tempered with an opposing perspective, as not all actors in the transforming economy see the transition so optimistically. Indeed, some managers and officials see the institution of *guanxi practice* as being as important as ever. One manager stated the issue simply, saying:

Now *guanxi* is more and more important. If your *guanxi* is good, you can get things done; if it's not, maybe you will, maybe you won't. Especially if you want to get things done procedurally, *guanxi* is extremely important. (Interview 43*, 1995)

Another manager said:

For getting projects approved, it is very important to have good connections in the administrative bureau. If you want to get procedures carried through, it is important to know the right people in the right places. This is especially true with smaller projects. Bigger projects can usually just be passed without any *guanxi*, because everyone wants those projects to go through. They are good for everyone, and they are usually judged just on their feasibility [*kexingxing*]. But the smaller projects are sometimes more trouble than they are worth for the government officials. For these projects, *guanxi* is very important. (Interview 49*, 1995)

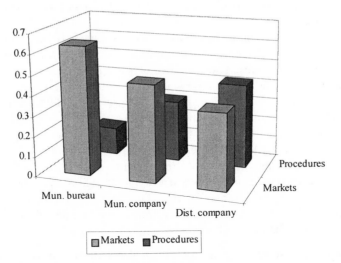

Figure 8.1: Proportion of Firms by Administrative Rank That Rely on *Guanxi* (in Markets) and *Guanxi Practice* (in Official Procedures) in Four Sectors in Industrial Shanghai, 1995

A government official expressed a similar sentiment:

Relying on *guanxi* to get procedural things done is still very important in China today. *Guanxi* really has a huge influence. If your *guanxi* is good, you may have a lot more power. In this respect things are really the same as they were in the past. *Guanxi* in China is just this way. I guess now things may be a little bit better, especially in Shanghai. In Shanghai the systems and rules are more concrete. And the people of Shanghai are more educated. But, overall, *guanxi* is still a very important factor in getting things done. (Interview 61, 1995)

It is pertinent, at this point, to raise the question of whether this variation of views on the importance and future of *guanxi practice* in the economic transition is simply random or if it is dependent on structural factors of the organization. Figure 8.1 shows the proportion of firms by government administrative rank that hold various views of the importance of *guanxi* in markets and the importance of *guanxi practice* for procedures [*ban shouxu*] in China's transition economy. As the figure shows, general managers' views on both these situations vary with an organization's administrative rank. The higher a firm is in China's administrative hierarchy, the less likely the firm's general manager is to view *guanxi practice* as important in the economic transition. The lower a firm is in the administrative hierarchy, the more likely it is that the firm's general manager will view *guanxi practice* as important to achieving success in the economic transition. Conversely, higher-ranked firms are more likely to view *guanxi* as an important part of business activity than lower-ranked firms.[19]

Two things are going on here. First, *guanxi* is inherently better for firms at the upper levels of China's administrative hierarchy. Irrespective of whether these firms actually resort to measures of *guanxi practice*, their social and political connections to state actors that really matter in decision-making processes are much better than those for firms at lower levels of the administrative hierarchy. These firms are positioned directly under the jurisdiction of the government organizational units that make decisions surrounding project and product approvals. Although bureaus are paying little attention to the administrative and economic decisions of firms under their jurisdictions, the bureaucrats in municipal bureaus naturally tend to favor the firms under their control. Even without any kind of explicit *guanxi practice* at work, these bureaucrats are likely to speed approvals along for firms under their jurisdictions. As one manager under the jurisdiction of a municipal bureau put it:

> *Guanxi* might speed up the approval process, but it has little impact on the actual outcome of the approval. (Interview 36*, 1995)

Managers at this level assume that because they do not have to use *guanxi practice* to get things done that connections are unimportant in the reform era. However, it is precisely because of these firms' position in the administrative hierarchy that managers in these firms do not need to pull *guanxi* strings [*la guanxi*] to make things happen for their organizations procedurally. The general managers in these firms are likely to be personally acquainted with the bureaucrats in municipal bureaus, which is sure to help procedural matters along without relying on *guanxi practice* [*kao guanxi xue*]. Firms that are further removed from offices that handle approvals have no personal connections with individuals operating at the upper levels of the government. It is not surprising, then, that general managers of these firms feel the need to use their personal connections to make things happen for their organizations.

Second, firms under the jurisdiction of municipal bureaus have significant advantages over those under municipal and district companies because of scale and scope. Firms at this level of the economy may not be as efficient as other firms, and many of them may be struggling to survive in the economic transition, but, in very basic terms, firms at the municipal bureau level simply have more—in terms of assets, market share, political power—than firms positioned at lower levels of the hierarchy. Their larger scale and scope, along with their proximity to the central government, make these firms targets of larger and more attractive projects. These larger-scale projects are often more attractive to everyone involved—including the bureaus and other approval organizations—than the small-scale projects that typically come to firms at lower levels of the administrative hierarchy (see quote from interview 49 above).[20]

The important message behind the associations presented in Figure 8.1 is

TABLE 8.1
Logistic Coefficients for Determinants of the View that *Guanxi Practice* Is Helpful in Procedural Matters among Managers in Organizations in Four Industrial Sectors, Shanghai, 1995

Independent variables	B	S.E.
Organizational variables[a]		
Chemicals	1.03	.63
Foods	.63	.49
Electronics	.40	.53
Active employees (ln)	−.29	.39
Organizational health	.10	.09
Products exported, 1990 (%)	.004	.01
Joint venture	.21	.35
Overall institutionalization[b]	**−.45****	.21
Governance variables		
GM w/bus./econ. backgrnd.	.43	.32
Municipal bureau	−.57	.45
Constant	2.87	2.55
χ^2		11.69
No. of cases		81

Note: See Appendix 4 for discussion of variables. B is the effect of the coefficient; S.E. is the standard error. ** $p < .05$ (two-tailed tests). Variables in bold are statistically significant.

[a] Reference category for sector is garments.

[b] Overall institutionalization is a variable derived by summing across the institutional categories that are the dependent variables in Table 3.1 (see also Table 3.2).

that while managers of some firms believe that the importance of *guanxi practice* is diminishing in the urban industrial economy, this attitude is highly contingent on the organization's position in the administrative hierarchy of the former command economy. Firms at upper levels of the administrative hierarchy have significant advantages over firms at lower levels of the hierarchy— in part because they have inherently closer connections to the administrative organs of the state that matter in the urban industrial economy—so there is less necessity for firms in this position to go out of their way to pull strings through connections. Here again, we see the theme of path dependency and the importance of a firm's position in the administrative hierarchy of the former command economy for how the firm experiences the economic transition.

Table 8.1 presents a full model of associations with regard to various independent variables and to a general manager's attitude toward the importance of *guanxi practice* for procedural matters in China's transition economy.[21] The table does not reveal much about the overall determinants of managers' viewpoints on the importance of *guanxi practice* (it should be noted that the model is not statistically significant). One interesting result that does emerge from the table, however, is that the overall institutionalization of the organization is negatively associated with the view that *guanxi practice* is important for procedural matters: Managers of organizations that are more "institutionalized" are significantly less likely to view *guanxi practice* as a necessary part of the official realm. Institutional structure is likely to affect attitudes toward *guanxi practice* because managers of firms that are more institutionalized have been more directly engaged in the project of constructing formal rational bureaucracies than managers of less-institutionalized firms (see chapter 3). They are likely to be engaged in processes that relate to observing and taking seriously the rational-legal system emerging at the state level. The firms that these managers run, to some extent, become the institutional environments in which they reside. It is not surprising, then, that managers in more institutionalized environments are likely to view *guanxi practice* as a system of the past. The causality may also work the other way: managers who already view *guanxi practice* as a withering convention in the economic transition are also likely to be the ones that decide to begin the project of constructing formal rational bureaucratic structures within their firms.

Views of the changing importance of *guanxi practice* differ from those of the importance of *guanxi* in markets and business. In the section that follows I explore managers' attitudes toward the use of *guanxi* (as opposed to *guanxi practice*) in markets in China's economic transition.

Connections and Networks in Markets and Business

Where many managers in the urban industrial economy increasingly view *guanxi practice* as diminishing in importance in the reform era, many other managers view social relations [*guanxi*] more generally, as a fundamental part of business relations in a market economic system. There are basically two categories of responses on the importance of *guanxi* in China's emerging market economy: those who view *guanxi* as increasingly important in the economic transition and those who view it as diminishing in importance, only to be replaced by an emphasis on price, quality, and service.

Of the first group, many managers not only view *guanxi* as an important aspect of market economies, but they believe this to be true not only for China but throughout the world. A manager in the foods sector said of this issue:

> For doing business, I think the role of connections is really the same everywhere. If people have a good feeling from you, and you do business based on that, this is a kind of *guanxi*. But this isn't a Chinese thing. This is the same everywhere. (Interview 83*, 1995)

And here are other informants' comments on this issue:

> I think that connections in markets are even more important than they are in proce-
> dures. If you have some customers with whom you have been working for a long
> time, this is the best situation for business. If you have a new product, they will trust
> that it is a good product because they have worked with you for a long time. They
> might even advertise for you. It's as if you are old friends helping each other out.
> These types of relationships are really important in business. (Interview 68*, 1995)

> In markets, relationships and connections are very important. Before, in the planned
> economy, business had nothing to do with connections or relations with customers.
> But now we are in a market economic system, and competition and relationships are
> very important. If you know me and trust me, I can better communicate to you about
> our products and services. You can tell me about any concerns or areas where you're
> unsatisfied. We still try to focus primarily on quality and price, but connections are
> also an important part of it. (Interview 93*, 1995)

> In markets and business, *guanxi* is still important. Relationships are important with
> customers and with business partners. Otherwise, why would they choose to do
> business with you. You might have an excellent product or the best factory, but if
> they can't work with you they will go elsewhere. There are other good products and
> other good factories out there. (Interview 104*, 1995)

The important message conveyed by these managers is that personal relationships enhance business; relationships with customers or business partners can
serve as an advantage in the increasingly competitive markets of the economic
transition.

As I mentioned above, a second category of managers views *guanxi* as unimportant in market economic systems. The commonly cited reasoning behind
this view is that price, quality, and service are the primary factors that shape
market relationships, and this is increasing in the economic transition. As a
manager in the foods sector put it:

> For doing business in China, connections really have no influence. Business depends
> on demand, price, and quality. There is really no need to rely on connections, espe-
> cially if you have a good product. I guess maybe it could have some influence in that
> if you know two people and their product is the same quality and the same price,
> you'll probably go with the person you know. But for the most part, it really depends
> on price and quality. (Interview 85*, 1995)

Several other managers agree that the leverage of social connections is decreasing in importance in a market economy, but they are less categorical in
their statements concerning the role of *guanxi*:

> I wouldn't say that there is no *guanxi* in China. We still have this; we still have
> people using connections to get things done. But it is much less so today than it has

been in the past. Especially in markets, *guanxi* is not an issue. Markets are completely based on competition and price, and *guanxi* plays no role in these. (Interview 45*, 1995)

Now that we are, for the most part, a market economy, we focus primarily on competition and quality. Of course, if you know people or have old customers, they might be more likely to come to you if your quality and service are the same as the person beside you. But if your price is high and your quality is not so good, that's all that matters. *Guanxi* only helps if you are competitive. (Interview 53*, 1995)

In business there are two sides: there's price and quality on one side and *guanxi* on the other side. It's our tradition to think about friends and the people you know first. So, of course, having connections in the business world helps. We often do business with friends. We work with them; when they give us more business, we give them better deals and more care and attention. But these days, more and more, quality, service, and price are really as important as anything. (Interview 94*, 1995)

In business, *guanxi* is perhaps somewhat important. Maybe it's important for making a first contact. But in the end, *guanxi* is not the main thing. Quality, price, service; these are the things that really matter in the business world. If there is *guanxi* in the business world here, it's really the same kind of *guanxi* that people use in market economies in other countries, isn't it? (Interview 98*, 1995)

What all these managers have in common is the view that the growing importance of price, quality, and service is rendering *guanxi* unimportant in the economic transition. Each of the managers concedes that *guanxi* still plays a role in economic relations in Chinese society but that its role is diminishing.

It is again useful here to consider how these attitudes vary as a function of a firm's position in the administrative hierarchy of the former command economy. Similar to the situation of attitudes surrounding *guanxi practice*, attitudes toward *guanxi* are path-dependent, but the pattern runs in the opposite direction from attitudes toward *guanxi practice* (see Figure 8.1): General managers in firms at higher levels of the administrative hierarchy have a stronger tendency to view *guanxi* as important in markets than those in firms at lower levels of the hierarchy.

Table 8.2 presents a more systematic analysis of the associations with regard to various organizational characteristics and general managers' attitudes toward *guanxi* in the reform era. General managers of firms in the chemicals and foods sectors are more likely than those in the garments sector to view *guanxi* as important in markets and business. This association is likely to be grounded in the type of markets the garments sector serves (i.e., markets that are more directly structured around price, quality, and speed) compared to other sectors.

Interestingly, managers of organizations that have joint ventures with foreign organizations are more likely than those without joint ventures to view

TABLE 8.2
Logistic Coefficients for Determinants of the View that *Guanxi*[a]
Is Important in Markets among Managers in Organizations in Four
Industrial Sectors, Shanghai, 1995

Independent variables	B	S.E.
Organizational variables[b]		
Chemicals	.98*	.58
Foods	.88*	.50
Electronics	.71	.49
Active employees (ln)	−.40	.35
Organizational health	.09	.08
Products exported (%)	.003	.01
Joint venture	.71**	.34
Overall institutionalization[c]	−.28	.18
Governance variables		
GM w/bus./econ. backgrnd.	.55*	.30
Municipal bureau	.39	.37
Constant	4.57*	2.34
χ^2	16.58*	
No. of cases	78	

Note: See Appendix 4 for discussion of variables. B is the effect of the coefficient; S.E. is the standard error. * $p < .1$ ** $p < .05$ (two-tailed tests). Variables in bold are statistically significant.

[a] *Guanxi*, meaning social relationships as opposed to *guanxi xue* (*guanxi practice*).

[b] Reference category for sector is garments.

[c] Overall institutionalization is a variable derived by summing across the institutional categories that are the dependent variables in Table 3.1 (see also Table 3.2).

guanxi as important for business in the reform era. Joint-venture relationships are complicated and are often forged over several months or even years. For many organizations, certain joint-venture relationships are among their most important alliances. Whether the venture means a new factory site (usually built with capital from the foreign partner), the transfer of technology, or greater access to international markets, the joint-venture relationship is often crucial for the firm's future.[22] General managers of organizations that have joint ventures have learned firsthand that good relations with prospective business partners is an essential ingredient of successful business deals. It is likely that these types of business deals and the relationship that went into forging them are foremost in these managers' minds. Thus they are more likely to view *guanxi* as an important part of the economic transition than managers of organizations without joint-venture relationships. Finally, general managers with backgrounds in business or economics are significantly more likely to view *guanxi* as important in the emerging market economic system. This association goes back to the issues of normative isomorphism and the professionalization that occurs in university settings.[23] Individuals who are trained (educationally) in similar settings and who, perhaps, are even part of networks that developed in these sites are likely to view the world in similar ways and also to guide their organizations to act in similar ways. The result is that general managers with similar types of educational backgrounds are significantly more likely to view networks and social relationships as an important part of doing business in the economic transition.

Concluding Remarks

While analyses of *guanxi* have taken on a number of different forms and themes, China scholars have generally not questioned the centrality of *guanxi* in Chinese society. It would be a stretch beyond the empirical data of this research for me to make generalizations which counter that view. However, it *is* within the scope of my data to argue that views and perceptions of *guanxi* are changing in important ways in the urban industrial economy and that these changes suggest a trend that does not fully fit with the argument that the role of *guanxi practice* is increasing throughout China in the economic transition. Whereas some scholars have argued that the importance of *guanxi* and *guanxi practice* is increasing in the reform era, I contend that this may not be true with respect to the urban industrial economy. There is a growing emphasis on the distinction between social relationships (*guanxi*) and the *use* of these social relationships in the gift economy (*guanxi practice*), and managers in the urban industrial economy are increasingly likely to distance themselves from the institution of *guanxi practice* in the economic transition.

Currently the Chinese government is engaged in the project of constructing a rational-legal system that will govern the decisions and practices of economic actors. This is especially true for large-scale organizations that the state monitors more closely than individuals or small-scale entrepreneurs. This rational-legal system will increasingly push actors—especially large-scale industrial firms—to conduct economic activities in ways that have a basis in this rational-legal system. The argument of this chapter is not that *guanxi* and the gift economy are insignificant in Chinese society. Clearly these institutions are important in other aspects of Chinese society. However, whether these institutions are important for "all types of commercial transactions" and whether their importance has "increased at an accelerated rate" in the economic transition are empirical questions of the reforms. To a large extent, the data presented in this chapter indicate that *guanxi practice* is diminishing in importance in China's urban industrial economy as the economic transition progresses.

Does corruption still exist in China? Of course. Do economic actors some-times rely on social connections to accomplish procedural tasks? Without question. The issue before us, however, is the direction these trends are head-ing. My position is that these problems, even if they are rampant in some parts of the country, are diminishing in China's transition economy. Setting up new institutions that fundamentally alter the structure of economic activity is a process that takes time—especially if the previous structure of the institutional system was a command economy. Laws and rational-legal institutions are new to this system, and naturally, as the state recedes from micromanagement and control of economic activity, there will be a period, as there was in the mid-1980s, in which economic actors abuse the opportunities created by this void. But is this something distinctively Chinese or is it a product of abrupt and wrenching institutional change? I argue the latter.

One final note on the Chu Shijians and the Deng Zhifangs (Deng Xiaoping's son, whose reputation for corruption precedes him) of this system: While these notorious figures in the Chinese economy are undeniable examples of corrup-tion, it is problematic to draw inferences from their situations. These individu-als became notorious (and rich) in large part *because* of their corruption and *because* of their privileged positions in society. Thus making inferences about trends in Chinese society based on these individuals amounts to selection on the dependent variable. If we are going to draw conclusions, based on a few cases, about those parts of the economy we do not observe, why not conclude that these individuals are the outliers their financial statements indicate they are? The empire that the Red Pagoda Cigarette Factory became under Chu's direction makes it, almost by definition, an outlier in this system. Few factories in China are even a fraction of the size of Red Pagoda. In a random sample of firms in China (such as the one on which my study is based), researchers are most likely to find a collection of somewhat successful organizations along with those that are struggling, on the verge of extinction, led by general man-agers who are straining to understand the uncertain environment in which their firms are now vulnerable. The more common story here, though less often told, is of organizations struggling to survive in the markets of China's transition economy. They are trying to make sense of the new rational-legal institutions the state has recently set in place, and they are trying to integrate them into daily organizational practices. Of course the Chus and the Dengs of this system provide a more exciting tale and surely they tell us something about the rich, infamous individuals they exemplify, but clearly they represent only a small segment of China's transition economy.

Nine _____

Conclusions and Implications

> In the past we focused on the moral ideal of the work unit
> organization: how things were done in the work unit, how
> clean it was, how it was organized. We thought of this in a
> moral and civil sense. The awards the government gave out
> to good organizations identified them as "civilized" work
> units [*wenming danwei*]. . . . Now we are starting to shift
> our way of thinking. Now we are also interested in an
> organization's adherence to laws and regulations. So now
> we have awards that designate an organization as one with
> a good history of contracts and trust [*zhong hetong shou
> xinyong danwei*] in economic relationships.
>   *(Government official; Interview 61, 1995)*

WALKING THROUGH the grounds of an old state-owned industrial firm in
Shanghai, one gets an almost eerie sense of the social life that used to thrive
within these gates. A basketball court is covered with weeds; the rusted old rim
gives the sense that no one has played basketball there in years. The on-site
work unit housing is still there, but it is no longer the hub of social and political
activity that it was in the prereform era. Many workers have moved elsewhere,
perhaps to the new suburbs, which can now be reached by Shanghai's fledg-
ling subway system. As is often the case, the firm simply no longer offers
housing as a workplace benefit for young employees. These work units were
the backbone of the social security system in Mao's China, but today, despite
the manufacturing areas still humming with activity, the facilities look
strangely vacant. During an interview in one such factory, I jokingly asked if
there were many basketball games on the basketball court; the manager somewhat wistfully replied:

> Not anymore. Actually, this place is a good example of what work units used to be
> like and how they have changed. We had this basketball court and many other kinds
> of activities on the factory grounds because all the workers lived here. Some people
> hardly ever left. This was the society they knew. The housing building was right over
> there [pointing to the run down building behind the basketball court]. People lived
> and worked and ate and slept all within this factory. Since the economic reform,
> things have really changed. Now no one lives in that housing unit; a few of the rooms
> have been converted into dorm rooms, and there are showering units so workers can

take showers if they want to. But no one lives here anymore. All the housing provided by the work unit is off the grounds at another site. And fewer people get housing from the work unit now. The part of the factory that has been given over to our joint venture really has nothing to do with housing and those types of benefits anymore. As for all the benefits you asked about earlier [commuter bus, retail shop, food service, etc.], as we become more and more like a company and less like a work unit, we are dealing with these benefits less and less. These things are not really part of our responsibility anymore. Now our main responsibility is to make money and be successful as an economic organization. Life here is really very different than it was before. (Interview 96*, 1995)

Clues of this shift in focus—from social security to economics—are apparent even before you enter these organizations. Hanging on the front gates of many industrial firms you will see a golden plaque announcing to the world that this organization is a "civilized" work unit [*wenming danwei*]. In the command economy, these "civilized" work unit awards were given to organizations that had good reputations for cleanliness, treatment of workers, and benefit packages, and, in general, upheld the ideals of China's communist system.[1] These signs served as a signal of state approval for upstanding "civilized" behavior on the part of the work unit, and organizations hung them on their gates with pride. Today, however, these signs are worn, rusted, and battered, and on the gates of some organizations, right beside the rusted awards for "civilized" behavior, hang shiny new golden plaques, which say something entirely different: "A Work Unit That Emphasizes Contracts and Trust" [*zhong hetong shou xinyong danwei*]. Some organizations have even taken down their old signs and replaced the plaques proclaiming "civilized" with those proclaiming "contract- and trustworthy." Introduced in the late 1980s, these new signs signal to the world that this organization is one that can be trusted in market relationships; this organization has a good history with contracts; this organization is one with which you can do business. Now, instead of working for the approval of bureaucrats, organizations spend time keeping books straight, for it is through upholding contracts and keeping accounting books accurate that an organization can win approval as a contract-worthy organization. The very conception of what makes an organization praiseworthy has shifted in the period of reform.

At the heart of these changes lies the essence of China's economic reforms. The transition from the civilized to the contractual symbolizes many of the changes organizations face in the new world of China's transition from a planned to a market economy. First, there is the shift in focus: Whereas organizations used to focus on socialist ideals, now they increasingly focus on the factors that are praiseworthy in markets. Where organizations under the old system advertised their good citizenry, today they advertise their practices and track records in markets. Second, the state-firm relationship has changed significantly under the economic reforms: Under the old system, state administrative offices made all administrative and economic decisions regarding organizational practices, and state officials awarded conduct based on personal relations and their own personal stake in a given firm. Increasingly today, the state has removed itself from the economic and administrative responsibilities of individual organizations, and, instead, has become an auditor and regulator of organizational practices. This is not to say that the state, as a major stakeholder in many industrial organizations, does not have significant influence over the economic decisions and actions of firms, but the role of state offices is increasingly one of inspection, approvals, and regulation. Third, the state-market relationship has changed significantly. Currently in China, the state is engaged in the project of constructing market institutions. From the broad, macroeconomic policies and laws that change the structure of market activity in China to microlevel institutions such as a reward system for outstanding contractual records, the state is forging new institutions that structure, define, and direct markets and the decisions and practices of economic actors within them. The state is constructing the very institutions that define markets and market activity in China today.

Yet, despite the magnitude of these changes, these changes also speak to another side of China's reforms: the path-dependent and state-driven nature of the reforms. New institutions are being built on the ruins of the old (and sometimes they exist side by side with the old). While factory managers recognize that there are new ways to gain notoriety in the new China, many are conflicted about enacting a set of changes that places markets and bottom-line statistics above all else. And the "heavy hand of the state" is everywhere in this example and everywhere throughout the reforms.[2] Some scholars speak of placing too much causal primacy on the state in studying economic transitions, but the simple fact is that the state is defining all the rules by which the new game is being played.[3] Economic actors can themselves decide whether they want to follow or break these rules, and that is also an important part of the story. But, as in the examples presented here, the state not only defines the new institutions that will shape market action (e.g., what practices will be praiseworthy), but it also defines the incentive system, which will reward actors for playing by the new rules, and then judges economic actors on their performance.

In urban China today, evidence of the economic transition abounds. The service sector has expanded to occupy a significant sector of the economy as well as of the urban labor force. Small private businesses line the main streets of urban areas. Neighborhood associations, the basic housing structure for urban citizens in prereform China, many of which occupy entire city blocks, are being swept away and replaced by thirty-story hotels and office buildings. Inside work units, it is common to see posters and banners exhorting workers to "study the Labor Law" [*xuexi laodonfa*] and to "exercise [your] democratic rights by attending the Workers' Representative Company Meetings" [*yi laodong minzhu quanli canjia zhigong diabiao dahui*].[4] It is now increasingly common to find workers who are tied to work units via labor contracts rather than the promise of lifetime employment. Instead of benefits, housing, and a long-term relationship with a prestigious Chinese industrial work unit, talented young workers seek high-paying jobs in joint ventures or wholly owned foreign companies. Beyond these changes, however, lie deeper issues relating to the transition, issues grounded in the actual nature of the reforms and the significant factors that drive them. Important questions about the political, economic, and social processes that define the observable changes require analyses that look deeper into the political structures and organizational characteristics that give rise to specific social and economic forms.

Throughout this study I have attempted to illuminate many hidden facets of China's reforms through direct observations of the decisions and practices of economic actors in the marketplace, as a way to explore the meaning of the broader political and institutional changes of the economic transition. My reasoning has been that if we are truly to understand the meaning of broader institutional changes, we must examine the ways that these institutional transformations have meaning for economic actors. Changes at the state level are important, but we can only begin to understand the true meaning of these changes by observing the ways they are adopted and employed by economic actors. In the previous chapters I explored a number of the different practices and market activities adopted by economic actors, specifically industrial organizations in Shanghai, in the transforming economy. I have explored the factors associated with the specification of arbitration clauses in joint-venture contracts, the determinants of autonomous price-setting and price-negotiation strategies, the adoption of the Company Law, and diversification strategies. Looking inside the firm, I have examined the organizational, political, and institutional characteristics associated with internal structure, including the institutionalization of organizational rules, job descriptions, grievance-filing procedures and mediation institutions, Worker Committee Meetings, promotion tests, formalized hiring procedures, changes in wages and nonwage benefits, and the institutionalization of labor contracts. In general, I have shown that a firm's position in the industrial hierarchy of the former command economy and whether a firm has a relationship with a foreign company significantly shape the decisions and practices the firm adopts in the reform era. Those at the upper levels of the economy are experiencing extreme uncertainty, and the strategies they adopt reflect this fact. Those that have formal relations with foreign firms are significantly more likely to adopt Western-style structures, suggesting that Chinese firms model themselves after those actors that are perceived to be the most successful in the marketplace.

In-depth analyses of these organizational practices highlight many aspects of China's reforms. They tell us a textured story about the dynamics of foreign investment, the effects of state institutions, and the complex ways that economic actors approach economic decision making in China's transition economy. Most important, however, analyses of these practices highlight the fact that we need a new set of tools to analyze transition economies, tools that paint a richer picture than individual-level data or various measures of productivity. In this concluding chapter I focus on three sets of implications that derive from the research presented here. First, I target the implications of this research for the theoretical and methodological approach we take in the study of transition economies. Second, while I have avoided analyses of economic outcomes in this study, here I address the implications of my research for the productivity of industrial organizations in China. Finally, I analyze the implications of this research for policy debates over foreign investment and the link between economic relations and China's human rights record.

An Economic Sociology of Transition Economies

One set of implications derived from this study relates to general issues in the study of economic transitions. With the wrenching social, political, and economic changes occurring throughout the world, study of societies in transition from planned to market economies is an area of research that has gained significant attention in recent years. From general theories of transition to more narrowly defined studies, a number of theoretical positions have been staked out and many important findings have been presented. Scholars such as Ivan Szelényi, Michael Burawoy, Victor Nee, Andrew Walder, David Stark, Barry Naughton, Jeffrey Sachs, and many others, have set the tone for theoretical and substantive debates over the nature of economic transitions, state-market and state-society relationships, who gains and who loses in economic transitions.[5] The empirical substance of these studies include changing mechanisms of stratification in transition economies, the changing nature of property rights, advantages of bureaucrats, and fundamental questions about the relationship between state control and production efficiency.[6]

All these studies have enhanced our understanding of important cases of economic transition. However, one problem with research on economic transitions is that we seem, to a large extent, to have taken our analytical cues from economics more than any other field; we have allowed economics to define the terms of the debate. Many studies in economic transitions begin with changes in income, entrepreneurial activity, changes in productivity, or the emergence of a private economy. Although these issues are certainly important, there are many more topics to explore in economic transitions.[7] Often, broad-based institutional changes have subtle but important effects on how economic actors understand their transforming social worlds. How economic actors choose to respond to and incorporate (or ignore) these institutional changes may provide important information about the meaning of the reforms. If institutional changes lead to rapid gains in income or productivity, that is certainly an important and noteworthy effect of the change. However, if there is not concurrent growth in income or productivity, a limited focus on economic indicators leaves us wondering if any below-the-surface changes are occurring at all. It is often likely that institutional changes do have a far-reaching impact on the structure of economic and social worlds, but this impact is not immediately reflected in economic indicators.

In chapter 1 I argued that an economic sociology of market transitions must do more than react to classical economic studies. I also outlined the essential parameters that an economic sociology of market transitions must embody. Economic sociology begins with the premise that economic actors are not necessarily the rational profit maximizers that neoclassical economic theories have posited them to be. Rational profit maximization may be one approach to economic decision making that economic actors take, but this is an empirical *question* for *research* not a social fact for theoretical suppositions or assumptions. The more interesting question for market transitions is *when* economic actors are rational profit maximizers and when their actions do not make sense in this framework and *why*.

An economic sociology of market action begins with the more general framework that economic actors strive to create stable worlds, and the strategies and practices they adopt reflect this effort.[8] It is through this lens that growth-oriented and survival strategies can be linked into one theory of economic action, as in both cases actors are striving to stabilize their market positions. One particular way that markets become unstable is through state-induced crises where state action radically changes the institutional environments in which economic actors operate. How economic actors react to these state-induced crises reflects their original market positions, their market strength, and the institutional environments and networks in which they are embedded. Following this approach, many researchers in organizational sociology often avoid a narrow focus on profit maximization and productivity by studying the strategies and structures that economic actors (organizations) adopt in response to changing political, institutional, and market environments. Paul DiMaggio and Walter Powell, Neil Fligstein, Lauren Edelman, John Sutton, Frank Dobbin, Richard Scott, and John Meyer have all shown the different ways that organizations respond to the uncertainty created by changing political, institutional, and market conditions. For each of these researchers, the focus is not on productivity, profits, or entrepreneurial activity but, rather, on the decisions and practices that economic actors adopt and the institutional changes that support those decisions and practices.

Economic sociology also posits that states are fundamental to the structure of markets. States make decisions and define the institutions that shape market structure and economic activity in transforming economies. Even in the so-called free markets of the United States, the decision to further deregulate many markets (and thereby favor those with the most resources) in the 1980s was unquestionably a political decision that resides in the world of government action and interest-group politics. It is in this sense that there is always a political element to economic action.[9] In addition, the historical legacy of the types of institutions—particularly state institutions—that define market structure and action play a fundamental role in shaping patterns of economic decision making. Theories of markets and economic action that deny the importance of politics or the legacy of past institutional structures are simply not in touch with the empirical world.

These theoretical propositions fit with the dynamics of change in China's transforming economy all too well. They allow us to take a step back from the somewhat exclusive focus on standard economic indicators and ask hard questions about how individuals and organizations are actually experiencing the reforms. For example, focusing on standard economic indicators and the assumption that economic actors will "pursue power and plenty" given the freedom to do so causes us to miss all the actors in the marketplace who have not conformed to this model of action. When I asked one general manager about the profitability of her organization, she defiantly replied:

> I don't *do* profits [*wo buzuo lirun*]. My goal is to raise the living standard of my employees as much as possible. So when we have an excess, I usually just reinvest some of the money in the factory and distribute the rest evenly among the employees. (Interview 54*, 1995)

Many other managers, such as the one who referred to profit maximization through price setting as a "black-hearted" practice (chapter 5) or those who proclaimed that it was more important to show loyalty to older workers (chapter 4), even if it were less profitable to do so, made clear that views of market action cannot be reduced to a simple rational profit-maximization framework.

As I have also argued throughout this study, by narrowly assuming that economic actors make decisions and adopt new practices solely to maximize profits we miss a dynamic that is fundamental to China's transforming economy: Chinese firms mimic the structures and practices of foreign organizational forms to appear legitimate and market savvy. They want more than anything to attract foreign investment, as often that means having access to international markets, capital, and technology. And if, in the early years of the reform, municipal bureaus and ministries could simply dictate which of the firms under their jurisdictions would be "married off" to a foreign partner, the process of joint-venture negotiations today involves a much more complex dance. Chinese managers know that attracting foreign investment involves presenting their firms as potential partners that will be accommodating and responsive to the needs and demands of the foreign partner. Many Chinese managers also know that they have much to learn about organizational management from their foreign partners. Chinese firms with foreign partners most readily have access to up-close examples of how foreign organizations are structured and run, and they model themselves accordingly. This dynamic is at the heart of the rhetoric of "getting on track with the international community" [*gen guoji jiegui*]. It is also at the core of the organizational decision to adopt many of the strategies and structures Chinese firms are embracing in the reform era, ranging from internal structures such as organizational rules, grievance-filing procedures, and formal hiring policies to rational price-setting practices, adoption of the Company Law, and the specification of arbitration clauses in joint-venture contracts.

Finally, I have shown throughout this study that the historical legacy of state institutions matter in fundamental ways for how organizations experience periods of economic change. Where a firm is positioned in the administrative hierarchy of the former command economy has powerful implications for the decisions and practices that firm will adopt; more generally, it colors the extent to which the firm experiences a sense of being set adrift by the state. Because resources were distributed in fundamentally different ways across this administrative system under the command economy, it is reasonable to assume that firms would experience sweeping changes in various ways. Accounting for part of this difference is that government organizations at the various levels of this hierarchy simply govern differently: Municipal bureaus are divesting themselves of administrative and economic responsibilities, while municipal and district companies are keeping tighter control over the firms under their jurisdictions. The research presented here suggests that organizations at the municipal and district company levels are far more likely to shun stability strategies, choosing instead to invest resources in upgrading their organizations. In contrast, the shock of being set adrift by municipal bureaus leads firms at this level of the hierarchy to adopt stability strategies that do not necessarily make the most sense in terms of the firm's long-term growth. Organizations under the jurisdiction of municipal bureaus are apparently experiencing markets most directly, and they are therefore the most likely to experiment with a variety of market strategies and practices; these include such rational market practices as rational price setting and such stability-seeking strategies as diversification into the service sector and the institutionalization of labor contracts. This analysis runs counter to studies that have predicted, based on slow gains in productivity in this sector of the economy, that these large state-owned organizations have been left largely unreformed. On the contrary, they are in many ways *more* reformed than their counterparts at lower levels of the industrial hierarchy, and they are struggling to survive as a result.

The general point here is that economic transition and the construction of new markets cannot be divorced from the social, political, and institutional contexts in which these processes occur. Firms' networks, the institutional and political environments in which the firms are embedded, and the historical legacies of institutions all matter for the decisions and practices economic actors adopt in periods of upheaval and reform. And in order to understand how these institutional, political, and social situations inform economic action, we need to look at specific cases of economic decision making in transition economies.

But What's the Bottom Line? Productivity in China's Urban Industrial Firms

Throughout this study I have argued that economic indicators tell a one-sided story about economic transitions. I have avoided discussions of economic indicators on both methodological and theoretical grounds, arguing that indicators other than income and productivity tell a richer story about the nature and dynamics of market reforms. Nevertheless, no matter how strong my argument for shifting the focus of this debate, economists, policy makers, and China investors will all inevitably ask a common question: What are the implications of these findings for the economic transformation of Chinese organizations? *What about productivity?* We already know from aggregate measures of productivity that rates of growth have been much faster in rural areas than in the urban industrial economy, but how do firms *within* the urban industrial economy compare to one another? What can this study of industrial Shanghai tell us about economic transitions more generally? I have already argued that contrary to suggestions that slow rates of growth imply a lack of reform in the upper levels of China's administrative hierarchy, my research shows that this sector of the economy is experiencing the greatest amount of market autonomy. I have also suggested that this sudden autonomy has led to a great deal of uncertainty for firms at this economic level. However, while this argument counters assumptions about the lack of reform in slow-growth sectors of the economy, it stops short of a positive answer to the productivity question.

The data I gathered in industrial Shanghai actually do point to a deeper, more radical answer to the productivity question. Jeffrey Sachs has championed the view that privatization is the only way to reform slow-growth, unproductive enterprises. His view is that reform in China has been successful *despite* the gradual hands-on approach to the transition; rapid privatization of the state sector will be a necessary final step in the process of reform. Other scholars have argued that it is precisely because of the hands-on nature of reform that rural China has grown so rapidly. My research on the urban industrial economy supports the latter view: I argue that firms actually benefit from and are more likely to succeed in the mixed economy.[10] The decisions and practices adopted by organizations in four sectors of industrial Shanghai suggest that despite the fact that firms at the highest levels of the industrial hierarchy are experiencing markets most directly, there is also evidence that they are adopting practices that will not lead to gains in productivity. Channeling assets into the service-sector economy as a form of fast-return investment helps to provide cash to cover costs, but it does little for the productivity of the

TABLE 9.1

Ordinary Least Squares Coefficients Predicting the Productivity of Organizations in Four Industrial Sectors, Shanghai, 1995

	Model I		Model II		Model III	
Independent variables	B	S.E.	B	S.E.	B	S.E.
Organizational variables[a]						
Chemicals	1.11*	.57	1.06*	.56	1.24**	.57
Electronics	−.20	.46	−.30	.44	−.29	.44
Foods	−.11	.99	−.14	.40	.04	.41
Active employees (ln)	−.07	.15	−.12	.14	−.18	.15
Joint venture	.54	.37	.49	.36	.37	.37
Governance variables						
GM w/bus./econ. backgrnd.	.19	.31	.07	.31	.16	.31
Municipal bureau	−.67	.60	—	—	—	—
Municipal company	—	—	.58*	.32	—	—
District company	—	—	—	—	−.55	.40
Constant	1.14	.80	1.28*	.74	1.94**	.87
R^2	.17		.20		.19	
No. of cases	81		81		81	

Note: See Appendix 4 for discussion of variables. B is the effect of the coefficient; S.E. is the standard error. Variables in bold are statistically significant. Productivity is calculated as follows: gross revenues/active employees. The mean, minimum, and maximum for this variable, respectively, are 114,045, 111, and 820,000 yuan per employee. The variable is divided by 100,000 to allow for manageable coefficients; coefficients should be multiplied by 100,000 for actual effects. * $p < .1$ ** $p < .05$ (two-tailed tests).
[a] Reference category for sector is garments.

organization. On the other hand, firms at the lower levels of the economy are changing their organizations in more fundamental ways. Qualitative accounts of managers under the jurisdiction of municipal and district companies, where the state offices maintain more of a hands-on approach to guiding firms through the transition, suggest that firms at this level of the economy are interested in upgrading their factories. At the bureau level, the shock of being set adrift leads to short-term stability strategies that do nothing for productivity; at the municipal and district company level, in the second, the gradual approach of the state's continued role leads to strategies that are more likely to foster long-term growth.

Table 9.1 shows which firms in China's urban industrial economy are doing the best in terms of productivity.[11] The models show that, controlling for size, sector, and the presence of a foreign-investment partner, the only variables that significantly affect a firm's productivity are location in the chemicals sector and location under the jurisdiction of a municipal company. It is the latter result that is the most intriguing for the analysis here: Net of other effects, firms under the jurisdiction of a municipal company, on average, bring in 58,087 yuan per employee (about U.S.$7,000) more than organizations under municipal bureaus and district companies. It is not the organizations that have been given the most market autonomy (those under municipal bureaus) that have gained the most in terms of productivity; nor have firms under government offices that take the most hands-on approach to the reforms (those under district companies) done comparatively well. Those under municipal companies (an administrative level in-between municipal bureaus and district companies—see Figure 2.1) have been the most successful at transforming themselves in Shanghai's urban industrial economy. Firms' success at this level of the economy fits with the findings presented in chapters 3 and 4, which show that these firms are the most likely to experiment with fundamentally altering work environments (they are the most likely to adopt rational internal structures) and incentive systems (they pay their employees significantly more than other firms). The success of firms at this economic level suggests that a mixture of political clout (being under the municipal as opposed to the district government) and hands-on management from state offices is the best recipe for reform. Thus there is little or no empirical support for the utility of a "shock therapy" approach to economic reform in the urban industrial economy.

Implications for Political Debates

I turn now to the implications of this study for the political debate over whether economic relations should be linked to China's record and progress on human rights. Recently, at Shanghai's airport, I bumped into one of my informants (Interview 35, 1995), who is now the head of China operations for a large American company that has a significant amount of its garment products manufactured in Chinese factories. After we exchanged pleasantries, I asked him where he was going. He told me he was on his way to conduct the factory visits and inspections that had become a routine part of his job in recent years. This raised my interest, so I asked a few more pointed questions and recorded what I remembered of the conversation as soon as we parted. According to this executive, his company has been conducting factory inspections since 1995. Since this multinational company is nervous about bad press over contracting out to exploitative factories, the practice was set up to monitor these organizations and ensure that they were treating workers in ways that were not problematic from a human rights standpoint. When I raised the counterpoint, which we so often hear from the Chinese, of interfering with China's internal affairs, the executive replied [I am paraphrasing here]:

> We're not trying to make them do anything that they don't already have on the books over here. We just want them to follow the laws that the Chinese government has already set up. The fact is, the Chinese government has, at this point, set in place a

good number of laws and institutions that protect workers' interests. The difficult part is getting people to follow them. We think we can play a positive role by emphasizing the importance of these laws. If we don't like the way they're running things, we can take our business elsewhere. They need the business, so they're generally pretty cooperative. . . . Believe me, we have our own interest in this. The last thing we want is the public relations disaster of allegations that our products are manufactured by a factory that violates human rights. It's just best for everyone that we make these visits.

Based on many conversations such as this one, and based on the empirical findings of this research, I view the role of on-the-ground foreign investment as an important part of the rationalization of Chinese society, having important implications for human rights in China. I argue here that if we want truly to understand the factors that affect the development of human rights, we need to look closely at the actual development of rational institutional structures with which people come into contact on a daily basis. Rational institutional structures here are viewed in contrast to particularistic authority relations that are dependent solely on the caprice of individuals in positions of power. We need to examine the extent to which rational institutional structures are replacing particularistic authority relations in ways that are meaningful for individuals. Further, we need to develop an empirically driven theory of the factors that influence the development of these local-level institutional structures. Because this is, in large part, what I have done throughout this study, I will discuss here the meaning of this study for informing political positions on the development of human rights in China.

The Most-Favored-Nation Debate

An important example is the implication this research has for the Most-Favored-Nation (MFN) debate, which has occupied the national stage annually since the Tiananmen crackdown in the spring of 1989. The issue is whether favorable trade status should be linked to China's record or progress in the area of human rights. Proponents of de-linking economic relations from issues of human rights have argued that it is only through continued contact with the international (Western) community of nations that the Chinese political and economic systems will become structured around a rational-legal framework. Dissenters argue that trade is a privilege and that if China wants to partake in this privilege, the government must show its commitment to legal institutional structures and frameworks in the realms of human rights, intellectual property rights, and the like. Implicit in the debate is a set of assumptions about the interrelated nature of development, economic change, and a society's institutional structure. Despite the resolve of advocates on both sides of the debate, the issues have still not been fully explored for the case of economic transition in China. In order to understand the impact of foreign investment, market reform, and economic change in China, we must answer the following questions: As the Chinese economy develops and becomes more globalized, what are the institutional structures that organize this society? What are the implications of an increasingly rationalized economic system that is more and more at odds with the particularistic and capricious authority relations of an authoritarian system? In general, we need to grasp the social, political, and economic factors associated with the adoption of institutional structures and systems. As the MFN debate has assumed, the issue of economic development has implications that go far beyond the economic world to several other realms of social life. The effects of economic development extend into the realm of the institutional legal structures that define human rights, labor law, and due process in the workplace, and to the general social structure of Chinese society.

The political positions on the MFN issue are problematic for several reasons, and these relate to the fundamental questions this study addresses. First and foremost, individuals and advocacy groups engaged in this debate have failed to clarify exactly what the goals of this debate are. Chinese political prisoners and dissidents get the most attention in the debate, but these individuals are only one component of the human rights issue. Of equal importance are the institutional environments that affect the lives of millions of Chinese workers every day. It is important to clarify specifically what this debate is about because, at least with respect to these two issues, achieving the various goals—release of political prisoners and respect for legal institutions that protect individual rights—may require different approaches. In other words, tactics that are effective in dealing with the issue of political prisoners may not be adequate in pushing for broad-based institutional change. Since my research primarily addresses the issue of institutional change at the factory level, my comments here pertain to the MFN debate as it relates to broad-based institutional change and the everyday experiences of Chinese workers.

Second, proponents from both sides of the debate take their positions in a veritable vacuum of empirical research on the topic. There has been a paucity of direct research on the factors associated with the adoption of institutional practices in the transforming Chinese society, yet politicians on both ends of the political spectrum have carved out a political rhetoric that is as uninformed as it is self-righteous. How can we form a policy on human rights and the rule of law in China when we have no empirical understanding of what social, political, and economic factors drive the process of institutional change?

On the surface, history and the nature of capitalism offer compelling arguments for the sanction and isolation positions. China would have much to lose if the international community was united on the issue of sanctions, and this approach has been successful in notable cases such as South Africa. Further, with many examples of exploitative practices among businesses seeking cheap labor, what reason do we have to expect that the case of foreign investment in

China would be any different? Yet, the Chinese case is unique in a number of ways, and the particularities of investment and economic development in China lead to an argument for engagement and the importance of foreign investment in systemic change. First of all, with vast untapped markets and much money to be made, it is inconceivable that the international community will ever by united on the sanctions position with respect to China. However, the most important fact of investment in China is that most foreign investors are more interested in setting up foreign-Chinese equity joint ventures and capturing a share of the domestic market in China than they are in seeking out cheap labor. Thus they are interested in stable, long-term investments—many joint ventures are twenty-year renewable agreements. Because foreign businesses setting up joint ventures are investing for the long term, finding a stable investment partner that understands rational-legal business and labor practices is among foreign investors' highest priorities. Chinese firms, for their part, want desperately to attract foreign joint-venture partners—which bring capital, technology, and status—so many of them are changing in radical ways to appear as stable investment partners that are savvy of Western business and labor practices. Despite the fact that foreign investors are not motivated by goals associated with human rights, the foreign-Chinese joint-venture relationship, coupled with the emergence of laws produced at the state level, has crucial consequences for labor relations, and therefore for human rights, in China.

Beyond the lack of research supporting either perspective in this debate, the argument for linking trade and human rights is backward in at least two ways. First, there is an implicit assumption in these political interchanges that the Chinese government should construct new laws, impose them, and rigorously enforce them. While nearly everyone—from investors to human rights advocates—would agree that the construction of a rational-legal institutional system would be a positive step toward dismantling a capricious authoritarian regime, the reasoning behind the political pressure position is flawed. The goal is to institutionalize a rational-legal system that dissuades the administrative and political fiat of an authoritarian government, yet only an authoritarian regime has the power to command such quick return on respect for laws or political decisions. While the construction and implementation of new laws are central to the overall institution-building project, the laws mean little on paper without a local-level institutional system to support the official institutions. Governments cannot simply demand that laws be respected; individuals must first understand these new institutions before they can be followed and meaningfully enforced. A particularly telling example of this dynamic occurred during the political pressure over the enforcement of intellectual property rights in the spring of 1995. As the United States put increasing pressure on the Chinese government to enforce trademark and copyright laws that existed primarily on paper, the government acted with the only means it had available. As pressure increased, so did the incidents of "knock-off" vendors getting beat up by Public Security Bureau police.[12] The method was effective for dealing with the problems of copyright violations but anathema for the larger issue of the pressure to create a strong institutional environment in which intellectual property rights, human rights, and due process are all protected under the law. In the void of local-level institutional structures, the paper-thin laws were enforced in the manner of totalitarian rule.

The point is that a broad-based institutional environment is likely to take significantly longer to construct than the simple production of laws in the official spheres. Virtually every manager and official with whom I spoke over the course of this research, including those who were sympathetic to the American push for rational-legality in China, expressed consternation and confusion at the expectation that institutional change should come about in China so quickly. As one government official put it:

It's ridiculous that the American government places these requirements on us that assume we suddenly have a developed legal infrastructure. We don't have two hundred years of legal development in this country; we have sixteen. And when the American government tells us to do the things it does, it completely assumes that we have developed legal infrastructure that can carry out the ideas that the American government decides on. It's impossible. . . . The most difficult part is changing the way people think. You Americans, as you grow up, become used to a legalistic way of thinking. You know the laws, and you understand the way people think. But this is not the case with the Chinese. We have grown up knowing one thing: Always listen to your leader. Changing the way people think about these things is the most difficult task of a developing nation. It takes a great amount of time; many things must be changed for a significant amount of time before people will start to think in a different way. (Interview 29, 1995)

Institutional change is a process that occurs over time, and, in research and policy making, we need to be attentive to both the institutional changes of the official sphere and the local-level institutional structures and practices that support these official changes. Thus, in a study of institutional change, we need to focus not only on the production of institutional changes at the state level but also on the local-level practices that coincide with, react to, and, in some cases, contradict the institutional changes in the official sphere. Not insignificantly, it should be noted that radical changes are occurring at the state level, from the construction of the Labor Law to the National Compensation Law, and the impact of these institutional changes were clearly present in Chinese factories in 1995.

The second problem with the perspectives surrounding the trade debate is the assumption that trade should be the reward for legal and institutional change when, in fact, economic exchanges may be the very engine—or at least a key component—that is driving the system toward the rational institutional structure that is so desired. The economic negotiations occurring at local levels often pressure organizational actors to respect institutional agreements. State-level institutional changes cannot be meaningful without the institutional structures to support them, and the changes cannot be viewed as meaningful if organizations (and people) do not incorporate them into everyday practices. But in order to understand the effects of economic negotiations and state-level institutional changes, we need to systematically observe local-level practices of economic actors and the ways that these practices are changing over the course of the economic transition. Where these changes are having the greatest impact will give us insight into the factors and characteristics that lead to institutional change.

Here again, radical changes are emerging at the factory level. In the research presented in these chapters, I have shown significant effects of joint-venture relationships on the emergence of formal rational institutional systems and practices at the firm level. In chapter 3 I showed that relationships with foreign partners have an impact on the emergence of a formal rational bureaucratic system in firms. Joint-venture relationships have a positive effect on the like-lihood that a firm will have formal organizational rules, grievance-filing procedures, and hiring procedures, and on the organization's overall institutionalization. In that chapter I also presented evidence suggesting that these institutional changes are more than symbolic, since the presence of these structures actually reduce the likelihood that individuals in an organization will seek external venues for filing grievances. In chapter 5 I showed that a formal relationship with a foreign investor has a significant impact on the types of price-setting practices that organizations adopt. In chapter 7 I showed that Western partners have an impact on the likelihood that an organization will agree to use CIETAC for dispute resolution. All these findings point to the importance of economic relationships with foreign companies for the emergence of formal rational structures and systems in China (in chapter 7 the findings indicate the importance of specifically Western investment).

The effects illuminated here have clear implications for the debate over linking trade and human rights. Institutional change in China is not coming solely from political pressure on the Chinese state to construct a rational-legal system. The state's construction of such institutions as the Labor Law, CIETAC, and the Labor Arbitration Commissions are necessary but not sufficient steps in the emergence of new institutions that touch the lives of individuals in China. Also necessary is the pressure that occurs at local levels in the markets of China's transforming economy. Political pressure is important, but individual and organizational actors are also influenced by the pressures they find across the negotiating table. Whether the pressure is direct negotiating pressure from foreign investors to take seriously an institution of international dispute arbitration (CIETAC) or simply competitive pressure to operate in a way that mimics foreign companies, these institutional changes arise as a result of economic relationships with foreign companies. The negotiations with foreign economic actors that seek and emphasize strong institutional environments are as important for meaningful institutional change as the frameworks defining these changes at the state level. In other words, political pressure at the state level is not meaningful without the pressure in the marketplace to take these institutional changes seriously. A fundamental component of the pressure for institutional change in China is the pressure of individual economic actors in the markets of China's transforming economic system.

The inference from this line of evidence and reasoning is that *economic relations and China's human rights record should not be linked*. The best hope for helping a formal rational-legal system emerge over the course of China's transition is to continue allowing the local-level negotiations between Chinese citizens and foreign companies to occur in China's markets. It is through a combination of broad-based, state-level institutional changes and pressure at local levels to take these changes seriously that meaningful institutional change will occur in China. Naturally, this tack does not preclude pressure from the international community; the two approaches, although separate, are by no means mutually exclusive. As one businessman-turned-human-rights activist put it:

> The international community has a right to question these issues, but these questions should not be linked to trade. This is something that still needs to be worked out in people's minds. Although [President] Clinton officially divorced the renewal of MFN from human rights, the 1972 Trade Act says that MFN has to be voted on by Congress every year. And, unfortunately, when Congress is voting, many are still linking trade to human rights. This is harmful because business can really be a powerful tool and leverage in changing these issues. But to hold out trade as a threat only backs China into a corner and gets nothing done. (Interview 28, 1995)

My point here is not to proselytize about the positive effects of foreign businesses in the process of China's economic transition. Businesses rarely, if ever, land in China with such high-minded intentions. My point is simply to emphasize the extent to which the causes of institutional change in China are empirical questions, and our assumptions and analyses of institutional change must be grounded in empirical research and the observations of business people who are experiencing this rapidly changing world firsthand. Policy and research should begin with the reality of Chinese citizens' actual experiences.

Concluding Remarks

The reforms of the last decade and a half in China have set in motion a number of radical transformations in China's economy and society. These range from the policies that touch rural, agricultural areas to those shaping economic action in urban industrial sectors to those transforming the very nature of the Chinese family and China's social demographics. The processes of change are driven by state reforms that have altered society's rules for social and economic actors. The state begins this gradual process with broad-based institutional changes constructed at the state level (in the form of laws and policies). As actors adapt to these new rules, they modify the social worlds in which they live and operate. When parents respond to the one-child policy and have fewer children than their parents did, their actions change the nature of the Chinese family; when farmers become petty entrepreneurs and alter their production, incentive systems, and incomes, they are changing the nature of what it means to be a farmer in rural China; and when industrial managers adopt practices at the firm level—be they economic strategies of the firm or changes in the firm's internal structure—they are transforming the social worlds in which workers operate as well as the very structures that defined the Chinese socialist organization. How social and economic actors choose to adopt (or resist or simply ignore) these broad-based institutional changes also has implications for the nature and path of the reform process.

Although the reforms of China's transition touch virtually every aspect of Chinese society, I have focused on one facet of this transition: the changes occurring among medium- and large-scale organizations in the urban industrial economy. This sector of the economy occupies a specific position in Chinese society, as it is the one sector, more than any other, that remains strongly in state hands, with the state closely monitoring its progression through the reforms. Further, Chinese industrial firms are embedded in the organizational hierarchy of the former command economy; this means that the institutional structure of state administration has a set of very particular consequences for the ways that firms at different levels of this hierarchy experience the reforms. The effects of this organizational hierarchy and the close relationship between the state and the urban industrial economy make the experiences of this economic sector a window onto important aspects of state-firm relationships in China's economic transition.

One of my goals has been to uncover some direct observations of the reforms. Where many studies of economic transition have focused somewhat narrowly on economically defined notions of productivity and growth to gauge the extent of the reforms, I have concentrated instead on the economic strategies and practices of firms. The decisions managers make regarding their firms' strategies are tied to the institutional environments in which they are embedded, the economic constraints they are experiencing, and the networks of firms in which they are situated. Although certain strategies may not make sense in profit-maximizing terms, and although they may not be reflected in patterns of growth or productivity, they do, nevertheless, reveal significant facts about how the environments in which firms are embedded are changing. Organizations experiencing extreme uncertainty will attempt to stabilize their worlds, and they will adopt strategies that reflect the uncertainties of their environments. Yet, these changes are often invisible to standard economic indicators. Chinese firms are adopting many strategies that reflect their experiences of uncertainty in the marketplace, even while economic indicators *seem* to indicate that little is changing for some firms in the economy. By focusing on the strategies of firms, I have attempted to expand the scope of indicators that can reveal significant findings about the process and path of China's reforms.

Attention on the internal structure of Chinese firms has also suggested significant notions about the path of China's reforms that are hidden from standard economic indicators. Here again, the structures and practices that managers adopt in their firms are reflections of the institutional environments and networks in which they are embedded. Formal rational bureaucracies are emerging at the firm level, and these bureaucracies have a significant impact on the decisions and practices that are carried out at the firm level. The emergence of these firm structures are tied to the organization's location in a particular sector, the general manager's background, and whether the firm has formal relations with a foreign company. These formal rational bureaucratic structures in Chinese organizations mark a radical departure from the structure of authority relations in prereform China.

The future of China's economic transition is difficult to predict, especially since the real challenges still lie ahead. But one thing is certain: The success of China's transition to a market economy largely hinges on the successful transformation of industrial organizations. Advocates of shock therapy will hail 1998 as a watershed year for the reform of state enterprises—between the Fifteenth Party Congress in the fall of 1997 and Zhu Rongji's pledge in the spring of 1998 to force state enterprises into solvency within three years, it seems that China's leadership is now more committed than ever to true enterprise reform. Yet, these announcements are less than the radical departure that they seem; indeed, they have been in the making since the mid-1980s when the gradual reforms of the industrial economy began. State-owned firms have been experiencing some level of market autonomy, experimenting with and adapting to market economic practices for more than a decade now.

If the future follows trends of the recent past, the picture I have sketched in these chapters suggests a few things. First, foreign investment will continue to have an impact that extends beyond the capital that individual companies invest. Foreign companies have a positive effect on the strength of rational-legal structures at the state level, as they push their partners to observe and take seriously such institutions as the Chinese International Economic Trade and Arbitration Commission in joint-venture agreements. They also have an impact on the internal structure of Chinese organizations, as firms both mimic the practices of their foreign partners and adopt formal rational bureaucratic structures to attract new partners. Second, market constraints not only mean that individual organizations are fully responsible for their own input costs and shortfalls but also that the state has little time to guide firms through the reforms. In the future, this reality will continue for all organizations; it will be most extreme, however, for organizations at the highest levels of China's administrative hierarchy, as they are the ones that have been truly set adrift in the transition economy. Local governments and low-level administrative offices continue to control the firms under their jurisdictions in ways that highlight the strengths of a mixed-economy approach to reforms. Thus transition in China will continue to be a path-dependent process in which firms' experiences of the reforms are highly contingent on the institutional structure of state administration and a firm's position in this administrative hierarchy, but it will also be shaped by the networks of firms and the models of economic action and organizational structure to which Chinese firms are exposed. As China continues to build new organizational models and market institutions on the foundations of the institutions that preceded the reforms, the resulting markets of China's transition economy will continue to become more global but will nevertheless remain distinctly Chinese.

Appendix One _____

Methodology and Sampling

TRAINED AS A sociologist, my ideas about research on economic transitions emerged primarily from the fields of organizational and economic sociology. Before I began my field research in the PRC, I knew that I wanted to study the ways that industrial firms were reacting to and incorporating the broad institutional reforms defined by the state. As is always the case in social science research, the approach I took to gathering data would shape the research in fundamental ways.

I had a few different options for carrying out my research on the changing nature of firms in reform-era China. A large-scale survey of firms conducted with the help of the municipal bureaus would allow me to see how a large portion of industrial firms is operating in the reform period.[1] This type of data (gathered through questionnaires sent to firms by the bureaus), however, would not allow me to see firsthand how the actual firms included in the survey were structured, as on-site visits would. Any substantive and contextual discussions regarding issues in the research would be unavailable. In addition, when managers are asked by government officials to fill out questionnaires, as has been the case in past studies, one has to wonder about the quality of information in the responses.[2] On the other hand, ethnographic research allows for the deepest contextual understanding of issues and questions that arise in the field. The researcher can gain a deep and textured perspective on the social, political, and institutional structure of one or more specific research sites.[3] However, the obvious question that arises from this type of research is the extent to which the specific cases examined are generalizable. One research tack that has been a mainstay for the China field is in-depth interviewing of factory managers and factory workers.[4] This type of research has many strong points: The interviews are in-depth, so, while they do not approach the depth of ethnography, the researcher can often learn more about context and thought processes than is possible in a large-scale survey. The researcher can probe, clarify, and ask follow-up questions about a given topic, question, or response. Exploring a subject across a large number of issues allows the researcher to examine ideas of political and institutional structure in a number of different contexts. The weakness of this type of research, however, is that, while the population of firms is larger than that explored in ethnographic research, it is impossible to know to what extent, if any, this population of organizations or managers is representative of any universe of Chinese firms. Since the firms and managers in these types of surveys are typically not selected in a random probability sample, it is likely that systematic biases are built in.

For this project, I wanted to conduct a study of a random sample of organizations, so I could legitimately draw inferences to a larger universe of organizations. As one of the basic assumptions behind inferential statistics, it is necessary to work with a random sample of organizations to make such inferences. A random sample is particularly important in organizational research, but especially in a place such as China because of the selection bias involved in this type of research. It is likely that organizations (and individuals) with particular characteristics (e.g., openness to the outside, strong performance) will be more willing to talk to foreign researchers than those without these traits. Whether these include attitudes toward foreigners, openness about China's transition, or specific aspects of the organization's institutional structure, they are likely to be correlated with the dependent variables. A random sample eliminates these problems because the errors are random and therefore uncorrelated with the dependent variables.

A second requirement of my research was to gather information through in-depth interviews. I had little confidence I could trust the data that would emerge from other data-gathering methods, such as a mailed questionnaire or reports collected by the state bureaus. Neither of these approaches would afford an opportunity for clarification or discussion over issues from the managers' points of view. I would never be certain that the managers were interpreting the question the way I originally intended it. Further, these data collection methods would not allow me to explore deeply what managers thought about a given issue. This proved to be crucial to my research because it is the managers' points of view that, to a large extent, raise my confidence in the data and in the causal arguments I make based on the statistical analyses I present.[5]

A third requirement was that I conduct interviews in private, and thus informally, in contrast to those that are either arranged or chaperoned by state officials. Andrew Walder, who has had much experience conducting in-depth interviews with Chinese industrial managers, points out that managers are far more open and candid in private interviews than they are in those that are public, formal, or set up by state officials.[6] This was my experience as well. In my preliminary research, the interviews arranged by or held in the presence of state officials simply did not achieve the candor and rapport I was often able to gain in private interviews. As recently as five or six years ago in China, many barriers still existed for foreign investigators conducting research independent of state control. In China today, although foreign researchers are permitted to set up private interviews without an official entrée or intervention, it is not a simple matter.[7] However, the more I talked to people in my preliminary interviews, the greater was my wish to arrange the survey on my own and hold the interviews in private.

Finally, I wanted to conduct the interviews on-site, that is, on the factory grounds themselves. An integral part of the interviews was actually being able to see what each of the firms I studied looked like. Although a mere two hours on the grounds of a factory hardly qualifies as ethnographic research, it allowed me to compare the manager's story with what I actually saw occurring in the factory. I also found, over the course of my preliminary interviews, that managers tended to be more at ease in their own setting. Occasionally, in my preliminary research, the Shanghai Academy of Social Sciences arranged for managers to meet with me at the academy, where I found them often to be extremely formal, tense, and hurried. In contrast, when I visited the managers alone at their factories, they were more open, less guarded, and less rushed. Naturally it was easier to build rapport in these situations.

When I arrived in China, I conducted formal interviews in order to construct a questionnaire and to get a feeling for the type of research that would be possible. While I was primarily interested in the ways that firms were reacting to the broader political and institutional changes of the reforms, I still needed to place these issues in the specific context of China's economic transition. Organizational practices that are interesting and consequential in one country or institutional context may not be so in another. A good example of this was my research on the practice of diversification among Chinese firms. Having read much of the diversification literature before my research in China, I was familiar with the view that diversification was a practice that firms adopted as a reaction to market uncertainty or, in some cases, institutional uncertainty. I wanted to test these hypotheses in the context of China's economic transition. However, the type of diversification most often discussed in the literature on U.S. organizations (i.e., firms investing first in related rather than in unrelated manufacturing sectors) is of little tangible interest in China's economic transition. Most organizations that are diversified across multiple manufacturing sectors have been so since before the reform era began. Thus there is little to learn about the changing institutional, political, and market contexts of firms from the classical vision of diversification. However, another, more specific type of diversification—what I call "service-sector diversification" (see chapter 6 and Guthrie 1997)—is closely tied to the economic transition. As I learned about this practice over the course of my preliminary research, it became clear that this was one of the organizational practices I should study in order to gain a sense of the meaning of the reforms at the firm level.

As I conducted the preliminary interviews (N = 35), two crucial aspects of the research took shape. First, the content of the questionnaire and the specific topics on which I should focus in a firm-level analysis became apparent. Second, as I spoke to more and more managers, I gained confidence in my ability to talk my way into Chinese organizations, and so I began to consider the possibility of actually arranging and conducting in-depth, on-site, private interviews with managers from a random sample of firms. Contrary to popular belief (and to the opinions expressed by my host organization) it *is* possible to set up interviews with upper-level managers in Chinese organizations without an official entrée or introduction. Such interviews require a great deal of explaining (usually over the phone or, on occasion, through letters), but I found managers amenable to meeting with me once they understood the purpose of my research.

The only obstruction at this point was the lack of a sampling frame. I needed complete lists of industrial sectors in Shanghai so I could randomly sample organizations from four specific sectors. Obviously, as the heads of industrial sectors, the bureaus possess such lists. However, because I wished to conduct my research independent of state control, I could not attain these lists from the bureaus.[8] Without any access to state offices, it is difficult to find systematic information or statistics on industrial organizations in China. At some point early on in my research, however, while searching for other materials deep in the stacks of the Shanghai municipal archives, I stumbled upon a three-volume reference book entitled *The Directory of Chinese Organizations and Institutions* [*Zhongguo qishiye minglu quanshu*], a complete listing of industrial organizations in Shanghai, Tianjin, Beijing, and five other provinces. Later I found another copy of this directory through personal contacts. It was a fortuitous find, to say the least. All regions were divided into sectors, and phone numbers were included for each organization. Through this directory I was able to conduct a random probability sample (stratified by sector) of industrial organizations in four sectors of Shanghai. The resulting sample on which all the quantitative work in this study is based is of eighty-one comparable organizations spread evenly across four industrial sectors. All the on-site, unaccompanied interviews at the eighty-one units were conducted between February and July 1995. Another seventy-four interviews were conducted during the pilot (1994–95) and follow-up (1995) stages of the research; these additional interviews, conducted with government officials, legal scholars, economists, and other managers whose organizations were not a part of the random sample, took place largely in Shanghai, but some were also conducted in various other settings, including Beijing, Shenyang, Dalian, Wuhan, Chongqing, Hangzhou, Luoyang, and Hong Kong. For a complete list of the interviewees and the type of organization they represent, see Appendix 2.

The 155 in-depth interviews I conducted over three research trips resulted in more than 250 interviewing hours and approximately 400 single-spaced pages of transcription. Interviews were transcribed by hand (during the interview) and then typed into a computer file on the same day. I did not use a tape recorder.[9] The data gathered in this research are both quantitative and qualitative. The quantitative data gathered from the eighty-one organizations included in the random sample are the basis for all the quantitative assessments presented throughout these pages. However, the words of the managers in these eighty-one firms and the words of the other seventy-four informants interviewed guide my understanding and interpretations of the findings. It is through a combination of quantitative and qualitative data that I was able to gain the clearest sense of the transformation that is occurring in four industrial sectors in Shanghai. However, I conducted a sufficient number of interviews with industrial managers and state officials in several other major cities to lead me to believe that, although the quantitative results can only provide inferences about the universes of firms in four sectors in Shanghai, the results point to trends occurring throughout industrial China.

Selection of Sectors and Sampling

Selection is a critical part of any study, both theoretically and methodologically. The selection of cases for this study included selecting the sectors to be studied and the organizational units within each sector. For selecting the industrial sectors I relied heavily on the theoretical factors that define and shape industrial organizational fields. While theoretical issues were important in the selection of the organizational units (e.g., selecting organizations of fifty or more individuals, production orientation), organizational selection relied to a greater extent on methodological decisions and distinctions. Both selection processes are described below. For discussion of the selection of Shanghai as the research site, see chapter 1.

Selection of the Sectors

Ideally, an organizational study should be conducted with a sample that is representative of the organizational makeup of the society, that is, one that represents all industries proportional to the number of organizations in each sector. If one cannot gather a large enough sample that will provide an adequate number of organizations across all sectors, another possibility is to choose sectors based on criteria of theoretical interest and then sample only within those sectors. This step in the sampling process resembles what some authors have described as "theoretical sampling," a measure whereby the researcher purposively chooses cases for theoretical and comparative reasons.[10] This type of sampling method is most appropriate for comparative studies where the goal is to analyze samples of populations that differ in substantively interesting ways.

In organizational studies the most common approach is to divide up populations of organizations by industrial sectors. Dobbin et al. (1993) gathered a sample of organizations spread evenly across thirteen sectors. Given that they ended up with about three hundred organizations in their sample, this translates roughly into twenty-three organizations per sector (assuming that the response rate is constant across sectors). In my own research I use a similar sampling technique—random sample stratified by sector—although Dobbin et al.'s overall sample is larger than mine. Crucial to the confidence of the data gathered for my study was that I conduct the interviews on site and in person (mailed questionnaires or telephone surveys are not appropriate for this type of research in China); thus time constraints only allowed me to interview managers in eighty-one comparable organizations. Selection of the sectors was an important issue because the sectors would have to allow me to develop a sample of organizations both somewhat representative of firms in China (or at least Shanghai) while allowing me to make comparisons of theoretical and substantive interest.

Several distinctions can be drawn for defining different types of industrial sectors. For example, industries can be either high- or low-tech. Some scholars have pointed to the institutional specificity of high-tech industries—pertaining to issues such as patents and technology transfer—as critical in the type of legal and institutional arrangements this type of industry fosters.[11] One possible approach, then, would be to compare patterns of institutionalization in organizations in high- and low-technology industrial sectors. Is the desire to protect intellectual property rights in high-tech sectors also an impetus for a stronger institutional or rational-legal environment in organizations in those sectors? Does the pressure from foreign firms to protect patents and technology create stronger institutional environments in high-tech than in low-tech industries?

A similar distinction in analyzing industry types might be between industries for which investments and contracts are capital-intensive or capital-nonintensive. To describe this distinction fully, I employ a simplified version of Williamson's (1986) concept of asset specificity. The basis of Williamson's concept has to do with the amount of assets invested in a contractual relationship in terms of location, machinery or other physical assets, and human capital in the form of training and learned experience. The greater the amount of time and capital invested in the contractual relationship, the greater is the asset specificity of the product. Because of the capital-intensive nature of investments necessary for contractual arrangements of high-asset specificity, organizations have more to lose in these types of dealings and therefore will have more interest in pushing for predictable and stable institutional arrangements. Investment in an arrangement of high-asset specificity also implies a commitment by the investor to maintain the relationship for an extended time because of the high cost of starting over. As Williamson puts it: "The reason why asset specificity is critical is that, once the investment has been made, [the two parties] are effectively operating in a bilateral (or quasi-lateral) exchange relation for a considerable period thereafter. . . . Accordingly, where asset specificity is great, [the two parties] will make special efforts to design an exchange relation that has good continuity properties."[12] Williamson is referring here to contractual agreements between two parties, but the argument could also be

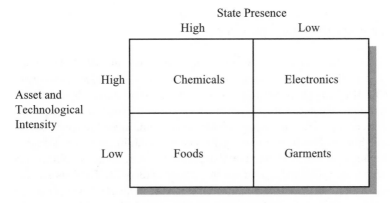

Figure A1.1: 2 × 2 Matrix of Selection Criteria for Sectors

extended to institutional environments within industries. As the case applies to investment and institutionalization in China, the contention would be that as asset specificity increases, so does the pressure for predictable and stable institutional arrangements; that is, the more capital and assets organizations have to invest in contractual relationships and projects in a given industry, the more the organizations will want to define the arrangements in a predictable and manageable fashion. Thus sectors that are more capital-intensive may be more likely to have strong institutional environments that have better "continuity properties" to temper the capricious administrative fiat of authoritarian state control.

Another parameter of interest as China makes the transition from a command to a market economy is the level of the state's presence in a given industrial sector. Once the quintessential example of a command economy, the Chinese state controlled all organizations within and across all industrial sectors. Since the beginning of the economic reforms, the extent to which the state has receded from control has varied across sectors. Therefore, in the economic transition, the level of state control in a given sector is a critical variable in the way organizations in that sector respond to the economic transition. State control in a given sector may have an impact on individual organizations' level of autonomy in that sector as well as on their institutional environment.

Selection of sectors for this study is based on a simplified matrix of these parameters that allow me to select for variation in the critical differences in the factors that structure an industry or sector. The matrix is a two-by-two table that cross-references state presence and technological/asset intensity. The levels of intensity were determined through preliminary interviews with officials in government bureaus overseeing each sector in Shanghai.[13] For comparative purposes across sectors, I selected one sector that was representative of the characteristics of each cell of the matrix. This matrix of parameters can be expanded, as shown in Figure A1.1.

Selection of the Organizational Units

Within each of the four sectors, organizations were randomly selected from the lists given in *Directory of Chinese Organizations and Institutions* [*Zhongguo Qi Shi Ye Ming Lu Quan Shu*] (1993).[14] As mentioned above, this reference book is a three-volume, 4,977-page directory of more than 160,000 organizations that are registered in Beijing, Shanghai, Tianjin, Inner Mongolia, Hebei Province, Shanxi Province, Liaoning Province, and Jilin Province. Roughly 8,800 organizations are listed in the Shanghai section. Each geographical area in the directory is divided into nineteen sectoral categories. The lists include the organization's address, telephone number(s), fax number (if available), and information on primary products and activities. With the rapid change and development occurring throughout China, it is impossible that this 1993 directory—containing information that was last updated on October 10, 1992—is a *complete* listing of organizations in the given geographical areas of China. I can say with a great deal of certainty, however, that this listing is among the most complete public directories of organizations in Shanghai. Further, as my focus was on the dynamics of the institutional practices of relatively large organizations (more than fifty employees—see Edelman 1990, 1992; Dobbin et al. 1993), we can be even more certain that this directory provides one of the most up-to-date lists of large organizations available.[15]

I treat the sectoral lists of organizations in the directory as the universes for this study. From the outset this approach may present a problem: For a study that has to do with institutional practices of organizations, drawing from a government-produced list of organizations may be a form of selection on the dependent variable. It may also be that organizations with a proclivity for certain institutional practices—for example, those that have not gone through the appropriate registration processes—may not be contained in this directory. Thus there would be a selection bias on the organizations that are relatively more institutionalized in terms of rules and procedures in Chinese society. This problem is diminished for two reasons, however. First, what interested me here is the variation as a function of the exogenous factors, as opposed to the absolute level of institutionalization. Second, the sector lists in the directory allowed me to conduct a random sample within each sector so that variation within the selected organizational sample populations was not a function of any selection bias. Thus we can assume that any errors within these selections are random. Further, the number of organizations in the Shanghai section of the directory (8,800) is very close to the total number of large- and medium-scale enterprises [*da zhong qiye*] in Shanghai (8,948), according to the *Statistical Yearbook of Shanghai* (1994).[16]

I limited the study geographically to the City of Shanghai, as opposed to Shanghai municipality (which includes the rural counties). This means that all organizations located in counties [*xian*] were eliminated from the study, and only those located in districts [*qu*] were included. This criterion was determined by the address given in the directory. Thus the study is one of organizations across four sectors in the nine districts in the city of Shanghai. In two cases in the foods sector, the selected organization was relocating from a city district to a county. These were still included, as the organizations, although in the process of relocating, still had operational factories located in their original city district. For these cases, the organizational unit was treated as one integrated organizational structure (with factories in both city district and county), much the same as other vertically integrated factories in the foods sector.[17]

Within each sector, each qualifying listed organization was assigned a number from 1 to *N*, in the order that the organizations are listed in the directory. I then used a random numbers table to select a random sample from the lists of organizations. For the cases with which I was unable to make contact or include as an organization in the sample, the next organization was selected to replace the one that was excluded. Three situations made it impossible to include a selected organization in the sample. First, if the listed phone number was incorrect and telephone information had no record of an organization under the name listed in the directory, I had no way of discovering what happened to the organization. It could be that the organization simply changed its name and phone number, yet was still located in the same place and conducting the same type of business. But short of going to every single organization for which a wrong number was listed (for electronics, N = 5; foods, N = 10; chemicals, N = 0; and garments, N = 14), there was no way I could track down these missing organizations. It is also likely that many of them had moved to other sites altogether, which was true, I was told in the contact call, for at least some of the organizations. Second, a few organizations simply refused an interview (electronics, N = 2; foods, N = 4; chemicals, N = 2; and garments, N = 1). Finally, in a few cases (electronics, N = 4; foods, N = 3; and chemicals and garments, N = 0), it turned out that the organization did not really belong in the sector given in the directory, or, if it did, it was not a comparable unit to the other industrial organizations in the sample.[18] With these occurrences, I calculate my response rate for the study to be 73 percent for the electronics sector, 58 percent for foods, 88 percent for chemicals, and 61 percent for garments. These rates are acceptable compared to other organizational studies.[19] However, the overall cooperation rate of the organizations I actually contacted, that is, those that had not changed phone numbers or moved, was 90 percent. In other words, eighty-one out of ninety organizations I contacted agreed to an interview at my first request. It was also the case that some of the organizations listed in the directory had shut down [*quxiao*]. This I was told (usually by security guards) when I contacted firms that came up in the original oversample. I do not include these firms in the response rates because, although they were listed in the directory, they did not exist in 1995.

Appendix Two _____

Interviews and Informants

THE QUANTITATIVE and qualitative data for this study were gathered through face-to-face interviews with factory directors/managers, government officials, legal scholars and experts, and a few other miscellaneous informants directly involved in the reform (see Appendix 1 for details on selection procedures).

The Managers

The core of this study is based on interviews with managers/directors of industrial organizations in Shanghai, China. To be sure, interviewing managers might lead to a somewhat one-sided view of life inside China's factories. However, because I wanted to include quantitative firm-level data in the study, it was necessary to interview the individuals who had access to that information for each firm in the data set. Thus all my interviews were with factory managers of the firms sampled in the data set, and more than half the additional (preliminary and follow-up) interviews I conducted were with managers. For the organizations included in the data set, the interviews, with few exceptions, were conducted with either the organization's general manager (director) or vice general managers. While I could not insist on exactly whom I interviewed in each organization—sometimes the general manager/director was away or unavailable—I did require that the interviewee be an upper-level manager who worked in the organization's central office.

Other Informants

While archival research revealed many of the official changes that had taken place over the course of the reforms, I needed to discuss these changes with all the players that were operative in and affected by the changes occurring in the reforms. Archival data were valuable, but of course there is no substitute for discussing the meaning of these changes with individuals who view the reforms from different perspectives and positions within the industrial economy. A government official may be able to discuss a policy as the government *intended* it to be implemented and carried out at the factory level, but a factory manager can reveal how that policy is *actually* carried out at the firm level.

Besides factory managers, I also interviewed government officials, legal scholars, and lawyers, workers, and expatriate businesspeople to get the fullest picture of the changes occurring at the organizational level in China's economic transition. The officials that oversee industry in China's economy were an invaluable source for the study that emerged for a number of reasons. Most important, through these interviews I was directed to the four industrial sectors that eventually became the substantive core of my research. Legal scholars and lawyers also proved to be essential to this study of institutional change because they were the ones who most often could discuss, with some analytical distance, the meaning of a law or institutional change. Expatriate businesspeople offered yet another perspective on the practical meaning of the institutional changes in China's economic transition. Through this collection of several different sources, I was able to piece together a multifaceted story of what is occurring at the organizational level of an important industrial center of China.

Protecting My Subjects

In this type of study the author owes a great debt to the informants who gave of their time and energy to the research. I would not have been able to complete the study I had envisioned had it not been for the interviewees who sat with me for more than 250 hours and patiently answered my questions. Clearly the anonymity of the discussions was important to many of the informants, and although I rarely could offer the informants anything in return for their time, I could promise them that their identities would be concealed.

Below I have listed the positions of all the individuals I interviewed. Each number (i.e., 1–155) indicates one interview. Certain interviews were conducted with more than one individual (sometimes from the same organization or office, sometimes from different ones). This is the case when more than one individual is listed below a number. For each informant I have provided a brief description of his or her occupation and position. An asterisk (*) following an interview number indicates those interviews that were randomly selected from the four industrial sectors and were therefore part of the organizational data set.

The Interviews and Informants

1. Manager, industrial factory, light-industry sector, Shanghai, 1994
   Manager, industrial factory, light-industry sector, Shanghai, 1994
2. Manager, industrial factory, construction and development, Shanghai, 1994
3. Expatriate manager, construction and development, Shanghai, 1994
4. Manager, business/import-export/investment company, Shanghai, 1994
5. Manager, shipping company, Shanghai, 1994
6. Manager, industrial factory, light-industry sector, Shanghai, 1994

7. Manager, business/import-export, Shanghai, 1994
   Manager, business/import-export, Shanghai, 1994
8. Manager, industrial factory, textiles sector, Shanghai, 1994
9. Manager, industrial factory, shipping and transportation, Shanghai, 1994
   Manager, industrial factory, shipping and transportation, Shanghai, 1994
10. Manager, industrial factory, textiles sector, Shanghai, 1994
11. Government official, government office (COFERT-Foreign Investment Office), Wuhan, 1994
12. Government official, government office (Provincial Bureau of Communications), Wuhan, 1994
13. Government official, government office (Light-Industry Bureau), Wuhan, 1994
    Lawyer, government office, Wuhan, 1994
14. Manager, industrial factory, construction and development, Wuhan, 1994
15. Government official, government office (COFERT), Wuhan, 1994
    Manager, industrial factory, light-industry sector, Wuhan, 1994
16. Manager, business/investment/consulting group, Wuhan, 1995
17. Government official, government office (COFERT), Shenyang, 1994
18. Government official, government office (Liaoning Provincial Planning Commission), Shenyang, 1994
    Government official, government office (Liaoning Provincial Planning Commission), Shenyang, 1994
19. Manager, industrial factory, heavy industry, Shenyang, 1994
20. Manager, industrial shipping company, Shenyang, 1994
21. Government official, government office (COFERT), Dalian, 1994
22. Manager, industrial factory, heavy industry, Dalian, 1994
23. Manager, industrial shipping company, Dalian, 1994
24. Manager, industrial factory, light-industry sector, Dalian, 1994
25. Government official, educational institution, Shanghai, 1995
26. Expatriate lawyer, foreign law firm, Hong Kong, 1995
27. Expatriate consultant, foreign consulting/investment firm/business, Hong Kong, 1995
28. Expatriate consultant, foreign consulting/investment firm/business, Hong Kong, 1995
29. Lawyer and legal scholar, educational institution, Shanghai, 1995
    Lawyer and legal scholar, educational institution, Shanghai, 1995
    Lawyer/legal scholar/government official, government office, Shanghai, 1995
    Lawyer/legal scholar, educational institution, Shanghai, 1995
30. Businessperson/investor, light industry, Shanghai, 1995
31a. Expatriate manager, business/investment/consulting, Shanghai, 1995
31b. Government official, government office (Labor Bureau), Shanghai, 1995
31c. Expatriate manager, business/investment, Shanghai, 1995
32. Professor, educational institution, Shanghai, 1995
33. Government official, government office (Labor Bureau), Shanghai, 1995
34. Manager, industry, electronics sector, Shanghai, 1995
    Professor, educational institution, Shanghai, 1995
35. Manager, business/consulting, Shanghai, 1995
36*. Manager, industry, electronics sector, Shanghai, 1995

37. Manager, industry, electronics sector, Shanghai, 1995
38*. Manager, industry, electronics sector, Shanghai, 1995
39*. Manager, industry, electronics sector, Shanghai, 1995
40. Government official, government office (Labor Bureau), Shanghai, 1995
41*. Manager, industry, electronics sector, Shanghai, 1995
Manager, industry, electronics sector, Shanghai, 1995
42. Professor, educational institution, Shanghai, 1995
43*. Manager, industry, electronics sector, Shanghai, 1995
44*. Manager, industry, electronics sector, Shanghai, 1995
45*. Manager, industry, electronics sector, Shanghai, 1995
46*. Manager, industry, electronics sector, Shanghai, 1995
47*. Manager, industry, electronics sector, Shanghai, 1995
48*. Manager, industry, electronics sector, Shanghai, 1995
Manager, industry, electronics sector, Shanghai, 1995
49*. Manager, industry, electronics sector, Shanghai, 1995
Manager, industry, electronics sector, Shanghai, 1995
50*. Manager, industry, electronics sector, Shanghai, 1995
51. Worker, business/consulting, Shanghai, 1995
52. Expatriate lawyer, foreign law firm, Shanghai, 1995
53*. Manager, industry, electronics sector, Shanghai, 1995
Manager, industry, electronics sector, Shanghai, 1995
54*. Manager, industry, electronics sector, Shanghai, 1995
Manager, industry, electronics sector, Shanghai, 1995
55*. Manager, industry, electronics sector, Shanghai, 1995
56*. Manager, industry, electronics sector, Shanghai, 1995
Manager, industry, electronics sector, Shanghai, 1995
57. Government official, government office (Labor Bureau), Shanghai, 1995
58*. Manager, industry, electronics sector, Shanghai, 1995
Manager, industry, electronics sector, Shanghai, 1995
59*. Manager, industry, electronics sector, Shanghai, 1995
60*. Manager, industry, electronics sector, Shanghai, 1995
61. Government official, government office (Electronics Bureau, currently "Electronics State-Owned Assets Management Company" [*guoyou zichan jingying gongsi*]), Shanghai, 1995
62. Government official, government office (Petro-Chemicals Bureau), Shanghai, 1995
63*. Manager, industry, electronics sector, Shanghai, 1995
Manager, industry, electronics sector, Shanghai, 1995
64*. Manager, industry, electronics sector, Shanghai, 1995
65. Government official, government office (Pharmaceuticals Management Bureau), Shanghai, 1995
66. Expatriate businessperson, consulting, Shanghai, 1995
67. Manager, industry, foods sector, Shanghai, 1995
68*. Manager, industry, foods sector, Shanghai, 1995
69*. Manager, industry, foods sector, Shanghai, 1995
70*. Manager, industry, foods sector, Shanghai, 1995
Manager, industry, foods sector, Shanghai, 1995

71*. Manager, industry, foods sector, Shanghai, 1995
72*. Manager, industry, foods sector, Shanghai, 1995
73. Government official, government office (Industrial Agriculture Commission), Shanghai, 1995
74*. Manager, industry, foods sector, Shanghai, 1995
75*. Manager, industry, foods sector, Shanghai, 1995
76*. Manager, industry, foods sector, Shanghai, 1995
77*. Manager, industry, foods sector, Shanghai, 1995
78*. Manager, industry, foods sector, Shanghai, 1995
79*. Manager, industry, foods sector, Shanghai, 1995
80. Government official, government office (municipal company in foods sector), Shanghai, 1995
81*. Manager, industry, foods sector, Shanghai, 1995
82*. Manager, industry, foods sector, Shanghai, 1995
83*. Manager, industry, foods sector, Shanghai, 1995
84*. Manager, industry, foods sector, Shanghai, 1995
85*. Manager, industry, foods sector, Shanghai, 1995
86*. Manager, industry, foods sector, Shanghai, 1995
87*. Manager, industry, foods sector, Shanghai, 1995
88*. Manager, industry, foods sector, Shanghai, 1995
89*. Manager, industry, foods sector, Shanghai, 1995
90*. Manager, industry, chemicals sector, Shanghai, 1995
Manager, industry, chemicals sector, Shanghai, 1995
91. Lawyer, government office (Chinese International Economic Arbitration Commission [*zhongguo guoji jingji zhongcai weiyuanhui*]), Beijing, 1995
Administrator, government office (Chinese International Economic Arbitration Commission [*zhongguo guoji jingji zhongcai weiyuanhui*]), Beijing, 1995
92. Worker, industry, light-industry sector, Beijing, 1995
93*. Manager, industry, chemicals sector, Shanghai, 1995
94*. Manager, industry, chemicals sector, Shanghai, 1995
95*. Manager, industry, chemicals sector, Shanghai, 1995
96*. Manager, industry, chemicals sector, Shanghai, 1995
97*. Manager, industry, chemicals sector, Shanghai, 1995
98*. Manager, industry, chemicals sector, Shanghai, 1995
99*. Manager, industry, chemicals sector, Shanghai, 1995
100*. Manager, industry, foods sector, Shanghai, 1995
101. Researcher, educational institution, Shanghai, 1995
102*. Manager, industry, chemicals sector, Shanghai, 1995
103*. Manager, industry, chemicals sector, Shanghai, 1995
104*. Manager, industry, chemicals sector, Shanghai, 1995
Manager, industry, chemicals sector, Shanghai, 1995
105*. Manager, industry, garments sector, Shanghai, 1995
106. Government official, government office (Institutional Reform Commission [*tizhigaige weiyuanhui*]), Shanghai, 1995
107*. Manager, industry, garments sector, Shanghai, 1995
108*. Manager, industry, garments sector, Shanghai, 1995

109*. Manager, industry, garments sector, Shanghai, 1995
Manager, industry, garments sector, Shanghai, 1995
Manager, industry, garments sector, Shanghai, 1995
Manager, industry, garments sector, Shanghai, 1995
110*. Manager, industry, garments sector, Shanghai, 1995
Manager, industry, garments sector, Shanghai, 1995
111*. Manager, industry, garments sector, Shanghai, 1995
112*. Manager, industry, garments sector, Shanghai, 1995
113*. Manager, industry, garments sector, Shanghai, 1995
114*. Manager, industry, garments sector, Shanghai, 1995
115*. Manager, industry, garments sector, Shanghai, 1995
116*. Manager, industry, garments sector, Shanghai, 1995
117*. Manager, industry, garments sector, Shanghai, 1995
118*. Manager, industry, garments sector, Shanghai, 1995
119*. Manager, industry, garments sector, Shanghai, 1995
120*. Manager, industry, garments sector, Shanghai, 1995
121*. Manager, industry, chemicals sector, Shanghai, 1995
122*. Manager, industry, garments sector, Shanghai, 1995
123*. Manager, industry, garments sector, Shanghai, 1995
124*. Manager, industry, garments sector, Shanghai, 1995
125*. Manager, industry, garments sector, Shanghai, 1995
126*. Manager, industry, garments sector, Shanghai, 1995
127*. Manager, industry, chemicals sector, Shanghai, 1995
128*. Manager, industry, chemicals sector, Shanghai, 1995
129*. Manager, industry, garments sector, Shanghai, 1995
130*. Manager, industry, electronics sector, Shanghai, 1995
131*. Manager, industry, electronics sector, Shanghai, 1995
Manager, industry, electronics sector, Shanghai, 1995
132*. Manager, industry, foods sector, Shanghai, 1995
133*. Manager, industry, garments sector, Shanghai, 1995
134. Taiwanese businessperson, industry/investment, construction/development,
Shanghai, 1995
135. Administrator, educational institution, Shanghai, 1995
136. Expatriate lawyer, foreign law firm, Beijing, 1995
137. Expatriate government official, foreign embassy, Beijing, 1995
138. Expatriate (Singapore) businessperson, industry, electronics sector, Beijing, 1995
139. Manager, industry, electronics sector, Beijing, 1995
140. Manager, business/accounting, Beijing, 1995
141. Manager, business/industry, electronics sector, Beijing, 1995
142. Manager, industry, electronics sector, Beijing, 1995
143. Government official, government office (Telecommunications Industrial Company [*gongye zonggongsi*]), Beijing, 1995
144. Government official, government office (Ministry of Electronics [*dianzi bu*]), Beijing, 1995
145. Businessperson, industry, electronics sector, Beijing, 1995
146. Manager, industry, electronics sector, Chongqing, 1995

147. Manager, industry, electronics sector, Chongqing, 1995
148. Manager, industry, electronics sector, Hangzhou, 1995
149. Manager, industry, electronics sector, Luoyang, 1995
150. Government official, government office (Ministry of Electronics [*dianzi bu*]), Beijing, 1995
151. Government official, government office (COFERT), Shanghai, 1995
152. Manager, business/industry, electronics sector, Shanghai, 1995
153. Government official, government office (Bureau of Electronics [*youdian ju*]), Shanghai, 1995
154. Manager, industry, electronics sector, Shanghai, 1995
155. Expatriate government official, foreign embassy, Beijing, 1995

Appendix Three _____

Complete Interview Schedule

ORGANIZATION (name): _____

RESPONDENT (name): _____

Date of interview: _____

Interview length (time): _____

Signed CPHS? (Y/N): _____

1. What *sector* is your organization officially a part of?
2. When was the organization founded (*age*)?
3. What are the *property rights* of the organization?
4. Have there been changes *in the property rights* since the founding of the organization?
5. What is the organization's *governing organization* [*zhuguan bumen*]?

(With the help of the interviewee, map out on paper the administrative structure of the organization; include details such as the administrative hierarchy leading up to the bureau, the total number of organizations the firm's governing administrative organization has jurisdiction over, etc.)

6. If the firm has control over more than one factory, is it a true *multidivisional firm*? (Assess this fact based on the following criteria: decentralized management structure; Limited Company [*youxian gongsi*] (as opposed to an administrative company); more than one factory underneath umbrella company; organized accordingly in terms of profit-pooling, internal pricing structure for business among factories underneath the parent company, overall budgetary information and allocation for the entire company; beware of companies that call themselves *multidivisional companies* [*jituan gongsi*] but have adopted the term in a nominal fashion only.)
7. How many *active employees* are in the organization?
8. How many *retired employees* are in the organization?
9. What percentage of the *employees* are *college graduates*?
10. What is the *average age* of organization's employees?
11. What is the *average salary* (yearly income—includes bonuses) of the organization's employees?
12. Please estimate the average amount spent on *medical insurance* per employee in 1994 (or the total amount spent in 1994).
13. *Factory director* (general manager) information:
    13.1. gender
    13.2. education (college/no) (Does the general manager have a college degree?)

13.3. specialized (y/n) (What was the general manager's field of specialization, i.e., engineer, chemist, economist, management, etc.?)

13.4. Internal Labor Market [ILM] (y/n) (Prompt: Was the general manager brought up through the ranks of the organization or was she or he brought in from the outside?)

14. What was the organization's *turnover* (gross sales) for *1994*?
15. What was the figure for *1990*?
16. What were the organization's *profits* for *1994*?
17. What was the figure for *1990*?
18. What is the current value of the organization's *fixed assets* (*1994* prices)?
19. What percentage of the organization's products was *exported* in *1994*?
20. What was the percentage in *1990*?
21. What percentage of the organization's *machinery/parts* was *imported*?
22. What percentage of the organization's *resources* is *imported*?
23. Is the organization *vertically integrated*? (Note: This question only applies to *jituan* and *lianhe gongsi*.)
    23.1. In terms of materials?
    23.2. Parts?
24. Does the *government allocate* any *resources* to the organization?
25. Does the organization have one *major product* (y = > 70 percent)?
26. How *many major kinds* [*da lei*] of *products* does the organization have?
27. What is the percentage of *production* for each major product kind [*da lei*]?
28. Does the organization have a *service-sector investment* [*disan chanye touzi*]?
    28.1. What percentage of the organization's turnover is derived from this investment? (Note: Some organizations claim to have these investments but they are not real investments; clarify the kind of investment—i.e., the service and sector of the economy—and then discuss the amount of start-up capital invested and the amount of turnover derived from the investment.)
29. Does the organization *rent factory space* to other organizations?
30. Does the organization have a *joint venture* [*hezi qiye*] or cooperative relationship [*hezuo*] with a foreign firm [if more than one, discuss earliest]?
    30.1. JV or coop. venture?
    30.2. Which country?
    30.3. When was it established?
    30.4. What is the (estimated) value of the contract?
    30.5. What provisions are made in the contract for disputes?
    30.6. Where will a dispute go to be resolved?
    30.7. Is there an arbitration clause specified in the contract? (If yes, where: CIE-TAC or out of the country?)
31. Does the organization generally sign *contracts* with *Chinese organizations*? (If yes, where does dispute resolution take place?)
32. Does the organization follow [*anzhao*] the *Company Law* [*gongsi fa*] or the *Enterprise Law* [*qiye fa*]?
    32.1. Is the factory officially a company or an enterprise? (If yes, when did the factory become a company?)
33. Does the *government control price setting* for *any* products of the organization?
34. (If no government control:) How does the organization go about *setting prices*?

35. Does the organization *negotiate prices* with customers?

36. Does the organization offer the following *benefits* to your employees:

    36.1. Housing? What percentage of employees is offered this benefit?

    36.2. Medical insurance? What percentage of employees is offered this benefit?

    36.3. Clinic?

    36.4. Cafeteria?

    36.5. Nursery?

    36.6. Kindergarten?

    36.7. Retail shop?

    36.8. Commuter bus?

    36.9. Library?

37. What is the organization's *new-workers'-search procedure*? (Prompt: How does the organization go about finding new employees? Does the organization rely on the government to distribute labor, or are there separate ways for the organization to find labor itself?)

    37.1. If the organization is hiring independent of the Labor Bureau, is there a formalized process for hiring? (Prompt: About when was this practice institutionalized?)

38. In your organization today, is it possible for workers who would like to work here to use *introductions* or *guanxi* to get a job in the organization?

39. Does the organization have formal, written *organizational rules*?

    39.1. If yes, when were these written organizational rules first adopted by the organization.

40. Does the organization have formal, written *job descriptions*? ((Prompt: About when were these institutionalized?)

41. Does the organization offer *job training* for the new employees? (Prompt: About when was this practice institutionalized?)

42. Does the organization have a formal *pay scale*?

    42.1. If yes, who sets the pay scale for the organization (governing organization or independently set by the organization)? (Prompt: When did the organization start operating autonomously with respect to this practice?)

43. Who controls the setting of salary *raises* (governing organization or independently set by the organization)?

44. How does the organization decide *promotions*? (What are the main criteria?)

    44.1. Does the organization have a promotion test? (Prompt: About when was this practice institutionalized?)

45. Does the organization have formal *grievance-filing procedures*? (Prompt: About when was this practice institutionalized?)

    45.1. What are the institutions in the firm that support grievance-filing procedures?

46. Does the organization have a *Workers' Representative Committee* [*zhigong daibiao dahui*]?

    46.1. How many general meetings does the committee have per year? (Prompt: About when was this practice institutionalized?)

47. Does the organization have a *mediation committee* [*tiaojie jigou*] (in the factory)? (Prompt: About when was this institutionalized?)

48. Has anyone from the organization ever applied to the *Labor Arbitration Commission* [*laodong zhongcai weiyuanhui*]?

49. Does the organization have a *labor union*? Is the labor union still significant today?
    49.1. What are the main responsibilities of the labor union today?
    49.2. Are these very different from the main responsibilities of the labor union before the economic reform began?
50. What percentage of the organization's employees is on *labor contracts [laodong hetong]*?
    50.1. If 100 percent, what year was this practice (of 100 percent of workers signing labor contracts) institutionalized?
    50.2. Can workers in your organization be fired [at the end of the contract or in cases of extreme transgression]?
51. What are the *taxes* that the organization paid in 1994?
    51.1. To what government organization does the firm pay taxes?
52. For this organization, is *guanxi* an important part of its activities in the *market economy*?
    52.1. For doing *business* in general?
    52.2. For carrying out government *procedures*?
53. Does the organization have its own *patents*?
54. Does the organization have its own *trademarks*?
55. Does the organization have a *time clock*?
56. Is the organization a "*civilized organization*" [*wenming danwei*]?
57. Is the organization a "*good contract record organization*" [*zhong hetong shou xinyong danwei*]?
58. Does the organization have a *personnel office*?
59. Is the organization *de-linked* [*tuogou*] from governing organization?

Rotating Subject I: *Guanxi*-Attitudinal

1. How important do you think *guanxi* is in markets in China? Do you think it is becoming less important? If so, why? What is taking its place?
2. If you wanted to get a business project approved, would you rely on law and procedures or would you rely on *guanxi*? Is this changing?
3. Why do you think *guanxi* is/has been important in Chinese society? Is it a Chinese (cultural) characteristic or is it the result of the government system that makes people think they cannot count on or trust anything in the system except for people they know?
4. Is *guanxi* like money? If you have a lot of *guanxi*, do you have a lot of power? If you have *guanxi*, can it effect resource exchanges?
5. Does *guanxi* affect people's lives and influence the way they act in other, more subtle ways?
6. What is capitalism; what are its most important characteristics?
7. In a capitalist system, do you think there should be a market for everything, or do you think some things should be left out of market processes? Examples?
8. What is socialism? What are the most important characteristics of socialism?
9. Do you think that some aspects of socialism will always exist beside capitalism, or do you think that eventually socialism will wither away and only capitalism will remain?

10. What do you think the role of law is in China right now? Do you think people are paying more and more attention to laws?

Rotating Subject II: Markets as Politics

1. What are the institutions/laws that organize the market in general; in this sector specifically?
2. How are property rights changing for your organization?
3. What are the rules that govern/influence action in this sector? Does anyone other than the state make these rules?
4. State-market linkage: Can you describe some ways in which the state controls the market?
5. Is the market well supported by physical infrastructure (i.e., roads, utilities, contracts, laws, etc.)? Which of these are the least developed? Which are the most?
6. Has the price-setting method changed over the past few years? How?
7. Institutions: When you are changing methods of production and practice, do companies in this sector pay close attention to the practices of the larger companies? If so, who? Examples?
8. Informal institutions? Practices?
9. Local culture?
10. What is the most important element in creating a market (e.g., creating stable worlds)?
11. Do the larger firms in this sector have more power to create practices and conceptions of control?
12. When you are looking for practices and market strategies, on whom do you focus in the market? On the state? On other large firms? Which ones?
13. How do new institutions emerge? How are they built?
(Note: Does the Fligstein "model for action" apply to this emerging market? . . . Contested nature of the rules of the market? Concrete examples? . . . How are social relations among suppliers, producers, and the state structured? Examples?)

For Garments

1. How has the international quota system [*peie*] affected your organization?

Appendix Four _____

Sample Characteristics and Variables

Production

Table A4.1 shows the main products of each of the firms included in the data set. The table also indicates the concentration of the firm's production in a single product. If the firm concentrated equal to or greater than 70 percent of its manufacturing in one product, the situation is indicated by a "yes" in that column. The information in Table A4.1 gives us a sense of the types of firms included in the sample and the types of products they manufacture, as well as the production strategies in which firms are engaged.[1]

Models and Variables

For each economic strategy, the specific models and the variables included in the analyses vary in subtle ways. However, the general models are the same for virtually all equations. Briefly I view the adoption of economic strategies by organizations as:

$$\Phi_{ij} = 1/(1 - p_{ij}) = f(\text{SECTOR}_j, \text{ORG}_i, \text{GOV}_i),$$

where Φ_{ij} is the log-of-the-odds that the ith firm will adopt a given organizational strategy, and p_{ij} is the probability of this dichotomous outcome. This outcome is a function of the industrial sector (SECTOR_j) in which the organization is located, a vector of organizational characteristics (ORG_i), and a vector of the governance environment (GOV_i) in which the organization is situated. From this general model, where appropriate, I estimate specific logistic regression models for the firm-level observations that show the log-odds probability that the ith organization will adopt a given strategy and the exogenous factors that are associated with that probability.[2] From these models, where appropriate, probabilities and odds are calculated, respectively, as:

$$p = [1/(1 + e^{-z})],$$

$$o = (\exp[\beta]),$$

where $z = \beta_0 + \beta_1 x_1 + \ldots + \beta_n x_n$, and β represents the effects of the variables in the model.

Basic definitions of the variables used throughout the analyses can be found in Table A4.2. Some variables, however, may require extended discussion here. Dummy variables capturing sector effects are defined according to an organization's location in a given sector, garments, electronics, foods, and chemicals. Organizational size is measured as the natural log of the number of active workers employed by the organizations; the term is logged because I expect that the effect of size increases at a diminishing rate. A composite measure of overall organizational health is calculated based on turnover, salary of the workers, and the constant rate that organizations are supposed to pay into the new official pension fund for retired workers (25.5 percent of the overall salary budget). To control for variation in input costs, and so on, the variable is standardized for the average of the organization's sector.[3] If an organization is doing well in terms of sales in relation to its labor burden, relative to the other organizations in its sector, the value of this variable will be positive; if an organization's health is average for its sector, the value will be close to zero; and if it is doing poorly relative to the other organizations in its sector, the value will be negative. The employee ratio of the organization is another measure of the burden that organizations face; the measure is the proportion of active employees for the total number of employees the organization has to support (active + retired). A low value indicates that an organization has to pay a significant amount of wages to nonproductive (retired) employees, and a high value indicates that the organization's burden, with respect to retired workers, is relatively small.[4] Like organizational health, I expect this variable to be negatively associated with the adoption of stability strategies such as diversification, as larger values indicate a more stable situation for that firm in over the last five to ten years. The economic strength of an organization must certainly have an impact on organizational strategies, and I have included several variables to capture this effect. Profit margins are calculated as profits relative to revenues; this term is then averaged from 1990 to 1994 to avoid problems of endogeneity. Loss terms were included in some equations as dummy variables. I use the 1990 variables, which indicate whether an organization lost money in 1990, again to avoid problems of endogeneity. Governing patterns and structures of organizations are critical for the economic decisions firms make. It may be that variation in organizational practices across sectors is a function of the different governing patterns and the various conceptions of control enacted at different levels of the administrative hierarchy. I observe the effects of the government administrative hierarchy in two ways. First, I observe the effects of a firm's location at different administrative levels by including them as dummy variables and comparing them to the other categories that are left out of the equation. The governance terms are included in the equations as dummy variables for governance by municipal bureau and municipal company; these are compared to district company governance. Second, I look at the effect of jurisdiction size by including a variable based on the number of firms a given firm's governing organization oversees. This variable is logged, as the effect is likely to increase at a diminishing rate.

Means, standard deviations, and brief definitions for several of the characteristics and variables of the organizations included in the sample are presented in Table A4.2.

TABLE A4.1

Main Products and Product Concentration for Firms in Samples from Four Industrial Sectors, Shanghai, 1995

Sector	Products	P ≥ 70%	Sector	Products	P ≥ 70 %
Electronics	electronic transformers, conductors	no	Foods	candy	yes
			Foods	edible oils (peanut, vegetable)	yes
Electronics	television bulbs	no	Foods	cakes (moon cakes)	yes
Electronics	electronic display lights, display boards	yes	Foods	candy, cookies	no
			Chemicals	intermediates of pesticides, plastics, pharmaceutical bases	no
Electronics	recorder/radio parts	yes			
Electronics	electrical equipment	yes	Chemicals	lithium bromide refrigerant	no
Electronics	telephones, telephone parts	yes	Chemicals	many chemical products	no
Electronics	many electrical products	no	Chemicals	agricultural pesticides	no
Electronics	semiconductor parts	yes	Chemicals	agricultural chemicals	no
Electronics	electronic components	yes	Chemicals	products used daily (soaps, etc.)	yes
Electronics	radios	no	Chemicals	coatings (polymers)	yes
Electronics	radios, radio parts	no	Chemicals	PVCs	no
Electronics	amplifiers	no	Chemicals	products used daily (soaps, etc.)	yes
Electronics	radios	no	Chemicals	paint, coatings	yes
Electronics	television tuners	yes	Chemicals	pesticides	no
Electronics	computers	yes	Chemicals	chlorine, alkali	no
Electronics	television tubes	no	Chemicals	plastics	no
Electronics	electronic components	no	Chemicals	chemicals used daily	no
Electronics	radio parts	no	Chemicals	industrial chemicals, pesticides	no
Electronics	radios, radio parts	no	Garments	dress shirts (men's)	yes
Electronics	electronic components	no	Garments	coats, parkas	no
Electronics	radios	no	Garments	sheets, covers, pillows	no
Electronics	televisions, television bulbs	yes	Garments	cloth shoes, slippers	no
Electronics	audio and video recorders	yes	Garments	robes, towels	yes
Foods	cakes	no	Garments	cloth shoes	no
Foods	breads, bakery items	yes	Garments	hats	yes
Foods	cakes	no	Garments	shirts	no
Foods	rice products	no	Garments	shirts	yes
Foods	meat products (pork)	yes	Garments	bed products (sheets, blankets)	yes
Foods	breads, bakery items	no	Garments	children's clothes	yes
Foods	meat products	no	Garments	handkerchiefs	yes
Foods	juice, canned fruit	no	Garments	bed products (sheets, blankets)	no
Foods	meat products (duck)	yes	Garments	silk shirts	no
Foods	starch	yes	Garments	robes, towels	yes
Foods	oil products (sesame)	no	Garments	children's clothes	yes
Foods	dried meats	no	Garments	dress shirts	yes
Foods	cookies, cakes	yes	Garments	sport shirts (casual wear)	no
Foods	cake products	yes	Garments	dresses (women's clothes)	no
Foods	starch (corn, beans)	yes	Garments	dress shirts (men's)	yes
Foods	cakes, candy (Japanese-style)	yes	Garments	blouses, women's jackets	yes
Foods	tofu and other soy products	yes	Garments	shirts, T-shirts	yes

Note: Each entry is an individual organization, so it is possible that two different organizations may have the same products. P = product concentration.

TABLE A4.2

Characteristics and Variables for Organizations from Four Industrial Sectors, Shanghai, 1995

	Mean	S.D.	Definition
Dependent variables			
Formal organizational rules	.642	.482	1 = organization has formal (written) organizational rules; 0 = no formal organizational rules
Formal job descriptions	.568	.499	1 = organization has formal (written) job descriptions; 0 = no formal job descriptions
Formal grievance filing procedures	.642	.482	1 = organization has formal grievance filing Procedures; 0 = no formal grievance procedures
Mediation institution in firm	.556	.500	1 = organization has an internal mediation institution; 0 = no mediation institution
Institutionalized WRC meetings	.852	.358	1 = organization has institutionalized Workers' Representative Committee meetings in a formal way; 0 = meetings have not been institutionalized
Promotion test	.284	.454	1 = organization uses promotion tests for worker advancement; 0 = no promotion tests
Pay scale	.642	.482	1 = organization has a formal pay scale; 0 = no formal pay scale
Formal hiring procedure	.269	.503	1 = organization has formal hiring procedures; 0 = no formal hiring procedures
Use connections to hire	.469	.502	1 = organization considers connections when making a hiring decision; 0 = formal rules against using connections in hiring decisions
Workers applied to outside arbitration	.263	.443	1 = workers in the firm have applied to the district Labor Arbitration Commission; 0 = no workers applied to outside arbitration
Overall institutionalization	3.630	1.907	Sum across all dummy variable categories for formal firm structure; the range of this variable is 0–7
Average salary	8996.914	2877.991	Average annual salary (inclusive of bonuses) in RMB; RMB-U.S.$ exchange is 8:1
Housing	.531	.502	1 = organization currently offers housing as a benefit for workers; 0 = housing is not offered as a benefit
Medical insurance	.975	.157	1 = organization offers medical insurance as a benefit for workers; 0 = medical insurance is not offered as a benefit
Family coverage[a]	1.148	.050	2 = organization offers full family coverage; 1 = partial coverage for family members; 0 = no coverage for family members
Medical clinic	.346	.479	1 = organization has a medical clinic on site as a benefit for workers; 0 = no medical clinic
Cafeteria	.815	.391	1 = organization has a cafeteria on site as a benefit for workers; 0 = no cafeteria
Child care	.173	.380	1 = organization offers child care as a benefit for workers; 0 = no child care
Kindergarten	.136	.345	1 = organization has a kindergarten as a benefit for workers; 0 = no kindergarten

TABLE A4.2 *cont.*

	Mean	*S.D.*	*Definition*
Retail shop	.469	.502	1 = organization has a retail shop as a benefit for workers; 0 = no retail shop
Commuter bus	.198	.401	1 = organization offers commuter bus service as a benefit for workers; 0 = no commuter bus service
Library	.210	.410	1 = organization has a library as a benefit for workers; 0 = no library
Total benefits	5.000	2.716	Sum across all of the benefit categories for the organization, where each category is assigned the value of the variable; the range of this variable is 0–11
100% of workers on labor contracts	.679	.470	1 = 100 percent of workers on labor contracts; 0 = <100 percent on labor contracts
Year 100% labor contracts	1992.421	1.253	The year 100 percent of workers were put on labor contracts; average taken only of firms that have already institutionalized labor contracts
% of workers on lab. contracts	77.645	35.462	Percentage of workers on labor contracts
Workers can be fired	.926	.264	1 = manager affirms that workers can be fired; 0 = workers cannot be fired despite contractual arrangement
Price setting[a]	.469	.502	2 = independent price setting w/formula; 1 = independent pricing, no formula ("market control"); 0 = government control of pricing
Price negotiation	.691	.465	1 = firm negotiates prices w/ customers; 0 = no negotiation
Company Law	.420	.497	1 = submitted application to become a company and adopted the Company Law; 0 = no adoption of the Company Law
Diversification	.395	.492	1 = investment in the service-sector economy; 0 = no investment
Specified arbitration clause	.521	.505	1 = specified arbitration clause in joint-venture contract with foreign partner; restricted sample: only firms with joint ventures (N = 48)
Guanxi in procedural matters	.279	.451	1 = General manager affirms that connections are important for accomplishing procedural matters; 0 = manager views connections as unimportant
Guanxi in markets	.487	.503	1 = General manager affirms that connections are important in business relations; 0 = manager views connections as unimportant
Organizational Variables			
Chemicals	.185	.391	Proportion of firms in sample located in chemicals sector.
Electronics	.284	.454	Proportion of firms in sample located in electronics sector.

Continues on next page

	Mean	S.D.	Definition
Foods	.259	.441	Proportion of firms in sample located in foods sector.
Garments	.272	.448	Proportion of firms in sample located in garments sector
Organizational size	1580.840	3724.745	Number of active (not retired) employees, year end, 1994
Organizational size (ln)	6.058	1.475	Natural log of active employees
Employee ratio	.754	.176	(active employees) / (active + retired employees)
Org. health (in millions)[b]	120.000	443.000	Revenues less labor cost less money paid into national pension fund; variable is then standardized to average value for sector, to control for sectoral variation in input costs (see text for discussion of this variable)
Profits (in millions)	22.000	120.000	Profits for year end, 1990, RMB
Profits (in millions)	20.554	113.078	Profits for year end, 1994, RMB
Profit margin, 1994	.070	.085	Profits divided by revenues
Profit margin, avg. 1990–1994	.073	.097	Average profit margin for 1990 and 1994
Losses, 1990	.235	.426	1 = firm lost money in 1990; 0 = no losses
Losses, 1994	.259	.441	1 = firm lost money in 1994; 0 = no losses
Loss trend	.457	.501	1 = firm with declining profits, i.e., [P (1994–1990)] < 0
% products exported, 1990	25.272	35.438	Percentage of products exported in 1990
% products exported, 1994	25.815	35.845	Percentage of products exported in 1994
Turnover (in millions)	201.927	542.653	Revenues, year end, 1994, RMB
Turnover (ln)	17.080	2.222	Natural log function of turnover
Fixed assets (in millions)	147.919	498.331	Fixed assets; estimated at 1994 values
Joint venture	.593	.494	1 = firm has a joint venture with a foreign firm; 0 = no joint venture
State-owned[c]	.580	.497	State-owned factory [*guoyou*]
Collectively owned	.333	.474	Collectively owned factory [*jiti*]
Other ownership	.086	.283	Privately owned [*sanzi qiye*]
Governance Variables			
General manager's education (college)	.790	.410	1 = has college degree; 0 = no college degree
General manager w/bus./econ. backgrnd.	.444	.500	1 = has background in business or economics; 0 = no background in business or economics
General manager through internal labor markets (ILM)	.568	.498	1 = rose through ILMs; 0 = brought in from outside
General manager's gender	.156	.345	1 = female; 0 = male
Municipal bureau	.296	.459	1 = firm under jurisdiction of municipal bureau; 0 = other
Municipal company	.296	.459	1 = firm under jurisdiction of municipal company; 0 = other

TABLE A4.2 *cont.*

	Mean	S.D.	Definition
District company	.321	.470	1 = firm under jurisdiction of municipal company; 0 = other
Jurisdiction size	46.963	72.257	Number of organizations competing for resources in the ith organization's government jurisdiction
Jurisdiction size (ln)	2.789	1.559	Natural log function of jurisdiction size

Note: See text for discussion of the variables and data collection.

[a] Recoded into dichotomous variables for binary logistic models.

[b] See text for discussion of this variable.

[c] Five of the state-owned factories are public shares companies [*gufen youxian gongsi*].

Notes _____

Chapter One
Firm Practices in China's Transforming Economy:
Efficiency or Mimicry?

1. For discussion of Deng Xiaoping's reforms, see, for example, Naughton (1993, 1995), Whyte (1993), and Lieberthal (1995). For discussion of the gradual nature of China's reforms, see, for example, Rawski (1995), Walder (1994b), and Naughton (1995).

2. For discussion, see especially Walder (1996, 1061).

3. Based on weak returns to education in urban areas, Xie and Hannum (1996, 984) conclude that "labor markets are virtually absent" in the Chinese economy. Many studies have drawn conclusions about cadre advantage based on income data (e.g., Nee 1989a, 1991, 1996; Róna-Tas 1994; Bian and Logan 1996; Parish and Michelson 1996). Strangely, in this body of research, despite cadres most often enjoying advantages through nonwage benefits and other perquisites hidden from income data, few studies have diverged from the focus on income as the primary indicator of returns to political capital; Walder (1995b) is an exception.

4. Based on slow rates of growth in productivity in the upper levels of China's administrative hierarchy, Walder (1995a, 270) has argued that reforms have been "relatively muted" in this economic sector. See Guthrie (1997) for further discussion.

5. For further discussion of the lack of convergence among modern capitalist economies, see Fligstein and Freeland (1995) and Whitley (1990, 1992a).

6. For the resolution converting Revolutionary Committees to People's Governments, see PRC (1979b); for Joint Venture Law, see PRC (1979a); for the resolution creating Special Economic Zones in Guangdong and Fujian, see PRC (1981b).

7. See North (1990, 3).

8. See especially Walder (1986a). See also Whyte and Parish (1984).

9. See Fligstein (1996b, 660). Fligstein uses the language of "state-building" to emphasize the ways that states and markets are inextricably intertwined. States may be regulatory or interventionist, thus varying in the *ways* they control markets, but through "property rights, governance structures, and rules of exchange . . . states are important to the formation and ongoing stability of markets" (Fligstein 1996b, 660). In other words, states shape the dynamics and structure of the markets that emerge under their guidance. I begin with a similar set of assumptions in this study.

10. See, for example, Naughton (1995), Lieberthal (1995), Field (1984, 1992), Yeh (1992), and C. Wong (1991, 1992).

11. For discussion of the relationship between institutions and performance, see North (1990). For discussions that focus on productivity, see Walder (1995a), Chen et al. (1988), and Woo et al. (1993). For discussion of the relationship between economic transition, institutions, and individual income, see Nee (1989a, 1991, 1996), Róna-Tas (1994), Domanski and Heyns (1995), Bian and Logan (1996), and Xie and Hannum (1996).

12. For discussion of firm practices and institutional environments as defined by the state, see Edelman (1990, 1992), Dobbin et al. (1993), Sutton et al. (1994), Fligstein (1996b), and Walder (1992a). For discussion of organizational practices related to survival and stability, see Fligstein (1991, 1996b), Stark (1996), and Guthrie (1997, 1998b). For discussion of the normative aspects of institutional environments, see Meyer and Rowan (1977) and DiMaggio and Powell (1983).

13. For examples of rationalist and efficiency theories of organizations, see Taylor (1923), Simon (1957), March and Simon (1958), Doeringer and Piore (1971), Williamson (1975, 1986). For further discussion of rationalist approaches to organizations, see Scott (1987).

14. For theoretical statements of "new institutional theory" in organizational analysis, see Meyer and Rowan (1977) and DiMaggio and Powell (1983); see also Powell and DiMaggio (1991). For other examples of "neoinstitutional" analysis, see Edelman (1990, 1992), Dobbin et al. (1993), Sutton et al. (1994), and Sutton and Dobbin (1996). For a politically grounded approach that focuses on economic strategies (as opposed to intra-organizational structures), see Fligstein (1990).

15. Sutton et al. (1994, 947–48); emphasis added.

16. Sachs and Woo (1997, 5).

17. Nee (1996, 945).

18. See Walder (1995a). For further discussion, see Guthrie (1997, 1268; 1998b). I will return to this issue in chapter 6.

19. Bian (1994b, 972).

20. See Yang (1994) and Bian (1994b, 1997); see also Bian and Ang (1997), Yan (1996), and Kipnis (1997).

21. See, for example, Xin and Pearce (1996), Wank (1996), Yeung and Tung (1996), Pye (1995), Hui and Graen (1997), and Tsui and Fahr (1997).

22. Walder (1996, 1068).

23. There are notable examples of studies that focus on organizations in the urban industrial economy. Studies by Schurmann (1968), Whyte and Parish (1984), and Walder (1986a) have become seminal examples of research on the organizational and institutional structure of China's prereform industrial economy. Lin and Bian (1991) and Bian (1994a) have explicitly linked the organizations in the urban industrial economy to processes of status attainment and social mobility. Groves et al. (1994, 1995) have used panel data to systematically study economic issues such as managerial labor markets and organizational autonomy in economic decision making for large organizations in the urban industrial economy (72 percent of their sample of eight hundred firms are in the urban industrial sector). Walder (1992a) used 1986 individual-level data in a study of urban industrial units focusing on structures and practices of the prereform period; Walder's (1995a) later work looks more directly at organizational structure in the economic transition. Other studies that have been important in advancing our understanding of Chinese organizations are Rawski (1994), Jefferson and Xu (1991), Reynolds (1987), and Lu and Perry (1997). In addition, some historians have traced the roots of the organizational and institutional structure of Chinese society to periods predating the PRC. Yeh's (1994, 1995) work shows that organizational and institutional forms that very much resembled the work unit under the CCP can, at the very least, be dated back to the 1930s. Similarly, Kirby's (1995) work on the Chinese Company Law and corporate organization relates contemporary organizational and legal structures on the

mainland and in Taiwan to their predecessors, dating back as far as 1904. As with the contemporary accounts, it is an underlying argument in both these historical works that an understanding of the organizational structures in historical Chinese society is essential to understanding social processes and social life.

24. For an example of research that draws inferences about market changes from shifting patterns of stratification, see Nee (1989a, 1991, 1996). For an example of research that draws conclusions from gains in productivity, see Walder (1995a).

25. See, for example, Nee (1996) and Walder (1995a).

26. While it used to be the case that the municipalities were significantly different from all other cities in terms of administrative power, this distinction is shrinking in the economic transition. For instance, the four official municipalities—Beijing, Shanghai, Tianjin, Chongqing (Chongqing is a recent addition to this administrative category)—all have the same autonomous approval rights as provinces, with the ability to independently approve investment projects of up to U.S.$30 million. In recent years, Wuhan, Shenyang, Guangdong, Hangzhou, Dalian, and others cities have also been given this level of autonomous approval.

27. An asterisk (*) next to the interview number indicates interviews conducted in those organizations that were randomly selected from the four industrial sectors in Shanghai. See Appendix 1 for discussion of selection procedures and Appendix 2 for a complete list of interviews.

28. For discussion, see Zucker (1991, postscript).

29. The interviews lasted an average of one hour and forty-five minutes. I visited each of the eighty-one factories included in the sample, and, in addition to going over quantitative information about the organization with the general manager, I discussed a number of issues and views with the interviewees about the economic transition more generally. See the appendixes for discussion of the methodology and interviews.

30. Owing to the random sampling procedures followed, I can, with confidence, infer my findings to the four sectors of organizations in Shanghai from which these samples were drawn. In addition, because I personally conducted the interviews and because they were unaccompanied (i.e., state officials were *not* present), I have high confidence in the quality of the data on which this study is based. I discuss these issues at greater length in the appendixes.

31. The reality of interviews in Chinese organizations is that there is no simple answer to any question. The most striking example was the seemingly straightforward profit question: During my pilot study I was alerted to the fact that factories commonly underreport (hide) profits to avoid paying a hefty income tax (33 percent). On more than one occasion the manager would tell me one profit figure, and then, when I explained that I knew how some organizations "hide" profits and asked if his or her organization had done so, in a number of cases the manager then told me the "true" profit figure. Almost without exception, there were clarification discussions surrounding *every* question in the survey.

32. In some cases, to find the best fitting model I relied on two criteria: McFadden's pseudo R^2 and the Bayesian Information Criterion (BIC). McFadden's pseudo R^2 is calculated as $1 - \ln L(B)/\ln L(a)$, where $\ln L(B)$ is the log-likelihood of the model and $\ln L(a)$ is the log-likelihood of an intercept model (Fischer et al. 1996). BIC is calculated as $D - (d.f.)\ln(N)$, where D is the residual deviance $(-2LL)$, d.f. is the model's degrees of freedom, and N is the number of cases (Brooks and Manza 1997). Generally, how-

ever, I simply present the full models—as opposed to the most parsimonious model—so that readers can observe which variables are significant and which are not.

33. Although I collected 1990 and 1994 fiscal data for each organization, in ten cases only 1994 data were available. The 1990 data are preferable to the 1994 data because of endogeneity issues: Since many of the practices I am examining were adopted in the 1990s, it is problematic to use 1994 data. However, for the ten cases with missing data I use the 1994 data. This approach is acceptable, as all the 1990 and 1994 fiscal variable pairs (profits, losses, turnover) are correlated at .85 or above, which implies that organizations' situations in 1990 were solid predictors of their economic situations in 1994. Thus, for these ten cases, using the 1994 data is not only an acceptable approach, but it also allows me to use the 1990 data (without losing ten cases), which is favorable, for theoretical reasons, to using the 1994 data.

34. In some cases the new organization is set up on the factory grounds of the Chinese partner. Even in these cases, however, the new organization is a separate legal entity.

35. The title "general manager" [jingli] is actually a term of the reform era. In pre-reform China, the term was not "manager" but "factory director" [changzhang]. Although, in my sample, some managers of less progressive factories still referred to themselves as directors, I use the term "general manager" to denote the person in the highest position in the organization.

36. For discussion, see Fligstein and Freeland (1995).

37. Fligstein (1996b, 657).

38. Ibid, 659.

39. Evans (1995, 10).

Chapter Two
Path Dependence in China's Economic Transition

1. See Stark (1992) and Walder (1995a). It should be noted here that although my use of the term "path dependence" fits with the way Stark and Walder use it, this notion differs considerably from the ways the term is used in the study of technology (see, e.g., Ruttan 1997) or in a number of studies of economic behavior (see, e.g., Balmann et al. 1996; Anderlini and Ianni 1996; Mueller 1997). The usage emphasizes the state's institutional structure and the variety of institutional forms that preceded China's reforms. Research in the field of comparative capitalisms also confirms the path-dependent perspective, arguing that although many countries are making transitions to market economic systems, there is no convergence among capitalist forms in the world economy. See Fligstein and Freeland (1995), Hamilton and Biggart (1988), Gerlach (1992), Whitley (1990, 1992a, 1992b), and Brinton, Lee, and Parish (1995).

2. Research that stresses path dependence often shares much in common with the "experimentalist" or "gradualist" approach to understanding China's economic transition; see, for example, Naughton (1994, 1995) and Rawski (1995). The central notion here is that politics, culture, and the institutional history of China's command economy have all played a hand in the course of China's reforms. These views stand in opposition to the "convergence" view (e.g., Sachs and Woo 1997), which focuses on universal notions of market institutions and regards politics and history as unimportant in market transitions.

3. It is on this point that Nee and Cao (1997) are correct in arguing that Market Transition Theory is not at odds with theories of path dependence. The theory is fundamentally about the ways that actors' positions in the state hierarchy will influence their opportunities in the reform era. The theory runs into trouble, however, when it makes assumptions about rational profit-maximizing actors in transforming societies and when it attempts to make claims about a generalizable pattern in the changing mechanisms of stratification across transforming societies.

4. As I noted in chapter 1, several important studies have examined the official policies that have defined China's reforms; see, for example, Naughton (1995), Lieberthal (1995), C. Wong (1991, 1992), and Field (1984, 1992). While many of the issues I cover in the following sections are tied to the official policies discussed in these studies, I focus on the issues as they are viewed by Chinese managers and local officials, rather than on the official changes as they are depicted in policy realms.

5. For example, although several scholars have sought to link their work to North's institutionalism and institutional theories in general, more than one reviewer has pointed out the failure to operationalize these variables in empirical analyses; see, for example, Fligstein (1996a) on Nee (1996), Cabestan (1995) on Lyons and Nee (1994), and Oberschall (1996) on Nee (1996) and Xie and Hannum (1996). Often when scholars factor in institutional change they focus on broad central tendencies rather than on what the institutional changes actually mean in practice. Criticizing the work of both Nee (1996) and Xie and Hannum (1996) for the broad inferences they make based on limited data, Oberschall (1996, 1039) points out the following:

> Institutional analysis . . . does not assume that "interests" are well-defined and obvious [as Nee clearly does]; on the contrary, ideologies, information costs, and cognitive processes bear close study. It treats collective action as problematic and expects a lot of institutional and social change to result from unintended unplanned actions. . . . *[A]ll of the action in the new institutional analysis takes place at the microlevel to derive and account for the meso- and macrolevel, including variance of norms and institutions, not just types and central tendencies.* . . . Merely borrowing some phrases . . . and incorporating them ad hoc in the usual social change discourse is not making use of institutional theory. (Emphasis added)

My study builds on the sentiments of this critique, as it is about the microlevel effects of specific state-level institutional changes; mine is an in-depth study of a specific institution that spans the period from the command economy through that of reform: the industrial administrative hierarchy in which firms are embedded (Figure 2.1).

6. Despite some scholars (e.g., Nee 1996, 943) having mistaken this study as illustrative of the period of economic transition, it is fundamentally about the economic structure of the redistributive system in prereform China. The reason for this has to do with the indicators: Although the data were collected in 1986, the study's dependent variables are the practices of organizations in the form of nonwage benefits that they offer to their employees. Since the majority of these practices were either instituted or carried out (in the case of housing distribution) before the economic reform began, it would be problematic to draw conclusions about the economic transition based on these indicators.

7. While Bian's discussion here is clearly about the structure of state administration as it applies to the overall industrial hierarchy, it should be noted that the "bureaucratic

rank" variable that appears throughout his analysis is based on the rank of an organization *within* a given jurisdiction as opposed to the rank of a firm's governing organization in the overall government hierarchy (as was analyzed by Walder 1992a, 1995a). Nevertheless, both approaches give a similar message—that a firm's position in the state industrial hierarchy has an impact on its available resources and how it experiences the economic transition.

8. See, for example, Lin and Bian (1991) and Peng (1992).

9. In my sample, municipal bureau governance is positively correlated with size ($r = .59$, $p < .01$), turnover ($r = .25$, $p < .05$), and fixed assets ($r = .24$, $p < .05$), whereas district company governance is negatively correlated with size ($r = -.25$, $p < .05$), turnover ($r = -.23$, $p < .05$), and fixed assets ($r = -.19$, not significant). In addition, municipal bureau governance is negatively correlated with collective ownership ($r = -.29$, $p < .01$) and positively correlated with state ownership ($r = .39$, $p < .01$); district companies are positively correlated with collective ownership (.28, $p < .05$) and negatively correlated with state ownership ($-.30$, $p < .01$). See also Walder (1995a) for discussion. However, this pattern varies by sector; for example, most firms in the foods sector are state-owned yet they are under district company governance.

10. For discussion of monitoring problems that give rise to soft-budget constraints see, especially, Walder (1995a, 287–89; 1992a, 530). For discussion of the attenuation of property rights at lower levels of the industrial hierarchy, see Walder (1994a). Note that the terms "soft-budget" and "hard-budget" constraint come out of Kornai's (1990) analysis of Hungary's command economy. In basic terms, soft budgets, which characterized firm budgets in planned economies, are flexible, usually allowing firms to draw without limits from state coffers; hard budgets are basically market-defined constraints, where firms must cover their own costs and losses. The transition from soft- to hard-budget constraints is one of the central problems of the transition from planned to market economies.

11. See Walder (1992a).

12. Naughton (1992) has argued that these changes initially gave rise to more complex state-firm bargaining relationships. My analysis is not in conflict with this view, though I do think that the complexity of state-firm bargaining relationships is diminishing as the economic transition progresses. My focus here, however, is on the rearrangement of administrative and economic responsibilities in the industrial hierarchy of the former command economy. For additional discussion on the shifting of responsibilities in the economic transition, see Groves et al. (1994).

13. This change in factory administration at the lower levels of the urban industrial hierarchy is similar to the changes Walder (1994a, 1995a) discussed regarding the township and village enterprise system.

14. For discussion of the work unit as the basis of the social security system in China, see Walder (1986a, 1995a), Whyte and Parish (1984), and Bian (1994a).

15. Neither the reinvigoration of the independent budget system nor the new self-responsibility policy is legal in nature (though they have become intertwined with subsequent laws). These changes are based on administrative policy ideas, which have been tested and eventually promulgated on a wide scale over the course of the economic transition; this stepwise process is at the heart of the gradualist approach adopted by the Chinese government. Many of these types of changes for the urban industrial economy were promoted heavily by Zhao Ziyang in 1984 (see Naughton 1995, chap. 5). But at

no point has there been an official [legal] requirement that the organizations adopt these changes. Thus there is considerable variation as to when and to what extent organizations have adopted the changes. Because these policy changes begin as internal communiqués, the actual moments of adoption and change at the organizational level are difficult to trace. Several of the important early documents that set the stage for the independent budget policy were issued by the 1979 State Council; among these documents were "Some Regulations on Enlarging the Management and Decision-Making Powers of State-Owned Industrial Enterprises" and "Provincial Regulations on Instituting Complete Reliance on Bank Credit for Working Capital in State-Owned Industrial Enterprises" (see Field 1984, 746; 1992). One internal (i.e., not public [*neibu*]) document that describes these changes in a broader, detailed fashion for the city of Shanghai is "The Practical Ways to Change the Management Institutions of State-Owned Enterprises for the City of Shanghai" [*Shanghai quanmin suoyouzhi gongye qiye zhuanhuan jingying jizhi shishi banfa*], which can be found in the internal reference book, *Shanghai Economic Institutional Change Yearbook, 1989–1993* [*Shanghai jingji tizhi gaige nianjian, 1989–1993*] (1994). Since 1979, the number of organizations on independent budgets has risen steadily from 5,866 to 10,254 in 1994 in the city of Shanghai (these data include counties; data on independent budgets in the nine city districts of Shanghai are not available). For medium and large-scale industrial organizations (mostly concentrated in city districts), the numbers have remained under 1,000 (see Shanghai Municipal Statistical Bureau 1990, 127–90; 1994, 140–68).

16. For factories on independent budgets, all "major" investment decisions must be approved by governing offices. However, the adherence to this approval process varies by investment size and type. Service-sector investments are often not monitored unless they are duly large investments; joint-venture investments with foreign partners are monitored much more rigidly. Even this approval process, however, varies across municipal boundaries (a function of the municipality's overall power): for example, Shanghai municipality can approve investment projects of up to U.S.$30,000,000 before the project approvals are turned over to the central ministry, whereas many other city governments can issue independent approvals of up to U.S.$10,000,000.

17. This policy also originated with a document issued by the 1979 State Council: "Regulations on the Retention of a Portion of Profits by State Enterprises" (see also Field 1984; Naughton 1995). The policy had virtually no meaning for organizations at that time. When and how the policy has come to have meaning for firms in practice is again an empirical question of the economic transition.

18. For discussion, see also Naughton (1992, 263).

19. For discussion of profit retention, see also Groves et al. (1994) and Field (1984). It should also be noted that the State Enterprise Law (PRC 1988a) is decidedly ambiguous on the nature and size of the residual profits left to enterprises (chap. 3, art. 28; see also Wang 1992). Wang (1992, 117) points out that "the state, as the owner, still decides the amount, if any, of such funds and the acceptable range of enterprise discretion." It is right that the size of residuals depends on the state, but in keeping with the perspective I present here, I argue that this factor, along with all other policies of the economic transition, varies across the nested organizational hierarchy of state administration. As with several of the economic policies and practices on which I present data below, it is likely that the size of residual profits left to an enterprise depends on the level of government organization that presides over the firm. Different levels of state admin-

istration have differing conceptions of control that they draw on to guide firms through the economic transition, and these conceptions of control are relevant for such crucial economic issues as the size of residual profits.

20. For discussion of gradualism, see Naughton (1995), Walder (1994b), and Raw-ski (1995).

21. Walder (1992a, 528; see also 1989, 1992b).

22. The multidivisional organizational firm—the type analyzed in Fligstein (1990; see, especially, Fligstein 1985, 378)—is beginning to emerge in the Chinese market, though it is still far from a common form, at least in the four industries sampled for this study. It is fairly common, however, for larger factories to *call* themselves multi-divisional firms, even though they are not. For my sample, in addition to a decentralized management structure and a central office, I also based classification of multidivisional firms on the following criteria: if the company (1) was a limited [economic] company [*youxian gongsi*] (as opposed to an administrative company) that (2) had control of more than one factory underneath its umbrella company and (3) organized itself accord-ingly in terms of profit-pooling, internal pricing structure for business among factories underneath the parent company, and overall budgetary information and allocation for the entire company; this final criterion is related to Fligstein's mention of centralized long-range planning and financial allocation (1985, 378). These distinctions were im-portant because many companies—especially in the chemicals sector—are calling themselves multidivisional companies [*jituan gongsi*] (literally, "group companies"), but for many of these cases they have done nothing more than change the name of the administrative company to indicate that they, too, are multidivisional companies. None of their practices have anything to do with what the true multidivisional firms are doing (i.e., no centralized long-range planning, allocations, profit-pooling). The five firms that fell into the category of true multidivisional organizations were treated as one large-scale organization for all data. Interestingly, two of the five multidivisional firms in-cluded in this sample started out as an administrative company and then applied to the government to become a limited company, giving them, in addition to administrative rights, profit rights, and, in some cases, actual property rights over the factories below them.

23. The situation regarding the No. 5 Factory gets even more interesting, as the manager of the firm that is underwriting loans for the No. 5 Factory informed me that his firm was planning on taking over the assets of this factory and becoming one large company in early 1996. According to the manager, his firm is not doing this because management thinks it is a smart move economically; on the contrary, they think the No. 5 Factory is somewhat of a lost cause. At the same time, however, they are wary of continuing to underwrite loans for the No. 5 Factory, as the factory has defaulted on these loans every year (the respondent organization, as the underwriter, had to pay back the loans). At the very least, they feel they could reorganize the management and pro-duction systems of the factory and perhaps make it more productive. The manager explained, "It's not the best situation. But I guess we think it would just be better if we were running the factory instead of just helping them with loans to meet costs. Maybe we can make it a better factory."

24. Walder (1995a, 248).

25. As I describe in Appendix 1, most of these cases were determined by contacting the organization's front office, which still usually employed a switchboard operator and

a security guard to watch over the grounds of the closed factory. These firms were not counted in the final sample (as they did not exist in 1995), but they were encountered over the course of the sampling process.

26. "Since the State-Owned Enterprise Second-Phase Profits Changed to the Tax Reform of 1985, enterprise profits are mainly extracted based on the standardized tax" [*1985 nian shixing guoyou qiye dierbu li gai shui banfa, qiye lirun zhuyao yi shui shou xingshi shangjiao*] (State Statistical Bureau 1994, 226; for other discussion, see the *Shanghai Economic Institutional Reform Yearbook* [Shanghai Reforms Collection Office 1994]). This practice first became official, however, with the "Decision of the Standing Committee of the National People's Congress on Authorizing the State Council to Reform the System of Industrial and Commercial Taxes and Issue Relevant Draft Tax Regulations for Trial Application," adopted September 18, 1984, at the Seventh Meeting of the Standing Committee of the Sixth National People's Congress. The document states that the standing committee and the State Council recommend "introducing the practice according to which state enterprises pay taxes instead of turning over their profit to the state and in the course reforming the system of industrial and commercial taxes" (PRC 1984a). See also Naughton (1995, 183–86) for further discussion of this reform.

27. See "The Practical Applications and Experimental Methods of 'The Separation of Taxes and Profits, Fees After Taxes, and Residuals After Taxes' for State-Owned Enterprises" [*Guoying qiye shixing "shuili fenliu, shuihou huandai, shuihou chengbao" de shidian banfa*], 64–66, in *The Shanghai Institutional Economic Yearbook, 1989–1993* (1994).

28. Naughton (1992) has argued that the implementation of this system has not been successful.

29. See Walder (1994b, 299); see also Walder (1986a), Whyte and Parish (1984), and Schurmann (1968).

30. Walder (1994b, 302). Walder further points out that the process of change in China's economic transition depends on the transformation of these "institutional pillars" and changes in the mechanisms through which these institutional pillars exert power (the mechanisms Walder specifys are dependence, monitoring capacity, and sanctioning capacity).

31. I should point out here that I am more interested in the organizational aspects of the Party in China's transforming economy than I am in Party power as Nee (1989a, 1991, 1996) has framed it: Nee is interested in the status and power that Party *membership* has accorded *individuals*. In this study, I am interested in the administrative power that the Party as an organizational apparatus has in Chinese society.

32. For discussion, see Zhao (1997).

33. As I pointed out in chapter 1, the responses of interviewees to this issue raises questions about the basis of Nee's work on the declining power of "redistributors" (i.e., Party members) in China's transition. Here again, the problem with Nee's research in this area is that he uses standard economic indicators (in this case, income) as the measure of power. But we have long known that there are many nonpecuniary advantages to working in government offices and large state-owned firms in China, particularly at the upper levels of these firms. Factory housing and factory cars, not to mention political power and prestige, are not reflected in income. If Party membership is still the path to administrative power, as the respondents in my study indicate, this may be true

irrespective of changes in income, but Nee's results would be the same either way (because he is only measuring income). These individuals are taking positions in low-paying (relative to entrepreneurial or service-sector jobs), high-status, high nonpecu-niary reward jobs. Ironically my interviews indicate that managers believe the Party's power comes into play specifically in the ways that Nee thinks Party power is declining (i.e., increasingly in the economic transition, Party membership matters for personal power).

34. See, for example, Nee (1989a).

Chapter Three
Formal Rational Bureaucracies in Chinese Firms:
Causes and Implications

1. The focus on intra-organizational structure in this chapter follows a number of organizational studies in sociology that have explored the organizational characteristics and institutional environments that influence firm structure. See, for example, Meyer and Rowan (1977), DiMaggio and Powell (1983), Sutton et al. (1994), Dobbin et al. (1993), and Edelman (1990, 1992).

2. For discussion of particularism in prereform Chinese organizations, see Walder (1986a).

3. As I discuss below, this relationship may, in fact, work both ways: Chinese firms may adopt Western-style practices to attract investors, and they may further mimic the practices of their joint-venture partners.

4. Among the broad institutional changes set in place to govern markets in a "ra-tional" way are the Accounting Law (PRC 1985a), the Enterprise Bankruptcy Law (PRC 1986d), the Enterprise Law (PRC 1988a), the Tax Collection Law (1992), the Company Law (PRC 1993), and the Commercial Banking Law (PRC 1995b), to name only a few. The entire battery of laws issued in the PRC since 1978 is too exhaustive to deal with here. According to Pei (1997, 76), the National People's Congress passed 175 laws between 1978 and 1994, and local people's congresses passed another 3,000. If we include "decisions," "resolutions," and "plans," I estimate that out of approximately 268 national-level official institutional reforms passed by the NPC from 1978 to 1994, at least thirty-eight deal directly (many more indirectly) with the organization and governance of emerging markets. See also Naughton (1995) for discussion of the "ra-tionalization" project.

5. Scott (1987, 33).

6. For discussion of internal labor markets and job structure, see Marsden et al. (1994), Dobbin et al. (1993), and Kalleberg et al. (1996); for discussion of incentives and remunerative practices, see Kalleberg and Van Buren (1996) and Sorensen (1994); for discussion of what formal institutions represent and how they diffuse across organi-zational fields, see Meyer and Rowan (1977) and DiMaggio and Powell (1983).

7. See Walder (1986a).

8. For extensive discussion, see Scott (1987). I focus on the rationalist and institu-tional perspectives here. For various other perspectives on organizational structures, see also scholars such as Roethlisberger and Dickson (1934), Gross (1953), and Pfeffer and Salancik (1978). Some scholars in the rationalist camp (e.g., Simon 1957 and March and Simon 1958) argue that individuals within the organizations operate in a world of

bounded rationality where the ultimate goals are clear (profit, growth) but the means for achieving those ends are murky. Nevertheless March and Simon, like such predecessors as Taylor (1923), view the structure and formalization of an organization as arising from rational (or boundedly rational) choices that actors make within the organizations.

9. See Edelman (1990, 1992), Dobbin et al. (1993), and Sutton et al. (1994). See also Meyer and Rowan (1977) and DiMaggio and Powell (1983).

10. See Walder (1986a, 10).

11. Walder (1986a, 11).

12. It is important to note that in my interviews, for managers who affirmed having adopted a given organizational practice, I made certain we were speaking of practices that had been adopted in the reform era. Some organizations did have simplistic organizational rules dating back to the Maoist era, but these were different from the extensive formalized rules I examine here. In my conversations with managers, I emphasized that we were speaking of formal written rules that had been produced in the reform era and made reference to or incorporated the broader institutional reforms of the economic transition. For all organizations that affirmed the existence of such institutions, these firm-level practices were adopted in the late 1980s or 1990s. I followed this protocol for discussions surrounding each specific organizational practice, though the issue is most relevant for the discussion of organizational rules.

13. See PRC (1995a).

14. For discussion of the symbolic aspects of organizational structures, see Meyer and Rowan (1977) and Edelman (1990, 1992).

15. Most organizations have WRCs, but only about half the organizations have formally established meeting times to allow the WRCs to participate in the organizational changes occurring over the course of the transition.

16. See Bian (1994b, 972).

17. The "talent market" is comprised of a set of organizations comparable to what we call "head-hunting firms," which function to help organizations find employees for a fee. These organizations are increasingly common in urban China.

18. In general, in Table 3.1, I follow the convention employed throughout the rest of this study and analyze the firm's external governance by looking at municipal bureau governance as compared to municipal company and district company governance. However, in Model 4 of Table 3.1 and for the model in Table 3.2, municipal company governance does have a significant effect; thus in these cases I have included this variable. To ensure that changing these variables in the equations does not alter the effects of other variables, each model (in both tables) was run with each separate governing category in the equation. Changing the governing category did not change the effects of other variables in any of the equations.

19. The firm's overall institutionalization is a variable that is calculated simply by adding up each of the dichotomous dependent variables analyzed in Table 3.1. The range of the variable is 0–7, the mean is 3.630, and the standard deviation is 1.907.

20. This discussion, where I talk about significant sector effects independent of all other effects, is based on models that have been rerun to isolate the effects of a given sector *compared to all other sectors*. The problem with talking about these sector effects based on Tables 3.1 and 3.2 is that the reference category in these tables is garments only, and therefore each sector effect is only significant relative to the garments sector. For the discussion in this section, however, I have rerun all models with all other

organizational variables but isolated each sector compared to all other sectors. For example, for organizational rules, the effect of location in the foods sector is significant, so the new tested model is $y = \beta_0 + \beta_1(\text{foods}) + \beta_2(\text{size}) + \beta_3(\text{employee ratio}) + \beta_4(\text{organizational health}) + \beta_5(\text{losses}) + \beta_6(\text{joint venture}) + \beta_7(\text{general manager's background}) + \beta_8(\text{bureau})$. Thus, in this section, when I speak of isomorphic effects, the effects are significant relative to all other sector categories (all three other sectors are left out of the equation), which is a stronger statement than that presented in the models in Tables 3.1 and 3.2. Nevertheless, there is still the question of diffusion, which is intimately tied to the phenomenon of isomorphism: While event history data on the adoption of organizational practices in a given sector or data on dyadic relationships and networks of general managers would provide more conclusive evidence of an isomorphic effect (particularly the mimetic effect), no such data were available for this research project. However, that many sector effects are significant independent of other organizational characteristics indicates that Chinese industrial organizations in similar social spaces tend to adopt comparable internal organizational practices in analogous ways (readers should note here that in many of the other analyses and chapters, sector effects generally disappear when other organizational characteristics are added to the equations).

21. For discussion of different types of isomorphism, see DiMaggio and Powell (1983).

22. DiMaggio and Powell (1991, 70).

23. This does not eliminate the possibility that there may be internal [*neibu*] policies that foreign researchers have no way of accessing. In my experience, when internal policies are raised in interviews, managers are often reluctant to talk about these issues. There are many such policies in China's economic transition, and *The Shanghai Economic Institutional Reform Yearbook* (Shanghai Reform Collections Office 1994) is filled with internal documents. An official in the Reform Collections Office allowed me to read this reference book and take notes on it for a short period. But I was not permitted to take the book out of the Reform Collections Office, nor was I allowed to photocopy any documents in the book. However, with the exception of labor contracts in the foods sector (see chapter 4), none of the practices I studied in this research were uniformly adopted in a given sector; even in the case of labor contracts, the timing of the adoption of this practice varied. The lack of uniformity of any of these practices indicates that their adoption is not guided by internal policies or mandates but rather by organizational characteristics; if it were simply a matter of the state mandating organizations in a given field to institutionalize a practice, we would expect that the adoption of this practice would not vary among organizations.

24. See Dobbin et al. (1993).

25. See DiMaggio and Powell (1991, 67).

26. For discussion, see Walder (1995a) and Guthrie (1997).

27. For discussion of variation in scale and scope across the hierarchy, see Walder (1995a); for discussion of budgetary allocation in the redistributive system, see Walder (1992a).

28. As I have noted above, the existence of new formal, nonparticularistic institutions in the firm does not guarantee that authority relations are necessarily going to change. I argue, however, that the construction of organizations around these nonparticularistic institutions cannot but transform authority relations within the firm, especially in the institutional context of broader changes such as the Labor Law and the Labor

Arbitration Commissions. As I show below, at least one set of these new institutions (the mediation committee) does appear to have an impact on worker discontent. Further, even if these institutions have not drastically altered the authority patterns of the past, even if they are, at this point, largely symbolic, real changes in authority relations are likely to emerge over time, as there is now an institutional context in which that transformation can occur.

29. DiMaggio and Powell (1991, 71).

30. It is not uncommon for upper-level managers of Chinese firms to have had some education in seminars, short courses, or degree programs in U.S. business schools.

31. Typically, the foreign partner's capital investment does not have a direct or immediate impact on the Chinese organization's economic well-being. Contracts clearly specify where capital is to go in setting up the venture, and the Chinese partner cannot simply funnel funds into its own organization (though I am sure this does happen). However, as a percentage partner in the venture, the Chinese partner stands to make profits proportional to its stake in the investment.

32. Given my assertion of this causal relationship, I should note here that the causal sequencing of these relationships exists in the opposite direction of those modeled in Tables 3.1 and 3.2 (the argument here is that firms which have adopted formalized institutional practices are more likely to land joint-venture contracts; the models above posit that joint-venture relationships give rise to formal organizational practices). Nevertheless, the associations among these variables, regardless of causal direction, are statistically significant, and once a company lands a joint venture, it is likely to engage in the type of mimicry described above. So for these companies, the causality probably runs both ways.

33. It is a general weakness of neoinstitutional theory that studies in this area often fail to explore what institutional structures mean for workers in the workplace. To some extent, this failure is related to the orienting questions and theories of research in this area, which often assume that organizational structures are primarily symbolic (see, for example, Edelman 1992; Meyer and Rowan 1977). In the following section I focus directly on the extent to which emerging structures in Chinese organizations matter for the decisions and practices adopted by organizations. In other words, I examine the extent to which these structures are *not* symbolic.

34. Bian (1994b, 999). This part of the analysis is set up in dialogue with Bian's argument that jobs will increasingly be manipulated by social networks and connections as the economic transition progresses. A few caveats should be noted here, however. First, whereas Bian's (1994b) research deals with individual-level data, my study is based on organizational-level data. Thus, where Bian's indicators are whether individuals used connections to get jobs, mine are whether the organization has formal hiring procedures, whether the organization has a formal stance on individuals using connections to get jobs in the organizations, and whether, in practice, the organization actually uses connections to hire new employees. Second, Bian's data reflect the role of connections in the pursuit of urban jobs in 1988, whereas my data pertain to 1995. Finally, Bian chose not to speak of *guanxi* directly in his survey because of the sensitivity of the word (see Bian 1994b, 984 n. 27), whereas I spoke directly with managers regarding the issue (see Appendix 3, question 38). This difference may be significant, but, as Bian points out, "although it would be inappropriate to use the word *guanxi* in a questionnaire, it is fine in personal interviews" (again, see 948 n. 27). Although my

interviews followed a set questionnaire format, as shown in Appendix 3, I personally administered the survey as in-depth interviews: I asked the questions directly and discussed each issue with the respondents at length for the sake of clarity and rapport.

35. The model in Table 3.3 is based on a reduced sample of organizations. In the survey I asked whether the Labor Bureau still allocates labor to the organization; thirty-six firms indicated that they are still under some form of state control in the allocation of labor. For these organizations, the institutionalization of formal hiring procedures is somewhat irrelevant. Therefore I have reduced the sample to the forty-five organizations that are not under any type of state control with respect to hiring decisions.

36. As with the sector effects in Tables 3.1 and 3.2 (discussed above), I have rerun this model with electronics as the only sector in the equation (all other sectors as the left out category). Results show that the effect is statistically significant at the $p < .05$ level ($\beta = -2.827$).

37. In this section, unless otherwise noted, information on the Labor Arbitration Commissions is based on an interview with a deputy division chief in the Shanghai Municipal Labor Bureau, who, at the time of the interview, oversaw the Office of Labor Disputes in the Shanghai Municipal Arbitration Committee (Interview 57, 1995).

38. Some officials and managers hold the view that legal frameworks have a direct impact on the use of outside arbitration. As one government official explained:

> We believe that the Labor Law will have a huge impact on the labor arbitration situation. We think this is already beginning to happen. Over the last few years there has been a steady increase of applications to the Labor Arbitration Commission. But this year we expect a huge increase because of the Labor Law. Because of the Labor Law, everyone will start to know what kind of personal power they have. The Labor Law is changing peoples' understanding of their rights. . . . We are hoping that the combination of the Labor Law and the Labor Arbitration Commission will force all types of organizations to focus on the laws more and more. Now that we are developing a market economy, changes are happening so quickly, and it's very important that everyone is protected by the laws. (Interview 57, 1995)

39. Individuals can also apply to serve in this group, but few do because it is not a paid position. Of those who volunteer, most are lawyers working at universities who want to gain experience with the legal changes occurring in China. According to officials, not enough individuals are working in this capacity, and, as a result, many cases are simply heard by the presiding government official.

40. Although there is a separate section in the LAC for disputes relating to benefits and pay, individuals generally rely on labor unions to solve such problems.

41. Survey question: "Has anyone from the organization ever applied to the Labor Arbitration Commission [*laodong zhongcai weiyuanhui*]?"

42. See *New York Times*, April 27, 1998, A1, 6.

43. See PRC (1995a) and PRC (1994), respectively.

44. For estimates of the number of cases brought before court, see *New York Times*, April 27, 1998, A1, 6. For discussion of the percentage rise in suits against the government, see Pei (1997, 76).

45. See Walder (1986a, 224).

46. This information is based on an interview with an official in the Labor Bureau (Interview 31b, 1995).

Chapter Four
Changing Labor Relations in the Period of Market Reform

1. See, for example, Róna-Tas (1994), Peng (1992), Xie and Hannum (1996), Bian and Logan (1996), Szelényi (1988), and Nee (1989a, 1991, 1996).

2. See Walder (1992a). The specific aspects of remuneration Walder examines are various nonwage benefits that organizations offer their workers.

3. See also Walder (1994a, 1995a).

4. Only the analysis of variance (ANOVA) in Table 6 (Xie and Hannum 1996, 982) includes an "ownership" term (presumably the same ownership terms Peng used—again ignoring Walder's work in this area), and there are no indicators that directly measure the structure of labor markets in China.

5. See Walder (1986a, chap. 6).

6. Naughton (1995, 32).

7. See Kornai (1980).

8. For further discussion of the shortage economy, see also Naughton (1995, 33); for discussion of Maoist asceticism, see Walder (1986a, chap. 6). Walder's work on the institutional structure of industry under the planned economy also discusses at length the importance of wages in the internal structure of firms and the relationships within firms for the maintenance of the patron-client relationships that were fundamental to the institutional structure of organizations in prereform China.

9. Naughton (1995, 103) connects the changes in wages to the institutional change of profit retention: "With the institution of profit retention, worker bonuses grew rapidly and became a major component of employee compensation. By 1980, bonuses amounted to 9 percent of total . . . wages, and the institution of bonuses accounted for the bulk of the 14 percent increase in real urban wages between 1978 and 1980."

10. See Naughton (1995, 104–5).

11. The objective of increasing urban income and living standards through wage increases was not without macroeconomic consequences: The rapid growth of real wages led to inflation because the growth had outrun the expanding production of consumer goods (Naughton 1995, 119).

12. For further discussion, see also Bian (1994a). As is the case with several other indicators of the economic transition, wages are higher in Shanghai than anywhere else in China. Once again, it could be argued that studying wages in the area that has experienced the most drastic changes may yield a skewed view of the changes that wages are undergoing in the economic transition. However, as I have argued earlier, studying these changes of the economic transition in a place that is experiencing rapid economic transformation such as Shanghai makes sense because these are changes that most places in China are eventually going to experience (see introduction).

13. The dependent variable for this part of the research is the natural log of wages. As Xie and Hannum (1996) have argued, an assessment of wages that decomposes actual wages and bonuses is appropriate for this type of analysis in the case of China (see also Bian 1994a). In my survey managers rarely had data on the average bonus awarded to employees across the organization, and some had no data on average wages across the organization. All the interviewees did, however, have data on the average amount of money paid to employees within the organization in 1994 (total wage costs / total no. of employees); the figure represents the average sum total of wages and

bonuses awarded to active employees in the organization in 1994. As a result, my measure is not as precise as the decomposed measures that Xie and Hannum or Bian used. Nevertheless, the measure does reveal the amount of money an organization awarded to its workers in 1994. As averages, the figures are fairly accurate representations of the general situations in each firm, because wage differentials within organizations are still relatively small.

14. Correlations between the electronics sector and losses in 1990 and 1994, respectively, are the following: $r = .305$ ($p < .01$); and $r = .190$ ($p < .1$).

15. While I generally do not include variables of ownership type in my analyses, focusing instead on a firm's position in the administrative hierarchy of the former command economy (see chapter 2 for discussion), Bian's (1994a) work indicates that state ownership is a significant predictor of higher wages. Therefore, in Table 4.1, the effect of state ownership is examined through a dummy variable for state ownership.

16. As I noted earlier, although some scholars have mistaken this study as being about the economic transition (the data were gathered in 1986), it is fundamentally about prereform China. See chapter 2 for discussion.

17. While Walder's (1992a) study creatively links the nonwage benefits to which an individual has access to the organizational and institutional aspects of the workplace, an organizational-level study is, in some ways, more appropriate than an individual-level survey. With regard to nonwage benefits such as meal service and infant day care, Walder et al.'s (1989) survey asked whether the organization provided the benefit. Regarding housing, however, the survey inquired about the source of the respondent's housing (as opposed to whether the respondent's work unit provided housing). For those who did not name their work unit as their source of housing, it could still be that the work unit provided housing but the respondent simply did not get his or her housing through the work unit. However, the study implicitly assumes that individuals who name another housing source were attached to work units that do not provide housing, which may or may not be true.

18. For example, employee ratio is correlated with the age of the organization at $r = -.42$ ($p < .01$), meaning that older organizations have significantly larger burdens in terms of retired employees than younger organizations.

19. It should be noted here that these are huge effects for logistic regression models: Effects of 2.23 and 4.08 translate into organizations at these levels of the industrial hierarchy being nine and fifty-nine times (respectively) more likely to offer the benefit of housing than those at lower levels of the hierarchy.

20. The Great Leap Forward (1958–60) provided a caveat to this system, as approximately sixteen million workers were laid off and sent down to the countryside during that campaign. This is the only period, however, where layoffs were not accompanied by reassignment (Walder 1986a).

21. For full translation, see Josephs (1989, Appendix A).

22. For discussion of "waiting for employment," see Gold (1980).

23. See Walder (1986a, 57, 68–74).

24. Despite the force of this manager's (and many other managers') statements regarding the importance of the labor contract, there is still significant variation surrounding the meaning of this institution in China today, and there are still places where the labor contract is viewed to have little meaning (see below). My argument here, however, is that the labor contract lays the foundation for fundamental changes in the labor

relationship, and these changes are already meaningful in many industrial organizations and will become increasingly meaningful in years to come.

25. See PRC (1986a, 1986b). See also *Statistical Yearbook of China* (State Statistical Bureau 1994, 131) and Josephs (1989).

26. My interviews with managers indicate that of these three, the fixed limited-term contract is the most stable in that it guarantees employment at an organization for the duration of the period defined in the contract. It is also the type of contract that workers in industrial factories are signing. The nonfixed limited-term contract and the project work limited-term contract are typically used in more project-oriented sectors, such as construction. Accordingly, I focus on the fixed limited-term contract.

27. See Naughton (1995, 210–12).

28. Although the official Provisional Regulations document (see PRC 1986a, 1986b) was promulgated in 1986, local governments began experimenting with contracts as early as 1983, by order of the Trial Implementation Notice of the State Council promulgated in 1983 (see PRC 1983a). Typically, this is the way broad institutional changes are set in motion in China: An institutional change begins with a policy idea that emerges as a "Notice" from the State Council, which is then experimented with in different localities and sectors of the economy. When the kinks have been worked out to some degree, the institutional change is legitimized through an official law, rule, regulation, or decree from the State Council.

29. As with most other indicators, there is significant variation across the administrative regions of China (the thirty-one administrative divisions of China include twenty-two provinces, five autonomous regions, and four municipalities): Shanghai has a considerably higher proportion of its laborers on labor contracts with 49.9 percent of its labor force (2,378,000 individuals) on labor contracts. The less developed areas of Tibet and Anhui Province are among the lowest with 10.5 percent (18,000 individuals) and 12.5 percent (621,000 individuals) of the labor force on labor contracts, respectively. It is also clear, however, that the implementation of the labor contract is not only a function of industrial development, since Tianjin—one of the major industrial municipalities in China—is also among the lowest with 13.8 percent (404,000 individuals) of the labor force on labor contracts.

30. Joint venture salaries are set at a minimum of 1.5 times the salary of workers in the Chinese factory that is the investment partner. Therefore, assuming that retirement salaries and active worker salaries are the same (they usually are not, but I do not have the data on retired workers incomes), then this factory's overhead is roughly six times that of the joint venture. It is likely that this figure underestimates the disparity, however, because joint ventures typically pay less overhead in additional nonwage benefits than do fully owned Chinese organizations.

31. For additional discussion, see *Zhongguo ribao* [China daily], May 24, 1996.

32. Three questions in the survey were relevant for establishing an organization's practices vis-à-vis labor contracts. The first question asked, "What percentage of the organization's employees are on labor contracts?" If the labor contract had been implemented on an organizationwide basis (i.e., 100 percent of workers were on contracts), a follow-up question inquired about the year in which this practice was implemented across the organization: "[If 100 percent,] what year was this practice institutionalized?" A third question inquired about the meaning of the labor contract for the labor relationship.

33. Six organizations answered no to this question. Analyses below show results for both the full sample and a sample adjusted to account for the organizations that had institutionalized labor contracts but did not view the labor relationship as having been transformed in any significant way.

34. Though he did modify Kornai's (1980) theory of soft-budget constraints significantly in his analysis of economic transition in China, Walder (1995a) left the "core" of Kornai's theory intact, arguing that it still applied to the large organizations positioned at the upper levels of China's administrative hierarchy. My study suggests, however, that firms at the upper levels of the hierarchy, while not becoming more productive, are in fact experiencing the reforms in significant ways. I will further extend the analysis of the issues I touch on here in chapter 6.

35. For discussion, see Guthrie (1997, 1998b).

36. For discussion of Hungary's economic transition and responses to uncertainty, see Stark (1996).

37. See, for example, Eswaran and Katwol (1985a, 1985b).

38. For discussion, see Walder (1986a).

Chapter Five
The Politics of Price Setting in China's Transitional Economy

1. See Friedman and Friedman (1979, 14–20).

2. Nee (1989a, 663).

3. Much important work has been done on price reform in economic studies of China's reforms. Scholars such as van Wijnbergen (1992), Wiemer (1992), K. Wong (1992), Parker (1995), Naughton (1995), and Guo (1992) have all dealt extensively with various aspects of price reform in China. While all these studies are useful for understanding price reform in China, most of them are either theoretical or based on macroeconomic data. With the exception of Naughton and Guo, I largely eschew discussion of this literature. My reasoning is that my focus here, as it was throughout my study, is on the empirical realities of the reform at the firm level.

4. For discussion of the 1984 Reform Declaration, see Naughton (1995, 248); for discussion of the "price reformers" and "enterprise reformers," see Naughton (1995, 188–96); for discussion of a lack of reform by the end of 1984, see Naughton (1995, 136).

5. For discussion, see Naughton (1995, 196–98) and Lieberthal (1995, 254).

6. Naughton (1995, 220).

7. Ibid., 289.

8. Fligstein (1996b, 659).

9. For discussion, see Naughton (1995, 221–22).

10. Naughton (1995, 232–33).

11. These results can also be interpreted in the opposite direction causally, as firms that are freer of state control may be more likely to be selected as joint-venture partners by foreign investors. Showing these results one way or the other would require time series data with dates of the adoption of price-setting practices and dates when a joint venture was set up. This type of data was unavailable for my study, and it is the main weakness of the results I present (see Appendix 1 for further discussion). However, the significance of the associations can be seen clearly enough from the results, and it is likely that causality runs in both directions.

12. See Walder (1995a).

13. For discussion, see Guthrie (1996, 1997, and chapters 2, 4, and 6 of this work).

14. Jurisdiction size and bureau governance cannot be placed in the same model owing to multicollinearity.

15. For discussion, see DiMaggio and Powell (1983).

Chapter Six
Economic Strategies in the Face of Market Reforms

1. Nee (1996, 945).

2. Walder (1995a, 294; see also ibid., 268–70; 1994a, 63).

3. One could argue that we should actually expect the opposite: Hard budget constraints would drastically alter the production patterns and protection that firms came to expect under the command economy, and it would not be surprising that many firms would be at risk of market failure. The point here is that slow gains in productivity are not sufficient evidence to conclude that changes in budget allocation have not occurred.

4. See, for example, Stark (1996) and Fligstein (1985, 1990, 1991).

5. For discussion, see Fligstein (1996b, 668–69; see also 1991, 314–15; 1990).

6. Three firms in my sample had applied to become companies but had not yet received approval. The idea of "adopting" the Company Law in the sense of deciding to become a company and aspiring to follow the Company Law applies to these firms as well. To assure that the issue is not one of state approvals, as opposed to a firm's decision to adopt the Company Law, models were run first with these firms coded as adopters and then coded as nonadopters; the size of the effects were different, but significance levels were the same as those reported in Table 6.1. Models were also run with these firms eliminated from the sample with no change to the results.

7. For discussion of the construction of laws in reform-era China, see Tanner (1995). For discussion of the political nature of laws in the European Union, see Fligstein and Mara-Drita (1996).

8. For discussion of the Company Law and its relation to China's socialist market economy, see Torbert (1994); for extensive discussion of the history of the Company, see Kirby (1995).

9. Pei (1997, 76).

10. See PRC (1988a).

11. To develop a more systematic understanding of what the Company Law means for firms in the economic transition, managers at each of the eighty-one organizations in the data set were asked two questions: "Does the organization follow [anzhao] the Company Law [gongsi fa] or the Enterprise Law [qiye fa]?" "Is the factory officially a company or an enterprise?" These questions are really two ways of inquiring about the same issue; both were asked to assure that there was no confusion in our discussions over the adoption of the Company Law. If a factory was officially still an enterprise but had applied to become a company (as was the case for three factories), that fact came out in the conversations engendered by these questions. If the manager answered that the entity was a company, one final question was asked: "When did the factory become a company?"

12. I address this issue in greater depth in the section on diversification.

13. I discuss this relationship in greater depth in the section on diversification.

14. Some scholars of diversification define the practice narrowly as the number of manufacturing markets served by a given manufacturing organization's output (Gort 1984). Others, however, define the term more broadly as "development based on [an organization's decision] to move into a completely new area of business in which the company has few (if any) skills" (Luffman and Reed 1984, 3). It is this latter, more broadly defined view of diversification that is the focus of this chapter. Throughout this section I refer to "diversification" or "service-sector diversification." In the case of China, some firms are diversified in the classical sense of the term, meaning that they have diversified production lines (see also Fligstein 1985, 1990, 1991; Chandler 1962). However, this classic type of diversification is not the most interesting practice to observe in China today vis-à-vis the economic transition (for one thing, it was happening long before the economic transition began; also, the multisector diversifiers are relatively rare). The discussion here refers to diversification investment in the service-sector economy [*disan chanye touzi*], a diversification practice that is fully disconnected from a given organization's manufacturing patterns or systems. Service-sector diversification involves any investment in the service economy [*disan chanye*], from hotels and office buildings to restaurants and Karaoke bars. This practice is intimately tied to the economic transition because, for all intents and purposes, it did not exist as an economic strategy or option before the economic transition began. One manager explained these investments as a "low-risk way for [firms] to make money in the fastest growing part of the economy."

15. For discussion of firms' desire to create stable worlds, see Fligstein (1996b).

16. See, for example, Fligstein (1991, 1996b) and Stark (1996).

17. Further, the service sector is an important area of research if only because it is one of the most rapidly expanding economies in China. Nationally, average daily transactions in the service sector rose more than 700 percent between 1985 and 1995 (State Statistical Bureau 1996, 5). In addition, this sector now comprises a significant portion of urban labor forces: In Shanghai's urban districts in 1993, 43 percent of the labor force was located in the service-sector economy; nationally, the figure was 26 percent (State Statistical Bureau 1994, 111, 108). Some firms are choosing to take advantage of this rapidly expanding economy by diversifying assets through investments into the service sector. An examination of service-sector diversification will help illuminate the structural and institutional situations that give rise to specific organizational decisions and practices in periods of economic upheaval and transformation.

18. For discussion of entry into rapidly expanding industries, see Gort (1962); for discussion of risk-spreading practices, see Williamson (1975).

19. Many organizations have small stores connected to them, literally called "our own service stores" [*zijide disan chanye*]. These range from retail stores run by the labor union (mostly set up for workers) to small stores connected to the factory to showcase factory products. But these types of retail centers are not set up as profit-returning investments and thus do not qualify as the type of market survival strategy pertinent to this discussion. Here again, to ensure we were talking about the same thing, this part of the interview required some in-depth discussion of the types of service-sector investments undertaken. Some common ventures included office buildings, hotels, construction development, restaurants, and the like.

20. While this question is relevant for all my analyses, it is more salient for the diversification issue: Do firms diversify because they are economically weak (as I con-

tend), or do firms become economically weak as a result of diversifying? Because this issue is so central to my contention of what service-sector diversification represents (i.e., a stability strategy adopted by weak or unstable firms experiencing uncertain market environments), Model II in Table 6.2 is set up specifically to address this concern. If indeed firms diversify because they are economically weak, then my argument carries weight, and we can use diversification strategies as an indicator of general uncertainty in emerging markets; if, on the other hand, firms become weak because of diversification, then my argument about the implications of the diversification strategy collapses.

21. The question, "When did your organization first invest in the service sector?" also appeared on the questionnaire. Although managers were often vague as to the exact date the firm adopted the strategy, virtually all were able to affirm that they had adopted the strategy within the last five years (i.e., since 1990).

22. See Walder (1995a).

23. It is not the case that simple variations in laws or rules define the differences in rates of adopting this strategy for different levels of the hierarchy. If the adoption of this strategy was simply a function of variant legal rules, we would find that no firms under a given administrative level (e.g., district company) were diversifying. This is not the case, however. While firms under municipal bureaus are most likely to diversify (and municipal companies are more likely than district companies), firms at each of these levels have adopted the strategy.

24. See chapter 2 for discussion of several important policies of the transitional period.

25. See Walder (1995a, 288–89).

Chapter Seven
Institutional Pressure, Rational Choice, and Contractual Relations:
Chinese-Foreign Negotiations in the Economic Transition

1. See, for example, Naughton (1995).

2. Nee (1996) makes a similar point, arguing that some studies focus exclusively on the causal primacy of state action in economic reform. However, Nee replaces an overwhelming focus on the state with a pervasive underlying assumption of the "pursuit of power and plenty" by autonomous economic actors in the marketplace, as well as emphasizing gains in income. From the perspective I advocate, state institutions, structures, and state action are all crucial; but the more interesting question for economic transitions is how economic actors (individuals or organizations) incorporate and react to state action and changing state institutions. Assuming that everyone is simply acting out a primal urge to pursue power and plenty does not add much here. Beyond individual greed, what are the social, political, economic, and institutional factors that drive economic decision making in transitional economies?

3. Some studies, such as the work of Heydebrand (1996), deal explicitly with the emergence of rational-legal institutional structures in Eastern Europe's economic transition. However, these studies are theoretical in nature and not based on empirical data.

4. While Weber's central thesis is that the existence of a formal rational-legal system alone did not give rise to capitalism, he did see a rational-legal system as a necessary part of the emergence of rational capitalism. According to Weber (1976, 25): "Modern rational capitalism has need, not only of the technical means of production,

but of a calculable legal system and of administration in terms of formal rules. Without it adventurous and speculative trading capitalism and all sorts of politically determined capitalisms are possible, but no rational enterprise under individual initiative, with fixed capital and certainty of calculations." In other places, Weber (1978, 814) wrote: "Capitalistic interests will fare best under a rigorously formal system of adjudication, which applies in all cases and operates under the adversary system of procedure." From Weber's view, one of the central requirements of a rational capitalist system is the ability of economic actors to calculate rational outcomes when entering an economic transaction. Necessary features of rational capitalism are freedom of contract and the promise that contractual relationships will be guaranteed by a legal body with the power to enforce legal institutions (Weber 1978, 668–69). Economic actors must be able to enter into the economic relationships they choose, and they must have the confidence in the existing institutional system that contracts will be protected in predictable ways with calculable outcomes. Economic systems plagued with unpredictable outcomes (e.g., those based on the capricious rule of administrative fiat) cannot develop into a rational capitalist system, because economic actors have no way of knowing whether their investments will be protected in a predictable manner. They will thus be unlikely to engage in economic action on the basis of a rational means-ends calculus. If rational action is inhibited, rational capitalism is impossible.

5. See, for example, Weber (1968) and Fairbank (1992).

6. For example, the Company Law; see Kirby (1995) for discussion.

7. Studies that include individual-level economic actors (such as petty agricultural entrepreneurs, e.g., Nee 1989a, 1991) typically analyze changes in income and mechanisms of stratification as the dependent variables. Studies of this genre are able to say little about the economic decisions and transactions per se; more to the point, they are able to say little about how the economic actors view the emerging rational-legal system (if one is indeed emerging).

8. The importance of foreign investment in China's transition extends beyond capital: In many high-tech sectors, foreign investment and the transfer of technology is as important to the development of the industrial sector as the investment of foreign capital.

9. See PRC (1979a, Article 1).

10. The following story is taken from *Time* magazine, October 10, 1994, 61.

11. Although the Patent Law (PRC 1984b), which was put into effect on April 1, 1985, may have been relevant for this dispute, the more pertinent question is which Chinese body (e.g., courts or CIETAC) was arbitrating this dispute and the extent to which that body chose seriously to consider DuPont's claims.

12. U.S.$16 million is not a huge sum as far as foreign investment goes. But it is a considerably large sum relative to the small ventures often set up by Taiwan and Hong Kong investors. In my sample of firms, the median joint-venture investment was U.S.$20.8 million; however, the median investment among Taiwan and Hong Kong investors was U.S.$7 million.

13. It is legal and possible for foreign companies to set up Wholly Owned Foreign Enterprises (WOFEs) in China, and some companies—for example, Motorola—have done this with great success. However, the export ratios of WOFEs are typically so high that if the foreign company wants to capture a share of the Chinese market (as many do), companies are usually pressured politically eventually to set up a joint venture to share

the technology and wealth with a local partner. For example, in 1996, after seven years of licensing production in China, Motorola was forced to set up a joint venture with the Hangzhou Telecommunications Equipment Factory. Though contracts and approval processes are involved in setting up a WOFE, the procedures and negotiations differ from those involved in setting up a joint venture (they are more directly between the state and foreign firms—no Chinese partner is involved). Since my sample is one of Chinese organizations and the contracts in which they are involved, my analysis in this chapter is confined to joint-venture contracts.

14. Municipal bureaus (in large industrial cities) approve joint-venture projects that are less that U.S.$30 million. If a joint-venture project exceeds this amount, approval must also come from the ministry (and, in some cases, the ministry-level State Planning Commission). If a joint contract exceeds U.S.$100 million, approval must come directly from the State Council. Because central government approvals are often slower and more difficult to predict, it is not uncommon for a contract in a given municipality to be set up for an amount of U.S.$29,999,999.

15. A good example is the government's recent decision to limit foreign returns in the power industry to 12 percent, which was apparently a reaction to Gordon Wu's bravado about his high returns on his Shenzhen venture in the power industry. Wu has since said that he will take future power industry investments elsewhere (e.g., Philippines, India) where the amount that foreign developers can earn through investments is unrestricted. See *Far Eastern Economic Review* 157 (May 12, 1994): 61.

16. See, for example, Petersen (1994).

17. See, for example, Cheng and Rosett (1991), Lubman and Wajnowski (1993), Hamilton and Biggart (1988), and Xin and Pearce (1996).

18. For extensive discussion of CIETAC as an institution, see Lubman and Wajnowski (1993).

19. See Clarke (1991).

20. Ibid., 267.

21. Clarke (1991).

22. For discussion of arbitration in China, see Lubman and Wajnowski (1993); for discussion of mediation institutions, see Clarke (1991); for discussion of contracts, see Cheng and Rosett (1991).

23. Size and revenues are significantly correlated at $r = .68$, $p < .01$.

24. Export ratios vary depending on the foreign company's bargaining power and on the level of government with which the foreign company is dealing directly. For example, as municipal bureaus handle most approvals of less than U.S.$30 million, if the foreign company is setting up a joint venture with a firm directly under the jurisdiction of a municipal bureau and the official overseeing the process has agreed to a given export ratio based on the results of the feasibility study (a part of the process that precedes the final application), the bureau is likely to approve this project. Also, if a foreign company has a technology of which the country is in dire need for development purposes, then it is likely that the foreign company will be able to negotiate a lower export ratio. There is no set figure on what export ratios must be—they are part of the negotiation—but it appears that they are typically around 15–20 percent.

25. General discussion of data and data collection can be found in the appendixes; see, especially, Appendix 4 for discussion of variables, definitions, and coding. However, a few specific variables may require extended discussion here. In the analysis

below, I view the specification of arbitration clauses (either CIETAC or third-country arbitration) in joint-venture contracts as diminishing Chinese sovereignty when compared to arbitration by the Chinese legal system. The dependent variable for the analysis is the contract that is formed in the partnership between a Chinese firm and a foreign company. The negotiation over these contracts will reveal the relative power over institutional outcomes among the actors involved. It will also help to illuminate the types of relationships among negotiating parties that give rise to different contractual outcomes. Further, it will reflect on the decision-making processes of the economic actors involved in the negotiations. Inasmuch as the dependent variable is the contractual outcome, it is important to note a few factors about the analysis of this variable. First, as some organizations have multiple joint-venture contracts, the survey specified a discussion about the *first* joint venture set up between the Chinese firm and a foreign partner. It was necessary to examine the structure of the first contract, because that could affect the structure of subsequent contracts (see, e.g., the comments of interviewee 131, quoted above). Second, the value of the joint-venture contract is logged, as the effect of this variable is likely to increase at a decreasing rate. Third, "Western partners" are defined as organizations that have ventures with any non-Asian country, including Australia; Australia was defined as a Western country because its cultural and institutional history resemble that of other Western countries more than Asian countries. "Chinese partners" refer to those countries with a culturally Chinese population, namely, Taiwan, Hong Kong, and Singapore.

26. Note that the proportions in Figure 7.1 are based on a sub-sample of the firms in the original random sample; the firms in the sub-sample are those that have joint-venture contracts with foreign partners. For firms that have more than one joint venture, the relationship examined is the *first* one the organization set up with a foreign partner. In these cases, I chose to focus on the first joint venture because, as I expressed above, the structure of first contracts may influence the structure of subsequent contracts.

27. According to Model I, controlling for all other effects, organizations under bureaus are less than one-twentieth as likely as organizations under district companies to have joint-venture contracts that contain arbitration clauses (exp[-3.465] = .03).

28. For example, the correlation between value of contract and Western investor is $r = .471, p < .01$.

29. Here again, in the sample, there is a firm that has a joint venture with a company from Australia. This company could be coded Western, in terms of customs, influences, and practices, or Asian, in terms of geographic location. For Model II, I follow the former approach, as I am interested in testing theories of Western institutional influences, not geographical location. However, changing the coding of the Australian company does not alter the results of the equations in any significant way.

Chapter Eight
The Declining Significance of Connections in China's Economic Transition

1. Seth Faison, "China's Paragon of Corruption: Meet Mr. Chu, a Hero to Some, an Embezzler to Others," *New York Times*, March 6, 1998.

2. Yang (1994) refers to these two institutions throughout her work as *guanxi* and *guanxi xue*; she also refers to the latter term as the "art of *guanxi*." To emphasize to

readers that the latter refers to a specific *practice* that employs *guanxi* (social networks) to exchange favors and gifts (hence "the gift economy" as it is also called by both Yang 1994 and Yan 1996), I refer to *guanxi xue* throughout this chapter as *guanxi practice*, which I have found to be less cumbersome than the "art of *guanxi*." Thus when I use the term *guanxi practice*, I am referring to the specific institution of *guanxi xue* (the gift economy).

3. See Guthrie (1998a).

4. Since Yang's work is the most complete formulation and analysis of the structure and practice of the "art of *guanxi*" in urban areas, my work in this realm engages primarily with her perspectives on the structure and future of *guanxi practice* in China's transforming economy. Yan (1996), Kipnis (1997), and Wilson (1997) also offer extensive analyses of China's "gift economy." These analyses, however, are based on rural China, which is likely to vary significantly from the situation in urban China (Yang 1994). As my work is about urban China, I focus on the arguments surrounding *guanxi* practice as they are laid out by Yang in her book *Gifts, Favors, and Banquets: The Art of Social Relationships in China*. Other important work on the changing nature of social relations in China's reform era can be found in Gold (1985) and Whyte and Parish (1984). There is also a sizable literature on the institutional nature of connections and their centrality in Chinese societies. Although I discuss some of the systematic research in this area (e.g., Bian 1994b, 1997; Yang 1994), I do not discuss the more general business literature (e.g., Xin and Pearce 1996; Wank 1996; Yeung and Tung 1996; Pye 1995; Hui and Graen 1997; Tsui and Fahr 1997). Nevertheless, my research has obvious implications on connections in business negotiations in Chinese society.

5. Yang (1994, 6).

6. For discussion of "increased at an accelerated rate," see Yang (1994, 147); for discussion of "all types of commercial transactions," see Yang (1994, 167).

7. For discussion, see Guthrie (1998a, 39–41).

8. See, for example, Schultz (1990), Whitley et al. (1996), Granovetter (1985), and Uzzi (1996).

9. For discussion, see Burawoy and Lukacs (1985, 723).

10. Bian (1994b, 972).

11. A final weakness of Yang's argument that the importance of *guanxi practice* is accelerating in the economic transition is that the pertinent data were gathered primarily in the 1980s: Although additional data were also gathered during trips in 1990, 1991, 1992, and 1993, according to Yang (1994, 15–16), her "fieldwork on *guanxi xue* took place mainly during [her] two years of residence in Beijing (in 1981–83 and in 1984–85)." Similarly, the data on which studies by Bian (1994b, 1997) are based were gathered in 1988. The problem with basing conclusions about the fate of *guanxi practice* in urban China on data gathered at this time, especially with regard to commercial and industrial economies, is that reforms really only turned to urban areas and specifically to industrial enterprises in 1984 (see Naughton 1995). In other words, Yang conducted her fieldwork either before the reforms turned to urban areas or at the precise time that this shift was beginning to occur. And Bian's research was conducted when the urban reforms were but four years old and organizations had only just begun to implement new bureaucratic structures. It is unreasonable to assume that the reforms of China's transition would have fully taken hold at that nascent stage of the transition. It is a common misconception of economic transitions that reforms are meaningful at the time

the state enacts them. On the contrary, it often takes years for the reforms to become meaningful for economic actors. Nevertheless, it is still remarkable that Yang's experiences depict situations in which the reforms were, in fact, diminishing the importance of *guanxi practice* in the industrial economy, even at this early stage of the transition (see the example of the printing factory discussed in Yang 1994, 167–69).

12. While I make no empirical claims about Yang's vision of Chinese society beyond my discussion of the urban industrial economy, in general I am dubious about the predictions Yang (and Bian) makes about the future of *guanxi practice* in Chinese society. It makes little sense to me, for example, how these rhizomatic networks, which seem to engulf all of society and which "stretch out indefinitely, and result in kaleidoscopic fluidity of social relations" (Fortes 1969, 108; quoted in Yang 1994, 311) fit with the construction of a rational-legal system and the emergence of formal rational bureaucracies at the firm level. My point here is not to question whether social relations are important in Chinese society; they certainly are, just as they are important in all societies. Nor is it to question whether *guanxi* and *guanxi practice* were extremely important in the 1980s. I think Yang's research makes that point clearly. It is simply that I have trouble fitting Yang's (and Bian's) view of the *guanxi*-over-all-else nature of Chinese society with the findings I have presented on the rationalizing (but not fully rational) world of China's urban industrial economy. The construction of a rational-legal system at the state level (this study, chapter 2), the emergence of formal rational bureaucracies at the firm level (this study, chapter 3), and economic agreements in growing markets that push actors to rationalize economic agreements and adopt contracts that rely on rationalized systems (this study, chapter 7) will all have growing implications for the importance of *guanxi* and *guanxi practice* as China's economic transition proceeds.

13. See Yang (1994, 6): "*Guanxi xue* involves the exchange of gifts, favors, and banquets; the cultivation of personal relationships and networks [*guanxi*]" (note that personal relationships and networks are a part of, but not synonymous with *guanxi xue*). According to Gold (1985, 660): "The technique of establishing and manipulating *guanxi* is *guanxi xue*." In Yan's (1996, 98) formulation, "Gift transactions and interpersonal relations are . . . closely related in a dialectical process of social integration"; here "gift transactions" refers to *guanxi xue*, while "interpersonal relations" refers to *guanxi*.

14. See Yang (1994, 58).

15. As I noted above, Yang's own research seems clearly to prove this point.

16. Again, Yang's own examples seem to illustrate this point: In one of her main interviews in the commercial sector, the general manager of a large marketing corporation was reluctant to conduct business with friends and stated clearly that the organization must make decisions which made sense from a business perspective. The manager stated that the firm could not afford to act according to anything other than "pure business principles" for an extended period of time (see Yang 1994, 170).

17. See Yang (1994, 58).

18. It could be argued that the concept of *guanxi* practice is so imbued with negative connotations (Yang 1994, 51–53) that managers would either not admit to having anything to do with the practice or that they would, at least, not be honest regarding their involvement and views surrounding it. Two points are relevant here. First, this is an issue that is always a problem in survey research, even if the method of data collection is in-depth interviewing. However, as Bian (1994b, 984 n. 27) points out, these issues

fare much better when presented and discussed in an in-depth interviewing format. My interviews were conducted this way, and I was careful to present the issues in a way that would make the interviewee least defensive about the topic. Second, if this issue were so deplorable that no one would want to be associated with it, we would not expect any variation on how managers discuss and admit to partaking in *guanxi practice* (no one would admit to it). But, in fact, my data reveal significant variation across the sample of respondents, showing that individuals *will* speak of or admit to partaking in *guanxi practice*.

19. The bivariate association between administrative rank and the use of *guanxi practice* is statistically significant at $p < .01$ (two-tailed test).

20. As I describe in chapter 7, firms at the upper levels of the administrative hierarchy are likely to land joint-venture projects, in part, precisely because they are positioned closely to the municipal bureaus. They land more important projects (because foreign investors rightly assume that approvals will be more likely to occur for ventures with firms at this level of the hierarchy), and, as a result, they have less actual need for the use of *guanxi practice* to push these projects through; they are the types of projects the state would like to see passed in the first place.

21. A problem with Tables 8.1 and 8.2 is that, to some extent, they are based on an ecological fallacy, and thus readers should approach the results of these tables with caution. The dependent variables are individual managers' views, and the independent variables are organizational. The problem here is that individuals' points of view cannot necessarily be taken as a characteristic of the organization; there may be variation across individual attitudes in the organization. Further, the errors here are systematic (nonrandom), as specific individuals within the organization were selected for the interview (by myself and the organization). Inasmuch as the general manager's or vice general manager's view is representative of some type of organizational characteristic (e.g., what the leadership of an organization thinks about a given issue), the findings can be viewed in that light.

22. The importance of a given joint venture for a Chinese firm varies with the size of the firm, as large, powerful firms often have multiple joint-venture relationships. However, even large, powerful firms have one or two joint-venture relationships that are essential to the success of the organization.

23. See DiMaggio and Powell (1983), and chapter 3 of this study.

Chapter Nine
Conclusions and Implications

1. Although there supposedly was a system for being awarded the status of *wenming danwei*, in interview after interview managers and bureaucrats alike informed me that, in practice, these awards were distributed unsystematically by bureau administrators. Needless to say, there was much room for the influence of personal relations within this system.

2. For discussion of the "heavy hand of the state," see Fligstein (1996a, 1075).

3. For discussion of placing too much causal primacy on the state, see Nee (1996).

4. The content depicted here was observed on a banner at the twentieth factory that I visited among those included in the random sample of firms. (Interview 64*, 1995).

5. A recent symposium on economic sociology in the *American Journal of Sociology* was important in this field not only for the substantive contributions (Nee 1996;

Stark 1996; Xie and Hannum 1996) but also for the insightful commentaries provided by a number of scholars (Oberschall 1996; Parish and Michelson 1996; Walder 1996; Fligstein 1996a; Szelényi and Kostello 1996).

6. Other examples of research in this area have broached issues of returns to education in transitional economies (Gerber and Hout 1995; Peng 1992; Xie and Hannum 1996; Hannum and Xie 1994), the emergence of legal institutions (Heydebrand 1996), changing mechanisms of stratification (Domanski and Heyns 1995) and the nature of entrepreneurship (Kennedy and Gianoplus 1994), bargaining relations among organizations in the former Soviet Union, and shop-floor politics (Lee 1995).

7. It should be noted that of those studies mentioned above, the articles of Burawoy and Krutov (1992), Lee (1995), and Stark (1996) do not focus on standard economic indicators. The pattern seems to be that quantitative studies are most often based on economic indicators, whereas qualitative studies are more likely to incorporate a number of different social and political indicators. One point of my research is to show that quantitative studies need not focus solely on income, income inequality, or productivity. As I discuss below, there is an explicit orientation in organizational sociology and in some areas of institutional economics that focuses on the decisions and practices of economic actors. Beyond the patterns of increasing income and productivity, it is also important to study what economic actors do in economic transitions, that is, the decisions and practices they adopt.

8. See Fligstein (1996b).

9. Hence Fligstein's (1996b) metaphor of "markets as politics."

10. For discussion of the shock therapy approach, see Sachs (1995b) and Sachs and Woo (1997). For discussion of the gradual approach, see Rawski (1995), Walder (1994b, 1995a), and Naughton (1995). As I have noted earlier, my argument here about the transformation of firms at the lower levels of China's administrative hierarchy is similar to Walder's (see, especialy, 1995a) argument about the dynamics of growth in rural China. Walder asserts that it is precisely *because* township and village governments are taking a hands-on approach to firm management—with clearer incentives and greater monitoring capacity—that the firms in the rural economy are thriving. The only point at which I differ with Walder is in his argument that slow rates of growth imply a lack of reform. I contend that, in fact, reforms are widespread in slow-growth sectors, but these sectors suffer from the absence of the hands-on approach of gradual reform.

11. Productivity is calculated here as $P = R/E$, where P is productivity, R is the firm's gross revenues, and E is the number of active employees. This measure of productivity is more simplistic than the measures of multi- and total-factor productivity that have been employed in other macroeconomic studies. However, based on the information available in my data set, this measure of productivity is the closest we can come to gauge a firm's efficiency.

12. See *South China Morning Post*, March 1, 1995, 1.

Appendix 1
Methodology and Sampling

1. For an example of this type of survey see, Groves et al. (1994, 1995).

2. As I noted in chapter 1, one remarkable situation I encountered a number of times epitomized the difference between information gathered through state channels and that

gathered independently: In one of my private preliminary interviews, a manager of an industrial firm (Interview 6, 1994) informed me that firms often underreport profits to avoid the income tax (33 percent) that had recently been instituted. In my data set of interviews, I systematically asked managers if the profit figure they had revealed to me was the actual figure for the organization or whether it was deflated as a result of the practice of underreporting profits. In a number of interviews, although the managers were surprised I was aware of this practice, they conceded that the figure did not truly reflect the firm's profits and they amended it accordingly. This information would never have been revealed in a state-sponsored questionnaire.

3. See, for example, Lee (1995), Burawoy (1979), Burawoy and Lukacs (1985), and Burawoy and Krutov (1992).

4. See, for example, Walder (1986a, 1989, 1992b) and Whyte and Parish (1984).

5. The importance of this point should not be underestimated. Although I was able to collect data for two time periods (1990 and 1994), I was not able to gather true time-series data (e.g., specific dates of when a given practice was adopted). Thus, even with statistically significant associations among variables and net effects in multivariate models, I am unable to say for certain which way the causality runs (do the independent variables cause the dependent variables, or vice versa?). For example, in the case of diversification, I have argued that for some firms, economic uncertainty leads to diversification; but the causality could run the other way—it could be that diversification leads to economic uncertainty. The models would show the same associations and effects, but this would be a very different story. Here is where the managers' views on these issues became absolutely crucial for my research. Following the data collection from the questionnaire, I would always return to discuss and clarify issues surrounding different organizational practices. (I tried to conduct these conversations after I had gone through the questionnaire to keep interactions surrounding the questionnaire somewhat consistent across the sample of organizations.) I would ask managers why their firm had decided to invest in the service-sector economy, why the firm had institutionalized labor contracts, why it had adopted the Company Law, or why it had institutionalized grievance-filing procedures. Invariably, these conversations guided the quantitative research, the specific models, and my interpretations of the results. For example, many of the managers who spoke of service-sector diversification discussed it in terms of economic uncertainty; managers of economically weak firms spoke of it in hopeful terms, as a possible way to help their firm survive; and managers of strong firms were disdainful of the practice, pointing out that only the weakest firms would participate in such a practice. It was these conversations and insights, possible only through in-depth interviews, that informed much of my analysis of this practice.

6. See Walder (1989, 247 n. 22). Like the discussion on official questionnaires (above), conversations on hidden profits could never have taken place in the presence of a third party, especially if the individual was a state official.

7. First, a researcher must have a host organization (for visa purposes) if she or he wants to conduct research over an extended period of time. The foreign affairs offices of the organizations are often arms of the Party-state, with the primary purpose of keeping watch over the activities of foreign researchers. They are concerned with the flow of information in and out of China. Second, there is still a conventional understanding—among Chinese and foreign researchers alike—that one needs introductions to get into an organization to talk to managers. Indeed, the first questions central offices

in organizations often asked were, "What organization are you with [*ni shi neige danwei*]?" and "How did you get the phone number to this organization [*ni zemma zhao women zheige danweide dianhua*]?"

8. The bureaus were willing to help with the sampling, but they required that they set up the interviews and send a representative to oversee them, a situation that was unacceptable to me for reasons I have noted above. As a result, I conducted the research without the help of the bureaus.

9. In a few of the early interviews I used a tape recorder, with disastrous results: The rapport and openness in these interviews were so different from those in which I did not use a tape recorder that I stopped the practice immediately. With the Cultural Revolution in relatively recent memory, it is not surprising that Chinese managers were reluctant to have their thoughts and opinions recorded.

10. For discussion of theoretical sampling, see Ragin (1994).

11. See Lubman (1986).

12. Williamson (1986, 142).

13. In the directory, both foods and garments are under the macrosectoral category of "light-industry sector" [*qinggongye*], which makes sense, given that both these sectors are viewed as "low" in terms of asset intensity. The electronics sector should not be confused with the telecommunications equipment sector. These are separate sectors in China, and they operate under very different levels of state control: The electronics sector is under relatively little state control for its level of asset intensity, whereas the telecommunications equipment sector operates under an extremely high level of state control.

14. The title *Directory of Chinese Organizations and Institutions* is the English title as translated on the cover of this directory. The directory was produced and published in 1993 by a special commission (⟨*Zhongguo Qi Shi Ye Ming Lu Quan Shu*⟩ *Bian Wei Hui*).

15. I also cross-checked this assertion with many of the government and organizational informants that were interviewed in the pilot and preliminary stages of the study. The majority of informants did not even know such a directory existed outside the bureaus' own lists, and when I showed them the content and extent of the sector lists, they were not only surprised but also certain that a more complete list of organizations did not exist in Shanghai or anywhere in China. Also, the size of the overall universe of organizations reported in the directory is compatible with the number of Shanghai municipal enterprises reported in the *Statistical Yearbook of Shanghai* (1994, 139), which is 8,948. However, as Aldrich et al. (1988) point out, this type of sampling frame is likely to underrepresent new organizations, an issue that is probably exaggerated in my study, given that the most recent version of the directory I was able to find was published in 1993.

16. It is somewhat difficult to speak of the number of organizations in a given sector within the directory for the following reasons: First, with the reorganization that is occurring across industrial sectors in China, one cannot know exactly how many organizations have been shut down or moved under the jurisdiction of a larger parent company or multidivisional company. Second, some of the factories listed are actually subdivisions of conglomerates or some type of multidivisional corporate organization within the sector. Since the only information given in the directory was the organization's name, address, and phone number, I could not determine which ones were part of

a larger corporate entity until I was personally informed, either on the phone or in the course of the interview. When I learned that the factory was part of a larger multidivisional company, I treated the entity as one multidivisional organizational unit (see Fligstein 1985, 1990) and conducted my interviews with the parent company. In all the interviews across the four sectors, this situation occurred five times.

17. That is, all organizational values—number of employees, fixed assets, turnover, profits, and so on—were treated as the sum of the two organizational parts (the same as a vertically integrated [*lianhe*] factory or a multidivisional company [*jituan gongsi*]).

18. For example, in one case an organization was drawn from the electronics sector, but the organization was actually a trading company that dealt primarily with products in the electronics sector. Although this organization is part of the electronics sector in terms of the broader organizational field as DiMaggio and Powell (1983) define it, it is seen more appropriately as a commerce organization rather than an industrial one, and thus was problematic for comparisons with other industrial organizations. For each of these types of cases, I replaced the "missing organization" with the next organization selected in the data set. Certain situations made it impossible to include a selected organization in the sample. For example, in two cases the factory director agreed to an interview, but when I arrived at the site I learned that only a shell of a factory remained; that is, these factories were no longer industrial factories in the electronics sector but, rather, the factory space had been rented out to any number of small projects operating completely independent of the original factory. In both these cases, the factory had been losing money long enough that the government shut it down, advising the directors to rent out the space. While these two interviews were informative as survival strategies during economic transition, neither was a comparable unit to the other industrial organizations in the sector. Certain other situations made it impossible to contact a selected organization. For example, in one case the head office of an organization was in the process of moving the office to another building. Thus their phone lines were not in place, and no one with whom I spoke knew how to get in touch with the appropriate individuals. Their best advice was that I send them a fax which they would pass on to their head office. I followed their suggestion, but the fax was never answered.

19. For example, Dobbin et al. (1993) had a response rate of 45 percent; Edelman (1992), a response rate of 54 percent.

Appendix 4
Sample Characteristics and Variables

1. Fligstein (1990, 261) defines a "dominant product strategy" as one in which "the firm produced 70 percent or more of its output in a single major industry." Similarly I define dominant production strategy in Chinese industry as one in which a firm concentrated 70 percent or more of its output in a single product.

2. In a few cases, I use the same general model to estimate OLS regression equations.

3. The equation for calculating the ith firm's organizational health is:

$$O_{hi} = \{[T_i - (S_iW_{ai} + .255S_iW_{ai})] - O_{s(avg)}\},$$

where T_i = turnover (gross income), S_i = average salary of workers in the ith organization, and W_{ai} = the number of active workers. The term $(.255S_iW_{ai})$ represents the amount every organization must pay into the new pension fund system [*yanglao jin*]. $O_{s\{avg\}}$ represents the average value for this variable for the ith organization's sector. Including this final term standardizes the value for the sector; this is a necessary step because firms vary by sector in terms of input costs, and, without direct data on input costs, the residual value of an organization's "health" after labor costs is simply less accurate. Organizations that are above average for their sector in terms of organizational health have positive values for this variable, those that are average for their sector have values of zero, and those that are below average in terms of organizational health have negative values for this variable. While this measure is a better overall indicator of an organization's economic health than the employee ratio figure, it is still problematic in that organizations have implemented payment into the new pension system at variable rates. As the pension system is not yet fully operational, some organizations are paying the money into the pension fund *in addition* to paying the full amount to support their retired workers. Thus the variable may, for some organizations, actually underestimate the importance of labor force burdens. Another problem with this term as a measure of organizational health is that it is incomplete: Ideally this equation should, at least, also include measures for costs such as medical insurance for both active and retired employees—a factor that has not yet been shifted to a general social system. The full equation should be $O_{hi} = \{T_i - [(S_iW_{ai} + .255S_iW_{ai}) + (M_iW_{ai} + W_{ri})] - O_{s\{avg\}}\}$, where M_i = average cost of medical insurance for workers and W_{ri} = the number of retired workers. Although I did collect data on each firm's average cost of medical insurance, the data were too sparse—and I had little confidence in the data factory managers provided for this parameter (many could only offer guesses, as the organizations often did not keep accurate figures on this)—for the parameter to be included in this variable.

4. While the organizational health variable may be the better overall measure of wage burdens than the employee ratio measure, the problem with that measure is that the pension system is a completely new system. Since we are dealing with the period of the past five to ten years (the time when organizations started adopting different practices), the employee ratio may tell us more about the burdens an organization has experienced during the period that is most salient for the dependent variables. In addition, many managers in the Chinese industrial economy believe that the burden of retired workers is the largest problem industrial organizations face; this variable examines the effect of that burden directly.

References

Cited Laws and Resolutions of the People's Republic of China

People's Republic of China [*Zhonghua renmin gongheguo*]. 1979a. "Law of the People's Republic of China on Chinese-Equity Joint Ventures." Adopted July 1, 1979, at the Second Session of the Fifth National People's Congress.

————. 1979b. "Resolution of the Standing Committee of the National People's Congress Authorizing Provinces, Autonomous Regions, and Municipalities Directly under the Central Government to Establish Standing Committees of People's Congresses and Change Revolutionary Committees to People's Governments in 1979." Adopted September 13, 1979, at the Eleventh Meeting of the Fifth National People's Congress.

————. 1981a. "Economic Contract Law of the People's Republic of China." Adopted on December 13, 1981, at the Fourth Session of the Fifth National People's Congress.

————. 1981b. "Resolution of the Standing Committee of the National People's Congress Authorizing the People's Congresses of Guangdong and Fujian Provinces and Their Standing Committees to Formulate Separate Economic Regulations for Their Respective Special Economic Zones." Adopted November 26, 1981.

————. 1983a. "Notice of the Ministry of Labor and Personnel on Active Trial Implementation of the Contract Employment System" [*Laodong renshi bu guanyu jiji shixing laodong hetong zhide tongzhi*]. *State Council Gazette* 6:213.

————. 1983b. "Decision of the Standing Committee of the National People's Congress on Authorizing the State Council to Make Partial Amendments and Supplements to the Measures Concerning the Retirement and Resignation of Staff Members and Workers." Adopted September 2, 1983.

————. 1984a. "Decision of the Standing Committee of the National People's Congress on Authorizing the State Council to Reform the System of Industrial and Commercial Taxes and Issue Relevant Draft Tax Regulations for Trial Application." Adopted September 18, 1984, at the Seventh Meeting of the Standing Committee of the Sixth National People's Congress.

————. 1984b. "Patent Law of the People's Republic of China." Adopted at the Fourth Meeting of the National People's Congress, promulgated by Order No. 11 of the President of the People's Republic of China on March 12, 1984, and effective as of April 1, 1985.

————. 1985a. "Accounting Law of the People's Republic of China." Adopted at the Ninth Meeting of the Standing People's Committee of the Sixth National People's Congress, promulgated by Order No. 21 of the President of the People's Republic of China on January 21, 1985, and effective as of May 1, 1985.

————. 1985b. "Law of the People's Republic of China on Economic Contracts Involving Foreign Interest." Adopted at the Tenth Session of the Standing Committee of the Sixth National People's Congress, promulgated by Order No. 22 of the President of the People's Republic of China on March 21, 1985, and effective as of July 1, 1985.

People's Republic of China. 1986a. "Provisional Regulations on the Implementation of the Contract Employment System in State Enterprises" [*Guoying qiye shixing laodong hetong zhanxing guiding*]. Promulgated by the State Council on July 12, 1986, effective October 1, 1986.

———. 1986b. "Provisional Regulations on the Dismissal of Workers and Staff for Work Violations in State Enterprises" [*Guoying qiye citui weiji zhigong zanxing guiding*]. Promulgated by the State Council on July 12, 1986, effective October 1, 1986.

———. 1986c. "Provisional Regulations on the Hiring of Workers in State Enterprises" [*Guoying qiye zhaoyong gongren zhanxing guiding*]. Promulgated by the State Council on July 12, 1986, effective October 1, 1986.

———. 1986d. "Law of the People's Republic of China on Enterprise Bankruptcy." Adopted at the Eighteenth Meeting of the Standing Committee of the Sixth National People's Congress and promulgated by Order No. 45 of the President of the People's Republic of China on December 2, 1986, for trial implementation for a period of three months after the Law on Industrial Enterprises with Ownership by the Whole People comes into effect.

———. 1987. "Law of the People's Republic of China on Technology Contracts." Adopted at the Twenty-First Meeting of the Standing Committee of the Sixth National People's Congress, promulgated by Order No. 53 of the President of the People's Republic of China on June 23, 1987, and effective as of November 1, 1987.

———. 1988a. "Law of the People's Republic of China on Industrial Enterprises Owned by the Whole People." Adopted at the First Session of the Seventh National People's Congress, promulgated by Order No. 3 of the President of the People's Republic of China on April 13, 1988, and effective as of August 1, 1988.

———. 1988b. "Law of the People's Republic of China on Chinese-Foreign Contractual Joint Ventures." Adopted at the First Session of the Seventh National People's Congress and promulgated by Order No. 4 of the President of the People's Republic of China on April 13, 1988.

———. 1992. "Law of the People's Republic of China on the Administration of Tax Collection." Adopted at the Twenty-Seventh Meeting of the Standing Committee of the Seventh National People's Congress on September 4, 1992, promulgated by Order No. 60 of the President of the People's Republic of China on September 4, 1992, and effective as of January 1, 1993.

———. 1993. "The Company Law of the People's Republic of China." Adopted at the Fifth Meeting of the Standing Committee of the Eighth National People's Congress on December 12, 1993, and effective as of July 1, 1994.

———. 1994. "The Labor Law of the People's Republic of China." Adopted at the Eighth Meeting of the Standing Committee of the National People's Congress on July 5, 1994, and effective as of January 1, 1995.

———. 1995a. "The National Compensation Law of the People's Republic of China." Adopted at the Seventh Meeting of the Standing Committee of the Eighth National People's Congress on May 5, 1994, and effective as of January 1, 1995.

———. 1995b. "Law of the People's Republic of China on Commercial Banking." Adopted at the Thirteenth Meeting of the Standing Committee of the Eighth National People's Congress on May 10, 1995 and effective as of July 7, 1995.

Other Sources

Aldrich, Howard. 1979. *Organizations and Environments*. Englewood Cliffs, NJ: Prentice-Hall.

Aldrich, Howard, Arne Kalleberg, Peter Marsden, and James Cassell. 1988. "In Pursuit of Evidence: Sampling Procedures for Locating New Businesses." *Journal of Business Venturing* 4:367–86.

Aldrich, Howard, and Jeffrey Pfeffer. 1976. "Environments and Organizations." *Annual Review of Sociology* 2:79–105.

Ali, Mubarik, and John C. Flinn. 1989. "Profit Efficiency Among Basmati Rice Producers in Pakistan Punjab." *American Journal of Agricultural Economics* (May 1989): 303–10.

Anderlini, L., and A. Ianni. 1996. "Path Dependence and Learning from Neighbors." *Games and Economic Behavior* 13 (2): 141–77.

Balmann, A., M. Odening, H. Weikard, and W. Brandes. 1996. "Path Dependence Without Increasing Returns to Scale and Network Externalities." *Journal of Economic Behavior and Organization* 29 (1): 159–72.

Bardhan, Pranab. 1984. *Land, Labor, and Rural Poverty: Essays in Development Economics*. Delhi: Oxford University Press.

Bell, Clive. 1989. "A Comparison of Principal-Agent and Bargaining Solutions: The Case of Tenancy Contracts." In *The Economic Theory of Agrarian Institutions*, edited by Pranab Bardhan, pp. 73–92 . Oxford: Clarendon.

Bian, Yanjie. 1994a. *Work and Inequality in Urban China*. Albany, NY: State University of New York Press.

———. 1994b. "*Guanxi* and the Allocation of Urban Jobs in China." *China Quarterly* 140:971–99.

———. 1997. "Bringing Strong Ties Back In: Indirect Ties, Network Bridges, and Job Searches in China." *American Sociological Review* 62:366–85.

Bian, Yanjie, and S. Ang. 1997. "*Guanxi* Networks and Job Mobility in China and Singapore." *Social Forces* 75 (3): 981–1005.

Bian, Yanjie, and John R. Logan. 1996. "Market Transition and the Persistence of Power: The Changing Stratification System in Urban China." *American Sociological Review* 61:739–58.

Blanchard, Oliver, Maxin Boycho, Marek Dabrowski, Rudiger Dorubusch, Richard Layard, and Andrei Shleifer. 1993. *Post Communist Reform: Pain and Progress*. Cambridge, MA: MIT Press.

Blau, Peter M. 1968. "The Hierarchy of Authority in Organizations." *American Journal of Sociology* 73:453–67.

Brinton, Mary C., Yean-Ju Lee, and William L. Parish. 1995. "Married Women's Employment in Rapidly Industrializing Societies: Examples from East Asia." *American Journal of Sociology* 100:1099–1130.

Brooks, Clem, and Jeff Manza. 1997. "The Social and Ideological Bases of Middle-Class Political Realignment in the United States, 1972 to 1992." *American Sociological Review* 62:191–208.

Burawoy, Michael. 1979. *Manufacturing Consent: Changes in the Labor Process under Monopoly Capitalism*. Chicago: University of Chicago Press.

Burawoy, Michael. 1985. *Politics of Production: Factory Regimes under Capitalism and Socialism*. London, England: Verso.

Burawoy, Michael, and János Lukacs. 1985. "Mythologies of Work: A Comparison of Firms in State Socialism and Advanced Capitalism." *American Sociological Review* 50:723–37.

Burawoy, Michael, and Pavel Krutov. 1992. "The Soviet Transition from Socialism to Capitalism: Worker Control and Economic Bargaining in the Wood Industry." *American Sociological Review* 57:16–38.

Cabestan, Jean-Pierre. 1995. "Review of *The Economic Transformation of South China: Reform and Development in the Post-Mao Era*, edited by Thomas P. Lyons and Victor Nee. *China Quarterly* 143:889–90.

Chandler, Alfred. 1962. *Strategy and Structure*. Cambridge, MA: MIT Press.

Chang, Jesse T. H., and Charles J. Conroy. 1987. "Trademark Law in the People's Republic of China." In *Foreign Trade, Investment, and the Law in the People's Republic of China*, edited by Michael J. Moser, pp. 427–52. New York: Oxford University Press.

Chen, Kuan, Wang Hongchang, Zheng Yuxin, Gary H. Jefferson, and Thomas G. Rawski. 1988. "Productivity Change in Chinese Industry: 1953–1985." *Journal of Comparative Economics* 12:570–91.

Cheng, Lucie, and Arthur Rosett. 1991. "Contract with a Chinese Face: Socially Embedded Factors in the Transformation from Hierarchy to Market, 1978–1989." *Journal of Chinese Law* 5:143–244.

China International Economic and Trade Arbitration Commission [CIETAC]. 1994. *Arbitration Rules*. Beijing.

Chinese Directory of Organizations and Institutions Publishing Committee [*Zhongguo qi shi ye ming lu quan shu bian wei hui*]. 1993. *Chinese Directory of Organizations and Institutions* [*Zhongguo qi shi ye ming lu quan shu*]. Beijing.

Christiansen, Flemming. 1992. "Market Transition in China: The Case of the Jiangsu Labor Market, 1978–1990." *Modern China* 18:72–93.

Clarke, Donald C. 1991. "Dispute Resolution in China." *Journal of Chinese Law* 5:245–96.

Cooper, Russell W. 1987. *Wage Employment Patterns in Labor Contracts: Microfoundations and Macroeconomic Implications*. New York: Harwood.

Curtis, Russell L., and Louise A. Zurcher Jr. 1973. "Stable Resources of Protest Movement: The Multi-organizational Field." *Social Forces* 52:53–60.

De Janvry, Alain. 1983. *The Agrarian Question and Reformism in Latin America*. Baltimore, MD: The Johns Hopkins University Press.

DiMaggio, Paul. 1983. "State Expansion and Organizational Fields." In *Organizational Theory and Public Policy*, edited by Richard H. Hall and Robert E. Quinn, pp. 147–61. Beverly Hills: Sage.

———. 1988. "Interest and Agency in Institutional Theory." In *Institutional Patterns and Organizations: Culture and Environment*, edited by Lynne Zucker, pp. 3–22. Cambridge: Ballinger.

———. 1991. "Constructing an Organizational Field as a Professional Project: U.S. Art Museums, 1920–1940." In *The New Institutionalism in Organizational Analysis*, edited by Walter W. Powell and Paul DiMaggio, pp. 267–92. Chicago: University of Chicago Press.

DiMaggio, Paul, and Walter Powell. 1983 [1991]. "The Iron Cage Revisited: Institutional Isomorphism and Collective Rationality in Organizational Fields." *American Sociological Review* 48:147–61.

———. 1991. "Introduction." In *The New Institutionalism in Organizational Analysis*, edited by Walter W. Powell and Paul DiMaggio, pp. 1–38. Chicago: University of Chicago Press.

Dobbin, Frank, John R. Sutton, John W. Meyer, and W. Richard Scott. 1993. "Equal Opportunity Law and the Construction of Internal Labor Markets." *American Journal of Sociology* 99:396–427.

Doeringer, Peter, and Michael Piore. 1971. *Internal Labor Markets and Manpower Analysis*. Lexington, MA: Heath.

Domanski, Henryk, and Barbara Heyns. 1995. "Toward a Theory of the Role of the State in Market Transition: From Bargaining to Markets in Post-Communism." *European Journal of Sociology* 36:317–51.

Dutta, Bhaskar, Debraj Ray, and Kunal Sengupta. 1989. "Contracts with Eviction in Infinitely Repeated Principal-Agent Relationships." In *The Economic Theory of Agrarian Institutions*, edited by Pranab Bardhan, pp. 93–121. Oxford: Clarendon.

Eccles, Robert G., and Harrison C. White. 1988. "Price and Authority in Inter-Profit Center Transactions." *American Journal of Sociology* 94 (Supplement): S17–S51.

Edelman, Lauren B. 1990. "Legal Environments and Organizational Governance: The Expansion of Due Process in the American Workplace." *American Journal of Sociology* 95:1401–40.

———. 1992. "Legal Ambiguity and Symbolic Structures: Organizational Mediation of Civil Rights Law." *American Journal of Sociology* 97:1531–76.

———. 1996. "Constructed Legalities: The Endogeneity of Law." Manuscript. Center for the Study of Law and Society, University of California, Berkeley.

Ericson, Richard E. 1991. "The Classical Soviet-Type Economy: Nature of the System and Implications for Reform." *Journal of Economic Perspectives* 5 (4): 11–27.

Eswaran, Mukesh, and Ashok Katwol. 1985a. "A Theory of Contractual Structure in Agriculture." *American Economic Review* 75:352–68.

———. 1985b. "A Theory of Two-Tier Labor Markets in Agrarian Economies." *American Economic Review* 75:162–78.

Evans, Peter. 1995. *Embedded Autonomy: States and Industrial Transformation*. Princeton, NJ: Princeton University Press.

Evans, Peter, Dietrich Rueschemeyer, and Theda Skocpol. 1985. *Bringing the State Back In*. Cambridge: Cambridge University Press.

Fabel, Oliver. 1990. *Insurance and Incentives in Labor Contracts: A Study in the Theory of Implicit Contracts*. Frankfurt, Germany: Anton Hain.

Fairbank, John King. 1992. *China: A New History*. Cambridge, MA: Belknap Press of Harvard University Press.

Faison, Seth. 1998. "China's Paragon of Corruption: Meet Mr. Chu, a Hero to Some, an Embezzler to Others." *New York Times*, March 6.

Field, Robert M. 1984. "Changes in Chinese Industry Since 1978." *China Quarterly* 100:742–61.

———. 1992. "China's Industrial Performance Since 1978." *China Quarterly* 131:577–607.

Fiorina, Morris. 1995. "Rational Choice and the New(?) Institutionalism." *Polity* 28:107–15.

Fischer, Claude, Michael Hout. Martin Sanchez Jankowski, Samuel Lucas, Ann Swidler, and Kim Voss. 1996. *Inequality by Design: Cracking the Bell Curve Myth.* Princeton, NJ: Princeton University Press.

Fischer, Stanley. 1992. "Privatization in Eastern European Transformation." In *The Emergence of Market Economies in Eastern Europe*, edited by Christopher Clague and Gordon C. Rausser, pp. 227–43. Cambridge, MA: Blackwell.

Fligstein, Neil. 1985. "The Spread of the Multidivisional Form Among Large Firms, 1919–1979." *American Sociological Review* 50:377–91.

———. 1987. "The Intraorganizational Power Struggle: Rise of Finance Personnel to Top Leadership in Large Corporations, 1919–1979." *American Sociological Review* 52:44–58.

———. 1990. *The Transformation of Corporate Control.* Cambridge, MA: Harvard University Press.

———. 1991. "The Structural Transformation of American Industry: An Institutional Account of the Causes of Diversification in the Largest Firms, 1919–1979." In *The New Institutionalism in Organizational Analysis*, edited by Walter W. Powell and Paul DiMaggio, pp. 311–36. Chicago: University of Chicago Press.

———. 1995. "Networks of Power or the Finance Conception of Control? Comment on Palmer, Barber, Zhou, and Soysal." *American Sociological Review* 60:500–503.

———. 1996a. "The Economic Sociology of the Transitions from Socialism." *American Journal of Sociology* 101:1074–81.

———. 1996b. "Markets as Politics: A Sociological View of Market Institutions." *American Sociological Review* 61:656–73.

———. 1996c. "Social Skill and Institutional Theory." *American Behavioral Scientist* 40:397–40.

Fligstein, Neil, and Peter Brantley. 1992. "Bank Control, Owner Control, or Organizational Dynamics: Who Controls the Large Modern Corporation?" *American Journal of Sociology* 98:280–307.

Fligstein, Neil, and Robert Freeland. 1995. "Theoretical and Comparative Perspectives on Corporate Organization." *Annual Review of Sociology* 21:21–43.

Fligstein, Neil, and Iona Mara-Drita. 1996. "How to Make a Market: Reflections on the Attempt to Make a Single Market in Western Europe." *American Journal of Sociology* 102:1–33.

Fortes, Meyer. 1969. *Kinship and the Social Order.* Chicago: Aldine.

Frideman, Milton, and Rose Friedman. 1979 [1990]. *Free to Choose: A Personal Statement.* San Diego, CA: Harcourt Brace.

Gelatt, Timothy A., and Richard D. Pomp. 1987. "China's Tax System: An Overview and Transactional Analysis." In *Foreign Trade, Investment, and the Law in the People's Republic of China*, edited by Michael J. Moser, pp. 42–89. New York: Oxford University Press.

Gerber, Theodore P., and Michael Hout. 1995. "Educational Stratification in Russia During the Soviet Period." *American Journal of Sociology* 101:611–60.

Gerlach, Michael L. 1992. *Alliance Capitalism: The Social Organization of Japanese Business.* Berkeley: University of California Press.

Gold, Thomas B. 1980. "Back to the City: The Return of Shanghai's Educated Youth." *China Quarterly* 84:55–70.

———. 1985. "After Comradeship: Personal Relations in China Since the Cultural Revolution." *China Quarterly* 104:657–75.

———. 1990. "Urban Private Business and Social Change." In *Chinese Society on the Eve of Tiananmen: The Impact of Reform*, edited by Deborah Davis and Ezra F. Vogel, pp. 157–78. Cambridge, MA: Harvard University Press.

———. 1991. "Urban Private Business and China's Reforms." In *Reform and Reaction in Post-Mao China: The Road to Tiananmen*, edited by Richard Baum, pp. 84–103. New York: Routledge.

Gort, M. 1962. *Diversification and Integration in American Industry*. Princeton, NJ: Princeton University Press.

———. 1984. *Diversification and Integration in American Industry*. Westport, CT: Greenwood.

Gouldner, Alvin W. 1959. "Organizational Analysis." In *Sociology Today*, edited by Robert K. Merton, Leonard Broom, and Leonard S Cottrell Jr., pp. 400–428. New York: Basic Books.

Granick, David. 1990. *Chinese State Enterprises: A Regional Property Rights Analysis*. Chicago: University of Chicago Press.

Granovetter, Mark. 1985. "Economic Action and Social Structure: The Problem of Embeddedness." *American Journal of Sociology* 91:481–510.

Gross, Edward. 1953. "Some Functional Consequences of Primary Controls in Formal Work Organizations." *American Sociological Review* 18:368–73.

Groves, Theodore, Yongmiao Hong, John McMillan, and Barry Naughton. 1994. "Autonomy and Incentives in Chinese State Enterprises." *Quarterly Journal of Economics* 109 (1): 193–209.

———. 1995. "China's Evolving Managerial Labor Market." *Journal of Political Economy* 103:873–92.

Guo, Jiann-Jong. 1992. *Price Reform in China, 1979–86*. Basingstoke, England: St. Martin's.

Guthrie, Doug. 1996. "Organizational Action and Institutional Reforms in China's Economic Transition: A Comparison of Two Industries." *Research in the Sociology of Organizations* 14:181–222.

———. 1997. "Between Markets and Politics: Organizational Responses to Reform in China." *American Journal of Sociology* 102 (5): 1258–1303.

———. 1998a. "The Declining Significance of *Guanxi* in China's Economic Transition." *China Quarterly* 154 (June): 31–62.

———. 1998b. "Organizational Uncertainty and the End of Lifetime Employment in China." *Sociological Forum* (September).

Hage, J., and M. Aiken. 1969. "Routine Technology, Social Structure, and Organizational Goals." *Administrative Science Quarterly* 14:366–76.

Hannan, Michael, and John Freeman. 1977. "The Population Ecology of Organizations." *American Journal of Sociology* 82:929–64.

Hannum, Emily, and Yu Xie. 1994. "Trends in Educational and Gender and Inequality in China." *Research in Social Stratification and Mobility* 13:73–98.

Hamilton, Gary, and Robert Feenstra. 1994. "Varieties of Hierarchies and Markets: An

Introduction." Paper presented at the American Sociological Association Annual Meetings, August 5–9, Los Angeles, CA.

Hamilton, Gary, and Nicole Woolsey Biggart. 1988. "Market, Culture, and Authority: A Comparative Analysis of Management and Organization in the Far East." *American Journal of Sociology* 94:S52–S94.

Heydebrand, Wolf. 1996. "The Dynamics of Legal Change in Eastern Europe." *Studies in Law, Politics, and Society* 15:263–313.

Hoff, Karla, and Joseph E. Stiglitz. 1990. "Introduction: Imperfect Information and Rural Credit Markets—Puzzles and Policy Perspectives." *World Bank Economic Review* 4 (3): 235–50.

Huang, Laiji, and Zhou Jingen, eds. 1994. *Gongsifa huiyi yu zujian gongsifa jingyan* [Answers to questions regarding the Company Law and the experience of constructing the Company Law]. Beijing: *Shijie tuanti chuban gongsi* [World Group Publishing Company].

Huang, Ruicai, and Xiaowen Cong. 1994. *Xiandai qiye caichan guanli* [Managing property in the modern enterprise]. Jinan: Jinan University Press.

Hui, C., and G. Graen. 1997. "*Guanxi* and Professional Leadership in Contemporary Sino-American Joint Ventures in Mainland China." *Leadership Quarterly* 8 (4): 451–65.

Jefferson, Gary H., and Thomas Rawski. 1994. "Enterprise Reform in Chinese Industry." *Journal of Economic Perspectives* 8 (2): 47–70.

Jefferson, Gary H., and Wenyi Xu. 1991. "The Impact of Reform on Socialist Enterprises in Transition: Structure, Conduct, and Performance in Chinese Industry." *Journal of Comparative Economics* 15:45–64.

Jepperson, Ronald L. 1991. "Institutions, Institutional Effects, and Institutionalism." In *The New Institutionalism in Organizational Analysis*, edited by Walter W. Powell and Paul DiMaggio, pp. 143–63. Chicago: University of Chicago Press.

Johnson, Chalmers. 1987. "Political Institutions and Economic Performance: The Government-Business Relationship in Japan, South Korea, and Taiwan." In *The Political Economy of the New Asian Industrialism*, edited by Frederic C. Deyo, pp. 136–64. Ithaca, NY: Cornell University Press.

Jones, William. 1994. "The Provenance and History of the Civil Code of 1929." Paper presented at the conference on China's Mid-Century Transitions, Fairbank Center for East Asian Research, Harvard University, September 8–10.

Josephs, Hilary K. 1989. *Labor Law in China: Choice and Responsibility*. Chatswood, Australia: Butterworth Legal Publishers.

Kalleberg, Arne L., David Knoke, Peter V. Marsden, and Joe L. Spaeth. 1996. *Organizations in America: Analyzing Their Structures and Human Resource Practices*. Thousand Oaks, CA: Sage.

Kalleberg, Arne L., and Mark E. Van Buren. 1996. "Is Bigger Better? Explaining the Relationship Between Organization Size and Job Rewards." *American Sociological Review* 61:47–66.

Kamm, John. 1989. "Reforming Foreign Trade." In *One Step Ahead in China: Guangdong under Reform*, Ezra Vogel, pp. 338–92. Cambridge, MA: Harvard University Press.

Kennedy, Michael D., and Pauline Gianoplus. 1994. "Entrepreneurs and Expertise: A

Cultural Encounter in the Making of Post-Communist Capitalism in Poland." *East European Politics and Societies* 8 (1): 58–93.

Kipnis, Andrew. 1997. *Producing Guanxi: Sentiment, Self, and Subculture in a North China Village*. Durham, NC: Duke University Press.

Kirby, William C. 1995. "China Unincorporated: Company Law and Business Enterprise in Twentieth-Century China." *Journal of Asian Studies* 54:43–63.

Kornai, János. 1980. *The Shortage Economy*. Amsterdam: North-Holland.

———. 1990. *The Road to a Free Economy*. New York: Norton.

Krug, Barbara. 1994. Review of "Price Reform in China, 1979–86," by Jiann-Jong Guo (Basingstoke, England: St. Martin's). *China Quarterly* 138:528–30.

Lardy, Nicholas R. 1992. *Foreign Trade and Economic Reform in China, 1978–1990*. New York: Cambridge University Press.

Lee, Ching Kwan. 1995. "Engendering the Worlds of Labor: Women Workers, Labor Markets, and Production Politics in the South China Economic Miracle." *American Sociological Review* 60:378–97.

Li, Cetao. 1993. *Gufen zhi lilun yu qiye gai zhi zao zuo* [The system and theory of stocks and enterprise reform]. Shanghai: Fudan University Press.

Li, Yushan. 1992. *Socialism and National Development: Reform and Development* [*Shehui zhuyi guojia jingji: gaige yu fazhan gongcheng*]. Dalian: Ligong University Press.

Lieberthal, Kenneth. 1995. *Governing China: From Revolution Through Reform*. New York: W. W. Norton.

Lin, Nan. 1995. "Market Socialism and Local Corporatism in Action in Rural China." *Theory and Society* 24:301–54.

Lin, Nan, and Bian Yanjie. 1991. "Getting Ahead in Urban China." *American Journal of Sociology* 97:657–88.

Lomborg, Bjorn. 1996. "Nucleus and Shield: The Evolution of Social Structure in the Iterated Prisoner's Dilemma." *American Sociological Review* 61:278–307.

Lu, Xiaobo, and Elizabeth Perry, eds. 1997. *Danwei: The Changing Chinese Workplace in Historical and Comparative Perspective*. Armonk, NY: M. E. Sharpe.

Lubman, Stanley. 1986. *China's Economy Looks Toward the Year 2000*, Vol. 1: *The Four Modernizations*, edited by the Joint Economic Committee. Washington, D.C.: Government Printing Office.

———. 1987. "Technology Transfer in China: Policies, Law, and Practice." In *Foreign Trade, Investment, and the Law in the People's Republic of China*, edited by Michael J. Moser, pp. 170–98. New York: Oxford University Press.

———. 1995. "Introduction: The Future of Chinese Law." *China Quarterly* 141:1–21.

Lubman, Stanley B., and Gregory C. Wajnowski. 1993. "International Commercial Dispute Resolution in China: A Practical Assessment." *American Review of International Arbitration* 4:107–78.

Luffman, George A., and Richard Reed. 1984. *The Strategy and Performance of British Industry, 1970–80*. New York: St. Martin's.

Luo, Xiaopeng. 1990. "Ownership and Status Stratification." In *China's Rural Industry: Structure, Development, and Reform*, edited by William A. Byrd and Lin Qingsong, pp. 134–71. New York: Oxford University Press.

Lyons, Thomas, and Victor Nee, eds. 1994. *The Economic Transformation of Rural China*. Ithaca, NY: The East Asian Program of Cornell University.

March, James G., and Herbert A. Simon. 1958. *Organizations*. New York: Wiley.

March, James G., and J. Olsen. 1989. *Rediscovering Institutions*. New York: Free Press.

Marsden, Peter V. 1994 "Selection Methods in U.S. Establishments." *Acta Sociologica* 37:287–301.

Marsden, Peter V., Cynthia R. Cook, and Arne L. Kallenberg. 1994. "Organizational Structures: Coordination and Control." *The American Behavioral Scientist* 37:911–29.

McKinnon, Ronald. 1992. "Taxation, Money, and Credit in a Liberalizing Socialist Economy." In *The Emergence of Market Economies in Eastern Europe*, edited by Christopher Clague and Gordon C. Rausser, pp. 109–127. Cambridge, MA: Blackwell.

Meyer, John W. 1977. "The Effects of Education as an Institution." *American Journal of Sociology* 83:53–77.

Meyer, John W., and Brian Rowan. 1977. "Institutionalized Organizations: Formal Structure as Myth and Ceremony." *American Journal of Sociology* 83:340–63.

Moser, Michael J. 1987. "Foreign Investment in China: The Legal Framework." In *Foreign Trade, Investment, and the Law in the People's Republic of China*, edited by Michael J. Moser, pp. 90–169. New York: Oxford University Press.

Mueller, D. 1997. "First-Mover Advantages and Path Dependence." *International Journal of Industrial Organization* 15 (6): 827–50.

Murphy, Michael. 1993. "Competition under the Laws Governing Soviet Producer Co-operatives During Peristroika." In *Capitalist Goals, Socialist Past: The Rise of the Private Sector in Command Economies*, edited by Perry L. Patterson, pp. 147–67. Boulder, CO: Westview.

Murrell, Peter. 1990. *The Nature of Socialist Economies: Lessons from Eastern Europe Foreign Trade*. Princeton, NJ: Princeton University Press.

———. 1992. "Evolution in Economics and in the Economic Reform of the Centrally Planned Economies." In *The Emergence of Market Economies in Eastern Europe*, edited by Christopher Clague and Gordon C. Rausser, pp. 35–53. Cambridge, MA: Blackwell.

Naughton, Barry. 1992. "Hierarchy and the Bargaining Economy: Government and Enterprise in the Reform Process." In *Bureaucracy, Politics, and Decision Making in Post-Mao China*, edited by Kenneth G. Lieberthal and David M. Lampton, pp. 245–79. Berkeley: University of California Press.

———. 1993. "Deng Xiaoping: The Economist." *China Quarterly* 135:491–512.

———. 1994. "What Is Distinctive about China's Economic Transition? State Enterprise Reform and Overall System Transformation." *Journal of Comparative Economics* 18:470–90.

———. 1995. *Growing Out of the Plan: Chinese Economic Reform 1978–1993*. New York: Cambridge University Press.

Nee, Victor. 1989a. "A Theory of Market Transition: From Redistribution to Markets in State Socialism." *American Sociological Review* 54:663–81.

———. 1989b. "Peasant Entrepreneurship and the Politics of Regulation in China." In *Remaking the Economic Institutions of Socialism: China and Eastern Europe*, edited by Victor Nee and David Stark, pp. 169–207. Stanford: Stanford University Press.

———. 1991. "Social Inequalities in Reforming State Socialism: Between Redistribution and Markets in China." *American Sociological Review* 56:267–82.

———. 1992. "Organizational Dynamics of Market Transition: Hybrid Forms, Property Rights, and Mixed Economy in China." *Administrative Science Quarterly* 37: 1–27.

———. 1996. "The Emergence of a Market Society: Changing Mechanisms of Stratification in China." *American Journal of Sociology* 101:908–49.

Nee, Victor, and Yang Cao. 1997. "Stratification in Path Dependent Societal Transformation." Unpublished manuscript.

Nee, Victor, and Rebecca Matthews. 1996. "Market Transition and Societal Transformation in Reforming State Socialism." *Annual Review of Sociology* 22:401–35.

North, Douglass C. 1990. *Institutions, Institutional Change, and Economic Performance.* New York: Cambridge University Press.

Oberschall, Anthony. 1996. "The Great Transition: China, Hungary, and Sociology Exit Socialism into the Market." *American Journal of Sociology* 101:1028–41.

Oi, Jean C. 1989. *State and Peasant in Contemporary China: The Political Economy of Village and Government.* Berkeley: University of California Press.

———. 1992. "Fiscal Reform and the Economic Foundations of Local State Corporatism." *World Politics* 45:99–126.

———. 1995. "The Role of the Local State in China's Transitional Economy." *China Quarterly* 144:1132–49.

Orrù, Marco, Nicole Woolsey Biggart, and Gary G. Hamilton. 1991. "Organizational Isomorphism in East Asia." In *The New Institutionalism in Organizational Analysis*, edited by Walter W. Powell and Paul DiMaggio, pp. 361–89. Chicago: University of Chicago Press.

Palmer, Michael. "The Re-emergence of Family Law in Post-Mao China: Marriage, Divorce, and Reproduction." *China Quarterly* 141:110–34.

Parish, William L., and Ethan Michelson. 1996. "Politics and Markets: Dual Transformations." *American Journal of Sociology* 4:1042–59.

Parker, Elliott. 1995. "Shadow Factor Price Convergence and the Response of Chinese State-Owned Construction Enterprises to Reform. *Journal of Comparative Economics* 21:54–81.

Pei, Minxin. 1994. *From Reform to Revolution: The Demise of Communism in China and the Soviet Union.* Cambridge, MA: Harvard University Press.

———. 1997. "Citizens v. Mandarins: Administrative Litigation in China." *China Quarterly* 152:832–62.

———. 1998. "Is China Democratizing?" *Foreign Affairs* (January/February): 68–82.

Peng, Yusheng. 1992. "Wage Determination in Rural and Urban China: A Comparison of Public and Private Industrial Sectors." *American Sociological Review* 57:198–213.

Pfeffer, Jeffrey, and Gerald Salancik. 1978. *The External Control of Organizations: A Resource Dependence Perspective.* New York: Harper and Row.

Perrow, Charles. 1967. "A Framework for the Comparative Analysis of Organizations." *American Sociological Review* 32:194–208.

———. 1991. "A Society of Organizations." *Theory and Society* 20:725–62.

Petersen, Trond. 1994. "On the Promise of Game Theory in Sociology." *Contemporary Sociology* 23 (4): 498–502.

Pfeffer, Jeffrey, and Gerald R. Salancik. 1978. *The External Control of Organizations.* New York: Harper and Row.

Polanyi, Karl. 1957. *The Great Transformation: The Political and Economic Origins of Our Time.* Boston: Beacon.

Potter, Pitman B. 1994. "Riding the Tiger: Legitimacy and Legal Culture in Post-Mao China." *China Quarterly* 138:325–58.

Powell, Walter W., and Paul DiMaggio, eds. 1991. *The New Institutionalism in Organizational Analysis.* Chicago: University of Chicago Press.

Pye, Lucian. 1995. "Factions and the Politics of *Guanxi*: Paradoxes in Chinese Administrative and Political Behaviour." *China Journal* 34:35–53.

Ragin, Charles C. 1994. *Constructing Social Research: The Unity and Diversity of Method.* Thousand Oaks, CA: Pine Forge.

Rawski, Thomas G. 1994. "Progress Without Privatization: The Reform of China's State Industries." In *Changing Political Economies: Privatization in Post-Communist and Reforming Communist States,* edited by Vedat Milor, pp. 27–52. Boulder, CO: Lynn Reinner.

———. 1995. "Implications of China's Reform Experience." *China Quarterly* 144:1150–73.

———. 1997. "Who Has Soft Budget Constraints?" *Global Economic Review* 26 (1): 29–49.

Reynolds, Bruce L., ed. 1987. *Reform in China: Challenges and Choices.* Amronk, NY: M. E. Sharpe.

Roethlisberger, F. J., and W. J. Dickson. 1934. *Management and the Worker: Technical vs. Social Organization in an Industrial Plant.* Cambridge, MA: Harvard University Press.

Róna-Tas, Ákos. 1994. "The First Shall Be Last? Enterpreneurship and Communist Cadres in the Transition from Socialism." *American Journal of Sociology* 100:40–69.

Ruttan, V. 1997. "Induced Innovation, Evolutionary Theory, and Path Dependence: Sources of Technical Change." *Economic Journal* 107 (444): 1520–29.

Sachs, Jeffrey D. 1992. "Privatization in Russia: Some Lessons from Eastern Europe." *American Economic Review* 80:43–48.

———. 1995a. "Consolidating Capitalism." *Foreign Policy* 98 (spring): 50–64.

———. 1995b. "Reforms in Eastern Europe and the Former Soviet Union in Light of the East Asian Experience." *Journal of the Japanese and International Economies* 9:454–85.

Sachs, Jeffrey D., and Wing Thye Woo. 1994. "Experiences in the Transition to a Market Economy." *Journal of Comparative Economics* 18 (3): 271–75.

———. 1997. "Understanding China's Economic Performance." Working Paper #5935, National Bureau of Economic Research, Working Paper series.

Schurmann, Franz. 1968. *Ideology and Organization in Communist China,* 2d ed. Berkeley: University of California Press.

Schultz, T. Paul. 1990. "Testing the Neoclassical Model of Family Labor Supply and Fertility." *Journal of Human Resources* 25 (4): 599–634.

Scott, W. Richard. 1987. *Organizations: Rational, Natural, and Open Systems,* 2d ed. Englewood Cliffs, NJ: Prentice-Hall.

———. 1992. "The Organization of Environments: Network, Cultural, and Historical

Elements." In *Organizational Environments: Ritual and Rationality*, edited by Richard Scott and John Meyer, pp. 155–175. Newbury Park, CA: Sage.

Scott, W. Richard, and John W. Meyer. 1991. "The Organization of Societal Sectors: Propositions and Early Evidence." In *The New Institutionalism in Organizational Analysis*, edited by Walter W. Powell and Paul DiMaggio, pp. 108–40. Chicago: University of Chicago Press.

———. 1992. "The Organization of Social Sectors." In *Organizational Environments: Ritual and Rationality*, edited by Richard Scott and John Meyer, pp. 129–54. Newbury Park, CA: Sage.

Sewell, William H. 1992. "A Theory of Structure: Duality, Agency, and Transformation." *American Journal of Sociology* 98:1–29.

Shanghai Academy of Social Sciences. 1994. *Shanghai jingji nianjian, 1994* [Economic Yearbook of Shanghai]. Shanghai: Shanghai Economic Yearbook Department [*Shanghai jingji nianjian chu*].

Shanghai Academy of Social Sciences. 1986. *Shanghai Academy of Social Sciences Papers* [*Shanghai shehui kexue yuan lunwen xuen*]. Shanghai: Shanghai Academy of Social Sciences Press.

———. 1988. *Shanghai Academy of Social Sciences Papers* [*Shanghai shehui kexue yuan lunwen xuen*]. Shanghai: Shanghai Academy of Social Sciences Press.

———. 1990. *Shanghai Academy of Social Sciences Papers*. Shanghai: Shanghai Academy of Social Sciences Press.

———. 1992. *Shanghai Academy of Social Sciences Papers*. Shanghai: Shanghai Academy of Social Sciences Press.

———. 1994. *Shanghai Academy of Social Sciences Papers*. Shanghai: Shanghai Academy of Social Sciences Press.

———. 1994. *The Institutional Structure of TVEs* [*Xiangzhen qiye yunxing jizhi yanjiu*]. Shanghai: Shanghai Academy of Social Sciences Press.

———. 1994. *Urban Progress, Business Development, and China's Modernization* [*Chengshi jinbu, qiye fazhan he zhongguo xiandaihua*]. Shanghai: Shanghai Academy of Social Sciences Press.

———. 1995. *Fifteen Years of Economic Development in Shanghai* [*Shanghai kaifang shiwu nian*]. Shanghai: Shanghai Academy of Social Sciences Press.

Shanghai Foreign Investment Commission. 1995. *Guide to Foreign Investment in China*. Shanghai: Shanghai Foreign Investment Commission.

Shanghai Municipal Statistical Bureau. 1990. *Shanghai tongji nianjian, 1990* [Statistical Yearbook of Shanghai, 1990]. Shanghai: Chinese Statistics Publishing House of the City of Shanghai's Statistical Bureau [*Shanghai shi tongjiju, Zhongguo tongji chubanshe*].

———. 1991. *Shanghai tongji nianjian, 1991* [Statistical Yearbook of Shanghai, 1991]. Shanghai: Chinese Statistics Publishing House of the City of Shanghai's Statistical Bureau [*Shanghai shi tongjiju, Zhongguo tongji chubanshe*].

———. 1993. *Shanghai tongji nianjian, 1993* [Statistical Yearbook of Shanghai, 1993]. Shanghai: Chinese Statistics Publishing House of the City of Shanghai's Statistical Bureau [*Shanghai shi tongjiju, Zhongguo tongji chubanshe*].

———. 1994. *Shanghai tongji nianjian, 1994* [Statistical Yearbook of Shanghai, 1994]. Shanghai: Chinese Statistics Publishing House of the City of Shanghai's Statistical Bureau [*Shanghai shi tongjiju, Zhongguo tongji chubanshe*].

Shanghai Reform Collections Office [*Shanghai gaige congshu bianzhuanbu*]. 1994. *Shanghai Economic Institutional Reform Yearbook, 1989–1993* [*Shanghai jingji tizhi gaige, 1989–1993*]. Shanghai.

Simon, Herbert A. 1957. *Administrative Behavior*, 2d ed. New York: Macmillan.

Skocpol, Theda. 1985. "Bringing the State Back In: Strategies of Analysis in Current Research." In *Bringing the State Back In*, edited by P. Evans, D. Reuschmeyer, and T. Skocpol, pp. 3–43. Cambridge: Cambridge University Press.

Smith, Adam. 1789 [1994]. *An Inquiry into the Nature and Causes of the Wealth of Nations*. New York: Random House.

Sorensen, Aage B. 1994. "Firms, Wages, and Incentives." In *Handbook of Economic Sociology*, edited by Neil J. Smelser and Richard Swedberg, pp. 504–28. Princeton, NJ: Princeton University Press.

Stark, David. 1992. "Path Dependence and Privatization Strategies in Eastern Europe." *Eastern European Politics and Societies* 6:17–54.

———. 1996. "Recombinant Property in East European Capitalism." *American Journal of Sociology* 101:993–1027.

Stark, David, and Victor Nee. 1989. *Remaking the Economic Institutions of Socialism*. Stanford: Stanford University Press.

State Statistical Bureau. 1994. *Zhongguo tongji nianjian, 1994* [Statistical Yearbook of China, 1994]. Beijing: Statistical Publishing House of China [*Zhongguo tongji chubanshe*].

State Statistical Bureau's City Social Survey Team [*Guojia tongjiju chengshi shehui jingji diaocha zongdui*]. 1990. Statistical Yearbook of Chinese Cities, 1990 [*Zhongguo chengshi tongji nianjian*]. Beijing: Chinese Statistical Publishing House [*Zhongguo tongji chubanshe*].

Steinmo, S., K. Thelen, and F. Longstreth. 1992. *Structuring Politics*. Cambridge: Cambridge University Press.

Stiglitz, Joseph E. 1992. "The Design of Financial Systems for the Newly Emerging Democracies of Eastern Europe." In *The Emergence of Market Economies in Eastern Europe*, edited by Christopher Clague and Gordon C. Rausser, pp. 161–84. Cambridge, MA: Blackwell.

Stiglitz, Joseph E., and A. Weiss. 1981. "Credit Rationing in Markets with Imperfect Information." *American Economic Review* 71 (3): 393–410.

Su, Si-jin. 1994. "Hybrid Organizational Forms in South China: 'One Firm, Two Systems.'" In *The Economic Transformation of South China: Reform and Development in the Post-Mao Era*, edited by Thomas P. Lyons and Victor Nee, pp. 199–213. Ithaca, NY: Cornell East Asia Program.

Sutton, John R., and Frank Dobbin. 1996. "The Two Faces of Governance: Responses to Legal Uncertainty in U.S. Firms, 1955–1985." *American Sociological Review* 61:794–811.

Sutton, John R., Frank Dobbin, John W. Meyer, and W. Richard Scott. 1994. "The Legalization of the Workplace." *American Journal of Sociology* 99:944–71.

Szelényi, Iván. 1978. "Social Inequalities in State Socialist Redistributive Economies." *International Journal of Comparative Sociology* 19:63–87.

———. 1983. *Urban Inequalities under State Socialism*. Oxford: Oxford University Press.

———. 1988. *Socialist Entrepreneurs: Embourgeoisement in Rural Hungary*. Madison: University of Wisconsin Press.

————. 1989. "Eastern Europe in Transition." In *Remaking the Economic Institutions of Socialism: China and Eastern Europe*, edited by Victor Nee and David Stark, pp. 208–32. Stanford: Stanford University Press.

Szelenyi, Ivan, and Eric Kostello. 1996. "The Market Transition Debate: Toward a Synthesis." *American Journal of Sociology* 101 (4): 1082–96.

Taizhou Property Rights Reform Leadership Group. 1994. *Chanquan Gaige* [Property Rights Reform]. Taizhou Economic Reforms Commission [*Taizhou diqu jingji tizhi gaige weiyuanhui*].

Tanner, Murray Scot. 1994. "The Erosion of Communist Party Control over Lawmaking in China." *China Quarterly* 138:381–403.

————. 1995. "How a Bill Becomes a Law in China: Stages and Processes in Lawmaking." *China Quarterly* 141:39–64.

Taylor, Frederick Winslow. 1923. *The Principles of Scientific Management*. New York: Harper and Brothers.

Thompson, J. D. 1967. *Organizations in Action*. New York: McGraw-Hill.

Torbert, Preston M. 1987. "Contract Law in the People's Republic of China." In *Foreign Trade, Investment, and the Law in the People's Republic of China*, edited by Michael J. Moser, pp. 321–42. New York: Oxford University Press.

————. 1994. "Broadening the Scope of Investment." *China Business Review* 21.3:48–55.

Tsui, Anne S., and Jing-lih Larry Fahr. 1997. "Where *Guanxi* Matters: Relational Demography and Guanxi in the Chinese Context." *Work and Occupations* 24 (1): 56–79.

Uzzi, Brian. 1996. "The Sources and Consequences of Embeddedness for the Economic Performance of Organizations: The Network Effect." *American Sociological Review* 61:674–98.

van Wijnbergen, Sweder. 1992. "Intertemperol Speculation, Shortages, and the Political Economy of Price Reform. *The Economic Journal* 102:1396–1406.

Walder, Andrew G. 1986a. *Communist Neo-Traditionalism: Work and Authority in Chinese Industry*. Berkeley: University of California Press.

————. 1986b. "The Informal Dimension of Enterprise Financial Reforms." Pp. 630–45 In *China's Economy Looks Toward the Year 2000*, Vol. 1: *The Four Modernizations*, edited by the Joint Economic Committee. Washington, D.C.: Government Printing Office.

————. 1989. "Factory and Manager in an Era of Reform." *China Quarterly* 118:242–64.

————. 1992a. "Property Rights and Stratification in Socialist Redistrubitive Economies." *American Sociological Review* 57:524–39.

————. 1992b. "Local Bargaining Relationships and Urban Industrial Finance." In *Bureaucracy, Politics, and Decision-Making in Post-Mao China*, edited by Kennth G. Lieberthal and David M. Lampton, pp. 308–33. Berkeley: University of California Press.

————. 1994a. "Corporate Organization and Local Government Property Rights in China." In *Changing Political Economies: Privatization in Post-Communist and Reforming Communist States*, edited by Vedat Milor, pp. 53–66. Boulder, CO: Lynn Reinner.

————. 1994b. "The Decline of Communist Power: Elements of a Theory of Institutional Change." *Theory and Society* 23:297–323.

Walder, Andrew G. 1995a. "Local Governments as Industrial Firms: An Organizational Analysis of China's Transitional Economy." *American Journal of Sociology* 101:263–301.

———. 1995b. "Career Mobility and the Communist Political Order." *American Sociological Review* 60:309–28.

———. 1996. "Markets and Inequality in Transitional Economies: Toward Testable Theories." *American Journal of Sociology* 4:1060–73.

Walder, Andrew, Zhou Lu, Peter M. Blau, Danching Ruan, and Zhang Yuchun. 1989. "The 1986 Survey of Work and Social Life in Tianjin, China: Aims, Methods, and Documentation." Harvard University, Department of Sociology, Center for Research on Politics and Social Organization, Working Paper series.

Wang, Wallace Wen-Yeu. 1992. "Reforming State Enterprises in China: The Case for Redefining Enterprise Operating Rights." *Journal of Chinese Law* 6:89–136.

Wank, David. 1996. "The Institutional Process of Market Clientelism: *Guanxi* and Private Business in a South China City." *China Quarterly* 147:820–38.

Weber, Max. 1968. *The Religion of China: Confucianism and Taoism*. Translated and edited by Hans H. Gerth. New York: Free Press.

———. 1976. *The Protestant Ethic and the Spirit of Capitalism*. Translated by Talcott Parsons with an introduction by Anthony Giddens. New York: Schribner's.

———. 1978. *Economy and Society: An Outline of Interpretive Sociology*, Vols. 1, 2. Edited by Guenther Roth and Claus Wittich. Berkeley: University of California Press.

Westney, D. Eleanor. 1987. *The Transfer of Western Organizational Patterns to Meiji Japan*. Cambridge, MA: Harvard University Press.

White, Harrison C. 1981. "Where Do Markets Come From?" *American Journal of Sociology* 87:517–47.

Whitley, Richard. 1990. "East Asian Enterprise Structures and the Comparative Analysis of Business Organizations." *Organization Studies* 8:125–47.

———. 1992a. *Business Systems in East Asia: Firms, Markets, and Societies*. Newbury Park, CA: Sage.

———, ed. 1992b. *European Business Systems: Firms and Markets in Their National Context*. Newbury Park, CA: Sage.

Whitley, R., J. Henderson, L. Czaben, and G. Langgel. 1996. "Trust and Contractual Relations in an Emerging Capitalist Economy: The Changing Trading Relationships of Ten Large Hungarian Enterprises." *Organization Studies* 17 (3): 397–420.

Whynes, David K. 1993. "Can Performance Monitoring Solve the Public Services' Principal-Agent Problem?" *Scottish Journal of Political Economy* 40:434–46.

Whyte, Martin K. 1993. "Deng Xiaoping: The Social Reformer." *China Quarterly* 135:513–33.

Whyte, Martin K., and William L. Parish. 1984. *Urban Life in Contemporary China*. Chicago: University of Chicago Press.

Wiemer, Calla. 1992. "Price Reform and Structural Change: Distributional Impediments to Allocative Gains." *Modern China* 18:171–96.

Williamson, Oliver E. 1975. *Markets and Hierarchies*. New York: Free Press.

———. 1986. *Economic Organization: Firms, Markets and Policy Control*. New York: New York University Press.

Wilson, Scott. 1997. "The Cash Nexus and Social Networks: Mutual Aid and Gifts in Contemporary Shanghai Villages." *The China Journal* 37:91–112.

Winship, Christopher, and Sherwin Rosen. 1988. "Introduction: Sociological and Economic Approaches to the Analysis of Social Structure." *American Journal of Sociology* 94 (Supplement): S1–S16.

Wong, Christine. 1991. "Central-Local Relations in an Era of Fiscal Decline: The Paradox of Fiscal Decentralization in Post-Mao China." *China Quarterly* 128:691–715.

———. 1992. "Fiscal Reform and Local Industrialization: The Problematic Sequencing of Reform in Post-Mao China." *Modern China* 18:197–227.

Wong, Kar-Yiu. 1992. "Inflation, Corruption, and Income Distribution: The Recent Price Reform in China." *Journal of Macroeconomics* 14:105–23.

Woo, Wing Thye, Wen Hai, Yibiao Jin, and Gang Fan. 1993. "How Successful Has Chinese Enterprise Reform Been? Pitfalls in Opposite Biases and Focus." *Journal of Comparative Economics* 18:410–37.

Xie, Yu, and Emily Hannum. 1996. "Regional Variation in Earnings Inequality in Reform-Era Urban China." *American Journal of Sociology* 101:950–92.

Xin, K., and J. Pearce. 1996. "*Guanxi*: Connections as Substitutes for Formal Institutional Support." *Academy of Management Journal* 39 (6): 1641–58.

Yan, Yunxiang. 1996. *The Flow of Gifts: Reciprocity and Social Networks in a Chinese Village*. Palo Alto, CA: Stanford University Press.

Yang, Mayfair Mei-hui. 1994. *Gifts, Favors, and Banquets: The Art of Social Relationships in China*. Ithaca, NY: Cornell University Press.

Yeh, K. C. 1992. "Macroeconomic Issues in China in the 1990s." *China Quarterly* 131:501–44.

Yeh, Wen-hsin. 1994. "Paper Paradise: Banking and Theater in Wartime Shanghai." Paper presented at the conference on China's Mid-Century Transitions, Fairbank Center for East Asian Research, Harvard University, September 8–10.

———. 1995. "Corporate Space, Communal Time: The Structure of Everyday Life in Shanghai's Bank of China." *American Historical Review* 100:97–122.

Yeung, I., And R. Tung. 1996. "Achieving Business Success in Confucian Societies: The Importance of *Guanxi* (Connections)." *Organizational Dynamics* 25 (2): 54–65.

Zhang, Wenxiang, and Fazhi Zhen. 1991. *Building Enterprise Participation: Letting "One Hundred Flowers Bloom"* [*Zengqing qiye huoli: baijai zhengming ji*]. Shanghai: Shanghai Academy of Social Sciences Press.

Zhao, Dingxin. 1997. "Decline of Political Control in Chinese Universities and the rise of the 1989 Chinese Student Movement." *Sociological Perspectives* 40:159–82.

Zhou, Xueguang. 1993a. "Unorganized Interests and Collective Action in Communist China." *American Sociological Review* 58:54–73.

———. 1993b. "The Dynamics of Organizational Rules." *American Journal of Sociology* 98:1134–66.

Zhou, Xueguang, Nancy Brandon Tuma, and Phyllis Moen. 1997. "Institutional Change and Job-Shift Patterns in Urban China, 1949 to 1994." *American Sociological Review* 62:339–65.

Zucker, Lynn G. 1977. "The Role of Institutionalization in Cultural Persistence." *American Sociological Review* 42:726–43.

———. 1991. "The Role of Institutionalization in Cultural Persistence (with postscript)." In *The New Institutionalism in Organizational Analysis*, edited by Walter W. Powell and Paul DiMaggio, pp. 83–107. Chicago: University of Chicago Press.

Index